PRINTED IN GREAT BRITAIN

EVERYMAN'S LIBRARY
EDITED BY ERNEST RHYS

TRAVEL AND
TOPOGRAPHY

THE JOURNAL OF A TOUR
TO THE HEBRIDES WITH
SAMUEL JOHNSON, LL.D.
BY JAMES BOSWELL

To the wise man all the world's a soil

BEN JONSON

The JOURNAL of a TOUR to the HEBRIDES with SAMUEL JOHNSON LL·D By JAMES · BOSWELL · Esq

LONDON & TORONTO
J·M·DENT & SONS
LTD. ℣ NEW YORK
E·P·DUTTON & CO

First Issue of this Edition . 1909
Reprinted 1910, 1914, 1920, 1926

INTRODUCTION

THERE are two books of travel in Scotland and the Hebrides which are the inevitable forerunners of Boswell's *Tour*. The one is Dr. Johnson's own account of the same adventure, his *Journey to the Western Islands ;* the other, Martin Martin's *Description* of that region. It was Martin's book which, according to Boswell, first gave Dr. Johnson his wish to visit the Hebrides. He said, in his *Journey*, it is true, he had had this wish so long that he scarcely remembered how it was excited; and he pointed to Boswell as his real inducement to the adventure, finding in him a companion " whose acuteness would help my inquiry and whose gaiety of conversation and civility of manners are sufficient to counteract the inconveniences of travel in countries less hospitable than we have passed." In this perfect instance of the Johnson equilibrated sentence, there is just so much of compliment to Boswell as may serve to cast the recollection of Martin into the shade. But Boswell's own references to Martin's book are explicit, both in the *Tour* and in the *Life ;* and an inscription in a copy at the Advocates' Library, Edinburgh, shows it to have been the very book that accompanied the travellers on their tour.

Martin's *Description*, in fact, although it has some dull intervals and faded pages, is a genuinely detailed record of the western isles, well contrived to whet the fancy of a boy in Lichfield to go exploring them

vii

whenever the day came. We know that long afterwards he said:—" No man now writes so ill as Martin's
Account of the Hebrides is written. A man could not
write so ill, if he should try. Set a merchant's clerk
now to write, and he'll do better." But the late Dr.
Birkbeck Hill, wisest of Johnsonians, protested in a
footnote against this summary conviction. The fact
is, Martin's short, concrete way of writing is excellent
for its purpose in rousing curiosity and stating sug-
gestive detail; and his *Description* may be compared,
to its own advantage, with Dr. Johnson's *Journey*.

The effect the book took on him is the proof of
its quality. The one special item that provoked his
utmost curiosity, the " St. Kilda man's notion that the
High Church of Glasgow had been hollowed out of a
rock," might be capped by many other passages in
which the traveller's imagination is pricked or set
agog. It is varied by inimitable passages of folklore
and the naïvest natural history, often admirably delivered. It tells of " a strange reciprocation of the
flux and reflux of the sea " off the east end of the isle
of Harries; of the tradition (which it helped to kill)
that a man must not be buried in St. Tarran's nor a
woman in St. Keith's; of the " marled salmon " of
Borera that no bait can allure and " that a shadow
frights away "; and of John Fake who lives in Pabble in
the parish of Kilmoor, who is constantly troubled with
a great sneezing a day or two before rain, and " therefore is he called the rain-almanack "; and of the ravens
of Heisker that elected a king.

Boswell's opening page that follows, where he speaks
of the simplicity and wildness and the wilder kind of
life that Martin's book led him and Dr. Johnson to
expect, might be complemented by many accounts
of the islanders. Of one island, Martin says, " The

natives have cows, sheep, barley and oats, and live a harmless life, being perfectly ignorant of most of those vices that abound in the world. They know nothing of money or gold, having no occasion for either; they neither sell nor buy, but only barter for such little things as they want; they covet no wealth, being fully content and satisfyed with food and raiment . . . they have an agreeable and hospitable temper for all strangers; they concern not themselves about the rest of mankind, except the inhabitants in the north part of Lewis. They take their surname from the colour of the sky, rainbow and clouds." It is such passages as this, coupled with others which give an ideal impression in transparent words, that leave us with so decisive a sense of Martin's book as a possible stimulator of Dr. Johnson's Scottish curiosity. Take one more instance:—

"As I came from South Uist, I perceived about sixty horsemen riding along the sands, directing their course for the east sea; and being between me and the sun, they made a great figure on the plain sands."

So much for the old Scottish travel-book that begat two others, both of them as famous as it is forgotten. Little remains to be said about Boswell's *Tour*, in which Dr. Johnson bulks bigger than all the Hebrides, and rightly, for he was Boswell's literary region and continent.

The present text is precisely that of the third edition of the book, published in 1786, following the Temple Classics reprint, edited by Mr. Arnold Glover. The map is a reduced copy of that in the same edition. The first edition of the *Journal* appeared in 1785, the year after Johnson's death, and the second in the same year. The work had been discreetly held over by Boswell, so as not to come into competition with Dr. Johnson's own *Journey to the Western Islands*.

The one delightful modern appendix to this triad of eighteenth-century Scottish travel-books is Dr. Birkbeck Hill's *Footsteps of Dr. Johnson* (Scotland) which appeared in 1890.

A note should perhaps have been added about a discussion in which Dr. Johnson showed an open mind, and argued both ways—that on the second sight. One of the most striking sections of Martin Martin's *Description*—which originally appeared, let us remember, in 1703—is his " Account of the Second Sight, in Irish called Taish," which was separately reprinted at a later date.

E. R.

1909.

Of Boswell's other publications, it is enough to mention the following, in verse and prose:—

Ode to Tragedy, 1761; Elegy on the Death of a Young Lady, with Commendatory Letters, 1761; Letters between Hon. Andrew Erskine and James Boswell, 1763; An Account of Corsica, and Memoirs of Pascal Paoli, 1768; British Essays in favour of the brave Corsicans, collected and published by J. B., 1769; The Essence of the Douglas Cause, 1767; The Hypochondriac, 27 articles in *London Magazine*, Oct. 1777-Dec. 1779; Letter to People of Scotland on State of Nation, 1783; Letter from Dr. Johnson to Ph. D. Stanhope, Earl of Chesterfield; and Conversation between George III. and Dr. Johnson, with notes by J. B., 1790; Life of Dr. Johnson, 1791.

DEDICATION

TO

EDMOND MALONE, Esq.

My dear Sir,

In every narrative, whether historical or biographical, authenticity is of the utmost consequence. Of this I have ever been so firmly persuaded, that I inscribed a former work to that person who was the best judge of its truth. I need not tell you I mean General Paoli; who, after his great, though unsuccessful, efforts to preserve the liberties of his country, has found an honourable asylum in Britain, where he has now lived many years the object of Royal regard and private respect; and whom I cannot name without expressing my very grateful sense of the uniform kindness which he has been pleased to shew me.

The friends of Doctor Johnson can best judge, from internal evidence, whether the numerous conversations which form the most valuable part of the ensuing pages, are correctly related. To them, therefore, I wish to appeal, for the accuracy of the portrait here exhibited to the world.

As one of those who were intimately acquainted with him, you have a title to this address. You have obligingly taken the trouble to peruse the original manuscript of this Tour, and can vouch for the strict fidelity of the present publication. Your literary alliance with our much lamented friend, in consequence of having undertaken to render one of his labours more complete, by your edition of Shakspeare, a work with I am confident will not disappoint the expectations of the publick, gives you another claim. But I have a still more powerful inducement to prefix your name to this volume, as it gives me an opportunity of letting the world know that I enjoy the honour and happiness of your friendship; and of thus publickly testifying the sincere regard with which I am,

My dear Sir,

Your very faithful

And obedient servant,

JAMES BOSWELL.

London,
20th September, 1785.

xi

ADVERTISEMENT

TO THE THIRD EDITION

Animated by the very favourable reception which two large impressions of this work have had, it has been my study to make it as perfect as I could in this edition, by correcting some inaccuracies which I discovered myself, and some which the kindness of friends or the scrutiny of adversaries pointed out. A few notes are added, of which the principal object is, to refute misrepresentation and calumny.

To the animadversions in the periodical Journals of criticism, and in the numerous publications to which my book has given rise, I have made no answer. Every work must stand or fall by its own merit. I cannot, however, omit this opportunity of returning thanks to a gentleman who published a Defence of my Journal, and has added to the favour by communicating his name to me in a very obliging letter.

It would be an idle waste of time to take any particular notice of the futile remarks, to many of which, a petty national resentment, unworthy of my countrymen, has probably given rise; remarks, which have been industriously circulated in the publick prints by shallow or envious cavillers, who have endeavoured to persuade the world that Dr. Johnson's character has been lessened by recording such various instances of his lively wit and acute judgment, on every topick that was presented to his mind. In the opinion of every person of taste and knowledge that I have conversed with, it has been greatly heightened; and I will venture to predict, that this specimen of the colloquial talents and extemporaneous effusions of my illustrious fellow-traveller will become still more valuable, when, by the lapse of time, he shall have become an ancient; when all those who can now bear testimony to the transcendent powers of his mind, shall have passed away; and no other memorial of this great and good man shall remain, but the following Journal, the other anecdotes and letters preserved by his friends, and those incomparable works, which have for many years been in the highest estimation, and will be read and admired as long as the English language shall be spoken or understood.

J. B.

LONDON, 15th *Aug.* 1786

MAP OF THE TOUR

THROUGH SCOTLAND AND THE HEBRIDES

MAP OF THE TOUR

through SCOTLAND and the HEBRIDES

by Samuel Johnson LLD and James Boswell Esq

in 1773

1773

CONTENTS

CONTENTS

HE WAS OF AN ADMIRABLE PREGNANCY OF WIT, AND
THAT PREGNANCY MUCH IMPROVED BY CONTINUAL
STUDY FROM HIS CHILDHOOD; BY WHICH HE HAD
GOTTEN SUCH A PROMPTNESS IN EXPRESSING HIS MIND,
THAT HIS EXTEMPORAL SPEECHES WERE LITTLE IN-
FERIOR TO HIS PREMEDITATED WRITINGS. MANY,
NO DOUBT, HAD READ AS MUCH, AND PERHAPS MORE
THAN HE; BUT SCARCE EVER ANY CONCOCTED HIS
READING INTO JUDGEMENT AS HE DID.

BAKER'S CHRONICLE.

The JOURNAL *of a*

TOUR TO THE HEBRIDES

WITH

SAMUEL JOHNSON, LL.D.

The *JOURNAL* of a

TOUR TO THE HEBRIDES

WITH

SAMUEL JOHNSON, LL.D.

D R. JOHNSON had for many years given me
hopes that we should go together, and visit
the Hebrides. Martin's Account of those islands
had impressed us with a notion that we might there
contemplate a system of life almost totally different
from what we had been accustomed to see ; and, to
find simplicity and wildness, and all the circumstances
of remote time or place, so near to our native great
island, was an object within the reach of reasonable
curiosity. Dr. Johnson has said in his "Journey,"
"that he scarcely remembered how the wish to visit
the Hebrides was excited;" but he told me, in
summer, 1763, that his father put Martin's Account
into his hands when he was very young, and that he
was much pleased with it. We reckoned there would
be some inconveniencies and hardships, and perhaps
a little danger ; but these we were persuaded were
magnified in the imagination of every body. When
I was at Ferney, in 1764, I mentioned our design
to Voltaire. He looked at me, as if I had talked

of going to the North Pole, and said, "You do not
insist on my accompanying you?"—"No, sir."—
"Then I am very willing you should go." I was
not afraid that our curious expedition would be prevented by such apprehensions; but I doubted that it
would not be possible to prevail on Dr. Johnson to
relinquish, for some time, the felicity of a London
life, which, to a man who can enjoy it with full
intellectual relish, is apt to make existence in any
narrower sphere seem insipid or irksome. I doubted
that he would not be willing to come down from
his elevated state of philosophical dignity; from a
superiority of wisdom among the wise, and of learning
among the learned; and from flashing his wit upon
minds bright enough to reflect it.

He had disappointed my expectations so long, that
I began to despair; but in spring, 1773, he talked of
coming to Scotland that year with so much firmness,
that I hoped he was at last in earnest. I knew
that, if he were once launched from the metropolis,
he would go forward very well; and I got our
common friends there to assist in setting him afloat.
To Mrs. Thrale in particular, whose enchantment
over him seldom failed, I was much obliged. It
was, "*I'll give thee a wind.*"—"*Thou art kind.*"—
To *attract* him, we had invitations from the chiefs
Macdonald and Macleod; and, for additional aid, I
wrote to Lord Elibank, Dr. William Robertson,
and Dr. Beattie.

To Dr. Robertson, so far as my letter concerned
the present subject, I wrote as follows:

"Our friend, Mr. Samuel Johnson, is in great health
and spirits; and, I do think, has a serious resolution
to visit Scotland this year. The more attraction, however, the better; and therefore, though I know he will

be happy to meet you there, it will forward the scheme, if, in your answer to this, you express yourself concerning it with that power of which you are so happily possessed, and which may be so directed as to operate strongly upon him."

His answer to that part of my letter was quite as I could have wished. It was written with the address and persuasion of the historian of America.

"When I saw you last, you gave us some hopes that you might prevail with Mr. Johnson to make out that excursion to Scotland, with the expectation of which we have long flattered ourselves. If he could order matters so, as to pass some time in Edinburgh, about the close of the summer session, and then visit some of the Highland scenes, I am confident he would be pleased with the grand features of nature in many parts of this country : he will meet with many persons here who respect him, and some whom I am persuaded he will think not unworthy of his esteem. I wish he would make the experiment. He sometimes cracks his jokes upon us ; but he will find that we can distinguish between the stabs of malevolence, and *the rebukes of the righteous, which are like excellent oil,*[1] *and break not the head*. Offer my best compliments to him, and assure him that I shall be happy to have the satisfaction of seeing him under my roof."

To Dr. Beattie I wrote, " The chief intention of this letter is to inform you, that I now seriously believe Mr. Samuel Johnson will visit Scotland this year : but I wish that every power of attraction may be employed

Dr. Robertson's letter

[1] Our friend Edmund Burke, who by this time had received some pretty severe strokes from Dr. Johnson, on account of the unhappy difference in their politicks, upon my repeating this passage to him, exclaimed, " Oil of vitriol ! "

Dr. to secure our having so valuable an acquisition, and
Beattie therefore I hope you will without delay write to me
what I know you think, that I may read it to the
mighty sage, with proper emphasis, before I leave London, which I must do soon.   He talks of you with
the same warmth that he did last year.   We are to see
as much of Scotland as we can, in the months of August
and September.   We shall not be long of being at
Marischal College.[1]   He is particularly desirous of
seeing some of the Western Islands."

Dr. Beattie did better : *ipse venit*.   He was, however, so polite as to wave his privilege of *nil mihi
rescribas*, and wrote from Edinburgh, as follows :

"Your very kind and agreeable favour of the 20th
of April overtook me here yesterday, after having
gone to Aberdeen, which place I left about a week
ago.   I am to set out this day for London, and hope
to have the honour of paying my respects to Mr. Johnson and you, about a week or ten days hence.   I shall
then do what I can, to enforce the topick you mention ;
but at present I cannot enter upon it, as I am in a very
great hurry ; for I intend to begin my journey within
an hour or two."

He was as good as his word, and threw some pleasing motives into the northern scale.   But, indeed, Mr.
Johnson loved all that he heard, from one whom he
tells us, in his Lives of the Poets, Gray found "a poet,
a philosopher, and a good man."

My Lord Elibank did not answer my letter to his
lordship for some time.   The reason will appear, when
we come to the isle of Sky.   I shall then insert my
letter, with letters from his lordship, both to myself
and Mr. Johnson.   I beg it may be understood, that I

[1] This, I find, is a Scotticism.   I should have said, "It
will not be long before we shall be at Marischal College."

insert my own letters, as I relate my own sayings, Johnson's
rather as keys to what is valuable belonging to others, character
than for their own sake.

Luckily Mr. Justice (now Sir Robert) Chambers,
who was about to sail for the East-Indies, was going
to take leave of his relations at Newcastle, and he
conducted Dr. Johnson to that town. Mr. Scott, of
University College, Oxford, (now Dr. Scott, of the
Commons,) accompanied him from thence to Edinburgh. With such propitious convoys did he proceed
to my native city. But, lest metaphor should make it
be supposed he actually went by sea, I choose to mention that he travelled in post-chaises, of which the rapid
motion was one of his most favourite amusements.

Dr. Samuel Johnson's character, religious, moral,
political, and literary, nay his figure and manner, are,
I believe, more generally known than those of almost
any man; yet it may not be superfluous here to attempt
a sketch of him. Let my readers then remember that
he was a sincere and zealous christian, of high church
of England and monarchical principles, which he would
not tamely suffer to be questioned; steady and inflexible
in maintaining the obligations of piety and virtue, both
from a regard to the order of society, and from a veneration for the Great Source of all order; correct, nay
stern in his taste; hard to please, and easily offended,
impetuous and irritable in his temper, but of a most
humane and benevolent heart; having a mind stored
with a vast and various collection of learning and knowledge, which he communicated with peculiar perspicuity
and force, in rich and choice expression. He united
a most logical head with a most fertile imagination,
which gave him an extraordinary advantage in arguing;
for he could reason close or wide, as he saw best
for the moment. He could, when he chose it, be

Boswell's the greatest sophist that ever wielded a weapon in
the schools of declamation; but he indulged this only
in conversation; for he owned he sometimes talked for
victory; he was too conscientious to make errour permanent and pernicious, by deliberately writing it.   He
was conscious of his superiority.   He loved praise
when it was brought to him; but was too proud to seek
for it.   He was somewhat susceptible of flattery.   His
mind was so full of imagery, that he might have been
perpetually a poet.   It has been often remarked, that in
his poetical pieces, which it is to be regretted are so few,
because so excellent, his style is easier than in his prose.
There is deception in this : it is not easier, but better
suited to the dignity of verse; as one may dance with
grace, whose motions, in ordinary walking,—in the
common step, are awkward.   He had a constitutional
melancholy, the clouds of which darkened the brightness
of his fancy, and gave a gloomy cast to his whole course
of thinking : yet, though grave and awful in his de-
portment, when he thought it necessary or proper,—
he frequently indulged himself in pleasantry and sportive sallies.   He was prone to superstition, but not to
credulity.   Though his imagination might incline him
to a belief of the marvellous, and the mysterious, his
vigorous reason examined the evidence with jealousy.
He had a loud voice, and a slow deliberate utterance,
which no doubt gave some additional weight to the
sterling metal of his conversation.   Lord Pembroke
said once to me at Wilton, with a happy pleasantry,
and some truth, that "Dr. Johnson's sayings would
not appear so extraordinary, were it not for his *bow-
wow way:*" but I admit the truth of this only on
some occasions.   The *Messiah*, played upon the *Can-
terbury organ*, is more sublime than when played upon
an inferior instrument : but very slight musick will seem

grand, when conveyed to the ear through that majestick medium. *While therefore Doctor Johnson's sayings are read, let his manner be taken along with them.* Let it however be observed, that the sayings themselves are generally great; that, though he might be an ordinary composer at times, he was for the most part a Handel. —His person was large, robust, I may say approaching to the gigantick, and grown unwieldy from corpulency. His countenance was naturally of the cast of an ancient statue, but somewhat disfigured by the scars of that *evil*, which, it was formerly imagined, the *royal touch* could cure. He was now in his sixty-fourth year, and was become a little dull of hearing. His sight had always been somewhat weak; yet, so much does mind govern, and even supply the deficiency of organs, that his perceptions were uncommonly quick and accurate. His head, and sometimes also his body, shook with a kind of motion like the effect of a palsy: he appeared to be frequently disturbed by cramps, or convulsive contractions,[1] of the nature of that distemper called *St. Vitus's* dance. He wore a full suit of plain brown clothes, with twisted-hair-buttons of the same colour, a large bushy greyish wig, a plain shirt, black worsted stockings, and silver buckles. Upon this tour, when journeying, he wore boots, and a very wide brown cloth great coat, with pockets which might have almost held the two volumes of his folio dictionary; and he

---

[1] Such they appeared to me; but since the first edition, Sir Joshua Reynolds has observed to me, "that Dr. Johnson's extraordinary gestures were only habits, in which he indulged himself at certain times. When in company, where he was not free, or when engaged earnestly in conversation, he never gave way to such habits, which proves that they were not involuntary." I still however think, that these gestures were involuntary; for surely had not that been the case, he would have restrained them in the publick streets.

Johnson's carried in his hand a large English oak stick.   Let me
prejudice not be censured for mentioning such minute particulars.
Every thing relative to so great a man is worth observing.   I remember Dr. Adam Smith, in his rhetorical
lectures at Glasgow, told us he was glad to know that
Milton wore latchets in his shoes, instead of buckles.
When I mention the oak stick, it is but letting *Hercules*
have his club; and, by-and-by, my readers will find
this stick will bud, and produce a good joke.

This imperfect sketch of " the COMBINATION and the
form " of that Wonderful Man, whom I venerated and
loved while in this world, and after whom I gaze with
humble hope, now that it has pleased ALMIGHTY GOD
to call him to a better world, will serve to introduce to
the fancy of my readers the capital object of the following journal, in the course of which I trust they will
attain to a considerable degree of acquaintance with
him.

His prejudice against Scotland was announced almost
as soon as he began to appear in the world of letters.
In his *London*, a poem, are the following nervous lines :

" For who would leave, unbrib'd, Hibernia's land ?
Or change the rocks of Scotland for the Strand ?
There none are swept by sudden fate away ;
But all, whom hunger spares, with age decay."

The truth is, like the ancient Greeks and Romans,
he allowed himself to look upon all nations but his own
as barbarians : not only Hibernia, and Scotland, but
Spain, Italy, and France, are attacked in the same
poem.   If he was particularly prejudiced against the
Scots, it was because they were more in his way ;
because he thought their success in England rather
exceeded the due proportion of their real merit ; and

because he could not but see in them that nationality **against** which I believe no liberal-minded Scotsman will deny. **Scotland** He was indeed, if I may be allowed the phrase, at bottom much of a *John Bull*; much of a blunt *true born Englishman*. There was a stratum of common clay under the rock of marble. He was voraciously fond of good eating; and he had a great deal of that quality called *humour*, which gives an oiliness and a gloss to every other quality.

I am, I flatter myself, completely a citizen of the world.—In my travels through Holland, Germany, Switzerland, Italy, Corsica, France, I never felt myself from home; and I sincerely love "every kindred and tongue and people and nation." I subscribe to what my late truly learned and philosophical friend Mr. Crosbie said, that the English are better animals than the Scots; they are nearer the sun; their blood is richer, and more mellow: but when I humour any of them in an outrageous contempt of Scotland, I fairly own I treat them as children. And thus I have, at some moments, found myself obliged to treat even Dr. Johnson.

To Scotland however he ventured; and he returned from it in great good humour, with his prejudices much lessened, and with very grateful feelings of the hospitality with which he was treated; as is evident from that admirable work, his "Journey to the Western Islands of Scotland," which, to my utter astonishment, has been misapprehended, even to rancour, by many of my countrymen.

To have the company of Chambers and Scott, he delayed his journey so long, that the court of session, which rises on the eleventh of August, was broke up before he got to Edinburgh.

On Saturday the fourteenth of August, 1773, late

*B 387

in the evening, I received a note from him, that he was arrived at Boyd's inn, at the head of the Canongate. I went to him directly. He embraced me cordially; and I exulted in the thought, that I now had him actually in Caledonia. Mr. Scott's amiable manners, and attachment to our *Socrates*, at once united me to him. He told me that, before I came in, the Doctor had unluckily had a bad specimen of Scottish cleanliness. He then drank no fermented liquor. He asked to have his lemonade made sweeter; upon which the waiter, with his greasy fingers, lifted a lump of sugar, and put it into it. The Doctor, in indignation, threw it out of the window. Scott said, he was afraid he would have knocked the waiter down. Mr. Johnson told me, that such another trick was played him at the house of a lady in Paris. He was to do me the honour to lodge under my roof. I regretted sincerely that I had not also a room for Mr. Scott. Mr. Johnson and I walked arm-in-arm up the High-street, to my house in James's court: it was a dusky night: I could not prevent his being assailed by the evening effluvia of Edinburgh. I heard a late baronet, of some distinction in the political world in the beginning of the present reign, observe, that "walking the streets of Edinburgh at night was pretty perilous, and a good deal odoriferous." The peril is much abated, by the care which the magistrates have taken to enforce the city laws against throwing foul water from the windows; but, from the structure of the houses in the old town, which consist of many stories, in each of which a different family lives, and there being no covered sewers, the odour still continues. A zealous Scotsman would have wished Mr. Johnson to be without one of his five senses upon this occasion. As we marched slowly along, he grumbled in my ear, "I smell you in the dark!" But he acknowledged that the breadth of the street, and the loftiness of the buildings on each side, made a noble appearance.

My wife had tea ready for him, which it is well known he delighted to drink at all hours, particularly when sitting up late, and of which his able defence against Mr. Jonas Hanway should have obtained him a magnificent reward from the East-India Company. He showed much complacency upon finding that the mistress of the house was so attentive to his singular habit; and as no man could be more polite when he chose to be so, his address to her was most courteous and engaging; and his conversation soon charmed her into a forgetfulness of his external appearance.

I did not begin to keep a regular full journal till some days after we had set out from Edinburgh; but I have luckily preserved a good many fragments of his *Memorabilia* from his very first evening in Scotland.

We had, a little before this, had a trial for murder, in which the judges had allowed the lapse of twenty years since its commission as a plea in bar, in conformity with the doctrine of prescription in the *civil* law, which Scotland and several other countries in Europe have adopted. He at first disapproved of this; but then he thought there was something in it, if there had been for twenty years a neglect to prosecute a crime which was *known*. He would not allow that a murder, by not being *discovered* for twenty years, should escape punishment. We talked of the ancient trial by duel. He did not think it so absurd as is generally supposed; "For (said he) it was only allowed when the question was *in equilibrio*, as when one affirmed and another denied; and they had a notion that Providence would interfere in favour of him who was in the right. But as it was found that

Sir
William
Forbes
in a duel, he who was in the right had not a better chance than he who was in the wrong, therefore society instituted the present mode of trial, and gave the advantage to him who is in the right.''

We sat till near two in the morning, having chatted a good while after my wife left us. She had insisted, that to shew all respect to the Sage, she would give up her own bed-chamber to him, and take a worse. This I cannot but gratefully mention, as one of a thousand obligations which I owe her, since the great obligation of her being pleased to accept of me as her husband.

Sunday, 15th August.

Mr. Scott came to breakfast, at which I introduced to Dr. Johnson, and him, my friend Sir William Forbes, now of Pitsligo ; a man of whom too much good cannot be said ; who, with distinguished abilities and application in his profession of a Banker, is at once a good companion, and a good christian ; which I think is saying enough. Yet it is but justice to record, that once, when he was in a dangerous illness, he was watched with the anxious apprehension of a general calamity ; day and night his house was beset with affectionate inquiries ; and, upon his recovery, *Te deum* was the universal chorus from the *hearts* of his countrymen.

Mr. Johnson was pleased with my daughter Veronica, [1] then a child of about four months old. She

[1] The saint's name of *Veronica* was introduced into our family through my great grandmother Veronica, Countess of Kincardine, a Dutch lady of the noble house of Sommelsdyck, of which there is a full account in Bayle's Dictionary. The family had once a princely right in Surinam. The governour of that settlement was appointed by the States General, the town of Amsterdam, and Sommelsdyck. The

had the appearance of listening to him. His motions The
seemed to her to be intended for her amusement; and **practice**
when he stopped, she fluttered, and made a little in- **of the**
fantine noise, and a kind of signal for him to begin **law**
again. She would be held close to him; which was
a proof, from simple nature, that his figure was not
horrid. Her fondness for him endeared her still more
to me, and I declared she should have five hundred
pounds of additional fortune.

We talked of the practice of the law. Sir William
Forbes said, he thought an honest lawyer should never
undertake a cause which he was satisfied was not a just
one. "Sir, (said Mr. Johnson,) a lawyer has no business with the justice or injustice of the cause which
he undertakes, unless his client asks his opinion, and
then he is bound to give it honestly. The justice or
injustice of the cause is to be decided by the judge.
Consider, sir; what is the purpose of courts of
justice? It is, that every man may have his cause
fairly tried, by men appointed to try causes. A
lawyer is not to tell what he knows to be a lie: he
is not to produce what he knows to be a false deed;
but he is not to usurp the province of the jury and of

States General have acquired Sommelsdyck's right; but the
family has still great dignity and opulence, and by inter-
marriages is connected with many other noble families.
When I was at the Hague, I was received with all the affection of kindred. The present Sommelsdyck has an important
charge in the Republick, and is as worthy a man as lives.
He has honoured me with his correspondence for these twenty
years. My great grandfather, the husband of Countess Veronica, was Alexander, Earl of Kincardine, that eminent *Royalist*
whose character is given by Burnet in his *History of his own
Times*. From him the blood of *Bruce* flows in my veins. Of
such ancestry who would not be proud? And, as *Nihil est,
nisi hoc sciat alter*, is peculiarly true of genealogy, who would
not be glad to seize a fair opportunity to let it be known?

Emigra-
tion

the judge, and determine what shall be the effect of
evidence,—what shall be the result of legal argument.
As it rarely happens that a man is fit to plead his own
cause, lawyers are a class of the community, who, by
study and experience, have acquired the art and power
of arranging evidence, and of applying to the points at
issue what the law has settled. A lawyer is to do for
his client all that his client might fairly do for himself,
if he could.   If, by a superiority of attention, of knowledge, of skill, and a better method of communication,
he has the advantage of his adversary, it is an advantage
to which he is entitled.   There must always be some
advantage, on one side or other ; and it is better that
advantage should be had by talents, than by chance.
If lawyers were to undertake no causes till they were
sure they were just, a man might be precluded altogether
from a trial of his claim, though, were it judicially
examined, it might be found a very just claim."—This
was sound practical doctrine, and rationally repressed
a too refined scrupulosity of conscience.

Emigration was at this time a common topick of discourse.   Dr. Johnson regretted it as hurtful to human
happiness : "For (said he) it spreads mankind which
weakens the defence of a nation, and lessens the comfort of living.   Men, thinly scattered, make a shift,
but a bad shift, without many things.   A smith is
ten miles off : they'll do without a nail or a staple.
A taylor is far from them : they'll botch their own
clothes.   It is being concentrated which produces high
convenience."

Sir William Forbes, Mr. Scott, and I, accompanied
Mr. Johnson to the chapel, founded by Lord Chief
Baron Smith, for the Service of the Church of
England.   The Reverend Mr. Carre, the senior
clergyman, preached from these words, "Because the

Lord reigneth, let the earth be glad."—I was sorry
to think Mr. Johnson did not attend to the sermon,
Mr. Carre's low voice not being strong enough to
reach his hearing. A selection of Mr. Carre's sermons has, since his death, been published by Sir
William Forbes, and the world has acknowledged their
uncommon merit. I am well assured Lord Mansfield
has pronounced them to be excellent.

Lord
Chief
Baron
Orde

Here I obtained a promise from Lord Chief Baron
Orde, that he would dine at my house next day. I
presented Mr. Johnson to his Lordship, who politely
said to him, " I have not the honour of knowing you;
but I hope for it, and to see you at my house. I am
to wait on you to-morrow." This respectable English
judge will be long remembered in Scotland, where he
built an elegant house, and lived in it magnificently.
His own ample fortune, with the addition of his salary,
enabled him to be splendidly hospitable. It may be
fortunate for an individual amongst ourselves to be
Lord Chief Baron; and a most worthy man now
has the office; but, in my opinion, it is better for
Scotland in general, that some of our publick em-
ployments should be filled by gentlemen of distinction
from the south side of the Tweed, as we have the
benefit of promotion in England. Such an interchange would make a beneficial mixture of manners,
and render our union more complete. Lord Chief
Baron Orde was on good terms with us all, in a
narrow country filled with jarring interests and keen
parties; and, though I well knew his opinion to be
the same with my own, he kept himself aloof at a
very critical period indeed, when the *Douglas cause*
shook the sacred security of *birthright* in Scotland to
its foundation; a cause, which had it happened before
the Union, when there was no appeal to a British

House of Lords, would have left the great fortress
of honours and of property in ruins.

When we got home, Dr. Johnson desired to see
my books.   He took down Ogden's Sermons on
Prayer, on which I set a very high value, having
been much edified by them, and he retired with them
to his room.   He did not stay long, but soon joined
us in the drawing room.   I presented to him Mr.
Robert Arbuthnot, a relation of the celebrated Dr.
Arbuthnot, and a man of literature and taste.   To
him we were obliged for a previous recommendation,
which secured us a very agreeable reception at St.
Andrews, and which Dr. Johnson, in his "Journey,"
ascribes to "some invisible friend."

Of Dr. Beattie, Mr. Johnson said, " Sir, he has
written like a man conscious of the truth, and feeling
his own strength.   Treating your adversary with respect, is giving him an advantage to which he is not
entitled.   The greatest part of men cannot judge of
reasoning, and are impressed by character ; so that,
if you allow your adversary a respectable character,
they will think, that though you differ from him,
you may be in the wrong.   Sir, treating your adversary with respect, is striking soft in a battle.   And
as to Hume,—a man who has so much conceit as
to tell all mankind that they have been bubbled for
ages, and he is the wise man who sees better than
they,—a man who has so little scrupulosity as to
venture to oppose those principles which have been
thought necessary to human happiness,—is he to be
surprised if another man comes and laughs at him ?
If he is the great man he thinks himself, all this
cannot hurt him : it is like throwing peas against a
rock."   He added " *something much too rough,*" both
as to Mr. Hume's head and heart, which I suppress.

Violence is, in my opinion, not suitable to the Christian David
cause. Besides, I always lived on good terms with Hume
Mr. Hume, though I have frankly told him, I was
not clear that it was right in me to keep company
with him. "But (said I) how much better are you
than your books!" He was cheerful, obliging, and
instructive; he was charitable to the poor; and many
an agreeable hour have I passed with him: I have
preserved some entertaining and interesting memoirs
of him, particularly when he knew himself to be dying,
which I may some time or other communicate to the
world. I shall not, however, extol him so very highly
as Dr. Adam Smith does, who says, in a letter to Mr.
Strahan the Printer (not a confidential letter to his
friend, but a letter which is published [1] with all formality) : "Upon the whole, I have always considered
him, both in his life time and since his death, as
approaching as nearly to the idea of a perfectly wise

[1] This letter, though shattered by the sharp shot of Dr.
Horne of Oxford's wit, in the character of "One of the People
called Christians," is still prefixed to Mr. Hume's excellent
History of England, like a poor invalid on the piquet guard,
or like a list of quack medicines sold by the same bookseller,
by whom a work of whatever nature is published; for it has
no connection with his *History*, let it have what it may with
what are called his *Philosophical* Works. A worthy friend
of mine in London was lately consulted by a lady of quality,
of most distinguished merit, what was the best History of
England for her son to read. My friend recommended Hume's.
But, upon recollecting that its usher was a superlative panegyrick on one, who endeavoured to sap the credit of our holy
religion, he revoked his recommendation. I am really sorry
for this ostentatious *alliance*; because I admire "The Theory
of Moral Sentiments," and value the greatest part of "An
Inquiry into the Nature and Causes of the Wealth of Nations."
Why should such a writer be so forgetful of human comfort,
as to give any countenance to that dreary infidelity which
would "make us poor indeed!"

Adam
Smith's
praise of
Hume

and virtuous man as perhaps the nature of human frailty will permit." Let Dr. Smith consider: Was not Mr. Hume blest with good health, good spirits, good friends, a competent and increasing fortune? And had he not also a perpetual feast of fame? But, as a learned friend has observed to me, "What trials did he undergo, to prove the perfection of his virtue? Did he ever experience any great instance of adversity?"—When I read this sentence, delivered by my old Professor of Moral Philosophy, I could not help exclaiming with the Psalmist, "Surely I have now more understanding than my teachers!"

While we were talking, there came a note to me from Dr. William Robertson.

"DEAR SIR,

"I have been expecting every day to hear from you, of Dr. Johnson's arrival. Pray, what do you know about his motions? I long to take him by the hand. I write this from the college, where I have only this scrap of paper. Ever yours,

"W. R."

"Sunday."

It pleased me to find Dr. Robertson thus eager to meet Dr. Johnson. I was glad I could answer, that he was come: and I begged Dr. Robertson might be with us as soon as he could.

Sir William Forbes, Mr. Scott, Mr. Arbuthnot, and another gentleman dined with us. "Come, Dr. Johnson, (said I,) it is commonly thought that our veal in Scotland is not good. But here is some which I believe you will like."—There was no catching him. —JOHNSON. "Why, sir, what is commonly thought, I should take to be true. *Your* veal may be good; but

that will only be an exception to the general opinion ; **Burke's**
not a proof against it." **wit**

Dr. Robertson, according to the custom of Edinburgh at that time, dined in the interval between the
forenoon and afternoon service, which was then later
than now ; so we had not the pleasure of his company
till dinner was over, when he came and drank wine
with us. And then began some animated dialogue, of
which here follows a pretty full note.

We talked of Mr. Burke.—Dr. Johnson said, he
had great variety of knowledge, store of imagery,
copiousness of language.—ROBERTSON. "He has wit
too."—JOHNSON. "No, sir ; he never succeeds there.
'Tis low ; 'tis conceit. I used to say, Burke never
once made a good joke.[1] What I most envy Burke

---

[1] This was one of the points upon which Dr. Johnson
was strangely heterodox. For, surely, Mr. Burke, with his
other remarkable qualities, is also distinguished for his wit,
and for wit of all kinds too ; not merely that power of language which Pope chooses to denominate wit,

(True wit is Nature to advantage drest ;
What oft was thought, but ne'er so well exprest.)

but surprising allusions, brilliant sallies of vivacity, and pleasant conceits. His speeches in parliament are strewed with
them. Take, for instance, the variety which he has given
in his wide range, yet exact detail, when exhibiting his
Reform Bill. And his conversation abounds in wit. Let
me put down a specimen.—I told him, I had seen, at a *Blue
stocking* assembly, a number of ladies sitting round a worthy
and tall friend of ours, listening to his literature. "Ay,
(said he) like maids round a May-pole."—I told him, I had
found out a perfect definition of human nature, as distinguished from the animal. An ancient philosopher said, Man
was "a two-legged animal without feathers," upon which
his rival Sage had a Cock plucked bare, and set him down in
the school before all the disciples, as a "Philosophick Man."
Dr. Franklin said, Man was "a tool-making animal," which
is very well ; for no animal but man makes a thing, by means

Instances
of Burke's
wit

for, is, his being constantly the same.   He is never
what we call hum-drum ; never unwilling to begin to
talk, nor in haste to leave off."—BOSWELL. "Yet he
can listen."—JOHNSON.   "No; I cannot say he is
good at that.   So desirous is he to talk, that, if one
is speaking at this end of the table, he'll speak to
somebody at the other end.   Burke, sir, is such a
man, that if you met him for the first time in the
street where you were stopped by a drove of oxen,
and you and he stepped aside to take shelter but for

of which he can make another thing.   But this applies to
very few of the species.   My definition of *Man* is, "a Cook-
ing Animal."   The beasts have memory, judgment, and all
the faculties and passions of our mind, in a certain degree ;
but no beast is a cook.   The trick of the monkey using the
cat's paw to roast a chestnut, is only a piece of shrewd malice
in that *turpissima bestia*, which humbles us so sadly by its similarity to us.   Man alone can dress a good dish ; and every man
whatever is more or less a cook, in seasoning what he himself eats.—Your definition is good, said Mr. Burke, and I now
see the full force of the common proverb, "There is *reason* in
roasting of eggs."—When Mr. Wilkes, in his days of tumul-
tuous opposition, was borne upon the shoulders of the mob,
Mr. Burke (as Mr. Wilkes told me himself, with classical
admiration,) applied to him what Horace says of Pindar,

   —— *numeris*que fertur
   LEGE *solutis.*

Sir Joshua Reynolds, who agrees with me entirely as to
Mr. Burke's fertility of wit, said, that this was "dignify-
ing a pun."   He also observed, that he has often heard
Burke say, in the course of an evening, ten good things,
each of which would have served a noted wit (whom he
named) to live upon for a twelvemonth.

I find, since the former edition, that some persons have
objected to the instances which I have given of Mr. Burke's
wit, as not doing justice to my very ingenious friend ; the spe-
cimens produced having, it is alledged, more of conceit than
real wit, and being merely sportive sallies of the moment,
not justifying the encomium which they think with me,

five minutes, he'd talk to you in such a manner, that, when you parted, you would say, this is an extraordinary man. Now, you may be long enough with me, without finding any thing extraordinary." He said, he believed Burke was intended for the law; but either had not money enough to follow it, or had not diligence enough. He said, he could not understand how a man could apply to one thing, and not to another. Robertson said, one man had more

Burke an extraordinary man

he undoubtedly merits. I was well aware, how hazardous it was to exhibit particular instances of wit, which is of so airy and spiritual a nature as often to elude the hand that attempts to grasp it. The excellence and efficacy of a *bon mot* depend frequently so much on the occasion on which it is spoken, on the particular manner of the speaker, on the person to whom it is applied, the previous introduction, and a thousand minute particulars which cannot be easily enumerated, that it is always dangerous to detach a witty saying from the group to which it belongs, and to set it before the eye of the spectator, divested of those concomitant circumstances, which gave it animation, mellowness, and relief. I ventured, however, at all hazards, to put down the first instances that occurred to me, as proofs of Mr. Burke's lively and brilliant fancy; but am very sensible that his numerous friends could have suggested many of a superior quality. Indeed, the being in company with him, for a single day, is sufficient to shew that what I have asserted is well founded; and it was only necessary to have appealed to all who know him intimately, for a complete refutation of the heterodox opinion entertained by Dr. Johnson on this subject. *He* allowed Mr. Burke, as the reader will find hereafter, to be a man of consummate and unrivalled abilities in every light except that now under consideration; and the variety of his allusions, and splendour of his imagery, have made such an impression on *all the rest* of the world, that superficial observers are apt to overlook his other merits, and to suppose that *wit* is his chief and most prominent excellence; when in fact it is only one of the many talents that he possesses, which are so various and extraordinary, that it is very difficult to ascertain precisely the rank and value of each.

White-
field and
Wesley

judgment, another more imagination.—JOHNSON. "No,
sir; it is only, one man has more mind than another.
He may direct it differently; he may, by accident, see
the success of one kind of study, and take a desire
to excel in it. I am persuaded that, had Sir Isaac
Newton applied to poetry, he would have made a very
fine epick poem. I could as easily apply to law as to
tragick poetry."—BOSWELL. "Yet, sir, you did apply
to tragick poetry, not to law."—JOHNSON. "Because,
sir, I had not money to study law. Sir, the man who
has vigour, may walk to the east, just as well as to the
west, if he happens to turn his head that way."—
BOSWELL. "But, sir, 'tis like walking up and down
a hill; one man will naturally do the one better than
the other. A hare will run up a hill best, from her
fore-legs being short; a dog down." JOHNSON. "Nay,
sir; that is from mechanical powers. If you make
mind mechanical, you may argue in that manner. One
mind is a vice, and holds fast; there's a good memory.
Another is a file; and he is a disputant, a controver-
sialist. Another is a razor; and he is sarcastical."—
We talked of Whitefield. He said, he was at the same
college with him, and knew him *before he began to be
better than other people* (smiling); that he believed he
sincerely meant well, but had a mixture of politicks and
ostentation: whereas Wesley thought of religion only.[1]
—Robertson said, Whitefield had strong natural elo-

[1] That cannot be said now, after the flagrant part which
Mr. John Wesley took against our American brethren, when,
in his own name, he threw amongst his enthusiastick flock,
the very individual combustibles of Dr. Johnson's "Taxation
no Tyranny;" and after the intolerant spirit which he manifested against our fellow-christians of the Roman Catholick
Communion, for which that able champion, Father O'Leary,
has given him so hearty a drubbing. But I should think
myself very unworthy, if I did not at the same time acknow-

quence, which, if cultivated, would have done great **Political**
things.—JOHNSON. "Why, sir, I take it, he was at the **parties**
height of what his abilities could do, and was sensible
of it.   He had the ordinary advantages of education ;
but he chose to pursue that oratory which is for the
mob."—BOSWELL. "He had great effect on the passions."—JOHNSON. "Why, sir, I don't think so. He
could not represent a succession of pathetick images.
He vociferated, and made an impression. *There*, again,
was a mind like a hammer."—Dr. Johnson now said,
a certain eminent political friend of our's was wrong,
in his maxim of sticking to a certain set of *men* on all
occasions.   "I can see that a man may do right to
stick to a party (said he) ; that is to say, he is a Whig,
or he is a Tory, and he thinks one of those parties upon
the whole the best, and that to make it prevail, it must
be generally supported, though, in particulars, it may
be wrong.   He takes its faggot of principles, in which
there are fewer rotten sticks than in the other, though
some rotten sticks to be sure ; and they cannot well be
separated.   But, to bind one's self to one man, or one
set of men, (who may be right to-day and wrong to-
morrow,) without any general preference of system, I
must disapprove." [1]

He told us of Cooke, who translated Hesiod, and
lived twenty years on a translation of Plautus, for which
he was always taking subscriptions ; and that he pre-

ledge Mr. John Wesley's merit, as a veteran " Soldier of Jesus
Christ," who has, I do believe, " turned many from darkness
into light, and from the power of Satan to the living GOD."
[1] If due attention were paid to this observation, there
would be more virtue, even in politicks. What Dr. Johnson
justly condemned, has, I am sorry to say, greatly increased
in the present reign.   At the distance of four years from
this conversation, 21st February 1777, My Lord Archbishop
of York, in his "Sermon before the Society for the Propa-

Arch-
bishop
Mark-
ham on
parties

sented Foote to a Club, in the following singular manner: "This is the nephew of the gentleman who was lately hung in chains for murdering his brother."

In the evening I introduced to Mr. Johnson [1] two

gation of the Gospel in Foreign Parts," thus indignantly describes the then state of parties:

"Parties once had a *principle* belonging to them, absurd perhaps, and indefensible, but still carrying a notion of *duty*, by which honest minds might easily be caught.

"But they are now *combinations of individuals*, who, instead of being the sons and servants of the community, make a league for advancing their *private interests*. It is their business to hold high the notion of *political honour*. I believe and trust, it is not injurious to say, that such a bond is no better than that by which the lowest and wickedest combinations are held together; and that it denotes the last stage of political depravity."

To find a thought, which just shewed itself to us from the mind of Johnson, thus appearing again at such a distance of time, and without any communication between them, enlarged to full growth in the mind of Markham, is a curious object of philosophical contemplation.—That two such great and luminous minds should have been so dark in one corner, —that *they* should have held it to be "Wicked rebellion in the British subjects established in America, to resist the abject condition of holding all their property at the mercy of British subjects remaining at home, while their allegiance to our common Lord the King was to be preserved inviolate,— is a striking proof to me, either that "He who sitteth in Heaven," scorns the loftiness of human pride,—or that the evil spirit, whose personal existence I strongly believe, and even in this age am confirmed in that belief by a Fell, nay, by a Hurd, has more power than some choose to allow.

[1] It may be observed, that I sometimes call my great friend, *Mr.* Johnson, sometimes *Dr.* Johnson; though he had at this time a doctor's degree from Trinity College, Dublin. The University of Oxford afterwards conferred it upon him by a diploma, in very honourable terms. It was some time before I could bring myself to call him Doctor; but, as he has been long known by that title, I shall give it to him in the rest of this Journal.

good friends of mine, Mr. William Nairne, Advocate, and Mr. Hamilton of Sundrum, my neighbour in the country, both of whom supped with us. I have preserved nothing of what passed, except that Dr. Johnson displayed another of his heterodox opinions,—a contempt of tragick acting. He said, "the action of all players in tragedy is bad. It should be a man's study to repress those signs of emotion and passion, as they are called." He was of a directly contrary opinion to that of Fielding, in his "Tom Jones"; who makes Partridge say, of Garrick, "why, I could act as well as he myself. I am sure, if I had seen a ghost, I should have looked in the very same manner, and done just as he did." For, when I asked him, "Would not you, sir, start as Mr. Garrick does, if you saw a ghost?" He answered, "I hope not. If I did, I should frighten the ghost."

Monday, 16th August.

Dr. William Robertson came to breakfast. We talked of Ogden on Prayer. Dr. Johnson said, "The same arguments which are used against GOD's hearing prayer, will serve against his rewarding good, and punishing evil. He has resolved, he has declared, in the former case as in the latter." He had last night looked into Lord Hailes's "Remarks on the History of Scotland." Dr. Robertson and I said, it was a pity Lord Hailes did not write greater things. His lordship had not then published his "Annals of Scotland."—JOHNSON. "I remember I was once on a visit at the house of a lady for whom I had a high respect. There was a good deal of company in the room. When they were gone, I said to this lady,

'What foolish talking have we had!'—'Yes, (said she,) but while they talked, you said nothing.'—I was struck with the reproof. How much better is the man who does any thing that is innocent, than he who does nothing. Besides, I love anecdotes. I fancy mankind may come, in time, to write all aphoristically, except in narrative; grow weary of preparation, and connection, and illustration, and all those arts by which a big book is made.—If a man is to wait till he weaves anecdotes into a system, we may be long in getting them, and get but few, in comparison of what we might get."

Dr. Robertson said, the notions of Eupham Macallan, a fanatick woman, of whom Lord Hailes gives a sketch, were still prevalent among some of the Presbyterians; and therefore it was right in Lord Hailes, a man of known piety, to undeceive them.

We walked out, that Dr. Johnson might see some of the things which we have to shew at Edinburgh. We went to the Parliament-House, where the Parliament of Scotland sat, and where the *Ordinary Lords* of Session hold their courts; and to the New Session-House adjoining to it, where our Court of Fifteen (the fourteen *Ordinaries*, with the Lord President at their head,) sit as a court of Review. We went to the Advocates' Library, of which Dr. Johnson took a cursory view, and then to what is called the *Laigh* (or under) Parliament-House, where the records of Scotland, which has an universal security by register, are deposited, till the great Register Office be finished. I was pleased to behold Dr. Samuel Johnson rolling about in this old magazine of antiquities. There was, by this time, a pretty numerous circle of us attending upon him. Somebody talked of happy moments for composition; and how a man can write at one time, and not at another.—"Nay (said Dr. Johnson) a man may write at any time, if he will set himself *doggedly* [1] to it."

I here began to indulge old Scottish sentiments, and to express a warm regret, that, by our Union with England, we were no more;—our independent kingdom was lost.—JOHNSON. "Sir, never talk of your independency, who could let your Queen remain twenty years in captivity, and then be put to death, without even a pretence of justice, without your ever attempting to rescue her; and such a Queen too! as every man of any gallantry of spirit would have sacrificed his life for."—Worthy Mr. JAMES KERR, Keeper of the Records. "Half our nation was bribed by English money."—JOHNSON. "Sir, that is no defence : that makes you worse."—Good Mr. BROWN, Keeper of the Advocates' Library. "We had better say nothing about it."—BOSWELL. "You would have been glad, however, to have had us last war, sir, to fight your battles!"—JOHNSON. "We should have had you for the same price, though there had been no Union, as we might have had Swiss, or other troops. No, no, I shall agree to a separation. You have only to *go home*."—Just as he had said this, I to divert the subject, shewed him the signed assurances of the three successive Kings of the Hanover family, to maintain the Presbyterian establishment in Scotland.—"We'll give you that (said he) into the bargain."

We next went to the great church of St. Giles, which has lost its original magnificence in the inside, by being divided into four places of Presbyterian worship. "Come, (said Dr. Johnson jocularly to Principal

---

[1] This word is commonly used to signify *sullenly, gloomily*; and in that sense alone it appears in Dr. Johnson's Dictionary. I suppose he meant by it, "with an *obstinate resolution*, similar to that of a sullen man."

Robertson,[1]) let me see what was once a church!"
We entered that division which was formerly called
the *New Church*, and of late the *High Church*, so well
known by the eloquence of Dr. Hugh Blair. It is
now very elegantly fitted up; but it was then shame-
fully dirty. Dr. Johnson said nothing at the time;
but when we came to the great door of the Royal
Infirmary, where, upon a board, was this inscription,
"*Clean your feet!*" he turned about slyly, and said,
"There is no occasion for putting this at the doors of
your churches!"

We then conducted him down the Post-house
stairs, Parliament-close, and made him look up from
the Cow-gate to the highest building in Edinburgh,
(from which he had just descended,) being thirteen
floors or stories from the ground upon the back
elevation; the front wall being built upon the edge of
the hill, and the back wall rising from the bottom of
the hill several stories before it comes to a level with
the front wall. We proceeded to the College, with
the Principal at our head. Dr. Adam Fergusson,
whose "Essay on the History of Civil Society" gives
him a respectable place in the ranks of literature, was
with us. As the College buildings are indeed very
mean, the Principal said to Dr. Johnson, that he must
give them the same epithet that a Jesuit did when
shewing a poor college abroad: "*Hæ miseriæ nostræ.*"
Dr. Johnson was, however, much pleased with the
library, and with the conversation of Dr. James Robertson, Professor of Oriental Languages, the Librarian.

---

[1] I have hitherto called him Dr. William Robertson, to
distinguish him from Dr. James Robertson, who is soon to
make his appearance. But *Principal*, from his being the
head of our college, is his usual designation, and is shorter;
so I shall use it hereafter

We talked of Kennicot's edition of the Hebrew Bible, Holy-
and hoped it would be quite faithful.—JOHNSON. "Sir, I rood-
know not any crime so great that a man could contrive house
to commit, as poisoning the sources of eternal truth."

I pointed out to him where there formerly stood an
old wall enclosing part of the college, which I remember bulged out in a threatening manner, and of
which there was a common tradition similar to that
concerning Bacon's study at Oxford, that it would
fall upon some very learned man.   It had some time
before this been taken down, that the street might be
widened, and a more convenient wall built.   Dr. Johnson, glad of an opportunity to have a pleasant hit at
Scottish learning, said, "they have been afraid it never
would fall."

We shewed him the Royal Infirmary, for which,
and for every other exertion of generous publick spirit
in his power, that noble-minded citizen of Edinburgh,
George Drummond, will be ever held in honourable
remembrance.   And we were too proud not to carry
him to the Abbey of Holyrood-house, that beautiful
piece of architecture, but, alas! that deserted mansion
of royalty, which Hamilton of Bangour, in one of his
elegant poems, calls

"A virtuous palace, where no monarch dwells."

I was much entertained while Principal Robertson
fluently harangued to Dr. Johnson, upon the spot, concerning scenes of his celebrated History of Scotland.
We surveyed that part of the palace appropriated to the
Duke of Hamilton, as Keeper, in which our beautiful
Queen Mary lived, and in which David Rizzio was
murdered; and also the State Rooms.   Dr. Johnson
was a great reciter of all sorts of things serious or
comical.   I over-heard him repeating here, in a kind

of muttering tone, a line of the old ballad, *Johnny Armstrong's Last Good-Night*:

"And ran him through the fair body!"[1]

We returned to my house, where there met him, at dinner, the Duchess of Douglas, Sir Adolphus Oughton, Lord Chief Baron, Sir William Forbes, Principal Robertson, Mr. Cullen, advocate. Before dinner, he told us of a curious conversation between the famous George Faulkner and him. George said that England had drained Ireland of fifty thousand pounds in specie, annually, for fifty years. "How so, sir! (said Dr. Johnson,) you must have a very great trade?" "No trade."—"Very rich mines?" "No mines."—"From whence, then, does all this money come?" "Come! why out of the blood and bowels of the poor people of Ireland!"

He seemed to me to have an unaccountable prejudice against Swift; for I once took the liberty to ask him, if Swift had personally offended him, and he told me, he had not. He said to-day, "Swift is clear, but he is shallow. In coarse humour, he is inferior to Arbuthnot; in delicate humour, he is inferior to Addison: So he is inferior to his contemporaries; without putting him against the whole world. I doubt if the 'Tale of a Tub' was his: it has so much more thinking, more knowledge, more power, more colour, than any of the works which are indisputably his. If it was his, I shall only say, he was *impar sibi*."

We gave him as good a dinner as we could. Our

---

[1] The stanza from which he took this line is,

"But then rose up all Edinburgh,
    They rose up by thousands three;
A cowardly Scot came John behind,
    And ran him through the fair body!"

Scotch muir-fowl, or growse, were then abundant, **Witch-** and quite in season; and, so far as wisdom and wit **craft** can be aided by administering agreeable sensations to the palate, my wife took care that our great guest should not be deficient.

Sir Adolphus Oughton, then our Deputy Commander in Chief, who was not only an excellent officer, but one of the most universal scholars I ever knew, had learned the Erse language, and expressed his belief in the authenticity of Ossian's Poetry. Dr. Johnson took the opposite side of that perplexed question; and I was afraid the dispute would have run high between them. But Sir Adolphus, who had a very sweet temper, changed the discourse, grew playful, laughed at Lord Monboddo's notion of men having tails, and called him a Judge, *à posteriori*, which amused Dr. Johnson; and thus hostilities were prevented.

At supper we had Dr. Cullen, his son the advocate, Dr. Adam Fergusson, and Mr. Crosbie, advocate. Witchcraft was introduced. Mr. Crosbie said, he thought it the greatest blasphemy to suppose evil spirits counteracting the Deity, and raising storms, for instance, to destroy his creatures.—JOHNSON. "Why, sir, if moral evil be consistent with the government of the Deity, why may not physical evil be also consistent with it? It is not more strange that there should be evil spirits, than evil men: evil unembodied spirits, than evil embodied spirits. And as to storms, we know there are such things; and it is no worse that evil spirits raise them, than that they rise."—CROSBIE. "But it is not credible, that witches should have effected what they are said in stories to have done."—JOHNSON. "Sir, I am not defending their credibility. I am only saying, that your arguments are not good, and

Lord Monboddo will not overturn the belief of witchcraft.—(Dr. Fergusson said to me, aside, 'He is right.')—And then, sir, you have all mankind, rude and civilized, agreeing in the belief of the agency of preternatural powers. You must take evidence : you must consider, that wise and great men have condemned witches to die."—CROSBIE. "But an act of parliament put an end to witchcraft."—JOHNSON. "No, sir ; witchcraft had ceased ; and therefore an act of parliament was passed to prevent persecution for what was not witchcraft. Why it ceased, we cannot tell, as we cannot tell the reason of many other things."—Dr. Cullen, to keep up the gratification of mysterious disquisition, with the grave address for which he is remarkable in his companionable as in his professional hours, talked, in a very entertaining manner, of people walking and conversing in their sleep.   I am very sorry I have no note of this.   We talked of the Ouran-Outang, and of Lord Monboddo's thinking that he might be taught to speak. Dr. Johnson treated this with ridicule.   Mr. Crosbie said, that Lord Monboddo believed the existence of every thing possible ; in short, that all which is in *posse* might be found in *esse.*—JOHNSON. "But, sir, it is as possible that the Ouran-Outang does not speak, as that he speaks.   However, I shall not contest the point. I should have thought it not possible to find a Monboddo ; yet *he* exists."—I again mentioned the stage. —JOHNSON. "The appearance of a player, with whom I have drunk tea, counteracts the imagination that he is the character he represents.   Nay, you know, nobody imagines that he is the character he represents.   They say, 'See Garrick ! how he looks to-night !   See how he'll clutch the dagger ! ' That is the buz of the theatre."

Tuesday, 17th August.

Sir William Forbes came to breakfast, and brought
with him Dr. Blacklock, whom he introduced to Dr.
Johnson, who received him with a most humane complacency; " Dear Dr. Blacklock, I am glad to see
you ! "—Blacklock seemed to be much surprized,
when Dr. Johnson said, " it was easier to him to write
poetry than to compose his Dictionary. His mind
was less on the stretch in doing the one than the other.
Besides ; composing a Dictionary requires books and
a desk : you can make a poem walking in the fields, or
lying in bed."—Dr. Blacklock spoke of scepticism in
morals and religion, with apparent uneasiness, as if he
wished for more certainty.[1] Dr. Johnson, who had
thought it all over, and whose vigorous understanding
was fortified by much experience, thus encouraged the
blind Bard to apply to higher speculations what we all
willingly submit to in common life : in short, he gave
him more familiarly the able and fair reasoning of
Butler's *Analogy* : " Why, sir, the greatest concern
we have in this world, the choice of our profession,
must be determined without demonstrative reasoning.
Human life is not yet so well known, as that we can
have it. And take the case of a man who is ill. I
call two physicians : they differ in opinion. I am not
to lie down, and die between them : I must do something."—The conversation then turned on Atheism ;
on that horrible book, *Système de la Nature* ; and on
the supposition of an eternal necessity, without design,
without a governing mind.—JOHNSON. " If it were so,
why has it ceased ? Why don't we see men thus
produced around us now ? Why, at least, does it not

---

[1] See his letter on this subject in the APPENDIX.

Lord keep pace, in some measure, with the progress of time?
Hailes If it stops because there is now no need of it, then it
is plain there is, and ever has been, an all-power-
ful intelligence. But stay! (said he, with one of
his satyrick laughs.) Ha! ha! ha! I shall suppose Scotchmen made necessarily, and Englishmen by
choice.''

At dinner this day, we had Sir Alexander Dick,
whose amiable character, and ingenious and cultivated
mind, are so generally known; (he was then on the
verge of seventy, and is now (1785) eighty-one, with his
faculties entire, his heart warm, and his temper gay;) Sir
David Dalrymple Lord Hailes; Mr. Maclaurin, advocate; Dr. Gregory, who now worthily fills his father's
medical chair; and my uncle, Dr. Boswell. This
was one of Dr. Johnson's best days. He was quite
in his element. All was literature and taste, without
any interruption. Lord Hailes, who is one of the best
philologists in Great-Britain, who has written papers
in the *World*, and a variety of other works in prose and
in verse, both Latin and English, pleased him highly.
He told him, he had discovered the Life of Cheynel,
in the *Student*, to be his.—JOHNSON. "No one else
knows it."—Dr. Johnson had, before this, dictated to
me a law-paper, upon a question purely in the law of
Scotland, concerning *vicious intromission*, that is to say,
intermeddling with the effects of a deceased person,
without a regular title; which formerly was understood to subject the intermeddler to payment of all the
defunct's debts. The principle has of late been re-
laxed. Dr. Johnson's argument was, for a renewal of
its strictness. The paper was printed, with additions
by me, and given into the Court of Session. Lord
Hailes knew Dr. Johnson's part not to be mine, and
pointed out exactly where it began, and where it ended.

Dr. Johnson said, " It is much, now, that his lordship can distinguish so."

In Dr. Johnson's *Vanity of Human Wishes*, there is the following passage :

> " The teeming mother, anxious for her race,
> Begs, for each birth, the fortune of a face :
> Yet *Vane* could tell, what ills from beauty spring ;
> And *Sedley* curs'd the charms which pleas'd a king."

Lord Hailes told him, he was mistaken in the instances he had given of unfortunate fair ones ; for neither *Vane* nor *Sedley* had a title to that description. His Lordship has since been so obliging as to send me a note of this, for the communication of which I am sure my readers will thank me.

" The lines in the tenth Satire of Juvenal, according to my alteration, should have run thus :

> " Yet *Shore* [1] could tell——— ;
> And *Valiere* [2] curs'd———.

" The first was a penitent by compulsion, the second by sentiment ; though the truth is, Mademoiselle de la Valiere threw herself (but still from sentiment) in the King's way.

" Our friend chose *Vane*, who was far from being well-looked ; and *Sedley*, who was so ugly, that Charles II. said, his brother had her by way of penance."

Mr. Maclaurin's learning and talents enabled him to do his part very well in Dr. Johnson's company. He produced two epitaphs upon his father, the celebrated mathematician. One was in English, of which Dr. Johnson did not change one word. In the other,

---

[1] Mistress of Edward IV.   [2] Mistress of Louis XIV

Epitaph
on Colin
Mac-
laurin
which was in Latin, he made several alterations.   In place of the very words of Virgil, " *Ubi luctus et pavor et plurima mortis imago*," he wrote " *Ubi luctus regnant et pavor*."   He introduced the word *prorsus* into the line " *Mortalibus prorsus non absit solatium*?" and after " *Hujus enim scripta evolve*," he added, " *Mentemque tantarum rerum capacem corpori caduco superstitem crede* ; " which is quite applicable to Dr. Johnson himself.[1]

Mr. Murray, advocate, who married a niece of Lord Mansfield's and is now one of the Judges of Scotland, by the title of Lord Henderland, sat with us a part of the evening ; but did not venture to say any thing, that I remember, though he is certainly possessed of talents which would have enabled him to have shewn himself to advantage, if too great anxiety had not prevented him.

At supper we had Dr. Alexander Webster, who, though not learned, had such a knowledge of mankind, such a fund of information and entertainment, so clear a head and such accommodating manners, that Dr. Johnson found him a very agreeable companion.

---

[1] Mr. ·Maclaurin's epitaph, as engraved on a marble tombstone, in the Gray-Friars church-yard, Edinburgh :

Infra situs est

COLIN MACLAURIN,

Mathes. olim in Acad. Edin. Prof.
Electus ipso Newtono suadente.
H. L. P. F.
Non ut nomini paterno consulat,
Nam tali auxilio nil eget;
Sed ut in hoc infelici campo,
Ubi luctus regnant et pavor.
Mortalibus prorsus non absit solatium :
Hujus enim scripta evolve,
Mentemque tantarum rerum capacem
Corpori caduco superstitem crede.

When Dr. Johnson and I were left by ourselves, I read to him my notes of the Opinions of our Judges upon the questions of Literary Property. He did not like them; and said, "they make me think of your Judges not with that respect which I should wish to do." To the argument of one of them, that there can be no property in blasphemy or nonsense, he answered, "then your rotten sheep are mine!—By that rule, when a man's house falls into decay, he must lose it." —I mentioned an argument of mine, that literary performances are not taxed.—As Churchill says, *Boswell's sketch of himself*

> "No statesman yet has thought it worth his pains
> To tax our labours, or excise our brains;"

and therefore they are not property.—"Yet, (said he,) we hang a man for stealing a horse, and horses are not taxed."—Mr. Pitt has since put an end to that argument.

Wednesday, 18th August.

On this day we set out from Edinburgh. We should gladly have had Mr. Scott to go with us; but he was obliged to return to England.—I have given a sketch of Dr. Johnson: my readers may wish to know a little of his fellow traveller. Think then, of a gentleman of ancient blood, the pride of which was his predominant passion. He was then in his thirty-third year, and had been about four years happily married. His inclination was to be a soldier; but his father, a respectable Judge, had pressed him into the profession of the law. He had travelled a good deal, and seen many varieties of human life. He had thought more than any body supposed, and had a pretty good stock of general learning and knowledge. He had all Dr.

Johnson's principles, with some degree of relaxation.
He had rather too little, than too much prudence ; and,
his imagination being lively, he often said things of
which the effect was very different from the intention.
He resembled sometimes

" The best good man, with the worst natur'd muse."

He cannot deny himself the vanity of finishing with
the encomium of Dr. Johnson, whose friendly partiality
to the companion of his Tour represents him as one,
" whose acuteness would help my inquiry, and whose
gaiety of conversation, and civility of manners, are sufficient to counteract the inconveniences of travel, in
countries less hospitable than we have passed."

Dr. Johnson thought it unnecessary to put himself to
the additional expence of bringing with him Francis
Barber, his faithful black servant ; so we were attended
only by my man, Joseph Ritter, a Bohemian ; a fine
stately fellow above six feet high, who had been over
a great part of Europe, and spoke many languages.   He
was the best servant I ever saw.   Let not my readers
disdain his introduction !   For Dr. Johnson gave him
this character : " Sir, he is a civil man, and a wise
man."

From an erroneous apprehension of violence, Dr.
Johnson had provided a pair of pistols, some gunpowder,
and a quantity of bullets : but upon being assured we
should run no risk of meeting any robbers, he left his
arms and ammunition in an open drawer, of which he
gave my wife the charge.   He also left in that drawer
one volume of a pretty full and curious Diary of his
Life, of which I have a few fragments ; but the book
had been destroyed.   I wish female curiosity had been
strong enough to have had it all transcribed, which
might easily have been done ; and I should think the

theft, being *pro bono publico*, might have been forgiven. But I may be wrong. My wife told me she never once looked into it.—She did not seem quite easy when we left her : but away we went !

Mr. Nairne, advocate, was to go with us as far as St. Andrews. It gives me pleasure that, by mentioning his *name*, I connect his title to the just and handsome compliment paid him by Dr. Johnson, in his book : " A gentleman who could stay with us only long enough to make us know how much we lost by his leaving us." When we came to Leith, I talked with perhaps too boasting an air, how pretty the Frith of Forth looked ; as indeed, after the prospect from Constantinople, of which I have been told, and that from Naples, which I have seen, I believe the view of that Frith and its environs, from the Castle-hill of Edinburgh, is the finest prospect in Europe. " Ay, (said Dr. Johnson,) that is the state of the world. Water is the same every where.

" Una est injusti cærula forma maris." [1]

I told him the port here was the mouth of the river or water of Leith. " Not *Lethe*," said Mr. Nairne.—" Why, sir, (said Dr. Johnson,) when a Scotchman sets out from this port for England, he forgets his native country."—NAIRNE. I hope, sir, you will forget England here."—JOHNSON. " Then 'twill be still more *Lethe*."—He observed of the Pier or Quay, " you have no occasion for so large a one : your trade does not require it : but you are like

---

[1] Non illic urbes, non tu mirabere silvas :
Una est injusti cærula forma maris.
OVID, *Amor*. L. II. El. xi.

Nor groves nor towns the ruthless ocean shows :
Unvaried still its azure surface flows.

Bare-
footed
Lairds
a shopkeeper who takes a shop, not only for what he
has to put into it, but that it may be believed he has a
great deal to put into it." It is very true, that there
is now, comparatively, little trade upon the eastern
coast of Scotland. The riches of Glasgow shew how
much there is in the west; and perhaps we shall find
trade travel westward on a great scale, as well as a
small.

We talked of a man's drowning himself.—JOHNSON.
" I should never think it time to make away with myself."—I put the case of Eustace Budgell, who was
accused of forging a will, and sunk himself in the
Thames, before the trial of its authenticity came on.
" Suppose, sir, (said I,) that a man is absolutely sure,
that, if he lives a few days longer, he shall be detected
in a fraud, the consequence of which will be utter disgrace and expulsion from society."—JOHNSON. "Then,
sir, let him go abroad to a distant country; let him go
to some place where he is *not* known. Don't let him
go to the devil where he *is* known! "

He then said, " I see a number of people barefooted
here: I suppose you all went so before the Union.
Boswell, your ancestors went so, when they had as
much land as your family has now. Yet Auchinleck is
the Field of Stones: there would be bad going bare-
footed there. The Lairds, however, did it."—I
bought some *speldings*, fish (generally whitings) salted
and dried in a particular manner, being dipped in the
sea and dried in the sun, and eaten by the Scots by
way of a relish. He had never seen them, though
they are sold in London. I insisted on *scottifying* [1] his
palate; but he was very reluctant. With difficulty I

[1] My friend, General Campbell, Governour of Madras,
tells me, that they make *speldings* in the East-Indies, particularly at Bombay, where they call them *Bambaloes*.

prevailed with him to let a bit of one of them lie in his Inch
Keith mouth. He did not like it.

In crossing the Frith, Dr. Johnson determined that we should land upon Inch Keith. On approaching it, we first observed a high rocky shore. We coasted about, and put into a little bay on the North-west. We clambered up a very steep ascent, on which was very good grass, but rather a profusion of thistles. There were sixteen head of black cattle grazing upon the island. Lord Hailes observed to me, that Brantome calls it *L'isle des Chevaux*, and that it was probably "a *safer* stable" than many others in his time. The fort, with an inscription on it, *Maria Re* 1564, is strongly built. Dr. Johnson examined it with much attention. He stalked like a giant among the luxuriant thistles and nettles. There are three wells in the island; but we could not find one in the fort. There must probably have been one, though now filled up, as a garrison could not subsist without it. But I have dwelt too long on this little spot. Dr. Johnson afterwards bade me try to write a description of our discovering Inch Keith, in the usual style of travellers, describing fully every particular; stating the grounds on which we concluded that it must have once been inhabited, and introducing many sage reflections; and we should see how a thing might be covered in words, so as to induce people to come and survey it. All that was told might be true, and yet in reality there might be nothing to see. He said, "I'd have this island. I'd build a house, make a good landing-place, have a garden, and vines, and all sorts of trees. A rich man, of a hospitable turn, here, would have many visitors from Edinburgh." When we had got into our boat again, he called to me, "Come, now, pay a classical compliment to the island on quitting it." I happened

Property
and in-
fluence
luckily, in allusion to the beautiful Queen Mary, whose name is upon the fort, to think of what Virgil makes Æneas say, on having left the country of his charming Dido :

Invitus, regina, tuo de littore cessi.[1]

"Very well hit off!" said he.

We dined at Kinghorn, and then got into a post-chaise. Mr. Nairne and his servant, and Joseph, rode by us. We stopped at Cupar, and drank tea. We talked of parliament; and I said, I supposed very few of the members knew much of what was going on, as indeed very few gentlemen know much of their own private affairs.—JOHNSON. "Why, sir, if a man is not of a sluggish mind, he may be his own steward. If he will look into his affairs, he will soon learn. So it is as to publick affairs. There must always be a certain number of men of business in parliament."—BOSWELL. "But consider, sir; what is the House of Commons? Is not a great part of it chosen by peers? Do you think, sir, they ought to have such an influence?"—JOHNSON. "Yes, sir. Influence must ever be in pro-portion to property; and it is right it should."—BOSWELL. "But is there not reason to fear that the common people may be oppressed?"—JOHNSON. "No, sir. Our great fear is from want of power in govern-ment. Such a storm of vulgar force has broke in."—BOSWELL. "It has only roared."—JOHNSON. "Sir, it has roared, till the Judges in Westminster-Hall have been afraid to pronounce sentence in opposition to the popular cry. You are frightened by what is no longer dangerous, like Presbyterians by Popery."—He then

[1] "Unhappy queen!
Unwilling I forsook your friendly state."
—*Dryden.*

repeated a passage, I think, in Butler's *Remains*, which ends, "and would cry, Fire! Fire! in Noah's flood." [1]

We had a dreary drive, in a dusky night, to St. Andrews, where we arrived late. We found a good supper at Glass's inn, and Dr. Johnson revived agreeably. He said, "the collection called 'The Muses' Welcome to King James,' (first of England, and sixth of Scotland,) on his return to his native kingdom, shewed that there was then abundance of learning in Scotland; and that the conceits in that collection, with which people find fault, were mere mode." He added, "we could not now entertain a sovereign so; that Buchanan had spread the spirit of learning amongst us, but we had lost it during the civil wars." He did not allow the Latin Poetry of Pitcairne so much merit as has been usually attributed to it; though he owned that one of his pieces, which he mentioned, but which I am sorry

The travellers at St. Andrews

---

[1] The passage quoted by Dr. Johnson is in the *Character of the Assembly-man*, Butler's *Remains*, p. 232, edit. 1754.—"He preaches, indeed, both in season and out of season; for he rails at Popery, when the land is almost lost in Presbytery; and would cry Fire! Fire! in Noah's flood."

There is reason to believe that this piece was not written by Butler, but by Sir John Birkenhead; for Wood, in his *Athenæ Oxonienses*, Vol. II. p. 640, enumerates it among that gentleman's works, and gives the following account of it:

"*The Assembly-man* (or the character of an Assembly-man) written 1647, Lond. 1662–3, in three sheets in qu. The copy of it was taken from the author by those who said they could not rob, because all was theirs; so excised what they liked not; and so mangled and reformed it, that it was no character of an Assembly, but of themselves. At length, after it had slept several years, the author published it, to avoid false copies. It is also reprinted in a book entit. *Wit and Loyalty revived*, in a collection of some smart satyrs in verse and prose on the late times, Lond. 1682, qu. said to be written by Abr. Cowley, Sir John Birkenhead, and Hudibras, alias Sam. Butler."—For this information I am indebted to Mr. Reed, of Staple Inn.

Learning and patronage

is not specified in my notes, was "very well." It is not improbable that it was the poem which Prior has so elegantly translated.

After supper, we made a *procession* to Saint Leonard's College, the landlord walking before us with a candle, and the waiter with a lantern. That college had some time before been dissolved; and Dr. Watson, a professor here, (the historian of Phillip II.) had purchased the ground, and what buildings remained. When we entered his court, it seemed quite academical; and we found in his house very comfortable and genteel accommodation.[1]

Thursday, 19th August.

We rose much refreshed. I had with me a map of Scotland, a Bible, which was given me by Lord Mountstuart when we were together in Italy, and Ogden's Sermons on Prayer. Mr. Nairne introduced us to Dr. Watson, whom we found a well-informed man, of very amiable manners. Dr. Johnson, after they were acquainted, said, "I take great delight in him." —His daughter, a very pleasing young lady, made breakfast. Dr. Watson observed, that Glasgow University had fewer home-students, since trade increased, as learning was rather incompatible with it. —JOHNSON. "Why, sir, as trade is now carried on by subordinate hands, men in trade have as much leisure as others; and now learning itself is a trade. A man goes to a bookseller, and gets what he can. We have done with patronage. In the infancy of learning, we find some great man praised for it. This diffused it among others. When it becomes

[1] My Journal from this day inclusive, was read by Dr. Johnson.

general, an author leaves the great, and applies to the **Changes** multitude."—BOSWELL. "It is a shame that authors **of man-** are not now better patronized."—JOHNSON. "No, sir. **ners** If learning cannot support a man, if he must sit with his hands across till somebody feeds him, it is as to him a bad thing, and it is better as it is. With patronage, what flattery! what falsehood! While a man is in equilibrio, he throws truth among the multitude, and lets them take it as they please : in patronage, he must say what pleases his patron, and it is an equal chance whether that be truth or falsehood."—WATSON. "But is not the case now, that, instead of flattering one person, we flatter the age?"—JOHNSON. "No, sir. The world always lets a man tell what he thinks, his own way. I wonder however, that so many people have written, who might have let it alone. That people should endeavour to excel in conversation, I do not wonder ; because in conversation praise is instantly reverberated."

We talked of change of manners. Dr. Johnson observed, that our drinking less than our ancestors was owing to the change from ale to wine. "I remember, (said he,) when all the *decent* people in Lichfield got drunk every night, and were not the worse thought of. Ale was cheap, so you pressed strongly. When a man must bring a bottle of wine, he is not in such haste. Smoking has gone out. To be sure, it is a shocking thing, blowing smoke out of our mouths into other people's mouths, eyes, and noses, and having the same thing done to us. Yet I cannot account, why a thing which requires so little exertion, and yet preserves the mind from total vacuity, should have gone out. Every man has something by which he calms himself: beating with his feet, or so.[1] I remember when people in England changed a shirt only once a week

[1] Dr. Johnson used to practice this himself very much.

The value of money — a Pandour, when he gets a shirt, greases it to make it last. Formerly, good tradesmen had no fire but in the kitchen; never in the parlour, except on Sunday. My father, who was a magistrate of Lichfield, lived thus. They never began to have a fire in the parlour, but on leaving off business, or some great revolution of their life."—Dr. Watson said, the hall was as a kitchen, in old squires' houses.—JOHNSON. "No, sir. The hall was for great occasions, and never was used for domestick refection."—We talked of the Union, and what money it had brought into Scotland. Dr. Watson observed, that a little money formerly went as far as a great deal now.—JOHNSON. "In speculation, it seems that a smaller quantity of money, equal in value to a larger quantity, if equally divided, should produce the same effect. But it is not so in reality. Many more conveniences and elegancies are enjoyed where money is plentiful, than where it is scarce. Perhaps a great familiarity with it, which arises from plenty, makes us more easily part with it."

After what Dr. Johnson had said of St. Andrews, which he had long wished to see, as our oldest university, and the seat of our Primate in the days of episcopacy, I can say little. Since the publication of Dr. Johnson's book, I find that he has been censured for not seeing here the ancient chapel of St. Rule, a curious piece of sacred architecture. But this was neither his fault nor mine. We were both of us abundantly desirous of surveying such sort of antiquities: but neither of us knew of this. I am afraid the censure must fall on those who did not tell us of it. In every place, where there is any thing worthy of observation, there should be a short printed directory for strangers, such as we find in all the towns of Italy, and in some of the towns in England. I was told that there is a manuscript account of St. Andrews, by **Retire-** Martin, secretary to Archbishop Sharp; and that one **ment** Douglas has published a small account of it. I in- **from the** quired at a bookseller's, but could not get it. Dr. **world** Johnson's veneration for the Hierarchy is well known. There is no wonder then, that he was affected with a strong indignation, while he beheld the ruins of religious magnificence. I happened to ask where John Knox was buried. Dr. Johnson burst out, "I hope in the high-way. I have been looking at his reformations."

It was a very fine day. Dr. Johnson seemed quite wrapt up in the contemplation of the scenes which were now presented to him. He kept his hat off while he was upon any part of the ground where the cathedral had stood. He said well, that "Knox had set on a mob, without knowing where it would end; and that differing from a man in doctrine was no reason why you should pull his house about his ears." As we walked in the cloisters, there was a solemn echo, while he talked loudly of a proper retirement from the world. Mr. Nairne said, he had an inclination to retire. I called Dr. Johnson's attention to this, that I might hear his opinion if it was right.—JOHNSON. "Yes, when he has done his duty to society. In general, as every man is obliged not only to 'love GOD, but his neighbour as himself,' he must bear his part in active life; yet there are exceptions. Those who are exceedingly scrupulous, (which I do not approve, for I am no friend to scruples,) and find their scrupulosity invincible, so that they are quite in the dark, and know not what they shall do,—or those who cannot resist temptations, and find they make themselves worse by being in the world, without making it better, may retire. I never read of a hermit, but in imagination I

Dinner with the Professors

kiss his feet; never of a monastery, but I could fall on my knees, and kiss the pavement. But I think putting young people there, who know nothing of life, nothing of retirement, is dangerous and wicked. It is a saying as old as Hesiod,

'Εργα νεῶν, βουλαίτε μέσων, ἔυχαιτε γερόντων.[1]

That is a very noble line: not that young men should not pray, or old men not give counsel, but that every season of life has its proper duties. I have thought of retiring, and have talked of it to a friend; but I find my vocation is rather to active life." I said, *some* young monks might be allowed, to shew that it is not age alone that can retire to pious solitude; but he thought this would only shew that they could not resist temptation.

He wanted to mount the steeples, but it could not be done. There are no good inscriptions here. Bad Roman characters he naturally mistook for half Gothick, half Roman. One of the steeples, which he was told was in danger, he wished not to be taken down; "for, said he, it may fall on some of the posterity of John Knox; and no great matter!"— Dinner was mentioned.——JOHNSON. "Ay, ay; amidst all these sorrowful scenes, I have no objection to dinner."

We went and looked at the castle, where Cardinal Beaton was murdered, and then visited Principal Murison at his college, where is a good library-room; but the principal was abundantly vain of it, for he seriously said to Dr. Johnson, "you have not such a one in England."

The professors entertained us with a very good dinner. Present: Murison, Shaw, Cooke, Hill, Haddo,

[1] Let youth in deeds, in counsel man engage;
Prayer is the proper duty of old age.

Watson, Flint, Brown. I observed, that I wondered to see him eat so well, after viewing so many sorrowful scenes of ruined religious magnificence. "Why," said he, "I am not sorry, after seeing these gentlemen; for they are not sorry."—Murison said, all sorrow was bad, as it was murmuring against the dispensations of Providence. — JOHNSON. "Sir, sorrow is inherent in humanity. As you cannot judge two and two to be either five, or three, but certainly four, so, when comparing a worse present state with a better which is past, you cannot but feel sorrow. It is not cured by reason, but by the incursion of present objects, which wear out the past. You need not murmur, though you are sorry."—MURISON. "But St. Paul says, 'I have learnt, in whatever state I am, therewith to be content.'"—JOHNSON. "Sir, that relates to riches and poverty; for we see St. Paul, when he had a thorn in the flesh, prayed earnestly to have it removed; and then he could not be content."—Murison, thus refuted, tried to be smart, and drank to Dr. Johnson, "Long may you lecture!"—Dr. Johnson afterwards, speaking of his not drinking wine, said, "The Doctor spoke of *lecturing* (looking to him). I give all these lectures on water."

Sorrow inherent in humanity

He defended requiring subscription in those admitted to universities, thus: "As all who come into the country must obey the king, so all who come into an university must be of the church."

And here I must do Dr. Johnson the justice to contradict a very absurd and ill-natured story, as to what passed at St. Andrews. It has been circulated, that, after grace was said in English, in the usual manner, he with the greatest marks of contempt, as if he had held it to be no grace in an university, would not sit down till he had said grace aloud in Latin. This

Im-
pressions
of St.
Andrews
would have been an insult indeed to the gentlemen
who were entertaining us. But the truth was precisely
thus. In the course of conversation at dinner, Dr.
Johnson, in very good humour, said, " I should have
expected to have heard a Latin grace, among so many
learned men : we had always a Latin grace at Oxford.
I believe I can repeat it." Which he did, as giving
the learned men in one place a specimen of what was
done by the learned men in another place.

We went and saw the church, in which is Archbishop Sharp's monument. I was struck with the
same kind of feelings with which the churches of Italy
impressed me. I was much pleased, to see Dr. Johnson actually in St. Andrews, of which we had talked
so long. Professor Haddo was with us this afternoon,
along with Dr. Watson. We looked at St. Salvador's
College. The rooms for students seemed very commodious, and Dr. Johnson said, the chapel was the
neatest place of worship he had seen. The key of
the library could not be found ; for it seems Professor
Hill, who was out of town, had taken it with him.
Dr. Johnson told a joke he had heard of a monastery
abroad, where the key of the library could never be
found.

It was somewhat dispiriting, to see this ancient archi-
episcopal city now sadly deserted. We saw in one of its
streets a remarkable proof of liberal toleration ; a nonjuring clergyman, strutting about in his canonicals, with
a jolly countenance and a round belly, like a well-fed
monk.

We observed two occupations united in the same
person, who had hung out two sign-posts. Upon one
was, " James Hood, White Iron Smith " (*i.e.* Tin-
plate Worker). Upon another, " The Art of Fencing
taught, by James Hood."—Upon this last were painted

some trees, and two men fencing, one of whom had
hit the other in the eye, to shew his great dexterity;
so that the art was well taught.—JOHNSON. "Were I
studying here, I should go and take a lesson. I remember Hope, in his book on this art, says, "'the
Scotch are very good fencers.'"

The danger of slow composition

We returned to the inn, where we had been entertained at dinner, and drank tea in company with some
of the Professors, of whose civilities I beg leave to add
my humble and very grateful acknowledgement to the
honourable testimony of Dr. Johnson, in his "Journey."

We talked of composition, which was a favourite
topick of Dr. Watson's, who first distinguished himself by lectures on rhetorick.—JOHNSON. "I advised
Chambers, and would advise every young man beginning to compose, to do it as fast as he can, to get a
habit of having his mind to start promptly; it is so
much more difficult to improve in speed than in accuracy."—WATSON. "I own I am for much attention to
accuracy in composing, lest one should get bad habits
of doing it in a slovenly manner."—JOHNSON. "Why,
sir, you are confounding *doing* inaccurately with the
necessity of doing inaccurately. A man knows when
his composition is inaccurate, and when he thinks fit
he'll correct it. But, if a man is accustomed to compose slowly, and with difficulty, upon all occasions,
there is danger that he may not compose at all, as we
do not like to do that which is not done easily; and,
at any rate, more time is consumed in a small matter
than ought to be."—WATSON. "Dr. Hugh Blair has
taken a week to compose a sermon."—JOHNSON. "Then,
sir, that is for want of the habit of composing quickly,
which I am insisting one should acquire."—WATSON.
"Blair was not composing all the week, but only such
hours as he found himself disposed for composition."

Johnson's
rapid
composition

—JOHNSON. "Nay, sir, unless you tell me the time he took, you tell me nothing. If I say I took a week to walk a mile, and have had the gout five days, and been ill otherwise another day, I have taken but one day. I myself have composed about forty sermons. I have begun a sermon after dinner, and sent it off by the post that night. I wrote forty-eight of the printed octavo pages of the Life of Savage at a sitting; but then I sat up all night. I have also written six sheets in a day of translation from the French."—BOSWELL. "We have all observed how one man dresses himself slowly, and another fast."—JOHNSON. "Yes, sir; it is wonderful how much time some people will consume in dressing; taking up a thing and looking at it, and laying it down, and taking it up again. Every one should get the habit of doing it quickly. I would say to a young divine, 'Here is your text; let me see how soon you can make a sermon.' Then I'd say, 'Let me see how much better you can make it.' Thus I should see both his powers and his judgement."

We all went to Dr. Watson's to supper. Miss Sharp, great grandchild of Archbishop Sharp, was there; as was Mr. Craig, the ingenious architect of the new town of Edinburgh, and nephew of Thomson, to whom Dr. Johnson has since done so much justice, in his "Lives of the Poets."

We talked of memory, and its various modes.— JOHNSON. "Memory will play strange tricks. One sometimes loses a single word. I once lost *fugaces* in the Ode *Posthume, Posthume.*" I mentioned to him, that a worthy gentleman of my acquaintance actually forgot his own name.—JOHNSON. "Sir, that was a morbid oblivion."

Friday, 20th August.

Dr. Shaw, the professor of divinity, breakfasted with us. I took out my "Ogden on Prayer," and read some of it to the company. Dr. Johnson praised him. "Abernethy (said he,) allows only of a physical effect of prayer upon the mind, which may be produced many ways, as well as by prayer; for instance, by meditation. Ogden goes farther. In truth, we have the consent of all nations for the efficacy of prayer, whether offered up by individuals, or by assemblies; and Revelation has told us, it will be effectual."—I said, "Leechman seemed to incline to Abernethy's doctrine." Dr. Watson observed, that Leechman meant to shew, that, even admitting no effect to be produced by prayer, respecting the Deity, it was useful to our own minds. He had given only a part of his system: Dr. Johnson thought he should have given the whole.

Dr. Johnson enforced the strict observance of Sunday. "It should be different (he observed) from another day. People may walk, but not throw stones at birds. There may be relaxation, but there should be no levity."

We went and saw Colonel Nairne's garden and grotto. Here was a fine old plane tree. Unluckily the colonel said, there was but this and another large tree in the county. This assertion was an excellent cue for Dr. Johnson, who laughed enormously, calling to me to hear it. He had expatiated to me on the nakedness of that part of Scotland which he had seen. His "Journey" has been violently abused, for what he has said upon this subject. But let it be considered, that, when Dr. Johnson talks of trees, he means trees of good size, such as he was accustomed to see in

Trees in
Scotland
England; and of these there are certainly very few upon the *eastern coast* of Scotland. Besides, he said, that he meant to give only a map of the road; and let any traveller observe how many trees, which deserve the name, he can see from the road from Berwick to Aberdeen. Had Dr. Johnson said, "there are *no* trees" upon this line, he would have said what is colloquially true; because, by no trees, in common speech, we mean few. When he is particular in counting, he may be attacked. I know not how Colonel Nairne came to say there were but *two* large trees in the county of Fife. I did not perceive that he smiled. There are certainly not a great many; but I could have shewn him more than two at Balmuto, from whence my ancestors came, and which now belongs to a branch of my family.

The grotto was ingeniously constructed. In the front of it were petrified stocks of fir, plane, and some other tree. Dr. Johnson said, " Scotland has no right to boast of this grotto; it is owing to personal merit. I never denied personal merit to many of you."— Professor Shaw said to me, as we walked, " This is a wonderful man: he is master of every subject he handles."—Dr. Watson allowed him a very strong understanding, but wondered at his total inattention to established manners, as he came from London.

I have not preserved, in my Journal, any of the conversation which passed between Dr. Johnson and Professor Shaw; but I recollect Dr. Johnson said to me afterwards, "I took much to Shaw."

We left St. Andrews about noon, and some miles from it observing, at Leuchars, a church with an old tower, we stopped to look at it. The *manse*, as the parsonage-house is called in Scotland, was close by. I waited on the minister, mentioned our names, and begged he would tell us what he knew about it. He was a very civil old man; but could only inform us, that it was supposed to have stood eight hundred years. He told us, there was a colony of Danes in his parish; that they had landed at a remote period of time, and still remained a distinct people. Dr. Johnson shrewdly inquired whether they had brought women with them. We were not satisfied as to this colony.

We saw, this day, Dundee and Aberbrothick, the last of which Dr. Johnson has celebrated in his "Journey." Upon the road we talked of the Roman Catholick faith. He mentioned (I think) Tillotson's argument against transubstantiation: "That we are as sure we see bread and wine only, as that we read in the Bible the text on which that false doctrine is founded. We have only the evidence of our senses for both." "If, (he added,) GOD had never spoken figuratively, we might hold that he speaks literally, when he says, 'This is my body.'"—BOSWELL. "But what do you say, sir, to the ancient and continued tradition of the church upon this point?"—JOHNSON. "Tradition, sir, has no place, where the Scriptures are plain; and tradition cannot persuade a man into a belief of transubstantiation. Able men, indeed, have *said* they believed it."

This is an awful subject. I did not then press Dr. Johnson upon it; nor shall I now enter upon a disquisition concerning the import of those words uttered by our Saviour,[1] which had such an effect upon many of his disciples, that they "went back, and walked no more with him." The Catechism and solemn office for Communion, in the Church of England, maintain

Transubstantiation

---

[1] *Then Jesus said unto them, Verily, verily, I say unto you, except ye eat the flesh of the Son of man, and drink his blood, ye have no life in you.* See St. John's Gospel, chap. vi. 53, and following verses.

a mysterious belief in more than a mere commemoration of the death of Christ, by partaking of the elements of bread and wine.

Dr. Johnson put me in mind, that, at St. Andrews, I had defended my profession very well, when the question had again been started, Whether a lawyer might honestly engage with the first side that offers him a fee. " Sir, (said I,) it was with your arguments against Sir William Forbes : but it was much that I could wield the arms of Goliath."

He said, our judges had not gone deep in the question concerning literary property. I mentioned Lord Monboddo's opinion, that if a man could get a work by heart, he might print it, as by such an act the mind is exercised.—JOHNSON. " No, sir ; a man's repeating it no more makes it his property, than a man may sell a cow which he drives home."—I said, printing an abridgement of a work was allowed, which was only cutting the horns and tail off the cow.—JOHNSON. " No, sir ; 'tis making the cow have a calf."

About eleven at night we arrived at Montrose. We found but a sorry inn, where I myself saw another waiter put a lump of sugar with his fingers into Dr. Johnson's lemonade, for which he called him " Rascal ! " It put me in great glee that our landlord was an Englishman. I rallied the Doctor upon this, and he grew quiet. Both Sir John Hawkins's and Dr. Burney's History of Musick had then been advertised. I asked if this was not unlucky : would not they hurt one another ? —JOHNSON. " No, sir. They will do good to one another. Some will buy the one, some the other, and compare them ; and so a talk is made about a thing, and the books are sold."

He was angry at me for proposing to carry lemons with us to Sky, that he might be sure to have his lemonade. "Sir, (said he,) I do not wish to be thought that feeble man who cannot do without any thing. Sir, it is very bad manners to carry provisions to any man's house, as if he could not entertain you. To an inferior, it is oppressive; to a superior, it is insolent." Johnson compared to a ghost

Having taken the liberty, this evening, to remark to Dr. Johnson, that he very often sat quite silent for a long time, even when in company with only a single friend, which I myself had sometimes sadly experienced, he smiled and said, "It is true, sir. Tom Tyers, (for so he familiarly called our ingenious friend, who, since his death, has paid a biographical tribute to his memory,) Tom Tyers described me the best. He once said to me, 'Sir, you are like a ghost: you never speak till you are spoken to.'" [1]

Saturday, 21st August.

Neither the Rev. Mr. Nisbet, the established minister, nor the Rev. Mr. Spooner, the episcopal minister, were in town. Before breakfast, we went and saw the town-hall, where is a good dancing-room, and other rooms for tea-drinking. The appearance of the town from it is very well; but many of the houses are built with their ends to the street, which looks awkward. When we came down from it, I met Mr. Gleg, a merchant here. He went with us to see the English chapel. It is situated on a pretty dry spot, and there is a fine walk to it. It is really an elegant building, both within and without. The organ is adorned with green and gold.

[1] This description of Dr. Johnson, appears to have been borrowed from "Tom Jones," Book XI. chap. ii. "The other, who like a ghost, only wanted to be spoke to, readily answered," &c.

Johnson and Lord Monboddo

Dr. Johnson gave a shilling extraordinary to the clerk, saying, "He belongs to an honest church." I put him in mind, that episcopals were but *dissenters* here; they were only *tolerated.* "Sir, (said he,) we are here, as Christians in Turkey."—He afterwards went into an apothecary's shop, and ordered some medicine for himself, and wrote the prescription in technical characters. The boy took him for a physician.

I doubted much which road to take, whether to go by the coast, or by Laurence Kirk and Monboddo. I knew Lord Monboddo and Dr. Johnson did not love each other: yet I was unwilling not to visit his lordship; and was also curious to see them together.[1] I mentioned my doubts to Dr. Johnson, who said, he would go two miles out of his way to see Lord Monboddo. I therefore sent Joseph forward, with the following note:

"Montrose, 21 August.

"MY DEAR LORD,

"THUS far I am come with Mr. Samuel Johnson. We must be at Aberdeen to-night. I know you do not admire him so much as I do; but I cannot be in this country without making you a bow at your old place, as I do not know if I may again have an opportunity of seeing Monboddo. Besides, Mr. Johnson says, he would go two miles out of his way to see Lord Monboddo. I have sent forward my servant, that we may know if your lordship be at home. I am ever, my dear lord,

"Most sincerely yours,

"JAMES BOSWELL."

[1] There were several points of similarity between them, learning, clearness of head, precision of speech, and a love of research on many subjects which people in general do not

As we travelled onwards from Montrose, we had Laurence Kirk the Grampion hills in our view, and some good land around us, but void of trees and hedges. Dr. Johnson has said ludicrously, in his "Journey," that the *hedges* were of *stone*; for, instead of the verdant *thorn* to refresh the eye, we found the bare *wall* or *dike* intersecting the Prospect. He observed, that it was wonderful to see a country so divested, so denuded of trees.

We stopped at Laurence Kirk, where our great Grammarian, Ruddiman, was once schoolmaster. We respectfully remembered that excellent man and eminent scholar, by whose labours a knowledge of the Latin language will be preserved in Scotland, if it shall be preserved at all. Lord Gardenston, one of our judges, collected money to raise a monument to him at this place, which I hope will be well executed. I know my father gave five guineas towards it. Lord Gardenston is the proprietor of Laurence Kirk, and has encouraged the building of a manufacturing village, of which he is exceedingly fond, and has written a pamphlet upon it, as if he had founded Thebes; in which, however, there are many useful precepts strongly expressed. The village seemed to be irregularly built, some of the houses being of clay, some of brick, and some of brick and stone. Dr. Johnson observed, they thatched well here.

I was a little acquainted with Mr. Forbes, the minister of the parish. I sent to inform him that a gentleman desired to see him. He returned for answer, "that he would not come to a stranger." I then gave my name, and he came. I remonstrated to him for not coming to a stranger; and, by pre-

---

investigate. Foote paid Lord Monboddo the compliment of saying, that he was "an Elzevir edition of Johnson."

It has been shrewdly observed that Foote must have meant a diminutive, or *pocket* edition.

senting him to Dr. Johnson, proved to him what a
stranger might sometimes be. His Bible inculcates
"be not forgetful to entertain strangers," and mentions the same motive. He defended himself by
saying, "He had once come to a stranger who sent
for him; and he found him 'a *little worth person*'!"

Dr. Johnson insisted on stopping at the inn, as I
told him that Lord Gardenston had furnished it with
a collection of books, that travellers might have entertainment for the mind, as well as the body. He praised
the design, but wished there had been more books, and
those better chosen.

About a mile from Monboddo, where you turn off
the road, Joseph was waiting to tell us my lord expected
us to dinner. We drove over a wild moor. It rained,
and the scene was somewhat dreary. Dr. Johnson
repeated, with solemn emphasis, Macbeth's speech on
meeting the witches. As we travelled on, he told
me, "Sir, you got into our club by doing what a
man can do.[1] Several of the members wished to
keep you out. Burke told me, he doubted if you
were fit for it: but, now you are in, none of them
are sorry. Burke says, that you have so much good
humour naturally, it is scarce a virtue."—BOSWELL.
"They were afraid of you, sir, as it was you who
proposed me."—JOHNSON. "Sir, they knew, that
if they refused you, they'd probably never have got
in another. I'd have kept them all out. Beauclerk
was very earnest for you."—BOSWELL. "Beauclerk
has a keenness of mind which is very uncommon."—
JOHNSON. "Yes, sir; and every thing comes from him

[1] This, I find, is considered as obscure. I suppose Dr.
Johnson meant, that I assiduously and earnestly recommended myself to some of the members, as in a canvass
for an election into parliament.

so easily. It appears to me that I labour, when I say a good thing."—BOSWELL. "You are loud, sir; but it is not an effort of mind."

Monboddo is a wretched place, wild and naked, with a poor old house; though, if I recollect right, there are two turrets which mark an old baron's residence. Lord Monboddo received us at his gate most courteously; pointed to the Douglas arms upon his house, and told us that his great-grandmother was of that family. "In such houses (said he,) our ancestors lived, who were better men than we."—"No, no, my lord (said Dr. Johnson). We are as strong as they, and a great deal wiser."—This was an assault upon one of Lord Monboddo's capital dogmas, and I was afraid there would have been a violent altercation in the very close, before we got into the house. But his lordship is distinguished not only for "ancient metaphysicks," but for ancient *politesse*, "*la vieille cour*," and he made no reply.

His lordship was drest in a rustick suit, and wore a little round hat; he told us, we now saw him as *Farmer Burnet*, and we should have his family dinner, a farmer's dinner. He said, "I should not have forgiven Mr. Boswell, had he not brought you here, Dr. Johnson." He produced a very long stalk of corn, as a specimen of his crop, and said, "You see here the *lætas segetes*:" he added, that Virgil seemed to be as enthusiastick a farmer as he, and was certainly a practical one.—JOHNSON. "It does not always follow, my lord, that a man who has written a good poem on an art, has practised it. Philip Miller told me, that in Philips's CYDER, a poem, all the precepts were just, and indeed better than in books written for the purpose of instructing; yet Philips had never made cyder."

I started the subject of emigration.—JOHNSON. "To a

man of mere animal life, you can urge no argument
against going to America, but that it will be some time
before he will get the earth to produce. But a man of
any intellectual enjoyment will not easily go and immerse
himself and his posterity for ages in barbarism."

He and my lord spoke highly of Homer.—JOHNSON.
"He had all the learning of his age. The shield of
Achilles shews a nation in war, a nation in peace;
harvest sport, nay stealing." [1]—MONBODDO. "Ay,
and what we (looking to me) would call a parliament-
house scene; a cause pleaded."—JOHNSON. "That is
part of the life of a nation in peace. And there are in
Homer such characters of heroes, and combinations of
qualities of heroes, that the united powers of mankind
ever since have not produced any but what are to
be found there."—MONBODDO. "Yet no character is
described."—JOHNSON. "No; they all develope themselves. Agamemnon is always a gentleman - like
character; he has always Βασιλικον τι. That the
ancients held so, is plain from this; that Euripides, in
his Hecuba, makes him the person to interpose." [2]—
MONBODDO. "The history of manners is the most

---

[1] My note of this is much too short. *Brevis esse laboro,
obscurus fio.* Yet as I have resolved that *the very Journal which
Dr. Johnson read*, shall be presented to the publick, I will not
expand the text in any considerable degree, though I may
occasionally supply a word to complete the sense, as I fill up
the blanks of abbreviation in the writing; neither of which
can be said to change the genuine Journal. One of the best
critics of our age conjectures that the imperfect passage
above has probably been as follows: "In his book we
have an accurate display of a nation in war, and a nation
in peace; the peasant is delineated as truly as the general;
nay, even harvest-sport, and the modes of ancient theft are
described."

[2] Dr. Johnson modestly said, he had not read Homer so
much as he wished he had done. But this conversation

valuable. I never set a high value on any other history."—JOHNSON. "Nor I; and therefore I esteem biography, as giving us what comes near to ourselves, what we can turn to use."—BOSWELL. "But in the course of general history, we find manners. In wars, we see the dispositions of people, their degrees of humanity, and other particulars."—JOHNSON. "Yes; but then you must take all the facts to get this; and it is but a little you get."—MONBODDO. "And it is that little which makes history valuable."—Bravo! thought I; they agree like two brothers.—MONBODDO. "I am sorry, Dr. Johnson, you were not longer at Edinburgh, to receive the homage of our men of learning."—JOHNSON. "My lord, I received great respect and great kindness."—BOSWELL. "He goes back to Edinburgh after our tour."—We talked of the decrease of learning in Scotland, and of the "Muses' Welcome." —JOHNSON. "Learning is much decreased in England, in my remembrance."—MONBODDO. "You, sir, have lived to see its decrease in England, I its extinction in Scotland." However, I brought him to confess that the High School of Edinburgh did well. —JOHNSON. "Learning has decreased in England, because learning will not do so much for a man as formerly. There are other ways of getting preferment. Few bishops are now made for their learning. To be a bishop, a man must be learned in a learned age,—factious in a factious age; but always of emi-

The decrease of learning

shews how well he was acquainted with the Mœonian bard; and he has shewn it still more in his criticism upon Pope's Homer, in his Life of that Poet. My excellent friend, Mr. Langton, told me, he was once present at a dispute between Dr. Johnson and Mr. Burke, on the comparative merits of Homer and Virgil, which was carried on with extraordinary abilities on both sides. Dr. Johnson maintained the superiority of Homer.

Warbur- nence. Warburton is an exception ; though his learn-
ton   ing alone did not raise him.   He was first an antagonist
to Pope, and helped Theobald to publish his Shak-
speare ; but, seeing Pope the rising man,—when Crousaz
attacked his 'Essay on Man,' for some faults which it
has, and some which it has not, Warburton defended
it in the Review of that time. This brought him
acquainted with Pope, and he gained his friendship.
Pope introduced him to Allen, Allen married him to
his niece : so, by Allen's interest and his own, he was
made a bishop.   But then his learning was the *sine quà
non* : He knew how to make the most of it ; but I
do not find by any dishonest means."—MONBODDO.
" He is a great man."—JOHNSON. " Yes ; he has great
knowledge,—great power of mind.   Hardly any man
brings greater variety of learning to bear upon his
point."—MONBODDO. "He is one of the greatest
lights of your church."—JOHNSON. "Why, we are
not so sure of his being very friendly to us.   He blazes,
if you will, but that is not always the steadiest light.—
Lowth is another bishop who has risen by his learning."

Dr. Johnson examined young Arthur, Lord Monboddo's son, in Latin.   He answered very well ;
upon which he said, with complacency, " Get you
gone !   When King James comes back,[1] you shall be
in the 'Muses' Welcome' ! "—My lord and Dr. Johnson disputed a little, whether the Savage or the London
Shopkeeper had the best existence ; his lordship, as
usual, preferring the Savage.—My lord was extremely
hospitable, and I saw both Dr. Johnson and him liking
each other better every hour.

Dr. Johnson having retired for a short time, his

[1] I find, some doubt has been entertained concerning Dr.
Johnson's meaning here.   It is to be supposed that he meant,
" when a king shall again be entertained in Scotland."

lordship spoke of his conversation as I could have Good
wished.   Dr. Johnson had said, "I have done greater breeding
feats with my knife than this;" though he had eaten
a very hearty dinner.—My lord, who affects or believes
he follows an abstemious system, seemed struck with
Dr. Johnson's manner of living.   I had a particular
satisfaction in being under the roof of Monboddo, my
lord being my father's old friend, and having been
always very good to me.   We were cordial together.
He asked Dr. Johnson and me to stay all night.
When I said we *must* be at Aberdeen, he replied,
"Well, I am like the Romans: I shall say to you,
' Happy to come ;—happy to depart ! ' "   He thanked
Dr. Johnson for his visit.—JOHNSON. "I little thought,
when I had the honour to meet your lordship in London, that I should see you at Monboddo."   After
dinner, as the ladies were going away, Dr. Johnson
would stand up.   He insisted that politeness was of
great consequence in society.   "It is, (said he,) fictitious benevolence.   It supplies the place of it amongst
those who see each other only in publick, or but little.
Depend upon it, the want of it never fails to produce
something disagreeable to one or other.   I have always
applied to good breeding, what Addison in his "Cato"
says of honour :

" ' Honour's a sacred tie ; the law of Kings ;
    The noble mind's distinguishing perfection,
    That aids and strengthens Virtue where it meets her,
    And imitates her actions where she is not.' "

When he took up his large oak stick, he said,
" My lord, that's *Homerick* ; " thus pleasantly alluding
to his lordship's favourite writer.

Gory, my lord's black servant, was sent as our
guide, to conduct us to the high road.   The cir-

Johnson
and Lord
Mon-
boddo

cumstance of each of them having a black servant
was another point of similarity between Johnson and
Monboddo. I observed how curious it was to see
an African in the north of Scotland, with little or
no difference of manners from those of the natives.
Dr. Johnson laughed to see Gory and Joseph riding
togéther most cordially. "Those two fellows, (said
he,) one from Africa, the other from Bohemia, seem
quite at home."—He was much pleased with Lord
Monboddo to-day. He said, he would have pardoned
him for a few paradoxes, when he found he had so
much that was good : but that, from his appearance in
London, he thought him all paradox ; which would
not do. He observed, that his lordship had talked no
paradoxes to-day. "And as to the savage and the
London shopkeeper, (said he,) I don't know but I
might have taken the side of the savage equally, had
any body else taken the side of the shopkeeper."—
He had said to my lord, in opposition to the value of
the savage's courage, that it was owing to his limited
power of thinking, and repeated Pope's verses, in which
" Macedonia's madman " is introduced, and the conclusion is,

" Yet ne'er looks forward farther than his nose."

I objected to the last phrase, as being low.—Johnson.
" Sir, it is intended to be low : it is satire. The
expression is debased, to debase the character."

When Gory was about to part from us, Dr. Johnson called to him, " Mr. Gory, give me leave to ask
you a question : are you baptised ? " Gory told him
he was,—and confirmed by the Bishop of Durham.
He then gave him a shilling.

We had tedious driving this afternoon, and were
somewhat drowsy. Last night I was afraid Dr.

Johnson was beginning to faint in his resolution; for he said, "If we must ride much, we shall not go; and there's an end on't."—To-day, when he talked of Sky with spirit, I said, "Why, sir, you seemed to me to despond yesterday. You are a delicate Londoner;—you are a maccaroni; you can't ride."—JOHNSON. "Sir, I shall ride better than you. I was only afraid I should not find a horse able to carry me."—I hoped then there would be no fear of getting through our wild Tour.

We came to Aberdeen at half an hour past eleven. The New Inn, we were told, was full. This was comfortless. The waiter, however, asked if one of our names was Boswell, and brought me a letter left at the inn: it was from Mr. Thrale, enclosing one to Dr. Johnson. Finding who I was, we were told they would contrive to lodge us by putting us for a night into a room with two beds. The waiter said to me in the broad strong Aberdeenshire dialect, "I thought I knew you, by your likeness to your father." —My father puts up at the New Inn, when on his circuit. Little was said to-night. I was to sleep in a little press-bed in Dr. Johnson's room. I had it wheeled out into the dining-room, and there I lay very well.

Sunday, 22nd August.

I sent a message to Professor Thomas Gordon, who came and breakfasted with us. He had secured seats for us at the English chapel. We found a respectable congregation, and an admirable organ, well played by Mr. Tait.

We walked down to the shore. Dr. Johnson laughed to hear that Cromwell's soldiers taught the Aberdeen people to make shoes and stockings, and to plant cab-

Publick
and
private
schools

bages. He asked, if weaving the plaids was ever a
domestick art in the Highlands, like spinning or knit-
ting. They could not inform him here. But he conjectured probably, that where people lived so remote
from each other, it was likely to be a domestick art;
as we see it was among the ancients, from Penelope.
—I was sensible to-day, to an extraordinary degree,
of Dr. Johnson's excellent English pronunciation. I
cannot account for its striking me more now than any
other day: but it was as if new to me; and I listened
to every sentence which he spoke, as to a musical composition.—Professor Gordon gave him an account of
the plan of education in his college. Dr. Johnson
said, it was similar to that at Oxford.—Waller the
poet's great grandson was studying here. Dr. Johnson
wondered that a man should send his son so far off,
when there were so many good schools in England.
He said, "At a great school there is all the splendour
and illumination of many minds; the radiance of all is
concentrated in each, or at least reflected upon each.
But we must own that neither a dull boy, nor an idle
boy, will do so well at a great school as at a private
one. For at a great school there are always boys
enough to do well easily, who are sufficient to keep
up the credit of the school; and after whipping being
tried to no purpose, the dull or idle boys are left at the
end of a class, having the appearance of going through
the course, but learning nothing at all. Such boys may
do good at a private school, where constant attention is
paid to them, and they are watched. So that the question of publick or private education is not properly a
general one; but whether one or the other is best for
my son."

We were told the present Mr. Waller was a plain
country gentleman; and his son would be such another.

I observed, a family could not expect a poet but in a **Sir Alex-** hundred generations.—" Nay, (said Dr. Johnson,) not **ander** one family in a hundred can expect a poet in a hundred **Gordon** generations." He then repeated Dryden's celebrated lines,

> Three poets in three distant ages born, &c.

and a part of a Latin translation of it done at Oxford : [1] he did not then say by whom.

He received a card from Sir Alexander Gordon, who had been his acquaintance twenty years ago in London, and who, " if forgiven for not answering a line from him," would come in the afternoon. Dr. Johnson rejoiced to hear of him, and begged he would come and dine with us. I was much pleased to see the kindness with which Dr. Johnson received his old friend Sir Alexander ; a gentleman of good family, Lismore, but who had not the estate. The King's College here made him Professor of Medicine, which affords him a decent subsistence. He told us that the value of the stockings exported from Aberdeen was, in peace, a hundred thousand pounds ; and amounted, in time of war, to one hundred and seventy thousand pounds. Dr. Johnson asked, What made the differ- ence ? Here we had a proof of the comparative saga- city of the two professors. Sir Alexander answered,

---

[1] London, *2nd May*, 1778.
Dr. Johnson acknowledged that he was himself the authour of the translation above alluded to, and dictated it to me as follows :

> Quos laudet vates Graius Romanus et Anglus
>   Tres tria temporibus secla dedere suis.
> Sublime ingenium Graius ; Romanus habebat
>   Carmen grande sonans ; Anglus utrumque tulit.
> Nil majus Natura capit : clarare priores
>   Quæ potuere duos tertius unus habet.

"Because there is more occasion for them in war."
Professor Thomas Gordon answered, "Because the
Germans, who are our great rivals in the manufacture
of stockings, are otherwise employed in time of war."—
JOHNSON. "Sir, you have given a very good solution."

At dinner, Dr. Johnson ate several plate-fulls of
Scotch broth, with barley and peas in it, and seemed
very fond of the dish. I said, "You never ate it
before."—JOHNSON. "No, sir; but I don't care how
soon I eat it again."—My cousin, Miss Dallas, formerly
of Inverness, was married to Mr. Riddoch, one of the
ministers of the English chapel here. He was ill, and
confined to his room; but she sent us a kind invitation
to tea, which we all accepted. She was the same
lively, sensible, cheerful woman, as ever. Dr. Johnson
here threw out some jokes against Scotland. He said,
"You go first to Aberdeen; then to Enbru (the
Scottish pronunciation of Edinburgh); then to Newcastle, to be polished by the colliers; then to York;
then to London." And he laid hold of a little girl,
Stuart Dallas, niece to Mrs. Riddoch, and, representing himself as a giant, said, he would take her with
him! telling her, in a hollow voice, that he lived in a
cave, and had a bed in the rock, and she should have a
little bed cut opposite to it!

He thus treated the point, as to prescription of murder in Scotland. "A jury in England would make
allowance for deficiencies of evidence, on account of
lapse of time : but a general rule that a crime should
not be punished, or tried for the purpose of punishment, after twenty years, is bad : It is cant to talk
of the King's advocate delaying a prosecution from
malice. How unlikely is it the King's advocate
should have malice against persons who commit murder, or should even know them at all.—If the son of

the murdered man should kill the murderer who got
off merely by prescription, I would help him to make
his escape; though, were I upon his jury, I would not
acquit him. I would not advise him to commit such
an act. On the contrary, I would bid him submit to
the determination of society, because a man is bound to
submit to the inconveniences of it, as he enjoys the
good: but the young man, though politically wrong,
would not be morally wrong. He would have to say,
' Here I am amongst barbarians, who not only refuse
to do justice, but encourage the greatest of all crimes.
I am therefore in a state of nature: for, so far as there
is no law, it is a state of nature: and consequently,
upon the eternal and immutable law of justice, which
requires that he who sheds man's blood should have his
blood shed, I will stab the murderer of my father.' "

We went to our inn, and sat quietly. Dr. Johnson
borrowed, at Mr. Riddoch's, a volume of Massillon's
" Discourses on the Psalms": but I found he read little
in it. Ogden too he sometimes took up, and glanced
at; but threw it down again. I then entered upon
religious conversation. Never did I see him in a better
frame: calm, gentle, wise, holy.—I said, "Would
not the same objection hold against the Trinity as
against Transubstantiation?"—"Yes, (said he,) if you
take three and one in the same sense. If you do so,
to be sure you cannot believe it: but the three persons in the Godhead are Three in one sense, and One
in another. We cannot tell how; and that is the
mystery!"

I spoke of the satisfaction of Christ. He said his
notion was, that it did not atone for the sins of the
world; but, by satisfying divine justice, by shewing
that no less than the Son of God suffered for sin, it
shewed to men and innumerable created beings, the

(marginal note: Religious conversation)

The doc-
trine of
atone-
ment

heinousness of it, and therefore rendered it unnecessary for divine vengeance to be exercised against sinners, as it otherwise must have been ; that in this way it might operate even in favour of those who had never heard of it : as to those who did hear of it, the effect it should produce would be repentance and piety, by impressing upon the mind a just notion of sin : that original sin was the propensity to evil, which no doubt was occasioned by the fall. He presented this solemn subject in a new light to me,[1] and rendered much more rational and clear the doctrine of what our Saviour has done for us ;—as it removed the notion of imputed righteousness in co-operating ; whereas by this view, Christ has done all already that he had to do, or is ever to do, for mankind, by making his great satisfaction ; the consequences of which will affect each individual according to the particular conduct of each. I would illustrate this by saying, that Christ's satisfaction resembles a sun placed to shew light to men, so that it depends upon themselves whether they will walk the right way or not, which they could not have done without that sun, "*the sun of righteousness.*" There is, however, more in it than merely giving light—*a light to lighten the Gentiles* : for we are told, there is *healing under his wings.* Dr. Johnson said to me, "Richard Baxter commends a treatise by Grotius, *De Satisfactione Christi.* I have never read it : but I intend to read it ; and you may read it." I remarked, upon the principle now laid down, we might explain the difficult

[1] My worthy, intelligent, and candid friend, Dr. Kippis, informs me, that several divines have thus explained the mediation of our Saviour. What Dr. Johnson now delivered, was but a temporary opinion ; for he afterwards was fully convinced of the *propitiatory sacrifice*, as I shall shew at large in my future work, THE LIFE OF SAMUEL JOHNSON, LL.D.

and seemingly hard text, "They that believe shall be saved; and they that believe not shall be damned:" They that believe shall have such an impression made upon their minds, as will make them act so that they may be accepted by GOD. **Johnson and Langton**

We talked of one of our friends taking ill, for a length of time, a hasty expression of Dr. Johnson's to him, on his attempting to prosecute a subject that had a reference to religion, beyond the bounds within which the Doctor thought such topicks should be confined in a mixed company.—JOHNSON. "What is to become of society, if a friendship of twenty years is to be broken off for such a cause?" As Bacon says,

> "Who then to frail mortality shall trust,
> But limns the water, or but writes in dust."

I said, he should write expressly in support of Christianity; for that, although a reverence for it shines through his works in several places, that is not enough. "You know, (said I,) what Grotius has done, and what Addison has done.—You should do also."—He replied, "I hope I shall."

Monday, 23rd August.

Principal Campbell, Sir Alexander Gordon, Professor Gordon, and Professor Ross, visited us in the morning, as did Dr. Gerard, who had come six miles from the country on purpose. We went and saw the Marischal College,[1] and at one o'clock we waited on the magistrates in the town hall, as they had invited us in order to present Dr. Johnson with the freedom of the town, which Provost Jopp did with a very good

[1] Dr. Beattie was so kindly entertained in England, that he had not yet returned home.

*D 387

Johnson a
burgess
of Aber-
deen
grace. Dr. Johnson was much pleased with this mark of attention, and received it very politely. There was a pretty numerous company assembled. It was striking to hear all of them drinking " Dr. Johnson ! Dr. Johnson ! " in the town-hall of Aberdeen, and then to see him with his burgess-ticket, or diploma,[1] in his hat, which he wore as he walked along the street, according to the usual custom.——It gave me great satisfaction to observe the regard, and indeed fondness too, which every body here had for my father.

While Sir Alexander Gordon conducted Dr. Johnson to old Aberdeen, Professor Gordon and I called on Mr. Riddoch, whom I found to be a grave worthy clergyman. He observed, that, whatever might be said of Dr. Johnson while he was alive, he would, after he was dead, be looked upon by the world with regard and astonishment, on account of his Dictionary.

Professor Gordon and I walked over to the Old College, which Dr. Johnson had seen by this time. I stepped into the chapel, and looked at the tomb of the founder, Archbishop Elphinston, of whom I shall have occasion to write in my History of James IV. of Scotland, the patron of my family.

We dined at Sir Alexander Gordon's. The Provost,

---

[1] Dr. Johnson's burgess-ticket was in these words:

" Aberdoniæ, vigesimo tertio die mensis Augusti, anno Domini millesimo septingentesimo septuagesimo tertio, in presentia honorabilium virorum, Jacobi Jopp, armigeri, præpositi, Adami Duff, Gulielmi Young, Georgii Marr, et Gulielmi Forbes, Balivorum, Gulielmi Rainie Decani guildæ, et Joannis Nicoll Thesaurarii dicti burgi.

" Quo die vir generosus et doctrina clarus, Samuel Johnson, LL.D. receptus et admissus fuit in municipes et fratres guildæ præfati burgi de Aberdeen. In deditissimi amoris et affectus ac eximiæ observantiæ tesseram, quibus dicti Magistratus eum amplectuntur. Extractum per me,

" ALEX. CARNEGIE."

Professor Ross, Professor Dunbar, Professor Thomas Gordon, were there. After dinner came in Dr. Gerard, Professor Leslie, Professor Macleod. We had little or no conversation in the morning; now we were but barren. The professors seemed afraid to speak.

Dr. Gerard told us that an eminent printer was very intimate with Warburton.—JOHNSON. "Why, sir, he has printed some of his works, and perhaps bought the property of some of them. The intimacy is such as one of the professors here may have with one of the carpenters who is repairing the college."—"But, (said Gerard,) I saw a letter from him to this printer, in which he says, that the one half of the clergy of the church of Scotland are fanaticks, and the other half infidels." — JOHNSON. "Warburton has accustomed himself to write letters just as he speaks, without thinking any more of what he throws out. When I read Warburton first, and observed his force, and his contempt of mankind, I thought he had driven the world before him; but I soon found that was not the case; for Warburton, by extending his abuse, rendered it ineffectual."

He told me, when we were by ourselves, that he thought it very wrong in the printer, to shew Warburton's letter, as it was raising a body of enemies against him. He thought it foolish in Warburton to write so to the printer; and added, "Sir, the worst way of being intimate, is by scribbling." He called Warburton's "Doctrine of Grace" a poor performance, and so he said was Wesley's Answer. "Warburton," he observed, "had laid himself very open. In particular, he was weak enough to say, that, in some disorders of the imagination, people had spoken with tongues, had spoken languages which they never knew

Locke's before ; a thing as absurd as to say, that, in some disorders of the imagination, people had been known
to fly."

I talked of the difference of genius, to try if I could
engage Gerard in a disquisition with Dr. Johnson ; but
I did not succeed.   I mentioned, as a curious fact, that
Locke had written verses.—Johnson. "I know of none,
sir, but a kind of exercise prefixed to Dr. Sydenham's
Works, in which he has some conceits about the dropsy,
in which water and burning are united ; and how Dr.
Sydenham removed fire by drawing off water, contrary
to the usual practice, which is to extinguish fire by
bringing water upon it.—I am not sure that there is a
word of all this ; but it is such kind of talk." [1]

[1] All this, as Dr. Johnson suspected at the time, was the
immediate invention of his own lively imagination ; for there
is not one word of it in Mr. Locke's complimentary performance.   My readers will, I have no doubt, like to be
satisfied, by comparing them ; and, at any rate, it may entertain them to read verses composed by our great metaphysician,
when a Bachelor in Physick.

AUCTORI, in Tractatum ejus de Febribus.

Febriles æstus, victumque ardoribus orbem
  Flevit, non tantis par Medicina malis.
Nam post mille artes, medicæ tentamina curæ,
  Ardet adhuc Febris; nec velit arte regi.
Præda sumus flammis ; solum hoc speramus ab igne,
  Ut restet paucus, quem capit urna, cinis.
Dum quærit medicus febris caussamque, modumque,
  Flammarum & tenebras, & sine luce faces;
Quas tractat patitur flammas, & febre calescens,
  Corruit ipse suis victima rapta focis.
Qui tardos potuit morbos, artusque trementes,
  Sistere, febrili se videt igne rapi.
Sic faber exesos fulsit tibicine muros;
  Dum trahit antiquas lenta ruina domos.
Sed si flamma vorax miseras incenderit ædes,
  Unica flagrantes tunc sepelire salus.

We spoke of Fingal.   Dr. Johnson said calmly, "If **Latin**
the poems were really translated, they were certainly **verses**
first written down.   Let Mr. Macpherson deposit the

Fit fuga, tectonicas nemo tunc invocat artes';
  Cum perit artificis non minus usta domus.
Se tandem Sydenham *febrisque Scholæque furori*
  Opponens, morbi quærit, & artis opem.
Non temere incusat tectæ putredinis ignes;
  Nec fictus, febres qui fovet, humor erit.
Non bilem ille movet, nulla hic pituita; Salutis
  Quæ spes, si fallax ardeat intus aqua?
Nec doctas magno rixas ostentat hiatu,
  Quis ipsis major febribus ardor inest.
Innocuas placide corpus jubet urere flammas,
  Et justo rapidos temperat igne focos.
Quid febrim exstinguat, varius quid postulat usus,
  Solari ægrotos, qua potes arte, docet.
Hactenus ipsa suum timuit Natura calorem,
  Dum sæpe incerto, quo calet, igne perit:
Dum reparat tacitos male provida sanguinis ignes,
  Prælusit busto, fit calor iste rogus.
Jam secura suas foveant præcordia flammas,
  Quem Natura negat, dat Medicina modum.
Nec solum faciles compescit sanguinis æstus,
  Dum dubia est inter spemque metumque salus;
Sed fatale malum domuit, quodque astra malignum
  Credimus, iratam vel genuisse Stygem.
Extorsit Lachesi *cultros, Pestique venenum*
  Abstulit, & tantos non sinit esse metus.
Quis tandem arte nova domitam mitescere Pestem
  Credat, & antiquas ponere posse minas?
Post tot mille neces, cumulataque funera busto,
  Victa jacet, parvo vulnere, dira Lues.
Ætheriæ quanquam spargunt contagia flammæ,
  Quicquid inest istis ignibus, ignis erit.
Delapsæ cælo flammæ licet acrius urant,
  Has gelida exstingui non nisi morte putas?
Tu meliora paras victrix Medicina; tuusque,
  Pestis quæ superat cuncta, triumphus erit.
Vive liber, victis febrilibus ignibus; unus
  Te simul & mundum qui manet, ignis erit.
          J. LOCK, *A.M.* Ex. Aede Christi, **Oxon.**

manuscript in one of the colleges at Aberdeen, where
there are people who can judge; and, if the professors
certify the authenticity, then there will be an end of
the controversy. If he does not take this obvious
and easy method, he gives the best reason to doubt;
considering too, how much is against it *à priori.*"

We sauntered after dinner in Sir Alexander's garden,
and saw his little grotto, which is hung with pieces of
poetry written in a fair hand. It was agreeable to
observe the contentment and kindness of this quiet,
benevolent man. Professor Macleod was brother to
Macleod of Talisker, and brother-in-law to the Laird
of Col. He gave me a letter to young Col. I was
weary of this day, and began to think wishfully of being
again in motion. I was uneasy to think myself too
fastidious, whilst I fancied Dr. Johnson quite satisfied.
But he owned to me that he was fatigued and teased
by Sir Alexander's doing too much to entertain him.
I said, it was all kindness.—JOHNSON. "True, sir: but
sensation is sensation."—BOSWELL. "It is so: we feel
pain equally from the surgeon's probe, as from the
sword of the foe."

We visited two booksellers' shops, and could not
find Arthur Johnston's Poems. We went and sat near
an hour at Mr. Riddoch's. He could not tell distinctly how much education at the college here costs,
which disgusted Dr. Johnson. I had pledged myself
that we should go to the inn, and not stay supper. They
pressed us, but he was resolute. I saw Mr. Riddoch
did not please him. He said to me, afterwards, "Sir,
he has no vigour in his talk." But my friend should have
considered that he himself was not in good humour;
so that it was not easy to talk to his satisfaction.—We
sat contentedly at our inn. He then became merry,
and observed how little we had either heard or said at

Aberdeen: That the Aberdonians had not started a A story single *mawkin* (the Scottish word for hare) for us to of Gold- pursue. smith

Tuesday, 24th August.

We set out about eight in the morning, and break-fasted at Ellon. The landlady said to me, " Is not this the great Doctor that is going about through the country ? "—I said, " Yes."—" Ay, (said she,) we heard of him, I made an errand into the room on purpose to see him. There's something great in his appearance : it is a pleasure to have such a man in one's house ; a man who does so much good. If I had thought of it, I would have shewn him a child of mine, who has had a lump on his throat for some time." —" But, (said I,) he is not a doctor of physick."—" Is he an oculist ? " said the landlord.—" No, (said I,) he is only a very learned man."——LANDLORD. " They say he is the greatest man in England, except Lord Mans-field."—Dr. Johnson was highly entertained with this, and I do think he was pleased too. He said, " I like the exception : to have called me the greatest man in England, would have been an unmeaning compliment : but the exception marked that the praise was in earnest ; and, in Scotland, the exception must be Lord Mansfield, or—Sir John Pringle."

He told me a good story of Dr. Goldsmith. Graham, who wrote " Telemachus, a Masque," was sitting one night with him and Dr. Johnson, and was half drunk. He rattled away to Dr. Johnson : " You are a clever fellow, to be sure ; but you cannot write an essay like Addison, or verses like the *Rape of the Lock.*" At last he said,[1] " Doctor, I should be happy to see you

[1] I am sure I have related this story exactly as Dr. Johnson told it to me ; but a friend who has often heard him tell it,

Slains
Castle
at Eaton."—"I shall be glad to wait on you," answered
Goldsmith.—"No, (said Graham,) 'tis not you I mean,
Dr. Minor; 'tis Dr. Major, there."—Goldsmith was
excessively hurt by this. He afterwards spoke of it
himself. "Graham, (said he,) is a fellow to make
one commit suicide."

We had received a polite invitation to Slains castle.
We arrived there just at three o'clock, as the bell for
dinner was ringing. Though, from its being just on
the North-east Ocean, no trees will grow here, Lord
Errol has done all that can be done. He has cultivated his fields so as to bear rich crops of every kind,
and he has made an excellent kitchen-garden, with a
hot-house. I had never seen any of the family: but
there had been a card of invitation written by the
honourable Charles Boyd, the earl's brother. We were
conducted into the house, and at the dining-room door
were met by that gentleman, whom both of us at first
took to be Lord Errol; but he soon corrected our mis-
take. My lord was gone to dine in the neighbourhood,
at an entertainment given by Mr. Irvine of Drum. Lady
Errol received us politely, and was very attentive to us
during the time of dinner. There was nobody at table
but her ladyship, Mr. Boyd, and some of the children,
their governour and governess. Mr. Boyd put Dr.
Johnson in mind of having dined with him at Cumming
the Quaker's, along with a Mr. Hall and Miss Williams:
this was a bond of connection between them. For me,
Mr. Boyd's acquaintance with my father was enough.
After dinner, Lady Errol favoured us with a sight of

informs me that he usually introduced a circumstance which
ought not to be omitted. "At last, sir, Graham, having now
got to about the pitch of looking at one man, and talking to
another, said Doctor, &c." "What effect (Dr. Johnson used
to add) this had on Goldsmith, who was as irascible as a
hornet, may be easily conceived."

her young family, whom she made stand up in a row.
There were six daughters and two sons. It was a very
pleasing sight.

Dr. Johnson proposed our setting out. Mr. Boyd
said, he hoped we would stay all night; his brother
would be at home in the evening, and would be very
sorry if he missed us. Mr. Boyd was called out of
the room. I was very desirous to stay in so comfortable a house, and I wished to see Lord Errol. Dr.
Johnson, however, was right in resolving to go, if we
were not asked again, as it is best to err on the safe
side in such cases, and to be sure that one is quite welcome. To my great joy, when Mr. Boyd returned,
he told Dr. Johnson that it was Lady Errol who had
called him out, and said that she would never let Dr.
Johnson into the house again, if he went away that
night; and that she had ordered the coach, to carry us
to view a great curiosity on the coast, after which we
should see the house. We cheerfully agreed.

Mr. Boyd was engaged, in 1745–6, on the same
side with many unfortunate mistaken noblemen and
gentlemen. He escaped, and lay concealed for a
year in the island of Arran, the ancient territory of
the Boyds. He then went to France, and was about
twenty years on the continent. He married a French
Lady, and now lived very comfortably at Aberdeen,
and was much at Slains castle. He entertained us with
great civility. He had a pompousness or formal pleni-
tude in his conversation, which I did not dislike. Dr.
Johnson said, "there was too much elaboration in his
talk." It gave me pleasure to see him, a steady branch
of the family, setting forth all its advantages with much
zeal. He told us that Lady Errol was one of the most
pious and sensible women in the island; had a good
head, and as good a heart. He said, she did not use

The force or fear in educating her children.—Johnson. "Sir,
Bullers of she is wrong; I would rather have the rod to be the
Buchan general terror to all, to make them learn, than tell a
child, if you do thus or thus, you will be more esteemed
than your brothers or sisters. The rod produces an
effect which terminates in itself. A child is afraid
of being whipped, and gets his task, and there's an
end on't; whereas, by exciting emulation, and comparisons of superiority, you lay the foundation of
lasting mischief; you make brothers and sisters hate
each other."

During Mr. Boyd's stay in Arran, he had found
a chest of medical books, left by a surgeon there,
and had read them till he acquired some skill in
physick, in consequence of which he is often consulted by the poor. There were several here waiting
for him as patients. We walked round the house
till stopped by a cut made by the influx of the sea.
The house is built quite upon the shore; the windows
look upon the main ocean, and the King of Denmark
is Lord Errol's nearest neighbour on the north-east.

We got immediately into the coach, and drove to
Dunbui, a rock near the shore, quite covered with
sea-fowls; then to a circular bason of large extent,
surrounded with tremendous rocks. On the quarter
next the sea, there is a high arch in the rock, which
the force of the tempest has driven out. This place
is called Buchan's Buller, or the Buller of Buchan, and
the country people call it the Pot. Mr. Boyd said it
was so called from the French *Bouloir*. It may be
more simply traced from *Boiler* in our own language.
We walked round this monstrous cauldron. In some
places, the rock is very narrow; and on each side there
is a sea deep enough for a man of war to ride in; so
that it is somewhat horrid to move along. However,

there is earth and grass upon the rock, and a kind of road marked out by the print of feet; so that one makes it out pretty safely: yet it alarmed me to see Dr. Johnson striding irregularly along. He insisted on taking a boat, and sailing into the Pot. We did so. He was stout, and wonderfully alert. The Buchan-men all shewing their teeth, and speaking with that strange sharp accent which distinguishes them, was to me a matter of curiosity. He was not sensible of the difference of pronunciation in the South, and North of Scotland, which I wondered at. Lord Errol and his surgeon

As the entry into the Buller is so narrow that oars cannot be used as you go in, the method taken is, to row very hard when you come near it, and give the boat such a rapidity of motion that it glides in. Dr. Johnson observed what an effect this scene would have had, were we entering into an unknown place. There are caves of considerable depth; I think, one on each side. The boatmen had never entered either of them far enough to know the size. Mr. Boyd told us that it is customary for the company at Peterhead well, to make parties, and come and dine in one of the caves here.

He told us, that, as Slains is at a considerable distance from Aberdeen, Lord Errol, who has a very large family, resolved to have a surgeon of his own. With this view he educated one of his tenants' sons, who is now settled in a very neat house and farm just by, which we saw from the road. By the salary which the earl allows him, and the practice which he has had, he is in very easy circumstances. He had kept an exact account of all that had been laid out on his education, and he came to his lordship one day, and told him that he had arrived at a much higher situation than ever he expected; that he was now able to repay

Entails what his lordship had advanced, and begged he would accept of it. The earl was pleased with the generous gratitude and genteel offer of the man; but refused it. —Mr. Boyd also told us, Cumming the Quaker first began to distinguish himself, by writing against Dr. Leechman on Prayer, to prove it unnecessary, as God knows best what should be, and will order it without our asking:—the old hackneyed objection.

When we returned to the house we found coffee and tea in the drawing-room. Lady Errol was not there, being, as I supposed, engaged with her young family. There is a bow-window fronting the sea. Dr. Johnson repeated the ode, *Jam satis terris*, while Mr. Boyd was with his patients. He spoke well in favour of entails, to preserve lines of men whom mankind are accustomed to reverence. His opinion was that so much land should be entailed as that families should never fall into contempt, and as much left free as to give them all the advantages of property in case of any emergency. "If (said he,) the nobility are suffered to sink into indigence, they of course become corrupt; they are ready to do whatever the king chooses; therefore it is fit they should be kept from becoming poor, unless it is fixed that when they fall below a certain standard of wealth they shall lose their peerages. We know the House of Peers have made noble stands, when the House of Commons durst not. The two last years of parliament they dare not contradict the populace."

This room is ornamented with a number of fine prints, and with a whole length picture of Lord Errol, by Sir Joshua Reynolds. This led Dr. Johnson and me to talk of our amiable and elegant friend, whose panegyrick he concluded by saying, "Sir Joshua Reynolds, sir, is the most invulnerable man I know; the man with whom if you should quarrel, you would find Lord
Errol the most difficulty how to abuse."

Dr. Johnson observed, the situation here was the noblest he had ever seen,—better than Mount Edgecumbe, reckoned the first in England; because, at Mount Edgecumbe, the sea is bounded by land on the other side, and, though there is there the grandeur of a fleet, there is also the impression of there being a dockyard, the circumstances of which are not agreeable. At Slains is an excellent old house. The noble owner has built of brick, along the square in the inside, a gallery, both on the first and second story, the house being no higher; so that he has always a dry walk, and the rooms, to which formerly there was no approach but through each other, have now all separate entries from the gallery, which is hung with Hogarth's works, and other prints. We went and sat a while in the library. There is a valuable numerous collection. It was chiefly made by Mr. Falconer, husband to the late Countess of Errol in her own right. This Earl has added a good many modern books.

About nine the Earl came home. Captain Gordon of Park was with him. His lordship put Dr. Johnson in mind of their having dined together in London, along with Mr. Beauclerk. I was exceedingly pleased with Lord Errol. His dignified person and agreeable countenance, with the most unaffected affability, gave me high satisfaction. From perhaps a weakness, or, as I rather hope, more fancy and warmth of feeling than is quite reasonable, my mind is ever impressed with admiration for persons of high birth, and I could, with the most perfect honesty, expatiate on Lord Errol's good qualities; but he stands in no need of my praise. His agreeable manners and softness of address prevented that constraint which the idea of his being Lord

High Constable of Scotland might otherwise have
occasioned.   He talked very easily and sensibly with
his learned guest.   I observed that Dr. Johnson,
though he shewed that respect to his lordship, which,
from principle, he always does to high rank, yet, when
they came to argument, maintained that manliness which
becomes the force and vigour of his understanding.   To
shew external deference to our superiors, is proper : to
seem to yield to them in opinion, is meanness.[1]   The
earl said grace, both before and after supper, with much
decency.   He told us a story of a man who was executed at Perth, some years ago, for murdering a woman
who was with child by him, and a former child he had

[1] Lord Chesterfield, in his letters to his son, complains of
one who argued in an indiscriminate manner with men of
all ranks.   Probably the noble lord had felt with some uneasiness what it was to encounter stronger abilities than his
own.   If a peer will engage at foils with his inferior in
station, he must expect that his inferior in station will avail
himself of every advantage; otherwise it is not a fair trial
of strength and skill.   The same will hold in a contest of
reason, or of wit.—A certain king entered the lists of genius
with Voltaire.   The consequence was, that, though the king
had great and brilliant talents, Voltaire had such a superiority that his majesty could not bear it; and the poet was
dismissed, or escaped, from that court.—In the reign of
James I. of England, Crichton, Lord Sanquhar, a peer of
Scotland, from a vain ambition to excel a fencing-master in
his own art, played at rapier and dagger with him.   The
fencing-master, whose fame and bread were at stake, put
out one of his lordship's eyes.   Exasperated at this, Lord
Sanquhar hired ruffians, and had the fencing-master assassi-
nated; for which his lordship was capitally tried, condemned, and hanged.   Not being a peer of England, he was
tried by the name of Robert Crichton, Esq. ; but he was
admitted to be a baron of three hundred years' standing.—
See the State Trials ; and the History of England by Hume,
who applauds the impartial justice executed upon a man of
high rank.

by her. His hand was cut off: he was then pulled
up; but the rope broke, and he was forced to lie an
hour on the ground, till another rope was brought from
Perth, the execution being in a wood at some distance,
—at the place where the murders were committed.
" *There*, (said my lord,) *I see the hand of Providence.*"
—I was really happy here. I saw in this nobleman
the best dispositions and best principles; and I saw
him, *in my mind's eye*, to be the representative of the
ancient Boyds of Kilmarnock. I was afraid he might
have urged drinking, as, I believe, he used formerly to
do, but he drank port and water out of a large glass
himself, and let us do as we pleased. He went with
us to our rooms at night; said, he took the visit very
kindly; and told me, my father and he were very old
acquaintance;—that I now knew the way to Slains,
and he hoped to see me there again.

I had a most elegant room; but there was a fire in
it which blazed; and the sea, to which my windows
looked, roared; and the pillows were made of the
feathers of some sea-fowl, which had to me a disagreeable smell: so that, by all these causes, I was kept
awake a good while. I saw, in imagination, Lord
Erroll's father, Lord Kilmarnock, (who was beheaded
on Tower-hill in 1746,) and I was somewhat dreary.
But the thought did not last long, and I fell asleep.

Wednesday, 25th August.

We got up between seven and eight, and found Mr.
Boyd in the dining-room, with tea and coffee before
him, to give us breakfast. We were in an admirable
humour. Lady Erroll had given each of us a copy of
an ode by Beattie, on the birth of her son, Lord
Hay. Mr. Boyd asked Dr. Johnson, how he liked it.

A
birthday
ode by
Beattie

Men of
family
and
Nabobs

Dr. Johnson, who did not admire it, got off very well, by taking it out, and reading the second and third stanzas of it with much melody. This, without his saying a word, pleased Mr. Boyd. He observed, however, to Dr. Johnson, that the expression as to the family of Errol,

> " *A thousand years* have seen it shine,"

compared with what went before, was an anti-climax, and that it would have been better

> Ages have seen, &c.

Dr. Johnson said, " So great a number as a thousand is better. *Dolus latet in universalibus.* Ages might be only two ages."—He talked of the advantage of keeping up the connections of relationship, which produce much kindness. " Every man (said he,) who comes into the world, has need of friends. If he has to get them for himself, half his life is spent, before his merit is known. Relations are a man's ready friends who support him. When a man is in real distress, he flies into the arms of his relations. An old lawyer, who had much experience in making wills, told me, that after people had deliberated long, and thought of many for their executors, they settled at last by fixing on their relations. This shews the universality of the principle.

I regretted the decay of respect for men of family, and that a Nabob now would carry an election from them.—JOHNSON. " Why, sir, the Nabob will carry it by means of his wealth, in a country where money is highly valued, as it must be where nothing can be had without money; but, if it comes to personal preference, the man of family will always carry it. There is generally a *scoundrelism* about a low man."—Mr. Boyd said, that was a good *ism*.

I said, I believed mankind were happier in the ancient feudal state of subordination, than they are in the modern state of independency.—JOHNSON. " To be sure, the *Chief* was : but we must think of the number of individuals. That *they* were less happy, seems plain ; for that state from which all escape as soon as they can, and to which none return after they have left it, must be less happy ; and this is the case with the state of dependance on a chief or great man." Subordination

I mentioned the happiness of the French in their subordination, by the reciprocal benevolence and attachment between the great and those in lower rank.—Mr. Boyd gave us an instance of their gentlemanly spirit. An old Chevalier de Malthe, of ancient *noblesse*, but in low circumstances, was in a coffee-house at Paris, where was Julien, the great Manufacturer at the Gobelins, of the fine tapestry, so much distinguished both for the figures and the *colours*. The chevalier's carriage was very old. Says Julien, with a plebeian insolence, " I think, sir, you had better have your carriage new painted." The chevalier looked at him with indignant contempt, and answered, " Well, sir, you may take it home and *dye* it ! "—All the coffee-house rejoiced at Julien's confusion.

We set out about nine. Dr. Johnson was curious to see one of those structures which northern antiquarians call a Druid's temple. I had a recollection of one at Strichen ; which I had seen fifteen years ago ; so we went four miles out of our road, after passing Old Deer, and went thither. Mr. Fraser, the proprietor, was at home, and shewed it to us. But I had augmented it in my mind ; for all that remains is two stones set up on end, with a long one laid upon them, as was usual, and one stone at a little distance from them. That stone was the capital one of the circle

The life of country gentlemen

which surrounded what now remains. Mr. Fraser was very hospitable.[1] There was a fair at Strichen; and he had several of his neighbours from it at dinner. One of them, Dr. Fraser, who had been in the army, remembered to have seen Dr. Johnson at a lecture on experimental philosophy, at Lichfield. The doctor recollected being at the lecture; and he was surprised to find here somebody who knew him.

Mr. Fraser sent a servant to conduct us by a short passage into the high road. I observed to Dr. Johnson, that I had a most disagreeable notion of the life of country gentlemen; that I left Mr. Fraser just now, as one leaves a prisoner in a jail.—Dr. Johnson said, that I was right in thinking them unhappy; for that they had not enough to keep their minds in motion.

I started a thought this afternoon which amused us a great part of the way. "If, (said I,) our club should come and set up in St. Andrews, as a college,

[1] He is the worthy son of a worthy father, the late Lord Strichen, one of our judges, to whose kind notice I was much obliged. Lord Strichen was a man not only honest, but highly generous; for after his succession to the family estate, he paid a large sum of debts contracted by his predecessor, which he was not under any obligation to pay. Let me here, for the credit of Ayrshire my own county, record a noble instance of liberal honesty in William Hutchison, drover, in Lanehead, Kyle, who formerly obtained a full discharge from his creditors upon a composition of his debts; but upon being restored to good circumstances, invited his creditors last winter to a dinner, without telling the reason, and paid them their full sums, principal and interest. They presented him with a piece of plate, with an inscription to commemorate this extraordinary instance of true worth, which should make some people in Scotland blush, while, though mean themselves, they strut about under the protection of great alliance, conscious of the wretchedness of numbers who have lost by them, to whom they never think of making reparation, but indulge themselves and their families in most unsuitable expence.

to teach all that each of us can, in the several depart- An ima-
ments of learning and taste, we should rebuild the city: ginary
we should draw a wonderful concourse of students."— university
Dr. Johnson entered fully into the spirit of this project.
We immediately fell to distributing the offices.   I was
to teach Civil and Scotch law; Burke, politicks and
eloquence; Garrick, the art of publick speaking; Langton was to be our Grecian, Colman our Latin professor;
Nugent to teach physick; Lord Charlemont, modern
history; Beauclerk, natural philosophy; Vesey, Irish
antiquities, or Celtick learning;[1] Jones, Oriental learning; Goldsmith, poetry and ancient history; Chamier,
commercial politicks; Reynolds, painting, and the arts
which have beauty for their object; Chambers, the law
of England.   Dr. Johnson at first said, " I'll trust
theology to nobody but myself."   But, upon due consideration, that Percy is a clergyman, it was agreed
that Percy should teach practical divinity and British
antiquities; Dr. Johnson himself, logick, metaphysicks,
and scholastick divinity.   In this manner did we amuse
ourselves;—each suggesting, and each varying or adding,
till the whole was adjusted.   Dr. Johnson said, we
only wanted a mathematician since Dyer died, who was
a very good one; but as to every thing else, we should
have a very capital university.[2]

[1] Since the first edition, it has been suggested by one of
the club, who knew Mr. Vesey better than Dr. Johnson and
I, that we did not assign him a proper place; for he was
quite unskilled in Irish antiquities and Celtick learning, but
might with propriety have been made professor of architecture, which he understood well, and has left a very good
specimen of his knowledge and taste in that art, by an elegant
house built on a plan of his own formation, at Lucan, a few
miles from Dublin.

[2] Our club, originally at the Turk's Head, Gerrard street,
then at Prince's, Sackville-street, now at Baxter's Dover-
street, which at Mr. Garrick's funeral acquired a *name* for the

Members
of The
Club
We got at night to Banff. I sent Joseph on to Duff-
house : but Earl Fife was not at home, which I regretted
much, as we should have had a very elegant reception
from his lordship. We found here but an indifferent
inn.[1] Dr. Johnson wrote a long letter to Mrs. Thrale.
I wondered to see him write so much so easily. He
verified his own doctrine that "a man may always write
when he will set himself *doggedly* to it."

Thursday, 26th August.

We got a fresh chaise here, a very good one, and
very good horses. We breakfasted at Cullen. They
set down dried haddocks broiled, along with our tea.
I ate one ; but Dr. Johnson was disgusted by the sight

first time, and was called THE LITERARY CLUB, was instituted
in 1764, and now consists of thirty-five members. It has,
since 1773, been greatly augmented ; and though Dr. John-
son with justice observed, that, by losing Goldsmith, Garrick,
Nugent, Chamier, Beauclerk, we had lost what would make
an eminent club, yet when I mention, as an accession, Mr.
Fox, Dr. George Fordyce, Sir Charles Bunbury, Lord Ossory,
Mr. Gibbon, Dr. Adam Smith, Mr. R. B. Sheridan, the
Bishops of Kilaloe and St. Asaph, Dean Marlay, Mr. Steevens,
Mr. Dunning, Sir Joseph Banks, Dr. Scott of the Commons,
Earl Spencer, Mr. Windham of Norfolk, Lord Elliott,
Mr. Malone, Dr. Joseph Warton, the Rev. Thomas Warton,
Lord Lucan, Mr. Burke junior, Lord Palmerston, Dr. Burney,
Sir William Hamilton, and Dr. Warren, it will be acknow-
ledged that we might establish a second university of high
reputation.

[1] Here, unluckily the windows had no pullies ; and Dr.
Johnson, who was constantly eager for fresh air, had much
struggling to get one of them kept open. Thus he had a
notion impressed upon him, that this wretched defect was
general in Scotland ; in consequence of which he has erroneously enlarged upon it in his "Journey." I regretted that
he did not allow me to read over his book before it was
printed. I should have changed very little ; but I should

of them, so they were removed. Cullen has a comfortable appearance, though but a very small town, and the houses mostly poor buildings.

I called on Mr. Robertson, who has the charge of Lord Findlater's affairs, and was formerly Lord Monboddo's clerk, was three times in France with him, and translated Condamine's Account of the Savage Girl, to which his lordship wrote a preface, containing several remarks of his own. Robertson said, he did not believe so much as his lordship did; that it was plain to him, the girl confounded what she imagined with what she remembered: that, besides, she perceived Condamine and Lord Monboddo forming theories, and she adapted her story to them.

Dr. Johnson said, " It is a pity to see Lord Monboddo publish such notions as he has done; a man of sense, and of so much elegant learning. There would be little in a fool doing it; we should only laugh; but when a wise man does it, we are sorry. Other people have strange notions; but they conceal them. If they have tails, they hide them; but Monboddo is as jealous of his tail as a squirrel."—I shall here put down some more remarks of Dr. Johnson's on Lord Monboddo, which were not made exactly at this time, but come in well from connection. He said, he did not approve of a judge's calling himself *Farmer* Burnett,[1] and going about with a little round hat. He laughed heartily at

have suggested an alteration in a few places where he has laid himself open to be attacked. I hope I should have prevailed with him to omit or soften his assertion, that " a Scotsman must be a sturdy moralist, who does not prefer Scotland to truth,"—for I really think it is not founded; and it is harshly said.

[1] It is the custom in Scotland for the judges of the Court of Session to have the title of *lords*, from their estates; thus Mr. Burnett is Lord Monboddo, as Mr. Home was Lord

Boswell's
praise of
enthusi-
asm

his lordship's saying he was an *enthusiastical* farmer;
"for, (said he,) what can he do in farming by his *enthusiasm?*" Here, however, I think Dr. Johnson mistaken.
He who wishes to be successful, or happy, ought to be
enthusiastical, that is to say, very keen in all the occupations or diversions of life. An ordinary gentleman-
farmer will be satisfied with looking at his fields once
or twice a day: an enthusiastical farmer will be constantly employed on them;—will have his mind earnestly
engaged; will talk perpetually of them. But Dr. Johnson has much of the *nil admirari* in smaller concerns.
That survey of life which gave birth to his *Vanity of
Human Wishes* early sobered his mind. Besides, so great
a mind as his cannot be moved by inferior objects: an
elephant does not run and skip like lesser animals.

Mr. Robertson sent a servant with us, to shew us
through Lord Findlater's wood, by which our way was
shortened, and we saw some part of his domain, which
is indeed admirably laid out. Dr. Johnson did not
choose to walk through it. He always said, that he
was not come to Scotland to see fine places, of which
there were enough in England; but wild objects,——
mountains,—— waterfalls,—— peculiar manners; in
short, things which he had not seen before. I have a
notion that he at no time has had much taste for rural
beauties. I have myself very little.

Dr. Johnson said, there was nothing more contemptible than a country gentleman living beyond his
income, and every year growing poorer and poorer.
He spoke strongly of the influence which a man has

Kames. There is something a little aukward in this; for
they are denominated in deeds by their *names*, with the addition of "one of the Senators of the College of Justice;" and
subscribe their Christian and sur-name, as James Burnett,
Henry Home, even in judicial acts.

by being rich. " A man, (said he,) who keeps his A rich money, has in reality more use from it, than he can man's have by spending it." I observed that this looked influence very like a paradox ; but he explained it thus : " If it were certain that a man would keep his money locked up for ever, to be sure he would have no influence ; but, as so many want money, and he has the power of giving it, and they know not but by gaining his favour they may obtain it, the rich man will always have the greatest influence. He again who lavishes his money, is laughed at as foolish, and in a great degree with justice, considering how much is spent from vanity. Even those who partake of a man's hospitality, have but a transient kindness for him. If he has not the command of money, people know he cannot help them, if he would ; whereas the rich man always can, if he will, and for the chance of that, will have much weight."—BOSWELL. " But philosophers and satirists have all treated a miser as contemptible."—JOHNSON. " He is so philosophically ; but not in the practice of life."—BOSWELL. " Let me see now :—I do not know the instances of misers in England, so as to examine into their influence."—JOHNSON. " We have had few misers in England."—BOSWELL. " There was Lowther."—JOHNSON. " Why, sir, Lowther, by keeping his money, had the command of the county, which the family has now lost, by spending it.[1] I take it, he lent a great deal ; and that is the way to have influence, and yet preserve one's wealth. A man may lend his money upon very good security, and yet have his debtor

[1] I do not know what was at this time the state of the parliamentary interest of the ancient family of Lowther ; a family before the Conquest ; but all the nation knows it to be very extensive at present. A due mixture of severity and kindness, œconomy and munificence, characterises its present Representative.

Elgin
Cathedral

much under his power."—BOSWELL. "No doubt, sir.
He can always distress him for the money; as no
man borrows, who is able to pay on demand quite
conveniently."

We dined at Elgin, and saw the noble ruins of the
cathedral. Though it rained much, Dr. Johnson
examined them with a most patient attention. He
could not here feel any abhorrence at the Scottish
reformers, for he had been told by Lord Hailes, that
it was destroyed before the Reformation, by the Lord
of Badenoch,[1] who had a quarrel with the bishop.
The bishop's house, and those of the other clergy,
which are still pretty entire, do not seem to have been
proportioned to the magnificence of the cathedral,
which has been of great extent, and had very fine
carved work. The ground within the walls of the
cathedral is employed as a burying-place. The family
of Gordon have their vault here; but it has nothing
grand.

We passed Gordon Castle[2] this forenoon, which

[1] NOTE, by Lord Hailes.

"The cathedral of Elgin was burnt by the Lord of Badenoch, because the Bishop of Moray had pronounced an award
not to his liking. The indemnification that the see obtained,
was, that the Lord of Badenoch stood for three days bare
footed at the great gate of the cathedral. The story is in
the Chartulary of Elgin."

[2] I am not sure whether the duke was at home. But, not
having the honour of being much known to his grace, I
could not have presumed to enter his castle, though to introduce even so celebrated a stranger. We were at any rate in
a hurry to get forward to the wildness which we came to
see. Perhaps, if this noble family had still preserved that
sequestered magnificence which they maintained when catho-
licks, corresponding with the Grand Duke of Tuscany, we
might have been induced to have procured proper letters
of introduction, and devoted some time to the contemplation
of venerable superstitious state.

has a princely appearance. Fochabers, the neighbour- The
ing village, is a poor place, many of the houses being piazzas
ruinous; but it is remarkable, they have in general at Elgin
orchards well stored with apple-trees. Elgin has what
in England are called piazzas, that run in many places
on each side of the street. It must have been a much
better place formerly. Probably it had piazzas all
along the town, as I have seen at Bologna. I approved
much of such structures in a town, on account of their
conveniency in wet weather. Dr. Johnson disapproved
of them, "because (said he) it makes the under story
of a house very dark, which greatly over-balances the
conveniency, when it is considered how small a part of
the year it rains; how few are usually in the street at
such times; that many who are might as well be at
home; and the little that people suffer, supposing them
to be as much wet as they commonly are in walking a
street."

We fared but ill at our inn here; and Dr. Johnson
said, this was the first time he had seen a dinner in
Scotland that he could not eat.

In the afternoon, we drove over the very heath
where Macbeth met the witches, according to tradition. Dr. Johnson again solemnly repeated—

How far is't called to Fores? What are these,
So wither'd, and so wild in their attire?
That look not like the inhabitants o' the earth,
And yet are on't?

He repeated a good deal more of *Macbeth*. His
recitation was grand and affecting, and, as Sir Joshua
Reynolds has observed to me, had no more tone than
it should have: it was the better for it. He then
parodied the *All-hail* of the witches to Macbeth,
addressing himself to me. I had purchased some land

E 387

Forres called Dalblair; and, as in Scotland it is customary
to distinguish landed men by the name of their estates,
I had thus two titles, Dalblair and Young Auchinleck.
So my friend, in imitation of

All hail Macbeth! hail to thee, Thane of Cawdor!

condescended to amuse himself with uttering—

All hail Dalblair! hail to thee, Laird of Auchinleck!

We got to Fores at night, and found an admirable
inn, in which Dr. Johnson was pleased to meet with
a landlord who styled himself "Wine-Cooper, from
London."

Friday, 27th August.

It was dark when we came to Fores last night; so
we did not see what is called King Duncan's monument.—I shall now mark some gleanings of Dr.
Johnson's conversation. I spoke of *Leonidas*, and
said there were some good passages in it.—Johnson.
"Why, you must *seek* for them."—He said, Paul
Whitehead's *Manners* was a poor performance.—
Speaking of Derrick, he told me "he had a kindness for him, and had often said, that if his letters
had been written by one of a more established name,
they would have been thought very pretty letters."

This morning I introduced the subject of the origin
of evil.—Johnson. "Moral evil is occasioned by free
will, which implies choice between good and evil.
With all the evil that there is, there is no man but
would rather be a free agent, than a mere machine
without the evil; and what is best for each individual,
must be best for the whole. If a man would rather
be the machine, I cannot argue with him. He is a

different being from me."—BOSWELL. "A man, as a Nairn
machine, may have agreeable sensations; for instance,
he may have pleasure in musick."—JOHNSON. "No,
sir, he cannot have pleasure in musick; at least no
power of producing musick; for he who can produce
musick may let it alone: he who can play upon a
fiddle may break it: such a man is not a machine."
This reasoning satisfied me. It is certain, there cannot
be a free agent, unless there is the power of being evil
as well as good. We must take the inherent possibilities of things into consideration, in our reasonings or
conjectures concerning the works of GOD.

We came to Nairn to breakfast. Though a county
town and a royal burgh, it is a miserable place. Over
the room where we sat, a girl was spinning wool with
a great wheel, and singing an Erse song: "I'll warrant
you, (said Dr. Johnson,) one of the songs of Ossian."
He then repeated these lines:

"Verse sweetens toil, however rude the sound.
   All at her work the village maiden sings;
Nor, while she turns the giddy wheel around,
   Revolves the sad vicissitude of things."

I thought I had heard these lines before.—JOHNSON.
"I fancy not, sir; for they are in a detached poem,
the name of which I do not remember, written by one
Giffard, a parson."

I expected Mr. Kenneth M'Aulay, the minister of
Calder, who published the history of St. Kilda, a book
which Dr. Johnson liked, would have met us here, as
I had written to him from Aberdeen. But I received a
letter from him, telling me that he could not leave home,
as he was to administer the sacrament the following
Sunday, and earnestly requesting to see us at his manse.
"We'll go," said Dr. Johnson; which we accordingly

Mac-   did.   Mrs. M'Aulay received us, and told us her
aulay's   husband was in the church distributing tokens.[1]   We
History of   arrived between twelve and one o'clock, and it was
St. Kilda   near three before he came to us.

Dr. Johnson thanked him for his book, and said "it
was a very pretty piece of topography."   M'Aulay did
not seem much to mind the compliment.   From his
conversation, Dr. Johnson was persuaded that he had
not written the book which goes under his name.   I
myself always suspected so; and I have been told it
was written by the learned Dr. John M'Pherson of
Sky, from the materials collected by M'Aulay.   Dr.
Johnson said privately to me, "There is a combination
in it of which M'Aulay is not capable."   However,
he was exceedingly hospitable; and, as he obligingly
promised us a route for our Tour through the Western
Isles, we agreed to stay with him all night.

After dinner, we walked to the old castle of Calder,
(pronounced Cawder) the Thane of Cawdor's seat.   I
was sorry that my friend, this "prosperous gentleman,"
was not there.   The old tower must be of great antiquity.   There is a draw-bridge,—what has been a
moat,—and an ancient court.   There is a hawthorn-
tree, which rises like a wooden pillar through the rooms
of the castle; for, by a strange conceit, the walls have
been built round it.   The thickness of the walls, the
small slaunting windows, and a great iron door at the

---

[1] In Scotland, there is a great deal of preparation before
administering the sacrament.   The minister of the parish
examines the people as to their fitness, and to those of whom
he approves gives little pieces of tin, stamped with the
name of the parish, as *tokens*, which they must produce before
receiving it.   This is a species of priestly power, and sometimes may be abused.   I remember a lawsuit brought by a
person against his parish minister, for refusing him admis-
sion to that sacred ordinance.

entrance on the second story as you ascend the stairs,
all indicate the rude times in which this castle was
erected. There were here some large venerable trees.

Creeds and confessions

I was afraid of a quarrel between Dr. Johnson and
Mr. M‘Aulay, who talked slightingly of the lower
English clergy. The Doctor gave him a frowning
look, and said, "This is a day of novelties : I have seen
old trees in Scotland, and I have heard the English
clergy treated with disrespect."

I dreaded that a whole evening at Calder-manse
would be heavy ; however, Mr. Grant, an intelligent
and well bred minister in the neighbourhood, was there,
and assisted us by his conversation. Dr. Johnson,
talking of hereditary occupations in the Highlands,
said, "There is no harm in such a custom as this ;
but it is wrong to enforce it, and oblige a man to be
a taylor or a smith, because his father has been one."
This custom, however, is not peculiar to our Highlands ; it is well known that in India a similar practice
prevails.

Mr. M‘Aulay began a rhapsody against creeds and
confessions. Dr. Johnson shewed, that "what he
called *imposition*, was only a voluntary declaration of
agreement in certain articles of faith, which a church
has a right to require, just as any other society can
insist on certain rules being observed by its members.
Nobody is compelled to be of the church, as nobody
is compelled to enter into a society."—This was a
very clear and just view of the subject : but, M‘Aulay
could not be driven out of his track. Dr. Johnson
said, "Sir, you are a *bigot to laxness*."

Mr. M‘Aulay and I laid the map of Scotland before us ; and he pointed out a route for us from Inverness,
by Fort Augustus, to Glenelg, Sky, Mull, Icolmkill,
Lorn, and Inverary, which I wrote down. As my

Family father was to begin the northern circuit about the 18th
worship of September, it was necessary for us either to make
our tour with great expedition, so as to get to Auchinleck before he set out, or to protract it, so as not to be
there till his return, which would be about the 10th
of October. By M'Aulay's calculation, we were not
to land in Lorn till the 20th of September. I thought
that the interruptions by bad days, or by occasional
excursions, might make it ten days later ; and I thought
too, that we might perhaps go to Benbecula, and visit
Clanranald, which would take a week of itself.

Dr. Johnson went up with Mr. Grant to the lib-
rary, which consisted of a tolerable collection ; but the
Doctor thought it rather a lady's library, with some Latin
books in it by chance, than the library of a clergyman.
It had only two of the Latin fathers, and one of the
Greek fathers in Latin. I doubted whether Dr. Johnson would be present at a Presbyterian prayer. I told
Mr. M'Aulay so, and said that the Doctor might sit
in the library while we were at family worship. Mr.
M'Aulay said, he would omit it, rather than give Dr.
Johnson offence : but I would by no means agree that
an excess of politeness, even to so great a man, should
prevent what I esteem as one of the best pious regulations. I know nothing more beneficial, more comfortable, more agreeable, than that the little societies of each
family should regularly assemble, and unite in praise and
prayer to our heavenly Father, from whom we daily
receive so much good, and may hope for more in a
higher state of existence. I mentioned to Dr. Johnson
the over-delicate scrupulosity of our host. He said,
he had no objection to hear the prayer. This was a
pleasing surprise to me ; for he refused to go and hear
Principal Robertson preach. " I will hear him, (said
he,) if he will get up into a tree and preach ; but I will

not give a sanction, by my presence, to a Presbyterian assembly." Servitors at Oxford

Mr. Grant having prayed, Dr. Johnson said, his prayer was a very good one; but objected to his not having introduced the Lord's Prayer. He told us, that an Italian of some note in London said once to him, "We have in our service a prayer called the *Pater Noster*, which is a very fine composition. I wonder who is the author of it."—A singular instance of ignorance in a man of some literature and general inquiry!

Saturday, 28th August.

Dr. Johnson had brought a Sallust with him in his pocket from Edinburgh. He gave it last night to Mr. M'Aulay's son, a smart young lad about eleven years old. Dr. Johnson had given an account of the education at Oxford, in all its gradations. The advantage of being a servitor to a youth of little fortune struck Mrs. M'Aulay much. I observed it aloud. Dr. Johnson very handsomely and kindly said, that, if they would send their boy to him, when he was ready for the university, he would get him made a servitor, and perhaps would do more for him. He could not promise to do more; but would undertake for the servitorship.[1]

I should have mentioned that Mr. White, a Welchman, who has been many years factor (*i.e.* steward) on the estate of Calder, drank tea with us last night, and upon getting a note from Mr. M'Aulay, asked us to

[1] Dr. Johnson did not neglect what he had undertaken. By his interest with the Rev. Dr. Adams, master of Pembroke College, Oxford, where he was educated for some time, he obtained a servitorship for young M'Aulay. But it seems he had other views; and I believe went abroad

Saying
grace at
breakfast

his house. We had not time to accept of his invitation. He gave us a letter of introduction to Mr. Ferne,
master of stores at Fort George. He shewed it to
me. It recommended "two celebrated gentlemen;
no less than Dr. Johnson, *author of his Dictionary*,—
and Mr. Boswell, known at Edinburgh by the name of
Paoli."—He said, he hoped I had no objection to
what he had written; if I had, he would alter it.   I
thought it was a pity to check his effusions, and acquiesced; taking care, however, to seal the letter, that it
might not appear that I had read it.

A conversation took place, about saying grace at
breakfast (as we do in Scotland) as well as at dinner
and supper; in which Dr. Johnson said, "It is enough
if we have stated seasons of prayer; no matter when.
A man may as well pray when he mounts his horse, or
a woman when she milks her cow, (which Mr. Grant
told us is done in the Highlands,) as at meals; and
custom is to be followed." [1]

We proceeded to Fort George. When we came
into the square, I sent a soldier with the letter to Mr.
Ferne. He came to us immediately, and along with
him came Major Brewse of the Engineers, pronounced
Bruce. He said he believed it was originally the
same Norman name with Bruce. That he had dined
at a house in London, where were three Bruces, one
of the Irish line, one of the Scottish line, and himself
of the English line. He said he was shewn it in the
Herald's office spelt fourteen different ways. I told
him the different spellings of my name. Dr. Johnson

[1] He could not bear to have it thought that, in any instance whatever, the Scots are more pious than the English.
I think grace as proper at breakfast as at any other meal.
It is the pleasantest meal we have. Dr. Johnson has allowed
the peculiar merit of breakfast in Scotland.

observed, that there had been great disputes about the **Fort** spelling of Shakspear's name; at last it was thought it **George** would be settled by looking at the original copy of his will; but, upon examining it, he was found to have written it himself no less than three different ways.

Mr. Ferne and Major Brewse first carried us to wait on Sir Eyre Coote, whose regiment, the 37th, was lying here, and who then commanded the fort. He asked us to dine with him, which we agreed to do.

Before dinner we examined the fort. The Major explained the fortification to us, and Mr. Ferne gave us an account of the stores. Dr. Johnson talked of the proportions of charcoal and salt-petre in making gunpowder, of granulating it, and of giving it a gloss. He made a very good figure upon these topics. He said to me afterwards, that "he had talked *ostentatiously*."—We reposed ourselves a little in Mr. Ferne's house. He had every thing in neat order as in England; and a tolerable collection of books. I looked into Pennant's Tour in Scotland. He says little of this fort; but that "the barracks, &c. form several streets." This is aggrandising. Mr. Ferne observed, if he had said they form a square, with a row of buildings before it, he would have given a juster description. Dr. Johnson remarked, "how seldom descriptions correspond with realities; and the reason is, that people do not write them till some time after, and then their imagination has added circumstances."

We talked of Sir Adolphus Oughton. The Major said, he knew a great deal for a military man.—JOHNSON. "Sir, you will find few men, of any profession, who know more. Sir Adolphus is a very extraordinary man; a man of boundless curiosity and unwearied diligence."

*E 387

Dinner
with
Sir Eyre
Coote

I know not how the Major contrived to introduce the contest between Warburton and Lowth.—Johnson. "Warburton kept his temper all along, while Lowth was in a passion. Lowth published some of Warburton's letters. Warburton drew *him* on to write some very abusive letters, and then asked his leave to publish them; which he knew Lowth could not refuse, after what *he* had done. So that Warburton contrived that he should publish, apparently with Lowth's consent, what could not but shew Lowth in a disadvantageous light." [1]

At three the drum beat for dinner. I, for a little while, fancied myself a military man, and it pleased me. We went to Sir Eyre Coote's, at the governour's house, and found him a most gentleman-like man. His lady is a very agreeable woman, with an uncommonly mild and sweet tone of voice. There was a pretty large company: Mr. Ferne, Major Brewse, and several officers. Sir Eyre had come from the East-Indies by land, through the Desarts of Arabia. He told us, the Arabs could live five days without victuals, and subsist for three weeks on nothing else but the blood of their camels, who could lose so much of it as would suffice for that time, without being exhausted. He highly praised the virtue of the Arabs; their fidelity, if they undertook to conduct any person; and said, they would sacrifice their lives rather than let him be robbed. Dr. Johnson, who is always for maintaining the superiority of civilized over uncivilized men, said, "Why, sir, I

[1] Here Dr. Johnson gave us part of a conversation held between a Great Personage and him, in the library at the Queen's Palace, in the course of which this contest was considered. I have been at great pains to get that conversation as perfectly preserved as possible. It may perhaps at some future time be given to the publick.

can see no superiour virtue in this.   A serjeant and The
twelve men, who are my guard, will die, rather than stage
that I shall be robbed."—Colonel Pennington, of the
37th regiment, took up the argument with a good deal of
spirit and ingenuity.—PENNINGTON. "But the soldiers
are compelled to this, by fear of punishment."—JOHN-
SON. "Well, sir, the Arabs are compelled by the
fear of infamy."—PENNINGTON. "The soldiers have
the same fear of infamy, and the fear of punishment
besides; so have less virtue; because they act less
voluntarily."—Lady Coote observed very well, that
it ought to be known if there was not, among the
Arabs, some punishment for not being faithful on such
occasions.

We talked of the stage.   I observed, that we had
not now such a company of actors as in the last age;
Wilks, Booth, &c. &c.—JOHNSON. "You think so,
because there is one who excels all the rest so much:
you compare them with Garrick, and see the deficiency.
Garrick's great distinction is his universality.   He can
represent all modes of life, but that of an easy fine bred
gentleman."—PENNINGTON. "He should give over
playing young parts."—JOHNSON. "He does not take
them now; but he does not leave off those which he
has been used to play, because he does them better than
any one else can do them.   If you had generations of
actors, if they swarmed like bees, the young ones might
drive off the old.   Mrs. Cibber, I think, got more
reputation than she deserved, as she had a great
sameness; though her expression was undoubtedly
very fine.   Mrs. Clive was the best player I ever saw.
Mrs. Pritchard was a very good one; but she had
something affected in her manner: I imagine she
had some player of the former age in her eye, which
occasioned it."

Colonel Pennington said, Garrick sometimes failed in emphasis; as for instance, in *Hamlet*,

> I will speak *daggers* to her; but use *none*,

instead of

> I will *speak* daggers to her; but *use* none.

We had a dinner of two complete courses, variety of wines, and the regimental band of musick playing in the square, before the windows, after it. I enjoyed this day much. We were quite easy and cheerful. Dr. Johnson said, " I shall always remember this fort with gratitude." I could not help being struck with some admiration, at finding upon this barren sandy point, such buildings,—such a dinner,—such company : it was like enchantment. Dr. Johnson, on the other hand, said to me more rationally, that " it did not strike *him* as any thing extraordinary ; because he knew, here was a large sum of money expended in building a fort ; here was a regiment. If there had been less than what we found, it would have surprized him." *He* looked coolly and deliberately through all the gradations : my warm imagination jumped from the barren sands to the splendid dinner and brilliant company, to borrow the expression of an absurd poet,

> " Without ands or ifs,
> I leapt from off the sands upon the cliffs."

The whole scene gave me a strong impression of the power and excellence of human art.

We left the fort between six and seven o'clock : Sir Eyre Coote, Colonel Pennington, and several more, accompanied us down stairs, and saw us into our chaise. There could not be greater attention paid to any visitors. Sir Eyre spoke of the hardships which Dr. Johnson had before him.—BOSWELL. "Considering what he Inverness has said of us, we must make him feel something rough in Scotland."—Sir Eyre said to him, "You must change your name, sir."—BOSWELL. "Ay, to Dr. M'Gregor."

We got safely to Inverness, and put up at Mackenzie's inn. Mr. Keith, the collector of Excise here, my old acquaintance at Ayr, who had seen us at the Fort, visited us in the evening, and engaged us to dine with him next day, promising to breakfast with us, and take us to the English chapel; so that we were at once commodiously arranged.

Not finding a letter here that I expected, I felt a momentary impatience to be at home. Transient clouds darkened my imagination, and in those clouds I saw events from which I shrunk; but a sentence or two of the Rambler's conversation gave me firmness, and I considered that I was upon an expedition for which I had wished for years, and the recollection of which would be a treasure to me for life.

Sunday, 29th August.

Mr. Keith breakfasted with us. Dr. Johnson expatiated rather too strongly upon the benefits derived to Scotland from the Union, and the bad state of our people before it. I am entertained with his copious exaggeration upon that subject; but I am uneasy when people are by, who do not know him as well as I do, and may be apt to think him narrow-minded.[1] I therefore diverted the subject.

The English chapel, to which we went this morning, was but mean. The altar was a bare fir table, with a

---

[1] It is remarkable that Dr. Johnson read this gentle remonstrance, and took no notice of it to me.

Mac-
beth's
castle
coarse stool for kneeling on, covered with a piece of thick sailcloth doubled, by way of cushion. The congregation was small. Mr. Tait, the clergyman, read prayers very well, though with much of the Scotch accent. He preached on " Love your Enemies." It was remarkable that, when talking of the connections amongst men, he said, that some connected themselves with men of distinguished talents, and since they could not equal them, tried to deck themselves with their merit, by being their companions. The sentence was to this purpose. It had an odd coincidence with what might be said of my connecting myself with Dr. Johnson.

After church, we walked down to the Quay. We then went to Macbeth's castle. I had a romantick satisfaction in seeing Dr. Johnson actually in it. It perfectly corresponds with Shakspeare's description, which Sir Joshua Reynolds has so happily illustrated, in one of his notes on our immortal poet :

" This castle hath a pleasant seat : the air
　　Nimbly and sweetly recommends itself
　　Unto our gentle sense," &c.

Just as we came out of it, a raven perched on one of the chimney-tops, and croaked. Then I repeated

" —— The raven himself is hoarse,
　　That croaks the fatal enterance of Duncan
　　Under my battlements."

We dined at Mr. Keith's. Mrs. Keith was rather too attentive to Dr. Johnson, asking him many questions about his drinking only water. He repressed that observation, by saying to me, " You may remember that Lady Errol took no notice of this."

Dr. Johnson has the happy art (for which I have heard my father praise the old Earl of Aberdeen) of instructing himself, by making every man he meets tell him something of what he knows best.   He led Keith to talk to him of the Excise in Scotland, and, in the course of conversation, mentioned that his friend Mr. Thrale, the great brewer, paid twenty thousand pounds a year to the revenue ; and that he had four casks, each of which holds sixteen hundred barrels,—above a thousand hogsheads.

Words coined by Johnson

After this there was little conversation that deserves to be remembered.   I shall therefore here again glean what I have omitted on former days.   Dr. Gerrard, at Aberdeen, told us, that when he was in Wales, he was shewn a valley inhabited by Danes, who still retain their own language, and are quite a distinct people. Dr. Johnson thought it could not be true, or all the kingdom must have heard of it.   He said to me, as we travelled, " these people, sir, that Gerrard talks of, may have somewhat of a *peregrinity* in their dialect, which relation has augmented to a different language." I asked him if *peregrinity* was an English word : he laughed, and said, " No."   I told him this was the second time that I had heard him coin a word.   When Foote broke his leg, I observed that it would make him fitter for taking off George Faulkner as Peter Paragraph, poor George having a wooden leg.   Dr. Johnson at that time said, " George will rejoice at the *depeditation* of Foote ; " and when I challenged that word, laughed, and owned he had made it, and added that he had not made above three or four in his dictionary.[1]

---

[1] When upon the subject of this *peregrinity*, he told me some particulars concerning the compilation of his Dictionary, and concerning his throwing off Lord Chesterfield's patronage, of which very erroneous accounts have been circulated.   These particulars, with others which he afterwards gave me,—as also his celebrated letter to Lord Chesterfield, which he dictated to me I reserve for his " LIFE."

The
travellers
begin
their
"equita-
tion"
Having conducted Dr. Johnson to our inn, I begged
permission to leave him for a little, that I might run
about and pay some short visits to several good people
of Inverness. He said to me, "You have all the old-
fashioned principles, good and bad." I acknowledge
I have. That of attention to relations in the remotest
degree, or to worthy persons, in every state whom I
have once known, I inherit from my father. It gave
me much satisfaction to hear every body at Inverness
speak of him with uncommon regard.—Mr. Keith
and Mr. Grant, whom we had seen at Mr. M'Aulay's,
supped with us at the inn. We had roasted kid, which
Dr. Johnson had never tasted before. He relished it
much.

Monday, 30th August.

This day we were to begin our *equitation*, as I said;
for *I* would needs make a word too. It is remarkable, that my noble, and to me most constant friend,
the Earl of Pembroke, (who, if there is too much ease
on my part, will please to pardon what his benevolent,
gay, social intercourse, and lively correspondence, have
insensibly produced,) has since hit upon the very same
word. The title of the first edition of his lordship's very useful book was, in simple terms, "A
Method of breaking Horses and teaching Soldiers to
ride." The title of the second edition is, "MILITARY
EQUITATION."

We might have taken a chaise to Fort Augustus,
but, had we not hired horses at Inverness, we should
not have found them afterwards: so we resolved to
begin here to ride. We had three horses, for Dr.
Johnson, myself, and Joseph, and one which carried
our portmanteaus, and two Highlanders who walked

along with us, John Hay and Lauchland Vass, whom **Loch**
Dr. Johnson has remembered with credit in his JOUR- **Ness**
NEY, though he has omitted their names. Dr. Johnson
rode very well.

About three miles beyond Inverness, we saw, just
by the road, a very complete specimen of what is called
a Druid's temple. There was a double circle, one of
very large, the other of smaller stones. Dr. Johnson
justly observed, that, "to go and see one druidical
temple is only to see that it is nothing, for there is
neither art nor power in it; and seeing one is quite
enough."

It was a delightful day. Lochness, and the road
upon the side of it, shaded with birch trees, and the
hills above it, pleased us much. The scene was as
sequestered and agreeably wild as could be desired,
and for a time engrossed all our attention.

To see Dr. Johnson in any new situation is always
an interesting object to me; and, as I saw him now
for the first time on horseback, jaunting about at his
ease in quest of pleasure and novelty, the very different
occupations of his former laborious life, his admirable
productions, his *London*, his *Rambler*, &c. &c. immediately presented themselves to my mind, and the contrast made a strong impression on my imagination.

When we had advanced a good way by the side of
Lochness, I perceived a little hut, with an old looking
woman at the door of it. I thought here might be a
scene that would amuse Dr. Johnson; so I mentioned
it to him. "Let's go in," said he. We dismounted,
and we and our guides entered the hut. It was a
wretched little hovel of earth only, I think, and for a
window had only a small hole, which was stopped with
a piece of turf, that was taken out occasionally to let
in light. In the middle of the room or space which

A hut on we entered, was a fire of peat, the smoke going out at
Loch a hole in the roof.   She had a pot upon it, with goat's
Ness flesh, boiling.   There was at one end under the same
roof, but divided by a kind of partition made of wattles,
a pen or fold in which we saw a good many kids.

Dr. Johnson was curious to know where she slept.
I asked one of the guides, who questioned her in Erse.
She answered with a tone of emotion, saying, (as he
told us,) she was afraid we wanted to go to bed to
her.   This coquetry, or whatever it may be called, of
so wretched a being, was truly ludicrous.   Dr. Johnson and I afterwards were merry upon it.   I said, it
was he who alarmed the poor woman's virtue.—" No,
sir, (said he,) she'll say, ' There came a wicked young
fellow, a wild dog, who I believe would have ravished
me, had there not been with him a grave old gentleman,
who repressed him : but when he gets out of the sight
of his tutor, I'll warrant you he'll spare no woman he
meets, young or old.' "—" No, sir, (I replied,) she'll
say, ' There was a terrible ruffian who would have
forced me, had it not been for a civil decent young
man who, I take it, was an angel sent from heaven to
protect me.' "

Dr. Johnson would not hurt her delicacy, by insisting on " seeing her bed-chamber," like Archer in the
Beaux Stratagem.   But my curiosity was more ardent ;
I lighted a piece of paper, and went into the place
where the bed was.   There was a little partition of
wicker, rather more neatly done than that for the fold,
and close by the wall was a kind of bedstead of wood
with heath upon it by way of bed ; at the foot of which
I saw some sort of blankets or covering rolled up in a
heap.   The woman's name was Fraser ; so was her
husband's.   He was a man of eighty.   Mr. Fraser of
Balnain allows him to live in this hut, and keep sixty

goats, for taking care of his woods, where he then was. **A**
They had five children, the eldest only thirteen. Two **contented**
were gone to Inverness to buy meal; the rest were **family**
looking after the goats. This contented family had
four stacks of barley, twenty-four sheaves in each.
They had a few fowls. We were informed that they
lived all the spring without meal, upon milk and curds
and whey alone. What they get for their goats, kids,
and fowls, maintains them during the rest of the year.

She asked us to sit down and take a dram. I saw
one chair. She said she was as happy as any woman
in Scotland. She could hardly speak any English
except a few detached words. Dr. Johnson was
pleased at seeing, for the first time, such a state of
human life. She asked for snuff. It is her luxury,
and she uses a great deal. We had none; but gave
her six pence a piece. She then brought out her
whisky bottle. I tasted it; as did Joseph and our
guides: so I gave her sixpence more. She sent us
away with many prayers in Erse.

We dined at a publick house called the General's
Hut, from General Wade, who was lodged there when
he commanded in the North. Near it is the meanest
parish Kirk I ever saw. It is a shame it should be
on a high road. After dinner, we passed through a
good deal of mountainous country. I had known
Mr. Trapaud, the deputy governour of Fort Augustus,
twelve years ago, at a circuit at Inverness, where my
father was judge. I sent forward one of our guides,
and Joseph, with a card to him, that he might know
Dr. Johnson and I were coming up, leaving it to him
to invite us or not. It was dark when we arrived.
The inn was wretched. Government ought to build
one, or give the resident governour an additional salary;
as in the present state of things, he must necessarily be

Fort
Augustus
put to a great expence in entertaining travellers.   Joseph announced to us, when we alighted, that the governour waited for us at the gate of the fort.   We walked to it.   He met us, and with much civility conducted us to his house.   It was comfortable to find ourselves in a well built little square, and a neatly furnished house, in good company, and with a good supper before us ; in short, with all the conveniencies of civilized life in the midst of rude mountains.   Mrs. Trapaud, and the governour's daughter, and her husband, Captain New-marsh, were all most obliging and polite.   The governour had excellent animal spirits, the conversation of a soldier, and somewhat of a Frenchman, to which his ex-traction entitles him.   He is brother to General Cyrus Trapaud.   We passed a very agreeable evening.

Tuesday, 31st August.

The governour has a very good garden.   We looked at it, and at the rest of the fort, which is but small, and may be commanded from a variety of hills around. We also looked at the galley or sloop belonging to the fort, which sails upon the Loch, and brings what is wanted for the garrison.   Captains Urie and Darippe, of the 15th regiment of foot, breakfasted with us. They had served in America, and entertained Dr. Johnson much with an account of the Indians.   He said, he could make a very pretty book out of them, were he to stay there.   Governour Trapaud was much struck with Dr. Johnson.   "I like to hear him, (said he,) it is so majestick.   I should be glad to hear him speak in your court."—He pressed us to stay dinner ; but I considered that we had a rude road before us, which we could more easily encounter in the morning, and that it was hard to say when we might get up,

were we to sit down to good entertainment, in good **Glen-**
company : I therefore begged the governour would **morison**
excuse us.—Here too, I had another very pleasing
proof how much my father is regarded. The governour expressed the highest respect for him, and bade
me tell him, that, if he would come that way on the
Northern circuit, he would do him all the honours of
the garrison.

Between twelve and one we set out, and travelled
eleven miles, through a wild country, till we came to
a house in Glenmorison, called Anoch, kept by a
M'Queen.[1] Our landlord was a sensible fellow : he
had learnt his grammar, and Dr. Johnson justly observed, that "a man is the better for that as long as
he lives." There were some books here : a Treatise
against Drunkenness, translated from the French ; a
volume of the Spectator ; a volume of Prideaux's
Connection, and Cyrus's Travels. M'Queen said he
had more volumes ; and his pride seemed to be much
piqued that we were surprised at his having books.

Near to this place we had passed a party of soldiers,
under a serjeant's command, at work upon the road.
We gave them two shillings to drink. They came to
our inn, and made merry in the barn. We went and
paid them a visit, Dr. Johnson saying, "Come, let's
go and give 'em another shilling a-piece." We did
so ; and he was saluted "MY LORD" by all of them.
He is really generous, loves influence, and has the way
of gaining it. He said, "I am quite feudal, sir."

[1] *A* M'Queen is a Highland mode of expression. An
Englishman would say *one* M'Queen. But where there are
clans or *tribes* of men, distinguished by *patronymick* surnames,
the individuals of each are considered as if they were of
different species, at least as much as nations are distinguished ;
so that a M'Queen, a M'Donald, a M'Lean, is said, as we
say a Frenchman, an Italian, a Spaniard.

Emigra-
tion

Here I agree with him.   I said, I regretted I was not
the head of a clan ; however, though not possessed of
such an hereditary advantage, I would always endeavour
to make my tenants follow me.   I could not be a *patriarchal* chief, but I would be a *feudal* chief.

The poor soldiers got too much liquor.   Some of
them fought, and left blood upon the spot, and cursed
whisky next morning.   The house here was built of
thick turfs, and thatched with thinner turfs and heath.
It had three rooms in length, and a little room which
projected.   Where we sat, the side-walls were wains-
cotted, as Dr. Johnson said, with wicker, very neatly
plaited.   Our landlord had made the whole with his
own hands.

After dinner, M'Queen sat by us a while, and talked
with us.   He said, all the Laird of Glenmorison's
people would bleed for him, if they were well used ; but
that seventy men had gone out of the Glen to America.
That he himself intended to go next year ; for that
the rent of his farm, which twenty years ago was only
five pounds, was now raised to twenty pounds.   That
he could pay ten pounds, and live ; but no more.—Dr.
Johnson said, he wished M'Queen laird of Glenmorison,
and the laird to go to America.   M'Queen very
generously answered, he should be sorry for it ; for
the laird could not shift for himself in America as he
could do.

I talked of the officers whom we had left to-day ;
how much service they had seen, and how little they
got for it, even of fame.—JOHNSON.   " Sir, a soldier
gets as little as any man can get."—BOSWELL.   " Goldsmith has acquired more fame than all the officers last
war, who were not Generals."—JOHNSON.   " Why,
sir, you will find ten thousand fit to do what they did,
before you find one who does what Goldsmith has

done. You must consider, that a thing is valued ac- A sailor's
cording to its rarity. A pebble that paves the street is life
in itself more useful than the diamond upon a lady's
finger."—I wish our friend Goldsmith had heard this.

I yesterday expressed my wonder that John Hay,
one of our guides, who had been pressed aboard a man
of war, did not choose to continue in it longer than
nine months, after which time he got off.—JOHNSON.
" Why, sir, no man will be a sailor, who has contrivance
enough to get himself into a jail ; for, being in a ship
is being in a jail, with the chance of being drowned."

We had tea in the afternoon, and our landlord's
daughter, a modest civil girl, very neatly drest, made it
for us. She told us, she had been a year at Inverness,
and learnt reading and writing, sewing, knotting, working
lace, and pastry. Dr. Johnson made her a present of
a book which he had bought at Inverness.[1]

---

[1] This book has given rise to much inquiry, which has
ended in ludicrous surprise. Several ladies, wishing to learn
the kind of reading which the great and good Dr. Johnson
esteemed most fit for a young woman, desired to know what
book he had selected for this Highland nymph. "They never
adverted, (said he,) that I had no choice in the matter. I have
said that I presented her with a book which I happened to
have about me."—And what was this book ?—My readers,
prepare your features for merriment. It was *Cocker's Arithmetick!*—Wherever this was mentioned, there was a loud
laugh, at which Dr. Johnson, when present, used sometimes
to be a little angry. One day, when we were dining at
General Oglethorpe's, where we had many a valuable day, I
ventured to interrogate him, " But, sir, is it not somewhat
singular that you should happen to have *Cocker's Arithmetick*
about you on your journey ? What made you buy such a
book at Inverness ? "—He gave me a very sufficient answer.
" Why, sir, if you are to have but one book with you upon
a journey, let it be a book of science. When you have read
through a book of entertainment, you know it, and it can do
no more for you ; but a book of science is inexhaustible."

The inn
at Anoch
The room had some deals laid across the joists, as a kind of ceiling.   There were two beds in the room, and a woman's gown was hung on a rope to make a curtain of separation between them.   Joseph had sheets, which my wife had sent with us, laid on them.   We had much hesitation, whether to undress, or lie down with our clothes on.   I said at last, "I'll plunge in! There will be less harbour for vermin about me, when I am stripped!"—Dr. Johnson said, he was like one hesitating whether to go into the cold bath.   At last he resolved too.   I observed, he might serve a campaign. —JOHNSON. "I could do all that can be done by patience: whether I should have strength enough, I know not."—He was in excellent humour.   To see the Rambler as I saw him to-night, was really an amusement.   I yesterday told him, I was thinking of writing a poetical letter to him, *on his return from Scotland,* in the stile of Swift's humorous epistle in the character of Mary Gulliver to her husband, Captain Lemuel Gulliver, on his return to England from the country of the Houyhnhnms :

> " At early morn I to the market haste,
>   Studious in ev'ry thing to please thy taste.
>   A curious *fowl* and *sparagrass* I chose ;
>   (For I remember you were fond of those :)
>   Three shillings cost the first, the last sev'n groats ;
>   Sullen you turn from both, and call for OATS."

He laughed, and asked in whose name I would write it.   I said, in Mrs. Thrale's.   He was angry.   "Sir, if you have any sense of decency or delicacy, you won't do that!"—BOSWELL. "Then let it be in Cole's, the landlord of the Mitre tavern; where we have so often sat together."—JOHNSON. "Ay, that may do."

After we had offered up our private devotions, and

had chatted a little from our beds, Dr. Johnson said, **Ground-** "GOD bless us both, for Jesus Christ's sake! Good **less fears** night!"—I pronounced "Amen."—He fell asleep immediately. I was not so fortunate for a long time. I fancied myself bit by innumerable vermin under the clothes; and that a spider was travelling from the wainscot towards my mouth. At last I fell into insensibility.

Wednesday, 1st September.

I awaked very early. I began to imagine that the landlord, being about to emigrate, might murder us to get our money, and lay it upon the soldiers in the barn. Such groundless fears will arise in the mind, before it has resumed its vigour after sleep! Dr. Johnson had had the same kind of ideas; for he told me afterwards, that he considered so many soldiers, having seen us, would be witnesses, should any harm be done, and that circumstance, I suppose, he considered as a security. When I got up, I found him sound asleep in his miserable *stye*, as I may call it, with a coloured handkerchief tied round his head. With difficulty could I awaken him. It reminded me of Henry the Fourth's fine soliloquy on sleep; for there was here as *uneasy a pallet* as the poet's imagination could possibly conceive.

A *red coat* of the 15th regiment, whether officer, or only serjeant, I could not be sure, came to the house, in his way to the mountains to shoot deer, which it seems the Laird of Glenmorison does not hinder any body to do. Few, indeed, can do them harm. We had him to breakfast with us. We got away about eight. M'Queen walked some miles to give us a convoy. He had, in 1745, joined the Highland army at Fort Augustus, and continued in it till after the battle

Glensheal of Culloden. As he narrated the particulars of that ill-advised, but brave attempt, I could not refrain from tears. There is a certain association of ideas in my mind upon that subject, by which I am strongly affected. The very Highland names, or the sound of a bagpipe, will stir my blood, and fill me with a mixture of melancholy and respect for courage ; with pity for an unfortunate and superstitious regard for antiquity, and thoughtless inclination for war ; in short, with a crowd of sensations with which sober rationality has nothing to do.

We passed through Glensheal, with prodigious mountains on each side. We saw where the battle was fought in the year 1719. Dr. Johnson owned he was now in a scene of as wild nature as he could see ; but he corrected me sometimes in my inaccurate observations.—" There, (said I,) is a mountain like a cone." —JOHNSON. " No, sir. It would be called so in a book ; and when a man comes to look at it, he sees it is not so. It is indeed pointed at the top ; but one side of it is larger than the other."—Another mountain I called immense.—JOHNSON. " No ; it is no more than a considerable protuberance."

We came to a rich green valley, comparatively speaking, and stopped a while to let our horses rest and eat grass.[1] We soon afterwards came to Auchnasheal, a

[1] Dr. Johnson, in his *Journey*, thus beautifully describes his situation here: " I sat down on a bank, such as a writer of romance might have delighted to feign. I had, indeed, no trees to whisper over my head ; but a clear rivulet streamed at my feet. The day was calm, the air soft, and all was rudeness, silence, and solitude. Before me, and on either side, were high hills, which, by hindering the eye from ranging, forced the mind to find entertainment for itself. Whether I spent the hour well, I know not ; for here I first conceived the thought of this narration."—The Critical Reviewers, with

kind of rural village, a number of cottages being built Auchna-
together, as we saw all along in the Highlands. We sheal
passed many miles this day without seeing a house, but
only little summer-huts, called *shielings*. Evan Campbell, servant to Mr. Murchison, factor to the Laird of
Macleod in Glenelg, ran along with us to-day. He
was a very obliging fellow. At Auchnasheal, we sat
down on a green turf-seat at the end of a house; they
brought us out two wooden dishes of milk, which we
tasted. One of them was frothed like a syllabub. I
saw a woman preparing it with such a stick as is used
for chocolate, and in the same manner. We had a
considerable circle about us, men, women and children,
all M'Craas, Lord Seaforth's people. Not one of them
could speak English. I observed to Dr. Johnson, it
was much the same as being with a tribe of Indians.
—JOHNSON. " Yes, sir; but not so terrifying." I gave
all who chose it, snuff and tobacco. Governour Trapaud had made us buy a quantity at Fort Augustus, and
put them up in small parcels. I also gave each person
a bit of wheat bread, which they had never tasted
before. I then gave a penny apiece to each child.
I told Dr. Johnson of this; upon which he called to
Joseph and our guides, for change for a shilling, and
declared that he would distribute among the children.

a spirit and expression worthy of the subject, say,—" We
congratulate the publick on the event with which this quotation concludes, and are fully persuaded that the hour in
which the entertaining traveller conceived this narrative
will be considered, by every reader of taste, as a fortunate
event in the annals of literature. Were it suitable to the talk
in which we are at present engaged, to indulge ourselves in a
poetical flight, we would invoke the winds of the Caledonian mountains to blow for ever, with their softest breezes,
on the bank where our author reclined, and request of Flora,
that it might be perpetually adorned with the gayest and
most fragrant productions of the year."

The
Macraes
Upon this being announced in Erse, there was a great stir; not only did some children come running down from neighbouring huts, but I observed one black-haired man, who had been with us all along, had gone off, and returned, bringing a very young child. My fellow traveller then ordered the children to be drawn up in a row; and he dealt about his copper, and made them and their parents all happy. The poor M'Craas, whatever may be their present state, were of considerable estimation in the year 1715, when there was a line in a song,

And aw the brave M'Craas are coming.[1]

There was great diversity in the faces of the circle around us: Some were as black and wild in their appearance as any American savages whatever. One woman was as comely almost as the figure of Sappho,

---

[1] The M'Craas, or Macraes, were since that time brought into the king's army, by the late Lord Seaforth. When they lay in Edinburgh castle in 1778, and were ordered to embark for Jersey, they with a number of other men in the regiment, for different reasons, but especially an apprehension that they were to be sold to the East-India Company, though enlisted not to be sent out of Great Britain without their own consent, made a determined mutiny, and encamped upon the lofty mountain, Arthur's seat, where they remained three days and three nights; bidding defiance to all the force in Scotland. At last they came down, and embarked peaceably, having obtained formal articles of capitulation, signed by Sir Adolphus Oughton, commander in chief, General Skene, deputy commander, the Duke of Buccleugh, and the Earl of Dunmore, which quieted them. Since the secession of the Commons of Rome to the Mons Sacer, a more spirited exertion has not been made. I gave great attention to it from first to last, and have drawn up a particular account of it. Those brave fellows have since served their country effectually at Jersey, and also in the East-Indies, to which, after being better informed, they voluntarily agreed to go.

as we see it painted.   We asked the old woman, the **Johnson** mistress of the house where we had the milk, (which **as a** by the bye, Dr. Johnson told me, for I did not observe **Chief** it myself, was built not of turf, but of stone,) what we should pay.   She said, what we pleased.   One of our guides asked her, in Erse, if a shilling was enough. She said, "Yes."   But some of the men bade her ask more.   This vexed me ; because it showed a desire to impose upon strangers, as they knew that even a shilling was high payment.   The woman, however, honestly persisted in her first price ; so I gave her half a crown. —Thus we had one good scene of life uncommon to us.   The people were very much pleased, gave us many blessings, and said they had not had such a day since the old Laird of Macleod's time.

Dr. Johnson was much refreshed by this repast.   He was pleased when I told him he would make a good Chief.   He said, "Were I a chief, I would dress my servants better than myself, and knock a fellow down if he looked saucy to a Macdonald in rags : but I would not treat men as brutes.   I would let them know why all my clan were to have attention paid to them.   I would tell my upper servants why, and make them tell the others."

We rode on well, till we came to the high mountain called the Rattakin, by which time both Dr. Johnson and the horses were a good deal fatigued.   It is a terrible steep to climb, notwithstanding the road is formed slanting along it ; however, we made it out. On the top of it we met Captain M'Leod of Balmenoch (a Dutch officer who had come from Sky) riding with his sword slung across him.   He asked, "Is this Mr. Boswell?" which was a proof that we were expected.   Going down the hill on the other side was no easy task.   As Dr. Johnson was a great

A
ludicrous
scene

weight, the two guides agreed that he should ride the
horses alternately.   Hay's were the two best, and the
Doctor would not ride but upon one or other of them,
a black or a brown.   But, as Hay complained much
after ascending the Rattakin, the Doctor was prevailed
with to mount one of Vass's greys.   As he rode upon
it down hill, it did not go well; and he grumbled.   I
walked on a little before, but was excessively entertained with the method taken to keep him in good
humour.   Hay led the horse's head, talking to Dr.
Johnson as much as he could; and (having heard him,
in the forenoon, express a pastoral pleasure on seeing
the goats browzing) just when the Doctor was uttering
his displeasure, the fellow cried, with a very Highland
accent, "See such pretty goats!"   Then he whistled,
whu! and made them jump.—Little did he conceive
what Doctor Johnson was.   Here now was a common
ignorant Highland clown imagining that he could divert,
as one does a child,—Dr. Samuel Johnson!—The ludi-
crousness, absurdity, and extraordinary contrast between
what the fellow fancied, and the reality, was truly comick.

It grew dusky; and we had a very tedious ride for
what was called five miles; but I am sure would
measure ten.   We had no conversation.   I was riding
forward to the inn at Glenelg, on the shore opposite
to Sky, that I might take proper measures, before Dr.
Johnson, who was now advancing in dreary silence,
Hay leading his horse, should arrive.   Vass also walked
by the side of his horse, and Joseph followed behind:
as therefore he was thus attended, and seemed to be
in deep meditation, I thought there could be no harm
in leaving him for a little while.   He called me back
with a tremendous shout, and was really in a passion
with me for leaving him.   I told him my intentions,
but he was not satisfied, and said, "Do you know, I

should as soon have thought of picking a pocket, as Johnson in a passion doing so."—BOSWELL. " I am diverted with you, sir." —JOHNSON. " Sir, I could never be diverted with incivility. Doing such a thing, makes one lose confidence in him who has done it, as one cannot tell what he may do next."—His extraordinary warmth confounded me so much, that I justified myself but lamely to him ; yet my intentions were not improper. I wished to get on, to see how we were to be lodged, and how we were to get a boat; all which I thought I could best settle myself, without his having any trouble. To apply his great mind to minute particulars, is wrong : it is like taking an immense balance, such as is kept on quays for weighing cargoes of ships,—to weigh a guinea. I knew I had neat little scales, which would do better; and that his attention to every thing which falls in his way, and his uncommon desire to be always in the right, would make him weigh, if he knew of the particulars : it was right therefore for me to weigh them, and let him have them only in effect. I however continued to ride by him, finding he wished I should do so.

As we passed the barracks at Bernéra, I looked at them wishfully, as soldiers have always every thing in the best order : but there was only a serjeant and a few men there. We came on to the inn at Glenelg. There was no provender for our horses ; so they were sent to grass, with a man to watch them. A maid shewed us up stairs into a room damp and dirty, with bare walls, a variety of bad smells, a coarse black greasy fir table, and forms of the same kind ; and out of a wretched bed started a fellow from his sleep, like Edgar in *King Lear*, " *Poor Tom's a cold.*" [1]

---

[1] It is amusing to observe the different images which this being presented to Dr. Johnson and me. The Doctor, in his JOURNEY, compares him to a Cyclops.

The
inn at
Glenelg

This inn was furnished with not a single article that we could either eat or drink; but Mr. Murchison, factor to the Laird of Macleod in Glenelg, sent us a bottle of rum and some sugar, with a polite message, to acquaint us, that he was very sorry that he did not hear of us till we had passed his house, otherwise he should have insisted on our sleeping there that night; and that, if he were not obliged to set out for Inverness early next morning, he would have waited upon us. —Such extraordinary attention from this gentleman, to entire strangers, deserves the most honourable commemoration.

Our bad accommodation here made me uneasy, and almost fretful. Dr. Johnson was calm. I said, he was so from vanity.—JOHNSON. "No, sir, it is from philosophy."—It pleased me to see that the Rambler could practise so well his own lessons.

I resumed the subject of my leaving him on the road, and endeavoured to defend it better. He was still violent upon that head, and said, "Sir, had you gone on, I was thinking that I should have returned with you to Edinburgh, and then have parted from you, and never spoken to you more."

I sent for fresh hay, with which we made beds for ourselves, each in a room equally miserable. Like Wolfe, we had a "choice of difficulties." Dr. Johnson made things easier by comparison. At M'Queen's, last night, he observed, that few were so well lodged in a ship. To-night he said, we were better than if we had been upon the hill. He lay down buttoned up in his great coat. I had my sheets spread on the hay, and my clothes and great coat laid over me, by way of blankets.

Thursday, 2nd September.

I had slept ill. Dr. Johnson's anger had affected me much. I considered that, without any bad intention, I might suddenly forfeit his friendship ; and was impatient to see him this morning. I told him how uneasy he had made me, by what he had said, and reminded him of his own remark at Aberdeen, upon old friendships being hastily broken off. He owned, he had spoken to me in passion ; that he would not have done what he threatened ; and that, if he had, he should have been ten times worse than I ; that forming intimacies, would indeed be " limning the water," were they liable to such sudden dissolution ; and he added, " Let's think no more on't."—BOSWELL. " Well then, sir, I shall be easy. Remember, I am to have fair warning in case of any quarrel. You are never to spring a mine upon me. It was absurd in me to believe you."—JOHNSON. " You deserved about as much, as to believe me from night to morning."

After breakfast, we got into a boat for Sky. It rained much when we set off, but cleared up as we advanced. One of the boatmen, who spoke English, said, that a mile at land was two miles at sea. I then observed, that from Glenelg to Armidale in Sky, which was our present course, and is called twelve, was only six miles : but this he could not understand. " Well, (said Dr. Johnson,) never talk to me of the native good sense of the Highlanders. Here is a fellow who calls one mile two, and yet cannot comprehend that twelve such imaginary miles make in truth but six."

We reached the shore of Armidale before one o'clock. Sir Alexander M'Donald came down to receive us. He and his lady, (formerly Miss Bosville of Yorkshire,) were then in a house built by a tenant

F 387

at this place, which is in the district of Slate, the family
mansion here having been burned in Sir Donald Macdonald's time.

The most ancient seat of the chief of the Macdonalds in the isle of Sky was at Duntulm, where
there are the remains of a stately castle. The principal residence of the family is now at Mugstot, at
which there is a considerable building. Sir Alexander
and lady Macdonald had come to Armidale in their
way to Edinburgh, where it was necessary for them to
be soon after this time.

Armidale is situated on a pretty bay of the narrow
sea, which flows between the main land of Scotland and
the Isle of Sky. In front there is a grand prospect of
the rude mountains of Moidart and Knoidart. Behind
are hills gently rising and covered with a finer verdure
than I expected to see in this climate, and the scene is
enlivened by a number of little clear brooks.

Sir Alexander Macdonald having been an Eton
scholar,[1] and being a gentleman of talents, Dr. Johnson
had been very well pleased with him in London. But
my fellow-traveller and I were now full of the old
Highland spirit, and were dissatisfied at hearing of racked
rents and emigration; and finding a chief not surrounded
by his clan. Dr. Johnson said, " Sir, the Highland
chiefs should not be allowed to go farther south than
Aberdeen. A strong-minded man, like Sir James Macdonald, may be improved by an English education ; but
in general, they will be tamed into insignificance."

We found here Mr. Janes of Aberdeenshire, a
naturalist. Janes said he had been at Dr. Johnson's
in London, with Ferguson the astronomer.—JOHNSON.
" It is strange that, in such distant places, I should

[1] See his Latin verses addressed to Dr. Johnson, in the
APPENDIX.

meet with any one who knows me. I should have
thought I might hide myself in Sky."

Friday, 3rd September.

This day proving wet, we should have passed our
time very uncomfortably, had we not found in the house
two chests of books, which we eagerly ransacked.
After dinner, when I alone was left at table with the
few Highland gentlemen who were of the company,
having talked with very high respect of Sir James
Macdonald, they were all so much affected as to shed
tears. One of them was Mr. Donald Macdonald,
who had been lieutenant of grenadiers in the Highland regiment, raised by Colonel Montgomery, now
Earl of Eglintoune, in the war before last; one of
those regiments which the late Lord Chatham prided
himself in having brought from " the mountains of the
North :" by doing which he contributed to extinguish
in the Highlands the remains of disaffection to the
present Royal Family. From this gentleman's conversation, I first learnt how very popular his Colonel
was among the Highlanders ; of which I had such
continued proofs, during the whole course of my Tour,
that on my return I could not help telling the noble
Earl himself, that I did not before know how great a
man he was.

We were advised by some persons here to visit
Rasay, in our way to Dunvegan, the seat of the Laird
of Macleod. Being informed that the Rev. Mr.
Donald M'Queen was the most intelligent man in Sky,
and having been favoured with a letter of introduction
to him, by the learned Sir James Foulis, I sent it to
him by an express, and requested he would meet us at
Rasay ; and at the same time enclosed a letter to the

The travellers' feudal enthusiasm

Laird of Macleod, informing him that we intended in a few days to have the honour of waiting on him at Dunvegan.

Dr. Johnson this day endeavoured to obtain some knowledge of the state of the country; but complained that he could get no distinct information about any thing, from those with whom he conversed.

Saturday, 4th September.

My endeavours to rouse the English-bred Chieftain, in whose house we were, to the feudal and patriarchal feelings, proving ineffectual, Dr. Johnson this morning tried to bring him to our way of thinking.—JOHNSON. "Were I in your place, sir, in seven years I would make this an independant island. I would roast oxen whole, and hang out a flag as a signal to the Macdonalds to come and get beef and whisky."—Sir Alexander was still starting difficulties.—JOHNSON. "Nay, sir; if you are born to object, I have done with you. Sir, I would have a magazine of arms."—SIR ALEXANDER. "They would rust."—JOHNSON. "Let there be men to keep them clean. Your ancestors did not use to let their arms rust."

We attempted in vain to communicate to him a portion of our enthusiasm. He bore with so polite a good-nature our warm, and what some might call Gothick, expostulations, on this subject, that I should not forgive myself, were I to record all that Dr. Johnson's ardour led him to say.—This day was little better than a blank.

Sunday, 5th September.

I walked to the parish church of Slate, which is a very poor one. There are no church bells in the island. I was told there were once some; what has become of

them, I could not learn.   The minister not being at
home, there was no service.   I went into the church,
and saw the monument of Sir James Macdonald, which
was elegantly executed at Rome, and has the following inscription, written by his friend, George Lord
Lyttelton :

Sir James
Mac-
donald's
monu-
ment

To the memory
Of Sir JAMES MACDONALD, Bart.
Who in the flower of youth,
Had attained to so eminent a degree of knowledge
In Mathematics, Philosophy, Languages,
And in every other branch of useful and polite learning,
As few have acquired in a long life
Wholly devoted to study :
Yet to this erudition he joined
What can rarely be found with it,
Great talents for business,
Great propriety of behaviour,
Great politeness of manners !
His eloquence was sweet, correct, and flowing ;
His memory vast and exact ;
His judgement strong and acute ;
All which endowments, united
With the most amiable temper
And every private virtue,
Procured him, not only in his own country,
But also from foreign nations,
The highest marks of esteem.
In the year of our Lord
1766,
The 25th of his life,
After a long and extremely painful illness,
Which he supported with admirable patience and fortitude,
He died at Rome,

Sir James
Macdonald's
monument

Where, notwithstanding the difference of religion,
Such extraordinary honours were paid to his memory,
As had never graced that of any other British subject,
Since the death of Sir Philip Sydney.
The fame he left behind him is the best consolation
To his afflicted family,
And to his countrymen in this isle,
For whose benefit he had planned
Many useful improvements,
Which his fruitful genius suggested,
And his active spirit promoted,
Under the sober direction
Of a clear and enlightened understanding.
Reader, bewail our loss,
And that of all Britain.
In testimony of her love,
And as the best return she can make
To her departed son,
For the constant tenderness and affection
Which, even to his last moments,
He shewed for her,
His much afflicted mother,
The LADY MARGARET MACDONALD,
Daughter to the EARL of EGLINTOUNE,
Erected this Monument,
A.D. 1768.[1]

[1] This extraordinary young man, whom I had the pleasure
of knowing intimately, having been deeply regretted by his
country, the most minute particulars concerning him must
be interesting to many. I shall therefore insert his two last
letters to his mother, Lady Margaret Macdonald, which her
ladyship has been pleased to communicate to me.

"MY DEAR MOTHER,   *Rome, 9th July,* 1766.
"Yesterday's post brought me your answer to the
first letter in which I acquainted you of my illness. Your
tenderness and concern upon that account are the same I

Dr. Johnson said, the inscription should have been His last
in Latin, as every thing intended to be universal and letters
permanent, should be.

This being a beautiful day, my spirits were cheered
by the mere effect of climate. I had felt a return of
spleen during my stay at Armidale, and had it not
been that I had Dr. Johnson to contemplate, I should

have always experienced, and to which I have often owed
my life. Indeed it never was in so great danger as it has
been lately; and though it would have been a very great
comfort to me to have had you near me, yet perhaps I
ought to rejoice, on your account, that you had not the
pain of such a spectacle. I have been now a week in
Rome, and wish I could continue to give you the same
good accounts of my recovery as I did in my last: but I
must own that, for three days past, I have been in a very
weak and miserable state, which however seems to give no
uneasiness to my physician. My stomach has been greatly
out of order, without any visible cause; and the palpitation
does not decrease. I am told that my stomach will soon
recover its tone, and that the palpitation must cease in time.
So I am willing to believe; and with this hope support the
little remains of spirits which I can be supposed to have, on
the forty-seventh day of such an illness. Do not imagine I
have relapsed;—I only recover slower than I expected. If my
letter is shorter than usual, the cause of it is a dose of physick, which has weakened me so much to-day, that I am not
able to write a long letter. I will make up for it next post,
and remain always

"Your most sincerely affectionate son,

"J. MACDONALD."

He grew gradually worse; and on the night before his
death he wrote as follows from Frescati:

"MY DEAR MOTHER,

"Though I did not mean to deceive you in my last
letter from Rome, yet certainly you would have very little
reason to conclude of the very great and constant danger I
have gone through ever since that time. My life, which is
still almost entirely desperate, did not at that time appear to
me so, otherwise I should have represented, in its true colours,

have sunk into dejection; but his firmness supported
me.   I looked at him, as a man whose head is turning
giddy at sea looks at a rock, or any fixed object.   I
wondered at his tranquillity.   He said, " Sir, when a
man retires into an island, he is to turn his thoughts
intirely to another world.   He has done with this."—
BOSWELL. "It appears to me, sir, to be very difficult to
unite a due attention to this world, and that which is to
come; for, if we engage eagerly in the affairs of life, we
are apt to be totally forgetful of a future state ; and, on
the other hand, a steady contemplation of the awful
concerns of eternity renders all objects here so insignificant, as to make us indifferent and negligent about
them."—JOHNSON. " Sir, Dr. Cheyne has laid down a
rule to himself on this subject, which should be im-
printed on every mind: ' *To neglect nothing to secure my
eternal peace, more than if I had been certified I should die
within the day: nor to mind any thing that my secular
obligations and duties demanded of me, less than if I had
been ensured to live fifty years more.*' "

I must here observe, that though Dr. Johnson
appeared now to be philosophically calm, yet his
genius did not shine forth as in companies, where I
have listened to him with admiration.   The vigour
of his mind was, however, sufficiently manifested,
by his discovering no symptoms of feeble relaxation

a fact which acquires very little horror by that means, and
comes with redoubled force by deception.   There is no circumstance of danger and pain of which I have not had
the experience, for a continued series of above a fortnight;
during which time I have settled my affairs, after my death,
with as much distinctness as the hurry and the nature of the
thing could admit of.   In case of the worst, the Abbé Grant
will be my executor in this part of the world, and Mr.
Mackenzie in Scotland, where my object has been to make
you and my younger brother as independent of the eldest as
possible."

in the dull, "weary, flat and unprofitable" state in which we now were placed.

I am inclined to think that it was on this day he composed the following Ode upon the Isle of Sky, which a few days afterwards he shewed me at Rasay:

O D A

Ponti profundis clausa recessibus,
Strepens procellis, rupibus obsita,
Quam grata defesso virentem
Skia sinum nebulosa pandis.

His cura, credo, sedibus exulat ;
His blanda certe pax habitat locis:
Non ira, non mæror quietis
Insidias meditatur horis.

At non cavata rupe latescere,
Menti nec ægræ montibus aviis
Prodest vagari, nec frementes
E scopulo numerare fluctus.

Humana virtus non sibi sufficit,
Datur nec æquum cuique animum sibi
Parare posse, ut Stoicorum
Secta crepet nimis alta fallax.

Exæstuantis pectoris impetum,
Rex summe, solus tu regis arbiter,
Mentisque, te tollente, surgunt,
Te recidunt moderante fluctus.[1]

[1] VARIOUS READINGS.

Line 2. In the manuscript, Dr. Johnson, instead of *rupibus obsita,* had written *imbribus uvida,* and *uvida nubibus,* but struck them both out.

Lines 15 & 16. Instead of these two lines, he had written, but afterwards struck out, the following:

Parare posse, utcunque jactet
Grandiloquus nimis alta Zeno.

Corricha-
tachin
After supper, Dr. Johnson told us, that Isaac
Hawkins Browne drank freely for thirty years, and
that he wrote his poem, *De Animi Immortalitate*, in
some of the last of these years.—I listened to this
with the eagerness of one, who, conscious of being
himself fond of wine, is glad to hear that a man of so
much genius and good thinking as Browne had the same
propensity.

Monday, 6th September.

We set out, accompanied by Mr. Donald M'Leod
(late of Canna) as our guide. We rode for some
time along the district of Slate, near the shore. The
houses in general are made of turf, covered with grass.
The country seemed well peopled. We came into
the district of Strath, and passed along a wild moorish
tract of land till we arrived at the shore. There we
found good verdure, and some curious whin-rocks, or
collections of stones like the ruins of the foundations of
old buildings. We saw also three Cairns of considerable size.

About a mile beyond Broadfoot, is Corrichatachin,
a farm of Sir Alexander Macdonald's, possessed by
Mr. M'Kinnon,[1] who received us with a hearty

[1] That my readers may have my narrative in the style of
the country through which I am travelling, it is proper to
inform them, that the chief of a clan is denominated by his
surname alone, as M'Leod, M'Kinnon, M'Intosh. To prefix *Mr.* to it would be a degradation from *the* M'Leod, &c.
My old friend, the Laird of M'Farlane, the great antiquary,
took it highly amiss, when General Wade called him Mr.
M'Farlane. Dr. Johnson said, he could not bring himself
to use this mode of address; it seemed to him to be too
familiar, as it is the way in which, in all other places, inti-
mates or inferiors are addressed. When the chiefs have
titles, they are denominated by them, as *Sir James Grant, Sir
Allan M'Lean.* The other Highland gentlemen, of landed
property, are denominated by their estates, as *Rasay, Bois-*

welcome, as did his wife, who was what we call in
Scotland a *lady-like* woman.   Mr. Pennant, in the
course of his tour to the Hebrides, passed two nights
at this gentleman's house.   On its being mentioned,
that a present had here been made to him of a curious
specimen of Highland antiquity, Dr. Johnson said, "Sir,
it was more than he deserved : the dog is a whig."

We here enjoyed the comfort of a table plentifully
furnished, the satisfaction of which was heightened by
a numerous and cheerful company ; and we for the
first time had a specimen of the joyous social manners
of the inhabitants of the Highlands.   They talked in
their own ancient language, with fluent vivacity, and
sung many Erse songs with such spirit, that, though
Dr. Johnson was treated with the greatest respect and
attention, there were moments in which he seemed to
be forgotten.   For myself, though but a *Lowlander*,
having picked up a few words of the language, I presumed to mingle in their mirth, and joined in the
chorusses with as much glee as any of the company.
Dr. Johnson being fatigued with his journey, retired
early to his chamber, where he composed the following
Ode, addressed to Mrs. Thrale :

O D A

Permeo terras, ubi nuda rupes
Saxeas miscet nebulis ruinas,
Torva ubi rident steriles coloni
                    Rura labores.

---

dale ; and the wives of all of them have the title of *ladies*.
The *tacksmen*, or principal tenants, are named by their
farms, as *Kingsburgh*, *Corrichatachin* ; and their wives are
called the *mistress* of Kingsburgh, the *mistress* of Corrichatachin.——Having given this explanation, I am at liberty
to use that mode of speech which generally prevails in the
Highlands and the Hebrides.

Pervagor gentes, hominum ferorum
Vita ubi nullo decorata cultu
Squallet informis, tugurique fumis
                        Fœda latescit.

Inter erroris salebrosa longi,
Inter ignotæ strepitus loquelæ,
Quot modis mecum, quid agat, requiro,
                        Thralia dulcis ?

Seu viri curas pia nupta mulcet,
Seu fovet mater sobolem benigna,
Sive cum libris novitate pascet
                        Sedula mentem ;

Sit memor nostri, fideique merces,
Stet fides constans, meritoque blandum
Thraliæ discant resonare nomen
                        Littora Skiæ.

Scriptum in Skiá, Sept. 6, 1773.

Tuesday, 7th September.

Dr. Johnson was much pleased with his entertainment here. There were many good books in the house : Hector Boethius in Latin ; Cave's Lives of the Fathers ; Baker's Chronicle ; Jeremy Collier's Church History ; Dr. Johnson's small Dictionary ; Craufurd's Officers of State, and several more :—a mezzotinto of Mrs. Brooks the actress (by some strange chance in Sky) ; and also a print of Macdonald of Clanranald, with a Latin inscription about the cruelties after the battle of Culloden, which will never be forgotten.

It was a very wet stormy day ; we were therefore obliged to remain here, it being impossible to cross the sea to Rasay.

I employed a part of the forenoon in writing this Journal. The rest of it was somewhat dreary, from the gloominess of the weather, and the uncertain state which we were in, as we could not tell but it might clear up every hour. Nothing is more painful to the mind than a state of suspence, especially when it depends upon the weather, concerning which there can be so little calculation. As Dr. Johnson said of our weariness on the Monday at Aberdeen, "Sensation is sensation:" Corrichatachin, which was last night a hospitable house, was, in my mind, changed to-day into a prison.—After dinner I read some of Dr. Macpherson's Dissertations on the Ancient Caledonians. I was disgusted by the unsatisfactory conjectures as to antiquity, before the days of record. I was happy when tea came. Such, I take it, is the state of those who live in the country. Meals are wished for from the cravings of vacuity of mind, as well as from the desire of eating. I was hurt to find even such a temporary feebleness, and that I was so far from being that robust wise man who is sufficient for his own happiness. I felt a kind of lethargy of indolence. I did not exert myself to get Dr. Johnson to talk, that I might not have the labour of writing down his conversation.—He enquired here, if there were any remains of the second sight. Mr. M'Pherson, Minister of Slate, said, he was *resolved* not to believe it, because it was founded on no principle.—JOHNSON. "There are many things then, which we are sure are true, that you will not believe. What principle is there, why a loadstone attracts iron? why an egg produces a chicken by heat? why a tree grows upwards, when the natural tendency of all things is downwards? Sir, it depends upon the degree of evidence that you have."——Young Mr. M'Kinnon mentioned one M'Kenzie, who is still alive, who had often fainted in his presence, and when he recovered, mentioned visions which had been presented to him.   He told Mr. M'Kinnon, that at such a place he should meet a funeral, and that such and such people would be the bearers, naming four ; and three weeks afterwards he saw what M'Kenzie had predicted.   The naming the very spot in a country where a funeral comes a long way, and the very people as bearers, when there are so many out of whom a choice may be made, seems extraordinary.   We should have sent for M'Kenzie, had we not been informed that he could speak no English.   Besides, the facts were not related with sufficient accuracy.

Mrs. M'Kinnon, who is a daughter of old Kingsburgh, told us that her father was one day riding in Sky, and some women, who were at work in a field on the side of the road, said to him, they had heard two *taiscks*, (that is, two voices of persons about to die,) and what was remarkable, one of them was an *English taisck*, which they never heard before.   When he returned, he at that very place met two funerals, and one of them was that of a woman who had come from the main land, and could speak only English.   This, she remarked, made a great impression upon her father.

How all the people here were lodged, I know not.   It was partly done by separating man and wife, and putting a number of men in one room, and of women in another.

Wednesday, 8th September.

When I waked, the rain was much heavier than yesterday ; but the wind had abated.   By breakfast, the day was better, and in a little while it was calm and clear.   I felt my spirits much elated.   The propriety of the expression, " the sunshine of the breast," now struck me with peculiar force; for the brilliant rays penetrated into my very soul. We were all in better humour than before. Mrs. M'Kinnon, with unaffected hospitality and politeness, expressed her happiness in having such company in her house, and appeared to understand and relish Dr. Johnson's conversation, as indeed all the company seemed to do. When I knew she was old Kingsburgh's daughter, I did not wonder at the good appearance which she made.

She talked as if her husband and family would emigrate, rather than be oppressed by their landlord; and said, "how agreeable would it be, if these gentlemen should come in upon us when we are in America."— Somebody observed that Sir Alexander Macdonald was always frightened at sea.—JOHNSON. "*He* is frightened at sea; and his tenants are frightened when he comes to land."

We resolved to set out directly after breakfast. We had about two miles to ride to the sea-side, and there we expected to get one of the boats belonging to the fleet of bounty herring-busses then on the coast, or at least a good country fishing-boat. But while we were preparing to set out, there arrived a man with the following card from the Reverend Mr. Donald M'Queen:

"Mr. M'Queen's compliments to Mr. Boswell, and begs leave to acquaint him that, fearing the want of a proper boat, as much as the rain of yesterday, might have caused a stop, he is now at Skianwden with Macgillichallum's[1] carriage, to convey him and Dr. Johnson to Rasay, where they will meet with a most hearty welcome, and where Macleod, being on a visit, now attends their motions.

"*Wednesday afternoon.*"

[1] The Highland expression for Laird of Rasay.

The Laird of Rasay's carriage

A High-
land
gentle-
man

This card was most agreeable; it was a prologue to that hospitable and truly polite reception which we found at Rasay. In a little while arrived Mr. Donald M'Queen himself; a decent minister, an elderly man with his own black hair, courteous, and rather slow of speech, but candid, sensible and well informed, nay learned. Along with him came, as our pilot, a gentleman whom I had a great desire to see, Mr. Malcolm Macleod, one of the Rasay family, celebrated in the year 1745-6. He was now sixty-two years of age, hale, and well proportioned,—with a manly countenance, tanned by the weather, yet having a ruddiness in his cheeks, over a great part of which his rough beard extended.—His eye was quick and lively, yet his look was not fierce, but he appeared at once firm and good-humoured. He wore a pair of brogues,—Tartan hose which came up only near to his knees, and left them bare,—a purple camblet kilt,—a black waistcoat,—a short green cloth coat bound with gold cord,—a yellowish bushy wig,—a large blue bonnet with a gold thread button. I never saw a figure that gave a more perfect representation of a Highland gentleman. I wished much to have a picture of him just as he was. I found him frank and *polite*, in the true sense of the word.

The good family at Corrichatachin said, they hoped to see us on our return. We rode down to the shore; but Malcolm walked with graceful agility.

We got into Rasay's *carriage*, which was a good strong open boat made in Norway. The wind had now risen pretty high, and was against us; but we had four stout rowers, particularly a Macleod, a robust, black-haired fellow, half naked, and bare-headed, something between a wild Indian and an English tar. Dr. Johnson sat high on the stern, like a magnificent Triton. Malcolm

sung an Erse song, the chorus of which was " *Hatyin* The sail
foam foam eri," with words of his own.   The tune to Rasay
resembled " Owr the muir amang the heather."   The
boatmen and Mr. M'Queen chorused, and all went
well.   At length Malcolm himself took an oar, and
rowed vigorously.   We sailed along the coast of Scalpa,
a rugged island, about four miles in length.   Dr. Johnson proposed that he and I should buy it, and found a
good school, and an episcopal church, (Malcolm said,
he would come to it,) and have a printing-press, where
he would print all the Erse that could be found.

Here I was strongly struck with our long projected
scheme of visiting the Hebrides being realized.   I
called to him, " We are contending with seas ;" which
I think were the words of one of his letters to me.
" Not much," said he ; and though the wind made the
sea lash considerably upon us, he was not discomposed.
After we were out of the shelter of Scalpa, and in the
sound between it and Rasay, which extended about a
league, the wind made the sea very rough.   I did not
like it.—JOHNSON. " This now is the Atlantick.   If
I should tell at a tea table in London, that I have
crossed the Atlantick in an open boat, how they'd
shudder, and what a fool they'd think me to expose
myself to such danger ! "   He then repeated Horace's
ode,

> *Otium Divos rogat in patenti*
> *Prensus Ægæo*——

In the confusion and hurry of this boisterous sail,
Dr. Johnson's spurs, of which Joseph had charge, were
carried over-board into the sea, and lost.   This was the
first misfortune that had befallen us.   Dr. Johnson was
a little angry at first, observing that " there was something wild in letting a pair of spurs be carried into the

Second sight sea out of a boat;" but then he remarked, "that, as Janes the naturalist had said upon losing his pocket-book, it was rather an inconvenience than a loss." He told us, he now recollected that he dreamt the night before, that he put his staff into a river, and chanced to let it go, and it was carried down the stream and lost. "So now you see, (said he,) that I have lost my spurs; and this story is better than many of those which we have concerning second sight and dreams." Mr M'Queen said he did not believe the second sight; that he never met with any well attested instances; and if he should, he should impute them to chance; because all who pretend to that quality often fail in their pre-dictions, though they take a great scope, and sometimes interpret literally, sometimes figuratively, so as to suit the events. He told us, that, since he came to be minister of the parish where he now is, the belief of witchcraft, or charms, was very common, insomuch that he had many prosecutions before his session (the parochial ecclesiastical court) against women, for having by these means carried off the milk from people's cows. He disregarded them; and there is not now the least vestige of that superstition. He preached against it; and in order to give a strong proof to the people that there was nothing in it, he said from the pulpit, that every woman in the parish was welcome to take the milk from his cows, provided she did not touch them.

Dr. Johnson asked him as to Fingal. He said he could repeat some passages in the original, that he heard his grandfather had a copy of it; but that he could not affirm that Ossian composed all that poem as it is now published. This came pretty much to what Dr. Johnson had maintained; though he goes farther, and contends that it is no better than such an epick poem as he could make from the song of Robin Hood; that The travellers at Rasay is to say, that, except a few passages, there is nothing truly ancient but the names and some vague traditions. Mr. M'Queen alledged that Homer was made up of detached fragments. Dr. Johnson denied this; observing, that it had been one work originally, and that you could not put a book of the Iliad out of its place; and he believed the same might be said of the Odyssey.

The approach to Rasay was very pleasing. We saw before us a beautiful bay, well defended by a rocky coast; a good family mansion; a fine verdure about it, —with a considerable number of trees;—and beyond it hills and mountains in gradation of wildness. Our boatmen sung with great spirit. Dr. Johnson observed, that naval musick was very ancient. As we came near the shore, the singing of our rowers was succeeded by that of reapers, who were busy at work, and who seemed to shout as much as to sing, while they worked with a bounding activity. Just as we landed, I observed a cross, or rather the ruins of one, upon a rock, which had to me a pleasing vestige of religion. I perceived a large company coming out from the house. We met them as we walked up. There were Rasay himself; his brother Dr. Macleod; his nephew the Laird of M'Kinnon; the Laird of Macleod; Colonel Macleod of Talisker, an officer in the Dutch service, a very genteel man, and a faithful branch of the family; Mr. Macleod of Muiravenside, best known by the name of Sandie Macleod, who was long in exile on account of the part which he took in 1745; and several other persons. We were welcomed upon the green, and conducted into the house, where we were introduced to Lady Rasay, who was surrounded by a numerous family, consisting of three sons and ten daughters. The laird of Rasay is a sensible, polite, and most hospitable

Dancing gentleman. I was told that his island of Rasay, and
at Rasay that of Rona, (from which the eldest son of the family
has his title,) and a considerable extent of land which
he has in Sky, do not altogether yield him a very large
revenue : and yet he lives in great splendour ; and so
far is he from distressing his people, that, in the present
rage for emigration, not a man has left his estate.

It was past six o'clock when we arrived. Some
excellent brandy was served round immediately, according to the custom of the Highlands, where a dram is
generally taken every day. They call it a *scalch*. On
a side-board was placed for us, who had come off the
sea, a substantial dinner, and a variety of wines. Then
we had coffee and tea. I observed in the room several
elegantly bound books and other marks of improved
life. Soon afterwards a fidler appeared, and a little
ball began. Rasay himself danced with as much spirit
as any man, and Malcolm bounded like a roe. Sandie
Macleod, who has at times an excessive flow of spirits,
and had it now, was, in his days of absconding, known
by the name of *M'Cruslick*, which it seems was the
designation of a kind of wild man in the Highlands,
something between Proteus and Don Quixotte ; and so
he was called here. He made much jovial noise. Dr.
Johnson was so delighted with this scene, that he said,
" I know not how we shall get away." It entertained
me to observe him sitting by, while we danced, sometimes in deep meditation, — sometimes smiling com-
placently,—sometimes looking upon Hooke's Roman
History,—and sometimes talking a little, amidst the
noise of the ball, to Mr. Donald M'Queen, who
anxiously gathered knowledge from him. He was
pleased with M'Queen, and said to me, " This is a
critical man, sir. There must be great vigour of mind
to make him cultivate learning so much in the isle of

Sky, where he might do without it.   It is wonderful A High-
how many of the new publications he has.   There must land
be a snatch of every opportunity."   Mr. M'Queen told breakfast
me that his brother (who is the fourth generation of the
family following each other as ministers of the parish
of Snizort,) and he joined together, and bought from
time to time such books as had reputation.   Soon after
we came in, a black cock and grey hen, which had been
shot, were shewn, with their feathers on, to Dr. Johnson, who had never seen that species of bird before.
We had a company of thirty at supper ; and all was
good humour and gaiety, without intemperance.

Thursday, 9th September.

At breakfast this morning, among a profusion of
other things, there were oat-cakes, made of what is
called *graddaned* meal, that is, meal made of grain
separated from the husks, and toasted by fire, instead
of being threshed and kiln dried.—This seems to be
bad management, as so much fodder is consumed by it.
Mr. M'Queen however defended it, by saying, that
it is doing the thing much quicker, as one operation
effects what is otherwise done by two.   His chief
reason however was, that the servants in Sky are,
according to him, a faithless pack, and steal what they
can ; so that much is saved by the corn passing but
once through their hands, as at each time they pilfer
some.   It appears to me, that the gradaning is a strong
proof of the laziness of the Highlanders, who will
rather make fire act for them, at the expence of fodder,
than labour themselves.   There was also, what I cannot help disliking at breakfast, cheese : it is the custom
over all the Highlands to have it ; and it often smells
very strong, and poisons to a certain degree the ele-

The
patri-
archal life
gance of an Indian repast. The day was showery; however, Rasay and I took a walk, and had some cordial conversation. I conceived a more than ordinary regard for this worthy gentleman. His family has possessed this island above four hundred years. It is the remains of the estate of Macleod of Lewis, whom he represents.—When we returned, Dr. Johnson walked with us to see the old chapel. He was in fine spirits. He said, "This is truly the patriarchal life : this is what we came to find."

After dinner, M'Cruslick, Malcolm, and I, went out with guns, to try if we could find any black-cock ; but we had no sport, owing to a heavy rain. I saw here what is called a Danish fort. Our evening was passed as last night was. One of our company, I was told, had hurt himself by too much study, particularly of infidel metaphysicians, of which he gave a proof, on second sight being mentioned. He immediately retailed some of the fallacious arguments of Voltaire and Hume against miracles in general. Infidelity in a Highland gentleman appeared to me peculiarly offensive. I was sorry for him, as he had otherwise a good character. I told Dr. Johnson that he had studied himself into infidelity.—JOHNSON. "Then he must study himself out of it again. That is the way. Drinking largely will sober him again."

Friday, 10th September.

Having resolved to explore the island of Rasay, which could be done only on foot, I last night obtained my fellow-traveller's permission to leave him for a day, he being unable to take so hardy a walk. Old Mr. Malcolm M'Cleod, who had obligingly promised to accompany me, was at my bedside between five and

six. I sprang up immediately, and he and I, attended
by two other gentlemen, traversed the country during
the whole of this day. Though we had passed over
not less than four-and-twenty miles of very rugged
ground, and had a Highland dance on the top of Dun
Can, the highest mountain in the island, we returned
in the evening not at all fatigued, and piqued ourselves
at not being outdone at the nightly ball by our less
active friends, who had remained at home.

My survey of Rasay did not furnish much which
can interest my readers; I shall therefore put into as
short a compass as I can, the observations upon it,
which I find registered in my Journal. It is about
fifteen English miles long, and four broad. On the
south side is the laird's family seat, situated on a
pleasing low spot. The old tower of three stories,
mentioned by Martin, was taken down soon after
1746, and a modern house supplies its place. There
are very good grass-fields and corn-lands about it, well-
dressed. I observed, however, hardly any inclosures,
except a good garden plentifully stocked with vegetables, and strawberries, raspberries, currants, &c.

On one of the rocks just where we landed, which
are not high, there is rudely carved a square, with a
crucifix in the middle. Here, it is said, the Lairds of
Rasay, in old times, used to offer up their devotions.
I could not approach the spot, without a grateful recollection of the event commemorated by this symbol.

A little from the shore, westward, is a kind of subterraneous house. There has been a natural fissure, or
separation of the rock, running towards the sea, which
has been roofed over with long stones, and above them
turf has been laid. In that place the inhabitants used
to keep their oars. There are a number of trees near
the house, which grow well; some of them of a pretty

A ruined chapel good size. They are mostly plane and ash. A little to the west of the house is an old ruinous chapel, unroofed, which never has been very curious. We here saw some human bones of an uncommon size. There was a heel-bone, in particular, which Dr. Macleod said was such, that if the foot was in proportion, it must have been twenty-seven inches long. Dr. Johnson would not look at the bones. He started back from them with a striking appearance of horrour. Mr. M'Queen told us, it was formerly much the custom, in these isles, to have human bones lying above ground, especially in the windows of churches. On the south of the chapel is the family burying-place. Above the door, on the east end of it, is a small bust or image of the Virgin Mary, carved upon a stone which makes part of the wall. There is no church upon the island. It is annexed to one of the parishes of Sky; and the minister comes and preaches either in Rasay's house, or some other house, on certain Sundays. I could not but value the family seat more, for having even the ruins of a chapel close to it. There was something comfortable in the thought of being so near a piece of consecrated ground. Dr. Johnson said, " I look with reverence upon every place that has been set apart for religion ; " and he kept off his hat while he was within the walls of the chapel.

The eight crosses, which Martin mentions as pyramids for deceased ladies, stood in a semicircular line, which contained within it the chapel. They marked out the boundaries of the sacred territory within which an asylum was to be had. One of them, which we observed upon our landing, made the first point of the semicircle. There are few of them now remaining. A good way farther north, there is a row of buildings about four feet high : they run from the shore on the

east along the top of a pretty high eminence, and so **Dun Can**
down to the shore on the west, in much the same direction with the crosses. Rasay took them to be the
marks for the asylum; but Malcolm thought them to
be false sentinels, a common deception, of which instances occur in Martin, to make invaders imagine an
island better guarded. Mr. Donald M'Queen, justly
in my opinion, supposed the crosses which form the
inner circle to be the church's land-marks.

The south end of the island is much covered with
large stones or rocky strata. The laird has enclosed
and planted part of it with firs, and he shewed me a considerable space marked out for additional plantations.

Dun Can is a mountain three computed miles from
the laird's house. The ascent to it is by consecutive
risings, if that expression may be used when vallies
intervene, so that there is but a short rise at once; but
it is certainly very high above the sea. The palm of
altitude is disputed for by the people of Rasay and
those of Sky; the former contending for Dun Can,
the latter for the mountains in Sky, over against it.
We went up the east side of Dun Can pretty easily.
It is mostly rocks all around, the points of which hem
the summit of it. Sailors, to whom it was a good
object as they pass along, call it Rasay's cap. Before
we reached this mountain, we passed by two lakes.
Of the first, Malcolm told me a strange fabulous tradition. He said, there was a wild beast in it, a sea-
horse, which came and devoured a man's daughter;
upon which the man lighted a great fire, and had a
sow roasted at it, the smell of which attracted the
monster. In the fire was put a spit. The man lay
concealed behind a low wall of loose stones, and he
had an avenue formed for the monster, with two rows
of large flat stones, which extended from the fire over

the summit of the hill, till it reached the side of the
loch.   The monster came, and the man with the red-
hot spit destroyed it.   Malcolm showed me the little
hiding-place, and the rows of stones.   He did not
laugh when he told this story.   I recollect having seen
in the *Scots Magazine*, several years ago, a poem upon
a similar tale, perhaps the same, translated from the
Erse, or Irish, called *Albin and the Daughter of Mey*.

There is a large tract of land, possessed as a common,
in Rasay.   They have no regulations as to the number
of cattle.   Every man puts upon it as many as he
chooses.   From Dun Can northward, till you reach
the other end of the island, there is much good natural
pasture unincumbered by stones.   We passed over a
spot, which is appropriated for the exercising ground.
In 1745, a hundred fighting men were reviewed here,
as Malcolm told me, who was one of the officers that
led them to the field.   They returned home all but
about fourteen.   What a princely thing is it to be able
to furnish such a band!   Rasay has the true spirit of
a chief.   He is, without exaggeration, a father to his
people.

There is plenty of lime-stone in the island, a great
quarry of free-stone, and some natural woods, but none
of any age, as they cut the trees for common country
uses.   The lakes, of which there are many, are well
stocked with trout.   Malcolm catched one of four-
and-twenty pounds weight in the loch next to Dun
Can, which, by the way, is certainly a Danish name,
as most names of places in these islands are.

The old castle, in which the family of Rasay formerly resided, is situated upon a rock very near the
sea.   The rock is not one mass of stone, but a con-
cretion of pebbles and earth, so firm that it does not
appear to have mouldered.   In this remnant of anti-

quity I found nothing worthy of being noticed, except **A cave on** a certain accommodation rarely to be found at the **the shore** modern houses of Scotland, and which Dr. Johnson and I sought for in vain at the Laird of Rasay's new-built mansion, where nothing else was wanting. I took the liberty to tell the Laird it was a shame there should be such a deficiency in civilized times. He acknow-ledged the justice of the remark. But perhaps some generations may pass before the want is supplied. Dr. Johnson observed to me, how quietly people will en-dure an evil, which they might at any time very easily remedy; and mentioned as an instance, that the pre-sent family of Rasay had possessed the island for more than four hundred years, and never made a commodious landing place, though a few men with pickaxes might have cut an ascent of stairs out of any part of the rock in a week's time.

The north end of Rasay is as rocky as the south end. From it I saw the little isle of Fladda, belong-ing to Rasay, all fine green ground;—and Rona, which is of so rocky a soil that it appears to be a pavement. I was told however that it has a great deal of grass, in the interstices. The Laird has it all in his own hands. At this end of the island of Rasay is a cave in a strik-ing situation. It is in a Recess of a great cleft, a good way up from the sea. Before it the ocean roars, being dashed against monstrous broken rocks; grand and aweful *propugnacula*. On the right hand of it is a longitudinal cave, very low at the entrance, but higher as you advance. The sea having scooped it out, it seems strange and unaccountable that the interior part, where the water must have operated with less force, should be loftier than that which is more immediately exposed to its violence. The roof of it is all covered with a kind of petrifications formed by drops, which per-

Wild life
in Rasay

petually distil from it. The first cave has been a place
of much safety. I find a great difficulty in describing
visible objects. I must own too that the old castle and
cave, like many other things, of which one hears much,
did not answer my expectations. People are every
where apt to magnify the curiosities of their country.

This island has abundance of black cattle, sheep,
and goats;—a good many horses, which are used for
ploughing, carrying out dung, and other works of husbandry. I believe the people never ride. There are
indeed no roads through the island, unless a few detached beaten tracks deserve that name. Most of the
houses are upon the shore; so that all the people have
little boats, and catch fish. There is great plenty of
potatoes here. There are black-cock in extraordinary
abundance, moor-fowl, plover and wild pigeons, which
seemed to me to be the same as we have in pigeon-
houses, in their state of nature. Rasay has no pigeon-
house. There are no hares nor rabbits in the island,
nor was there ever known to be a fox, till last year,
when one was landed on it by some malicious person,
without whose aid he could not have got thither, as
that animal is known to be a very bad swimmer. He
has done much mischief. There is a great deal of fish
caught in the sea round Rasay; it is a place where one
may live in plenty, and even in luxury. There are no
deer; but Rasay told us he would get some.

They reckon it rains nine months in the year in this
island, owing to its being directly opposite to the western
coast of Sky, where the watery clouds are broken by
high mountains. The hills here, and indeed all the
heathy grounds in general, abound with the sweet-
smelling plant which the Highlanders call *gaul*, and
(I think) with dwarf juniper in many places. There
is enough of turf, which is their fuel, and it is thought

there is a mine of coal.—Such are the observations Bentley
which I made upon the island of Rasay, upon comparing it with the description given by Martin, whose
book we had with us.

There has been an ancient league between the families of Macdonald and Rasay. Whenever the head
of either family dies, his sword is given to the head of
the other. The present Rasay has the late Sir James
Macdonald's sword. Old Rasay joined the Highland
army in 1745, but prudently guarded against a forfeiture,
by previously conveying his estate to the present gentleman, his eldest son. On that occasion, Sir Alexander, father of the late Sir James Macdonald, was
very friendly to his neighbour. "Don't be afraid,
Rasay," said he; "I'll use all my interest to keep
you safe; and if your estate should be taken, I'll buy
it for the family."—And he would have done it.

Let me now gather some gold dust,—some more
fragments of Dr. Johnson's conversation, without regard to order of time. He said, "he thought very
highly of Bentley; that no man now went so far in
the kinds of learning that he cultivated; that the many
attacks on him were owing to envy, and to a desire of
being known, by being in competition with such a man;
that it was safe to attack him, because he never answered his opponents, but let them die away. It was
attacking a man who would not beat them, because his
beating them would make them live the longer. And
he was right not to answer; for, in his hazardous
method of writing, he could not but be often enough
wrong; so it was better to leave things to their general
appearance, than own himself to have erred in particulars."—He said, "Mallet was the prettiest drest puppet
about town, and always kept good company. That,
from his way of talking, he saw, and always said, that

The Duchess of Marlborough he had not written any part of the Life of the Duke of Marlborough, though perhaps he intended to do it at some time, in which case he was not culpable in taking the pension. That he imagined the Duchess furnished the materials for her Apology, which Hooke wrote, and Hooke furnished the words and the order, and all that in which the art of writing consists. That the duchess had not superior parts, but was a bold frontless woman, who knew how to make the most of her opportunities in life. That Hooke got a *large* sum of money for writing her Apology. That he wondered Hooke should have been weak enough to insert so profligate a maxim, as that to tell another's secret to one's friend, is no breach of confidence; though perhaps Hooke, who was a virtuous man, as his *History* shews, and did not wish her well, though he wrote her Apology, might see its ill tendency, and yet insert it at her desire. He was acting only ministerially."—I apprehend, however, that Hooke was bound to give his best advice. I speak as a lawyer. Though I have had clients whose causes I could not, as a private man, approve; yet, if I undertook them, I would not do any thing that might be prejudicial to them, even at their desire, without warning them of their danger.

Saturday, 11th September.

It was a storm of wind and rain; so we could not set out. I wrote some of this Journal, and talked awhile with Dr. Johnson in his room, and passed the day, I cannot well say how, but very pleasantly. I was here amused to find Mr. Cumberland's comedy of the *Fashionable Lover*, in which he has very well drawn a Highland character, Colin M'Cleod, of the same name with the family under whose roof we now were.

Dr. Johnson was much pleased with the Laird of Macleod, who is indeed a most promising youth, and with a noble spirit struggles with difficulties, and endeavours to preserve his people.   He has been left with an incumbrance of forty thousand pounds debt, and annuities to the amount of thirteen hundred pounds a year.   Dr. Johnson said, " If he gets the better of all this, he'll be a hero ; and I hope he will.   I have not met with a young man who had more desire to learn, or who has learnt more.   I have seen nobody that I wish more to do a kindness to than Macleod." —Such was the honourable eulogium, on this young chieftain, pronounced by an accurate observer, whose praise was never lightly bestowed.

The heritable jurisdictions

There is neither justice of peace, nor constable in Rasay.   Sky has Mr. M'Cleod of Ulinish, who is the sheriff substitute, and no other justice of peace.   The want of the execution of justice is much felt among the islanders.   Macleod very sensibly observed, that taking away the heritable jurisdictions had not been of such service in the islands, as was imagined.   They had not authority enough in lieu of them.   What could formerly have been settled at once, must now either take much time and trouble, or be neglected.   Dr. Johnson said, " A country is in a bad state, which is governed only by laws ; because a thousand things occur for which laws cannot provide, and where authority ought to interpose.   Now destroying the authority of the chiefs set the people loose.   It did not pretend to bring any positive good, but only to cure some evil ; and I am not well enough acquainted with the country to know what degree of evil the heritable jurisdictions occasioned."—I maintained hardly any ; because the chiefs generally acted right, for their own sakes.

Dr. Johnson was now wishing to move.   There was

Johnson's
curiosity
not enough of intellectual entertainment for him, after he had satisfied his curiosity, which he did, by asking questions, till he had exhausted the island ; and where there was so numerous a company, mostly young people, there was such a flow of familiar talk, so much noise, and so much singing and dancing, that little opportunity was left for his energetick conversation.   He seemed sensible of this ; for when I told him how happy they were at having him there, he said, " Yet we have not been able to entertain them much."—I was fretted, from irritability of nerves, by M'Cruslick's too obstreperous mirth.   I complained of it to my friend, observing we should be better if he was gone.—" No, sir (said he). He puts something into our society, and takes nothing out of it."—Dr. Johnson, however, had several opportunities of instructing the company ; but I am sorry to say, that I did not pay sufficient attention to what passed, as his discourse now turned chiefly on mechanicks, agriculture and such subjects, rather than on science and wit.—Last night Lady Rasay shewed him the operation of *wawking* cloth, that is, thickening it in the same manner as is done by a mill.   Here it is performed by women, who kneel upon the ground, and rub it with both their hands, singing an Erse song all the time. He was asking questions while they were performing this operation, and, amidst their loud and wild howl, his voice was heard even in the room above.

They dance here every night.   The queen of our ball was the eldest Miss Macleod, of Rasay, an elegant well-bred woman, and celebrated for her beauty over all those regions, by the name of Miss Flora Rasay.[1]

[1] She had been some time at Edinburgh, to which she again went, and was married to my worthy neighbour, Colonel Mure Campbell, now Earl of Loudoun ; but she died soon afterwards, leaving one daughter.

There seemed to be no jealousy, no discontent The
among them; and the gaiety of the scene was such, travellers
that I for a moment doubted whether unhappiness leave
had any place in Rasay. But my delusion was soon Rasay
dispelled, by recollecting the following lines of my
fellow-traveller :

> "Yet hope not life from pain or danger free,
> Or think the doom of man revers'd for thee!"

Sunday, 12th September.

It was a beautiful day, and although we did not
approve of travelling on Sunday, we resolved to set
out, as we were in an island from whence one must
take occasion as it serves. Macleod and Talisker sailed
in a boat of Rasay's for Sconser, to take the shortest
way to Dunvegan. M'Cruslick went with them to
Sconser, from whence he was to go to Slate, and so to
the main land. We were resolved to pay a visit at
Kingsburgh, and see the celebrated Miss Flora Macdonald, who is married to the present Mr. Macdonald
of Kingsburgh ; so took that road, though not so near.
All the family, but Lady Rasay, walked down to the
shore to see us depart. Rasay himself went with us in
a large boat, with eight oars, built in his island ; as did
Mr. Malcolm M'Cleod, Mr. Donald M'Queen, Dr.
Macleod, and some others. We had a most pleasant
sail between Rasay and Sky ; and passed by a cave,
where Martin says fowls were caught by lighting fire
in the mouth of it. Malcolm remembers this. But it
is not now practised, as few fowls come into it.

We spoke of Death. Dr. Johnson on this subject
observed, that the boastings of some men, as to dying

A short
sermon
on death
easily, were idle talk, proceeding from partial views. I mentioned Hawthornden's Cypress-grove, where it is said that the world is a mere show; and that it is unreasonable for a man to wish to continue in the show-room, after he has seen it. Let him go cheerfully out, and give place to other spectators.—JOHNSON. "Yes, sir, if he is sure he is to be well, after he goes out of it. But if he is to grow blind after he goes out of the show-room, and never to see any thing again; or if he does not know whither he is to go next, a man will not go cheerfully out of a show-room. No wise man will be contented to die, if he thinks he is to go into a state of punishment. Nay, no wise man will be contented to die, if he thinks he is to fall into annihilation: for however unhappy any man's existence may be, he yet would rather have it, than not exist at all. No; there is no rational principle by which a man can die contented, but a trust in the mercy of GOD, through the merits of Jesus Christ."—This short sermon, delivered with an earnest tone, in a boat upon the sea, which was perfectly calm, on a day appropriated to religious worship, while every one listened with an air of satisfaction, had a most pleasing effect upon my mind.

Pursuing the same train of serious reflection, he added, that it seemed certain that happiness could not be found in this life, because so many had tried to find it, in such a variety of ways, and had not found it.

We reached the harbour of Portree, in Sky, which is a large and good one. There was lying in it a vessel to carry off the emigrants, called the *Nestor*. It made a short settlement of the differences between a chief and his clan:

——*Nestor* componere lites
Inter Peleiden festinat & inter Atriden.

We approached her, and she hoisted her colours. Dr. **Portree**
Johnson and Mr. M'Queen remained in the boat : Rasay
and I, and the rest went on board of her.   She was a
very pretty vessel, and, as we were told, the largest in
Clyde.   Mr. Harrison, the captain shewed her to us.
The cabin was commodious, and even elegant.   There
was a little library, finely bound.   Portree has its name
from King James the Fifth having landed there in his
tour through the Western Isles, *Ree* in Erse being King,
as *Re* is in Italian ; so it is *Port-Royal*.   There was here
a tolerable inn.   On our landing, I had the pleasure of
finding a letter from home ; and there were also letters
to Dr. Johnson and me, from Lord Elibank, which
had been sent after us from Edinburgh.——His lordship's
letter to me was as follows :

"DEAR BOSWELL,
   "I FLEW to Edinburgh the moment I heard of Mr.
Johnson's arrival ; but so defective was my intelligence,
that I came too late.
   "It is but justice to believe, that I could never forgive myself, nor deserve to be forgiven by others, if I
was to fail in any mark of respect to that very great
genius.——I hold him in the highest veneration ; for that
very reason I was resolved to take no share in the
merit, perhaps guilt, of enticing him to honour this
country with a visit.——I could not persuade myself
there was anything in Scotland worthy to have a
Summer of Samuel Johnson bestowed on it ; but since
he has done us that compliment, for heaven's sake
inform me of your motions.   I will attend them most
religiously ; and though I should regret to let Mr.
Johnson go a mile out of his way on my account, old
as I am, I shall be glad to go five hundred miles to
enjoy a day of his company.   Have the charity to send

a council-post [1] with intelligence; the post does not suit us in the country.—At any rate write to me. I will attend you in the north, when I shall know where to find you.

> " I am,
>> " My dear Boswell,
>>> " Your sincerely
>>>> " Obedient humble servant,
>>>>> " ELIBANK."

" *August* 21*st*, 1773."

The letter to Dr. Johnson was in these words :

" DEAR SIR,

" I WAS to have kissed your hands at Edinburgh, the moment I heard of you ; but you was gone.

" I hope my friend Boswell will inform me of your motions. It will be cruel to deprive me an instant of the honour of attending you. As I value you more, than any King in Christendom, I will perform that duty with infinitely greater alacrity than any courtier. I can contribute but little to your entertainment ; but, my sincere esteem for you gives me some title to the opportunity of expressing it.

" I dare say you are by this time sensible that things are pretty much the same, as when Buchanan complained of being born *solo et seculo inerudito*. Let me hear of you, and be persuaded that none of your admirers is more sincerely devoted to you, than,

> " Dear Sir,
>> " Your most obedient,
>>> " And most humble servant,
>>>> " ELIBANK."

---

[1] A term in Scotland for a special messenger, such as was formerly sent with dispatches by the lords of the council.

Dr. Johnson, on the following Tuesday, answered for both of us, thus : Johnson's reply

"MY LORD,

"ON the rugged shore of Skie, I had the honour of your Lordship's letter, and can with great truth declare, that no place is so gloomy but that it would be cheered by such a testimony of regard, from a mind so well qualified to estimate characters, and to deal out approbation in its due proportions. If I have more than my share, it is your Lordship's fault; for I have always reverenced your judgment too much, to exalt myself in your presence by any false pretensions.

"Mr. Boswell and I are at present at the disposal of the winds, and therefore cannot fix the time at which we shall have the honour of seeing your lordship. But we should either of us think ourselves injured by the supposition that we would miss your lordship's conversation, when we could enjoy it; for I have often declared that I never met you without going away a wiser man.

"I am, my Lord,
"Your lordship's most obedient
"And most humble servant,
"SAM. JOHNSON."

"Skie, Sept. 14th, 1773."

At Portree, Mr. Donald M'Queen went to church and officiated in Erse, and then came to dinner. Dr. Johnson and I resolved that we should treat the company, so I played the landlord, or master of the feast, having previously ordered Joseph to pay the bill.

Sir James Macdonald intended to have built a village here, which would have done great good. A village is like a heart to a country. It produces a perpetual circulation, and gives the people an opportunity to make

Kings-
burgh
profit of many little articles, which would otherwise be in a good measure lost. We had here a dinner, *et præterea nihil*. Dr. Johnson did not talk. When we were about to depart, we found that Rasay had been before-hand with us, and that all was paid: I would fain have contested this matter with him, but seeing him resolved, I declined it. We parted with cordial embraces from him and worthy Malcolm. In the evening Dr. Johnson and I remounted our horses, accompanied by Mr. M'Queen and Dr. Macleod. It rained very hard. We rode what they call six miles, upon Rasay's lands in Sky, to Dr. Macleod's house. On the road Dr. Johnson appeared to be somewhat out of spirits. When I talked of our meeting Lord Elibank, he said, " I cannot be with him much. I long to be again in civilized life ; but can stay but a short while ; " (he meant at Edinburgh). He said, " let us go to Dunvegan to-morrow."—" Yes, (said I,) if it is not a deluge."—" At any rate," he replied.—This shewed a kind of fretful impatience ; nor was it to be wondered at, considering our disagreeable ride. I feared he would give up Mull and Icolmkill, for he said something of his apprehensions of being detained by bad weather in going to Mull and Iona. However I hoped well. We had a dish of tea at Dr. Macleod's, who had a pretty good house, where was his brother, a half-pay officer. His lady was a polite, agreeable woman. Dr. Johnson said, he was glad to see that he was so well married, for he had an esteem for physicians. The doctor accompanied us to Kingsburgh, which is called a mile farther ; but the computation of Sky has no connection whatever with real distance.

I was highly pleased to see Dr. Johnson safely arrived at Kingsburgh, and received by the hospitable Mr. Macdonald, who, with a most respectful attention,

supported him into the house. Kingsburgh was com- Flora Mac-donald
pletely the figure of a gallant Highlander,—exhibiting
"the graceful mien and manly looks," which our popular
Scotch song has justly attributed to that character. He
had his Tartan plaid thrown about him, a large blue
bonnet with a knot of black ribband like a cockade, a
brown short coat of a kind of duffil, a Tartan waistcoat
with gold buttons and gold button-holes, a bluish philibeg, and Tartan hose. He had jet black hair tied behind, and was a large stately man, with a steady sensible
countenance.

There was a comfortable parlour with a good fire,
and a dram went round. By and by supper was served,
at which there appeared the lady of the house, the celebrated Miss Flora Macdonald. She is a little woman,
of a genteel appearance, and uncommonly mild and well
bred. To see Dr. Samuel Johnson, the great champion
of the English Tories, salute Miss Flora Macdonald in
the isle of Sky, was a striking sight; for though somewhat congenial in their notions, it was very improbable
they should meet here.

Miss Flora Macdonald (for so I shall call her) told
me, she heard upon the main land, as she was returning
home about a fortnight before, that Mr. Boswell was
coming to Sky, and one Mr. Johnson, a young English
buck, with him. He was highly entertained with this
fancy. Giving an account of the afternoon which we
passed at Anock, he said, "I, being a *buck*, had miss
in to make tea."—He was rather quiescent to-night,
and went early to bed. I was in a cordial humour,
and promoted a cheerful glass. The punch was excellent. Honest Mr. M'Queen observed that I was in
high glee, "my *governour* being gone to bed." Yet
in reality my heart was grieved, when I recollected
that Kingsburgh was embarrassed in his affairs, and

Prince
Charles's
room
intended to go to America. However, nothing but
what was good was present, and I pleased myself in
thinking that so spirited a man would be well every
where. I slept in the same room with Dr. Johnson.
Each had a neat bed, with Tartan curtains, in an upper
chamber.

Monday, 13th September.

The room where we lay was a celebrated one. Dr.
Johnson's bed was the very bed in which the grandson
of the unfortunate King James the Second [1] lay, on one
of the nights after the failure of his rash attempt in
1745-6, while he was eluding the pursuit of the emis-
saries of government, which had offered thirty thousand
pounds as a reward for apprehending him. To see Dr.
Samuel Johnson lying in that bed, in the isle of Sky, in
the house of Miss Flora Macdonald, struck me with
such a group of ideas as it is not easy for words to
describe, as they passed through the mind. He smiled,
and said, " I have had no ambitious thoughts in it.[2]—

[1] I do not call him the Prince of Wales, or the Prince,
because I am quite satisfied that the right which the House
of Stuart had to the throne is extinguished. I do not call
him the Pretender, because it appears to me as an insult to
one who is still alive, and, I suppose, thinks very differently.
It may be a parliamentary expression; but it is not a gentlemanly expression. I *know*, and I exult in having it in my
power to tell, that THE ONLY PERSON in the world who is
intitled to be offended at this delicacy, "thinks and feels as I
do;" and has liberality of mind and generosity of sentiment
enough to approve of my tenderness for what even *has been*
Blood Royal. That he is a *prince* by *courtesy*, cannot be
denied; because his mother was the daughter of Sobiesky,
king of Poland. I shall, therefore, *on that account alone*, distinguish him by the name of Prince Charles Edward.

[2] This perhaps, was said in allusion to some lines ascribed
to Pope, on his lying, at John Duke of Argyle's, at Adder-

The room was decorated with a great variety of maps at Kings-
and prints. Among others, was Hogarth's print of burgh
Wilkes grinning, with the cap of liberty on a pole
by him. That too was a curious circumstance in the
scene this morning; such a contrast was Wilkes to
the above group. It reminded me of Sir William
Chambers's Account of Oriental Gardening, in which
we are told all odd, strange, ugly, and even terrible
objects, are introduced, for the sake of variety; a wild
extravagance of taste which is so well ridiculed in the
celebrated Epistle to him. The following lines of that
poem immediately occurred to me;

> "Here too, O king of vengeance! in thy fane,
> Tremendous Wilkes shall rattle his gold chain."

Upon the table in our room I found in the morning
a slip of paper, on which Dr. Johnson had written
with his pencil these words:

> "Quantum cedat virtutibus aurum." [1]

What he meant by writing them I could not tell.[2]
He had caught cold a day or two ago, and the rain
yesterday having made it worse, he was become very

bury, in the same bed in which Wilmot, Earl of Rochester,
had slept.
> "With no poetick ardour fir'd,
>   I press the bed where Wilmot lay;
> That here he liv'd, or here expir'd,
>   Begets no numbers, grave or gay."

[1] With virtue weigh'd, what worthless trash is gold!
[2] Since the first edition of this book, an ingenious friend
has observed to me, that Dr. Johnson had probably been
thinking on the reward which was offered by government
for the apprehension of the grandson of King James II. and
that he meant by these words to express his admiration of
the Highlanders, whose fidelity and attachment had resisted
the golden temptation that had been held out to them.

*G 387

Prince
Charles's
adven-
tures
deaf. At breakfast he said, he would have given a good deal rather than not have lain in that bed. I owned he was the lucky man; and observed, that without doubt it had been contrived between Mrs. Macdonald and him. She seemed to acquiesce; adding, "You know young *bucks* are always favourites of the ladies." He spoke of Prince Charles being here, and asked Mrs. Macdonald, "*Who* was with him? We were told, madam, in England, there was one Miss Flora Macdonald with him."—She said, "they were very right;" and perceiving Dr. Johnson's curiosity, though he had delicacy enough not to question her, very obligingly entertained him with a recital of the particulars which she herself knew of that escape, which does so much honour to the humanity, fidelity, and generosity, of the Highlanders. Dr. Johnson listened to her with placid attention, and said, "All this should be written down."

From what she told us, and from what I was told by others personally concerned, and from a paper of information which Rasay was so good as to send me, at my desire, I have compiled the following abstract, which, as it contains some curious anecdotes, will, I imagine, not be uninteresting to my readers, and even, perhaps, be of some use to future historians.

Prince Charles Edward, after the battle of Culloden, was conveyed to what is called the Long Island, where he lay for some time concealed. But intelligence having been obtained where he was, and a number of troops having come in quest of him, it became absolutely necessary for him to quit that country without delay. Miss Flora Macdonald, then a young lady, animated by what she thought the sacred principle of loyalty, offered, with the magnanimity of a Heroine, to

accompany him in an open boat to Sky, though the Dis-
coast they were to quit was guarded by ships. He guised as
dressed himself in women's clothes, and passed as her an Irish
supposed maid, by the name of Betty Bourke, an Irish girl
girl. They got off undiscovered, though several shots
were fired to bring them to, and landed at Mugstot,
the seat of Sir Alexander Macdonald. Sir Alexander
was then at Fort Augustus, with the Duke of Cumberland; but his lady was at home. Prince Charles
took his post upon a hill near the house. Flora Macdonald waited on Lady Margaret, and acquainted her
of the enterprise in which she was engaged. Her
ladyship, whose active benevolence was ever seconded
by superior talents, shewed a perfect presence of mind,
and readiness of invention, and at once settled that
Prince Charles should be conducted to old Rasay,
who was himself concealed with some select friends.
The plan was instantly communicated to Kingsburgh,
who was dispatched to the hill to inform the Wanderer,
and carry him refreshments. When Kingsburgh approached, he started up, and advanced, holding a large
knotted stick, and in appearance ready to knock him
down, till he said, "I am Macdonald of Kingsburgh, come to serve your highness." The Wanderer
answered, "It is well," and was satisfied with the
plan.

Flora Macdonald dined with Lady Margaret, at
whose table there sat an officer of the army, stationed
here with a party of soldiers, to watch for Prince
Charles in case of his flying to the isle of Sky. She
afterwards often laughed in good humour with this
gentleman, on her having so well deceived him.

After dinner, Flora Macdonald on horseback, and
her supposed maid, and Kingsburgh, with a servant
carrying some linen, all on foot, proceeded towards

The
Prince
at Kings-
burgh
that gentleman's house. Upon the road was a small
rivulet which they were obliged to cross. The Wanderer, forgetting his assumed sex, that his clothes might
not be wet, held them up a great deal too high. Kingsburgh mentioned this to him, observing, it might make
a discovery. He said he would be more careful for
the future. He was as good as his word ; for the next
brook they crossed, he did not hold up his clothes at
all, but let them float upon the water. He was very
awkward in his female dress. His size was so large,
and his strides so great, that some women whom they
met reported that they had seen a very big woman,
who looked like a man in woman's clothes, and that
perhaps it was (as they expressed themselves) the
Prince, after whom so much search was making.

At Kingsburgh he met with a most cordial reception ; seemed gay at supper, and after it indulged himself in a cheerful glass with his worthy host. As he
had not had his clothes off for a long time, the comfort
of a good bed was highly relished by him, and he slept
soundly till next day at one o'clock.

The mistress of Corrichatachin told me, that in the
forenoon she went into her father's room, who was also
in bed, and suggested to him her apprehensions that a
party of the military might come up, and that his guest
and he had better not remain here too long. Her
father said, " Let the poor man repose himself after
his fatigues ; and as for me, I care not, though they
take off this old grey head ten or eleven years sooner
than I should die in the course of nature." He then
wrapped himself in the bed-clothes, and again fell fast
asleep.

On the afternoon of that day, the Wanderer, still
in the same dress, set out for Portree, with Flora
Macdonald and a man servant. His shoes being very

bad, Kingsburgh provided him with a new pair, and **A** taking up the old ones, said, " I will faithfully keep **dilemma** them till you are safely settled at St. James's. I will then introduce myself by shaking them at you, to put you in mind of your night's entertainment and protection under my roof."—He smiled, and said, " Be as good as your word ! "—Kingsburgh kept the shoes as long as he lived. After his death, a zealous Jacobite gentleman gave twenty guineas for them.

Old Mrs. Macdonald, after her guest had left the house, took the sheets in which he had lain, folded them carefully, and charged her daughter that they should be kept unwashed, and that, when she died, her body should be wrapped in them as a winding sheet. Her will was religiously observed.

Upon the road to Portree, Prince Charles changed his dress, and put on man's clothes again; a tartan short coat and waistcoat, with philibeg and short hose, a plaid, and a wig and bonnet.

Mr. Donald M'Donald, called Donald Roy, had been sent express to the present Rasay, then the young laird, who was at that time at his sister's house, about three miles from Portree, attending his brother, Dr. Macleod, who was recovering of a wound he had received at the battle of Culloden. Mr. M'Donald communicated to young Rasay the plan of conveying the Wanderer to where old Rasay was; but was told that old Rasay had fled to Knoidart, a part of Glengary's estate. There was then a dilemma what should be done. Donald Roy proposed that he should conduct the Wanderer to the main land; but young Rasay thought it too dangerous at that time, and said it would be better to conceal him in the island of Rasay, till old Rasay could be informed where he was, and give his advice what was best. But the difficulty was, how to get

him to Rasay. They could not trust a Portree crew,
and all the Rasay boats had been destroyed, or carried
off by the military, except two belonging to Malcolm
M'Leod, which he had concealed somewhere.

Dr. Macleod being informed of this difficulty, said
he would risk his life once more for Prince Charles;
and it having occurred, that there was a little boat
upon a fresh-water lake in the neighbourhood, young
Rasay and Dr. Macleod, with the help of some women,
brought it to the sea, by extraordinary exertion, across
a Highland mile of land, one half of which was bog,
and the other a steep precipice.

These gallant brothers, with the assistance of one
little boy, rowed the small boat to Rasay, where they
were to endeavour to find Captain M'Leod, as Malcolm
was then called, and get one of his good boats, with
which they might return to Portree, and receive the
Wanderer; or, in case of not finding him, they were
to make the small boat serve, though the danger was
considerable.

Fortunately, on their first landing, they found their
cousin Malcolm, who, with the utmost alacrity, got
ready one of his boats, with two strong men, John
M'Kenzie, and Donald M'Friar. Malcolm, being
the oldest man, and most cautious, said, that as young
Rasay had not hitherto appeared in the unfortunate
business, he ought not to run any risk; but that Dr.
Macleod and himself, who were already publickly engaged, should go on this expedition. Young Rasay
answered, with an oath, that he would go, at the risk
of his life and fortune.—" In God's name then (said
Malcolm) let us proceed." The two boatmen, however, now stopped short, till they should be informed
of their destination; and M'Kenzie declared he would
not move an oar till he knew where they were going.

Upon which they were both sworn to secrecy; and the **The**
business being imparted to them, they were eager to **Prince in**
put off to sea without loss of time.   The boat soon **Rasay**
landed about half a mile from the inn at Portree.

All this was negotiated before the Wanderer got
forward to Portree.   Malcolm M'Leod, and M'Friar,
were dispatched to look for him.   In a short time he
appeared, and went into the publick house.   Here
Donald Roy, whom he had seen at Mugstot, received
him, and informed him of what had been concerted.
He wanted silver for a guinea, but the landlord had
only thirteen shillings.   He was going to accept of
this for his guinea; but Donald Roy very judiciously
observed, that it would discover him to be some great
man; so he desisted.   He slipped out of the house,
leaving his fair protectress, whom he never again saw;
and Malcolm Macleod was presented to him by Donald
Roy, as a captain in his army.   Young Rasay and
Dr. Macleod had waited, in impatient anxiety, in the
boat.   When he came, their names were announced to
him.   He would not permit the usual ceremonies of
respect, but saluted them as his equals.

Donald Roy staid in Sky, to be in readiness to get
intelligence, and give an alarm in case the troops should
discover the retreat to Rasay; and Prince Charles was
then conveyed in a boat to that island in the night.   He
slept a little upon the passage, and they landed about
day-break.   There was some difficulty in accommodating him with a lodging, as almost all the houses in the
island had been burnt by the soldiery.   They repaired to
a little hut, which some shepherds had lately built, and
having prepared it as well as they could, and made a bed
of heath for the stranger, they kindled a fire, and partook
of some provisions which had been sent with him from
Kingsburgh.   It was observed, that he would not taste

A council wheat-bread, or brandy, while oat-bread and whisky
of war lasted; "for these," said he, "are my own country
bread and drink."—This was very engaging to the
Highlanders.

Young Rasay being the only person of the company
that durst appear with safety, he went in quest of something fresh for them to eat; but though he was amidst
his own cows, sheep, and goats, he could not venture
to take any of them for fear of a discovery, but was
obliged to supply himself by stealth. He therefore
caught a kid, and brought it to the hut in his plaid,
and it was killed and drest, and furnished them a meal
which they relished much. The distressed Wanderer,
whose health was now a good deal impaired by hunger,
fatigue, and watching, slept a long time, but seemed to
be frequently disturbed. Malcolm told me he would
start from broken slumbers, and speak to himself in
different languages, French, Italian, and English. I
must however acknowledge, that it is highly probable
that my worthy friend Malcolm did not know precisely the difference between French and Italian. One
of his expressions in English was, " O GOD! poor
Scotland!"

While they were in the hut, M'Kenzie and M'Friar,
the two boatmen, were placed as sentinels upon different eminences; and one day an incident happened,
which must not be omitted. There was a man wandering about the island, selling tobacco. Nobody knew
him, and he was suspected to be a spy. M'Kenzie
came running to the hut, and told that this suspected
person was approaching. Upon which the three gentlemen, young Rasay, Dr. Macleod, and Malcolm, held
a council of war upon him, and were unanimously of
opinion that he should instantly be put to death. Prince
Charles, at once assuming a grave and even severe

countenance, said, "GOD forbid that we should take King and
away a man's life, who may be innocent, while we can Parlia-
preserve our own." The gentlemen however persisted ment
in their resolution, while he as strenuously continued
to take the merciful side. John M'Kenzie, who sat
watching at the door of the hut, and overheard the
debate, said in Erse, "Well, well; he must be shot.
You are the king, but we are the parliament, and will
do what we choose."——Prince Charles, seeing the gentlemen smile, asked what the man had said, and being
told it in English, he observed that he was a clever
fellow, and, notwithstanding the perilous situation in
which he was, laughed loud and heartily. Luckily
the unknown person did not perceive that there were
people in the hut, at least did not come to it, but
walked on past it, unknowing of his risk. It was
afterwards found out that he was one of the Highland
army, who was himself in danger. Had he come to
them, they were resolved to dispatch him; for, as
Malcolm said to me, "We could not keep him with
us, and we durst not let him go. In such a situation, I
would have shot my brother, if I had not been sure of
him."——John M'Kenzie was at Rasay's house, when
we were there.[1] About eighteen years before, he hurt
one of his legs when dancing, and being obliged to have
it cut off, he now was going about with a wooden leg.
The story of his being a *member of parliament* is not yet
forgotten. I took him out a little way from the house,
gave him a shilling to drink Rasay's health, and led
him into a detail of the particulars which I have just
related. — With less foundation, some writers have
traced the idea of a parliament, and of the British constitution, in rude and early times. I was curious to

[1] This old Scottish *member of parliament*, I am informed, is
still living (1785).

The Highland army at Culloden know if he had really heard, or understood, any thing of that subject, which, had he been a greater man, would probably have been eagerly maintained. " Why, John, (said I,) did you think the king should be controuled by a parliament ? "—He answered, " I thought, sir, there were many voices against one."

The conversation then turning on the times, the Wanderer said, that, to be sure, the life he had led of late was a very hard one ; but he would rather live in the way he now did, for ten years, than fall into the hands of his enemies. The gentlemen asked him, what he thought his enemies would do with him, should he have the misfortune to fall into their hands. He said, he did not believe they would dare to take his life publickly, but he dreaded being privately destroyed by poison or assassination.—He was very particular in his inquiries about the wound which Dr. Macleod had received at the battle of Culloden, from a ball which entered at one shoulder, and went cross to the other. The doctor happened still to have on the coat which he wore on that occasion. He mentioned, that he himself had his horse shot under him at Culloden ; that the ball hit the horse about two inches from his knee, and made him so unruly that he was obliged to change him for another. He threw out some reflections on the conduct of the disastrous affair at Culloden, saying, however, that perhaps it was rash in him to do so.—I am now convinced that his suspicions were groundless ; for I have had a good deal of conversation upon the subject with my very worthy and ingenious friend, Mr. Andrew Lumisden, who was under secretary to Prince Charles, and afterwards principal secretary to his father at Rome, who, he assured me, was perfectly satisfied both of the abilities and honour of the generals who commanded the High-

land army on that occasion. Mr. Lumisden has written
an account of the three battles in 1745-6, at once
accurate and classical.—Talking of the different Highland corps, the gentlemen who were present wished to
have his opinion which were the best soldiers. He
said, he did not like comparisons among those corps :
they were all best.

He told his conductors, he did not think it advisable
to remain long in any one place ; and that he expected
a French ship to come for him to Lochbroom, among
the Mackenzies.   It then was proposed to carry him
in one of Malcolm's boats to Lochbroom, though the
distance was fifteen leagues coastwise.   But he thought
this would be too dangerous, and desired that at any
rate, they might first endeavour to obtain intelligence.
Upon which young Rasay wrote to his friend, Mr.
M'Kenzie of Applecross, but received an answer, that
there was no appearance of any French ship.

It was therefore resolved that they should return to
Sky, which they did, and landed in Strath, where they
reposed in a cow-house belonging to Mr. Niccolson of
Scorbreck.   The sea was very rough, and the boat
took in a good deal of water.   The Wanderer asked if
there was danger, as he was not used to such a vessel.
Upon being told there was not, he sung an Erse song
with much vivacity. He had by this time acquired a
good deal of the Erse language.

Young Rasay was now dispatched to where Donald
Roy was, that they might get all the intelligence they
could ; and the Wanderer, with much earnestness,
charged Dr. Macleod to have a boat ready, at a certain
place about seven miles off, as he said he intended it
should carry him upon a matter of great consequence ;
and gave the doctor a case, containing a silver spoon,
knife, and fork, saying, " keep you that till I see you,"

which the doctor understood to be two days from that time.   But all these orders were only blinds; for he had another plan in his head, but wisely thought it safest to trust his secrets to no more persons than was absolutely necessary.   Having then desired Malcolm to walk with him a little way from the house, he soon opened his mind, saying, "I deliver myself to you. Conduct me to the Laird of M'Kinnon's country." —Malcolm objected that it was very dangerous, as so many parties of soldiers were in motion.   He answered, "There is nothing now to be done without danger." —He then said, that Malcolm must be the master, and he the servant; so he took the bag, in which his linen was put up, and carried it on his shoulder; and observing that his waistcoat, which was of scarlet tartan, with a gold twist button, was finer than Malcolm's, which was of a plain ordinary tartan, he put on Malcolm's waistcoat, and gave him his; remarking at the same time, that it did not look well that the servant should be better dressed than the master.

Malcolm, though an excellent walker, found himself excelled by Prince Charles, who told him, he should not much mind the parties that were looking for him, were he once but a musquet shot from them; but that he was somewhat afraid of the Highlanders who were against him.   He was well used to walking in Italy, in pursuit of game; and he was even now so keen a sportsman, that, having observed some partridges, he was going to take a shot; but Malcolm cautioned him against it, observing that the firing might be heard by the tenders who were hovering upon the coast.

As they proceeded through the mountains, taking many a circuit to avoid any houses, Malcolm, to try his resolution, asked him what they should do, should they fall in with a party of soldiers: he answered,

"Fight, to be sure!"—Having asked Malcolm if he should be known in his present dress, and Malcolm having replied he would, he said, "Then I'll blacken my face with powder."—"That," said Malcolm, "would discover you at once."—"Then," said he, "I must be put in the greatest dishabille possible." So he pulled off his wig, tied a handkerchief round his head, and put his nightcap over it, tore the ruffles from his shirt, took the buckles out of his shoes, and made Malcolm fasten them with strings; but still Malcolm thought he would be known. "I have so odd a face, (said he) that no man ever saw me but he would know me again." ^{in M'Kinnon's country}

He seemed unwilling to give credit to the horrid narrative of men being massacred in cold blood, after victory had declared for the army commanded by the Duke of Cumberland. He could not allow himself to think that a general could be so barbarous.

When they came within two miles of M'Kinnon's house, Malcolm asked if he chose to see the laird. "No, (said he) by no means. I know M'Kinnon to be as good and as honest a man as any in the world, but he is not fit for my purpose at present. You must conduct me to some other house; but let it be a gentleman's house."—Malcolm then determined that they should go to the house of his brother-in-law, Mr. John M'Kinnon, and from thence be conveyed to the main land of Scotland, and claim the assistance of Macdonald of Scothouse. The Wanderer at first objected to this, because Scothouse was cousin to a person of whom he had suspicions. But he acquiesced in Malcolm's opinion.

When they were near Mr. John M'Kinnon's house, they met a man of the name of Ross, who had been a private soldier in the Highland army. He fixed his eyes steadily on the Wanderer in his disguise, and having

"One Lewis Caw from Crieff" at once recognized him, he clapped his hands, and exclaimed, "Alas! is this the case?" Finding that there was now a discovery, Malcolm asked "What's to be done?"—"Swear him to secrecy," answered Prince Charles. Upon which Malcolm drew his dirk, and on the naked blade, made him take a solemn oath, that he would say nothing of his having seen the Wanderer, till his escape should be made publick.

Malcolm's sister, whose house they reached pretty early in the morning, asked him who the person was that was along with him. He said it was one Lewis Caw, from Crieff, who being a fugitive like himself, for the same reason, he had engaged him as his servant, but that he had fallen sick. "Poor man! (said she) I pity him. At the same time my heart warms to a man of his appearance."—Her husband was gone a little way from home; but was expected every minute to return. She set down to her brother a plentiful Highland breakfast. Prince Charles acted the servant very well, sitting at a respectful distance, with his bonnet off. Malcolm then said to him, "Mr. Caw, you have as much need of this as I have; there is enough for us both: you had better draw nearer and share with me."—Upon which he rose, made a profound bow, sat down at table with his supposed master, and eat very heartily. After this there came in an old woman, who, after the mode of ancient hospitality, brought warm water, and washed Malcolm's feet. He desired her to wash the feet of the poor man who attended him. She at first seemed averse to this, from pride, as thinking him beneath her, and in the periphrastick language of the Highlanders and the Irish, said warmly, "Though I wash your father's son's feet, why should I wash his father's son's feet?"—She was however persuaded to do it.

They then went to bed, and slept for some time;

and when Malcolm awaked, he was told that Mr. John M'Kinnon, his brother-in-law, was in sight. He sprang out to talk to him before he should see Prince Charles. After saluting him, Malcolm, pointing to the sea, said, " What, John, if the prince should be prisoner on board one of those tenders ? "—" GOD forbid ! " replied John.—" What if we had him here ? " said Malcolm.—" I wish we had," answered John ; " we should take care of him."—" Well, John," said Malcolm, " he is in your house."—John, in a transport of joy, wanted to run directly in, and pay his obeisance ; but Malcolm stopped him, saying, " Now is your time to behave well, and do nothing that can discover him."—John composed himself, and having sent away all his servants upon different errands, he was introduced into the presence of his guest, and was then desired to go and get ready a boat lying near his house, which, though but a small leaky one, they resolved to take, rather than go to the Laird of M'Kinnon. John M'Kinnon, however, thought otherwise ; and upon his return told them, that his Chief and lady M'Kinnon were coming in the laird's boat. Prince Charles said to his trusty Malcolm, " I am sorry for this, but must make the best of it."—M'Kinnon then walked up from the shore, and did homage to the Wanderer. His lady waited in a cave, to which they all repaired, and were entertained with cold meat and wine.—Mr. Malcolm M'Leod being now superseded by the Laird of M'Kinnon, desired leave to return, which was granted him, and Prince Charles wrote a short note, which he subscribed James Thompson, informing his friends that he had got away from Sky, and thanking them for their kindness ; and he desired this might be speedily conveyed to young Rasay and Dr. Macleod, that they might not wait longer in expectation of seeing him

The
Prince
reaches
the main-
land

again.   He bade a cordial adieu to Malcolm, and insisted on his accepting of a silver stock-buckle, and ten
guineas from his purse, though, as Malcolm told me, it
did not appear to contain above forty.   Malcolm at
first begged to be excused, saying, that he had a few
guineas at his service; but Prince Charles answered,
" You will have need of money.   I shall get enough
when I come upon the main land."

The Laird of M‘Kinnon then conveyed him to the
opposite coast of Knoidart.   Old Rasay, to whom intelligence had been sent, was crossing at the same time
to Sky; but as they did not know of each other, and
each had apprehensions, the two boats kept aloof.

These are the particulars which I have collected concerning the extraordinary concealment and escapes of
Prince Charles, in the Hebrides.   He was often in im-
minent danger.   The troops traced him from the Long
Island, across Sky, to Portree, but there lost him.

Here I stop,—having received no farther authentic
information of his fatigues and perils before he escaped
to France.—Kings and subjects may both take a lesson
of moderation from the melancholy fate of the House
of Stuart; that Kings may not suffer degradation and
exile, and subjects may not be harrassed by the evils of
a disputed succession.

Let me close the scene on that unfortunate House
with the elegant and pathetick reflections of Voltaire,
in his *Histoire Generale*.—" Que les hommes privés
(says that brilliant writer, speaking of Prince Charles)
qui se croyent malheureux, jettent les yeux sur ce
prince et ses ancêtres."

In another place he thus sums up the sad story of
the family in general :—" Il n'y a aucun exemple dans
l'histoire d'une maison si longtems infortunée.   Le
premier des Rois d'Ecosse, qui eut le nom de Jacques,

apres avoir êtê dix-huit ans prisonnier en Angleterre, Voltaire
mourut assassiné, avec sa femme, par la main de ses on the
sujets.   Jacques II. son fils, fut tué à vingt-neuf ans Stuarts
en combattant contre les Anglois.   Jacques III. mis
en prison par son peuple, fut tué ensuite par les revoltés,
dans une battaille.   Jacques IV. perit dans un combat
qu'il perdit.   Marie Stuart, sa petite fille, chassèe de
son trone, fugitivê en Angleterre, ayant langui dix-huit
ans en prison, se vit condamnée à mort par des juges
Anglais, et eut la téte tranchée.   Charles I. petit fils
de Marie, Roi d'Ecosse et d'Angleterre, vendu par les
Ecossois, et jugé à mort par les Anglais, mourut sur
un échaffaut dans la place publique.   Jacques, son fils,
septiéme du nom, et deuxieme en Angleterre, fut chassé
de ses trois royaumes; et pour comble de malheur on
contesta à son fils sa naissance; le fils ne tenta de
remonter sur le trone de ces peres, que pour faire périr
ses amis par des bourreaux ; et nous avons vu le Prince
Charles Edouard, reunuissant en vain les vertus de ses
peres, et le courage do Roy Jean Sobieski, son ayeul
maternel, executer les exploits et essuyer les malheurs
les plus incroyables.   Si quelque chose justifie ceux qui
croyent une fatalité à laquelle rien ne peut se soustraire,
c'est cette suite continuelle de malheurs qui a persecuté
la maison de Stuart, pendant plus de trois-cent années.''

The gallant Malcolm was apprehended in about ten
days after they separated, put aboard a ship and carried
prisoner to London.   He said, the prisoners in general
were very ill treated in their passage ; but there were
soldiers on board who lived well, and sometimes
invited him to share with them : that he had the good
fortune not to be thrown into jail, but was confined in
the house of a messenger, of the name of Dick.   To
his astonishment, only one witness could be found
against him, though he had been so openly engaged ;

and therefore, for want of sufficient evidence, he was
set at liberty. He added, that he thought himself in
such danger, that he would gladly have compounded
for banishment. Yet, he said, "he should never be so
ready for death as he then was."—There is philosophical truth in this. A man will meet death much
more firmly at one time than another. The enthusiasm
even of a mistaken principle warms the mind, and sets
it above the fear of death; which in our cooler
moments, if we really think of it, cannot but be terrible, or at least very awful.

Miss Flora Macdonald being then also in London,
under the protection of Lady Primrose, that lady provided a post-chaise to convey her to Scotland, and desired
she might choose any friend she pleased to accompany
her. She chose Malcolm. "So (said he, with a
triumphant air) I went to London to be hanged, and
returned in a post-chaise with Miss Flora Macdonald."

Mr. Macleod of Muiravenside, whom we saw at
Rasay, assured us that Prince Charles was in London
in 1759, and that there was then a plan in agitation
for restoring his family. Dr. Johnson could scarcely
credit this story, and said, there could be no probable
plan at that time. Such an attempt could not have
succeeded, unless the King of Prussia had stopped the
army in Germany; for both the army and the fleet
would, even without orders, have fought for the King,
to whom they had engaged themselves."

Having related so many particulars concerning the
grandson of the unfortunate King James the Second;
having given due praise to fidelity and generous attachment, which, however erroneous the judgement may be,
are honourable for the heart; I must do the Highlanders the justice to attest, that I found every where
amongst them a high opinion of the virtues of the

King now upon the throne, and an honest disposition
to be faithful subjects to his majesty, whose family has
possessed the sovereignty of this country so long, that
a change, even for the abdicated family, would now
hurt the best feelings of all his subjects.

The *abstract* point of *right* would involve us in a
discussion of remote and perplexed questions; and
after all, we should have no clear principle of decision.
That establishment, which, from political necessity,
took place in 1688, by a breach in the succession of
our kings, and which, whatever benefits may have
accrued from it, certainly gave a shock to our monarchy,
—the able and constitutional Blackstone, wisely rests
on the solid footing of authority.—" Our ancestors
having most indisputably a competent jurisdiction to
decide this great and important question, and having,
in fact, decided it, it is now become our duty, at this
distance of time, to acquiesce in their determination."[1]

Mr. Paley, the present Archdeacon of Carlisle, in
his *Principles of Moral and Political Philosophy*, having,
with much clearness of argument, shown the duty of
submission to civil government to be founded neither
on an indefeasible *jus divinum*, nor on *compact*, but on
expediency, lays down this rational position :—" Irre-
gularity in the first foundation of a state, or subsequent
violence, fraud, or injustice, in getting possession of the
supreme power, are not sufficient reasons for resistance,
after the government is once peaceably settled. No
subject of the British empire conceives himself engaged
to vindicate the justice of the Norman claim or conquest, or apprehends that his duty in any manner
depends upon that controversy. So likewise, if the
house of Lancaster, or even the posterity of Cromwell,
had been at this day seated upon the throne of Eng-

[1] COMMENTARIES on the laws of England, Book I. chap. 3.

land, we should have been as little concerned to enquire how the founder of the family came there." [1]

In conformity with this doctrine, I myself, though fully persuaded that the House of Stuart had originally no right to the crown of Scotland; for that Baliol, and not Bruce, was the lawful heir; should yet have thought it very culpable to have rebelled, on that account, against Charles the First, or even a prince of that house much nearer the time, in order to assert the claim of the posterity of Baliol.

[1] B. VI. chap. 3. Since I have quoted Mr. Archdeacon Paley upon one subject, I cannot but transcribe, from his excellent work, a distinguished passage in support of the Christian Revelation.—After shewing, in decent but strong terms, the unfairness of the *indirect* attempts of modern infidels to unsettle and perplex religious principles, and particularly the irony, banter, and sneer, of one whom he politely calls "an eloquent historian," the archdeacon thus expresses himself:

"Seriousness is not constraint of thought; nor levity, freedom. Every mind which wishes the advancement of truth and knowledge, in the most important of all human researches, must abhor this licentiousness, as violating no less the laws of reasoning than the rights of decency. There is but one description of men to whose principles it ought to be tolerable. I mean that class of reasoners who can see *little* in Christianity even supposing it to be true. To such adversaries we address this reflection.—Had Jesus Christ delivered no other declaration than the following, 'The hour is coming in the which all that are in the graves shall hear his voice, and shall come forth,—they that have done well unto the resurrection of life, and they that have done evil unto the resurrection of damnation,' he had pronounced a message of inestimable importance, and well worthy of that splendid apparatus of prophecy and miracles with which his mission was introduced and attested:—a message in which the wisest of mankind would rejoice to find an answer to their doubts, and rest to their inquiries. It is idle to say that a future state had been discovered already.—It had been discovered as the Copernican System was;—it was one guess amongst many. He alone discovers who *proves*; and no man

However convinced I am of the justice of that Highland principle, which holds allegiance and protection to be loyalty reciprocal, I do however acknowledge, that I am not satisfied with the cold sentiment which would confine the exertions of the subject within the strict line of duty. I would have every breast animated with the *fervour* of loyalty; with that generous attachment which delights in doing somewhat more than is required, and makes "service perfect freedom." And, therefore, as our most gracious Sovereign, on his accession to the throne, gloried in being *born a Briton*; so, in my more private sphere, *Ego me nunc* denique natum, *gratulor.* I am happy that a disputed succession no longer distracts our minds; and that a monarchy, established by law, is now so sanctioned by time, that we can fully indulge those feelings of loyalty which I am ambitious to excite. They are feelings which have ever actuated the inhabitants of the Highlands and the Hebrides. The plant of loyalty is there in full vigour, and the Brunswick graft now flourishes like a native shoot. To that spirited race of people I may with propriety apply the elegant lines of a modern poet, on the "facile temper of the beauteous sex : "

"Like birds new-caught, who flutter for a time,
And struggle with captivity in vain;
But by-and-by they rest, they smooth their plumes,
And to *new masters* sing their former notes." [1]

can prove this point but the teacher who testifies by miracles that his doctrine comes from GOD."—Book V. chap. 9.

If infidelity be disingenuously dispersed in every shape that is likely to allure, surprise, or beguile the imagination, —in a fable, a tale, a novel, a poem,—in books of travels, of philosophy, of natural history,—as Mr. Paley has well observed,—I hope it is fair in me thus to meet such poison with an unexpected antidote, which I cannot doubt will be found powerful.   [1] *Agis,* a tragedy, by John Home.

Emigra-
tion

Surely such notes are much better than the queru-
lous growlings of suspicious Whigs and discontented
Republicans.

Kingsburgh conducted us in his boat, across one of
the lochs, as they call them, or arms of the sea, which
flow in upon all the coasts of Sky,—to a mile beyond
a place called Grishinish. Our horses had been sent
round by land to meet us. By this sail we saved eight
miles of bad riding. Dr. Johnson said, "When we
take into the computation what we have saved, and
what we have gained, by this agreeable sail, it is a great
deal." He observed, "it is very disagreeable riding in
Sky. The way is so narrow, one only at a time can
travel, so it is quite unsocial; and you cannot indulge
in meditation by yourself, because you must be always
attending to the steps which your horse takes."—This
was a just and clear description of its inconveniencies.

The topick of emigration being again introduced,
Dr. Johnson said, that "a rapacious chief would make
a wilderness of his estate." Mr. Donald M'Queen
told us, that the oppression, which then made so much
noise, was owing to landlords listening to bad advice
in the letting of their lands; that interested and de-
signing people flattered them with golden dreams of
much higher rents than could reasonably be paid; and
that some of the gentlemen *tacksmen*, or upper tenants,
were themselves in part the occasion of the mischief,
by over-rating the farms of others. That many of the
tacksmen, rather than comply with exorbitant demands,
had gone off to America, and impoverished the country,
by draining it of its wealth; and that their places were
filled by a number of poor people, who had lived
under them, properly speaking, as servants, paid by a
certain proportion of the produce of the lands,

though called sub-tenants. I observed, that if the
men of substance were once banished from a Highland estate, it might probably be greatly reduced
in its value; for one bad year might ruin a set of
poor tenants, and men of any property would not
settle in such a country, unless from the temptation
of getting land extremely cheap; for an inhabitant
of any good county in Britain, had better go to
America than to the Highlands or the Hebrides.
Here, therefore, was a consideration that ought to induce a Chief to act a more liberal part, from a mere
motive of interest, independent of the lofty and honourable principle of keeping a clan together, to be in
readiness to serve his king. I added, that I could not
help thinking a little arbitrary power in the sovereign,
to control the bad policy and greediness of the Chiefs,
might sometimes be of service. In France a Chief
would not be permitted to force a number of the king's
subjects out of the country.—Dr. Johnson concurred
with me, observing, that "were an oppressive chieftain
a subject of the French king, he would probably be
admonished by a *letter*."

During our sail, Dr. Johnson asked about the use
of the dirk, with which he imagined the Highlanders
cut their meat. He was told, they had a knife and
fork besides, to eat with. He asked, how did the
women do? and was answered, some of them had a
knife and fork too; but in general the men, when they
had cut their meat, handed their knives and forks to
the women, and they themselves eat with their fingers.
The old tutor of Macdonald always eat fish with his
fingers, alledging that a knife and fork gave it a bad
taste. I took the liberty to observe to Dr. Johnson,
that he did so. "Yes," said he; "but it is because
I am short-sighted, and afraid of bones, for which

Marginal note: Bad policy of the Chiefs

reason I am not fond of eating many kinds of fish, because I must use my fingers."

Dr. M'Pherson's *Dissertations on Scottish Antiquities*, which he had looked at when at Corrichatachin, being mentioned, he remarked, that "you might read half an hour, and ask yourself what you had been reading: there were so many words to so little matter, that there was no getting through the book."

As soon as we reached the shore, we took leave of Kingsburgh, and mounted our horses. We passed through a wild moor, in many places so soft that we were obliged to walk, which was very fatiguing to Dr. Johnson. Once he had advanced on horseback to a very bad step. There was a steep declivity on his left, to which he was so near, that there was not room for him to dismount in the usual way. He tried to alight on the other side, as if he had been a *young buck* indeed, but in the attempt he fell at his length upon the ground; from which, however, he got up immediately without being hurt. During this dreary ride, we were sometimes relieved by a view of branches of the sea, that universal medium of connection amongst mankind. A guide, who had been sent with us from Kingsburgh, explored the way (much in the same manner as, I suppose, is pursued in the wilds of America,) by observing certain marks known only to the inhabitants. We arrived at Dunvegan late in the afternoon. The great size of the castle, which is partly old and partly new, and is built upon a rock close to the sea, while the land around it presents nothing but wild, moorish, hilly, and craggy appearances, gave a rude magnificence to the scene. Having dismounted, we ascended a flight of steps, which was made by the late Macleod, for the accommodation of persons coming to him by land, there formerly being, for security, no other access to the castle but from the sea; so that Sir Roderick Macleod visitors who came by the land were under the necessity of getting into a boat, and sailed round to the only place where it could be approached. We were introduced into a stately dining-room, and received by Lady Macleod, mother of the laird, who, with his friend Talisker, having been detained on the road, did not arrive till some time after us.

We found the lady of the house a very polite and sensible woman, who had lived for some time in London, and had there been in Dr. Johnson's company. After we had dined, we repaired to the drawing-room, where some of the young ladies of the family, with their mother, were at tea. This room had formerly been the bed-chamber of Sir Roderick Macleod, one of the old Lairds; and he chose it, because, behind it, there was a considerable cascade, the sound of which disposed him to sleep. Above his bed was this inscription : " Sir Rorie M'Leod of Dunvegan, Knight. God send good rest ! "—Rorie is the contraction of Roderick. He was called Rorie More, that is, great Rorie, not from his size, but from his spirit.—Our entertainment here was in so elegant a style, and reminded my fellow-traveller so much of England, that he became quite joyous. He laughed, and said, " Boswell, we came in at the wrong end of this island."— " Sir, (said I,) it was best to keep this for the last."—He answered, " I would have it both first and last."

Tuesday, 14th September.

Dr. Johnson said in the morning, " Is not this a fine lady ? "—There was not a word now of his " impatience to be in civilized life ; "—though indeed I should

H 387

The importance of chastity

beg pardon,—he found it here. We had slept well, and lain long. After breakfast we surveyed the castle, and the garden. Mr. Bethune, the parish minister,— Magnus M'Leod, of Claggan, brother to Talisker, and M'Leod, of Bay, two substantial gentlemen of the clan, dined with us. We had admirable venison, generous wine; in a word, all that a good table has. This was really the hall of a chief. Lady M'Leod had been much obliged to my father, who had settled by arbitration, a variety of perplexed claims between her and her relation, the Laird of Brodie, which she now repaid by particular attention to me.—M'Leod started the subject of making women do penance in the church for fornication.—JOHNSON. "It is right, sir. Infamy is attached to the crime, by universal opinion, as soon as it is known. I would not be the man who would discover it, if I alone knew it, for a woman may reform; nor would I commend a parson who divulges a woman's first offence; but being once divulged, it ought to be infamous. Consider, of what importance to society the chastity of women is. Upon that all the property in the world depends. We hang a thief for stealing a sheep; but the unchastity of a woman transfers sheep, and farm and all, from the right owner. I have much more reverence for a common prostitute than for a woman who conceals her guilt. The prostitute is known. She cannot deceive: she cannot bring a strumpet into the arms of an honest man, without his knowledge."—BOSWELL. "There is, however, a great difference between the licentiousness of a single woman, and that of a married woman."—JOHNSON. "Yes, sir; there is a great difference between stealing a shilling, and stealing a thousand pounds; between simply taking a man's purse, and murdering him first, and then taking it. But when one begins to be vicious, it is easy to go on. Where single women are licentious, you rarely find faithful married women."—Boswell. "And yet we are told that in some nations in India, the distinction is strictly observed."—Johnson. "Nay, don't give us India. That puts me in mind of Montesquieu, who is really a fellow of genius too in many respects; whenever he wants to support a strange opinion, he quotes you the practice of Japan or of some other distant country, of which he knows nothing. To support polygamy, he tells you of the island of Formosa, where there are ten women born for one man. He had but to suppose another island, where there are ten men born for one woman, and so make a marriage between them." [1]

At supper, Lady Macleod mentioned Dr. Cadogan's book on the gout.—Johnson. "It is a good book in general, but a foolish one in particulars. It is good in general, as recommending temperance and exercise, and cheerfulness. In that respect it is only Dr. Cheyne's book told in a new way; and there should come out such a book every thirty years, dressed in the mode of the times. It is foolish, in maintaining that the gout is not hereditary, and that one fit of it, when gone, is like a fever when gone."—Lady Macleod objected that the author does not practice what he teaches.[2]—Johnson. "I cannot help that, madam.

[1] What my friend treated as so wild a supposition, has actually happened in the Western islands of Scotland, if we may believe Martin, who tells it of the islands of Col and Tyr-yi, and says that it is proved by the parish registers.

[2] This was a general reflection against Dr. Cadogan, when his very popular book was first published. It was said, that whatever precepts he might give to others, he himself indulged freely in the bottle. But I have since had the pleasure of becoming acquainted with him, and, if his own testimony may be believed, (and I have never heard it impeached,) his course of life has been conformable to his doctrine.

Principle
and prac-
tice
That does not make his book the worse. People are influenced more by what a man says, if his practice is suitable to it,—because they are blockheads. The more intellectual people are, the readier will they attend to what a man tells them. If it is just, they will follow it, be his practice what it will. No man practises so well as he writes. I have, all my life long, been lying till noon; yet I tell all young men, and tell them with great sincerity, that nobody who does not rise early will ever do any good. Only consider! You read a book; you are convinced by it; you do not know the authour. Suppose you afterwards know him, and find that he does not practice what he teaches; are you to give up your former conviction? At this rate you would be kept in a state of equilibrium, when reading every book, till you knew how the authour practised." —"But," said Lady M'Leod, "you would think better of Dr. Cadogan, if he acted according to his principles."—JOHNSON. "Why, madam, to be sure, a man who acts in the face of light, is worse than a man who does not know so much; yet I think no man should be the worse thought of for publishing good principles. There is something noble in publishing truth, though it condemns one's self."—I expressed some surprize at Cadogan's recommending good humour, as if it were quite in our own power to attain it.— JOHNSON. "Why, sir, a man grows better humoured as he grows older. He improves by experience. When young, he thinks himself of great consequence, and every thing of importance. As he advances in life, he learns to think himself of no consequence, and little things of little importance; and so he becomes more patient, and better pleased. All good-humour and complaisance are acquired. Naturally a child seizes directly what it sees, and thinks of pleasing itself only. By degrees,

it is taught to please others, and to prefer others; and
that this will ultimately produce the greatest happiness.
If a man is not convinced of that, he never will practice it. Common language speaks the truth as to this:
we say, a person is well bred. As it is said, that all
material motion is primarily in a right line, and is never
per circuitum, never in another form, unless by some
particular cause; so it may be said intellectual motion
is."—Lady M'Leod asked, if no man was naturally
good?—JOHNSON. " No, madam, no more than a wolf."
—BOSWELL. " Nor no woman, sir?"—JOHNSON. "No,
sir."—Lady M'Leod started at this, saying, in a low
voice, " This is worse than Swift."

M'Leod of Ulinish had come in the afternoon. We
were a jovial company at supper. The Laird, surrounded by so many of his clan, was to me a pleasing
sight. They listened with wonder and pleasure, while
Dr. Johnson harangued. I am vexed that I cannot
take down his full strain of eloquence.

Wednesday, 15th September.

The gentlemen of the clan went away early in the
morning to the harbour of Lochbradale, to take leave
of some of their friends who were going to America.
It was a very wet day. We looked at Rorie More's
horn, which is a large cow's horn, with the mouth of
it ornamented with silver curiously carved. It holds
rather more than a bottle and a half. Every Laird of
M'Leod, it is said, must, as a proof of his manhood,
drink it off full of claret, without laying it down.—
From Rorie More many of the branches of the family
are descended; in particular, the Talisker branch; so
that his name is much talked of. We also saw his
bow, which hardly any man now can bend, and his

No man is natu-rally good

Glaymore, which was wielded with both hands, and is of a prodigious size. We saw here some old pieces of iron armour, immensely heavy. The broadsword now used, though called the Glaymore, (*i.e.* the great sword,) is much smaller than that used in Rorie More's time. There is hardly a target now to be found in the Highlands. After the disarming act, they made them serve as covers to their butter-milk barrels; a kind of change, like beating spears into pruning-hooks.

Sir George Mackenzie's Works (the folio edition) happened to lie in a window in the dining-room. I asked Dr. Johnson to look at the *Characteres Advocatorum*. He allowed him power of mind, and that he understood very well what he tells; but said, that there was too much declamation, and that the Latin was not correct. He found fault with *appropinquabant*, in the character of Gilmour. I tried him with the opposition between *gloria* and *palma*, in the comparison between Gilmour and Nisbet, which Lord Hailes, in his Catalogue of the Lords of Session, thinks difficult to be understood. The words are, "*penes illum gloria, penes hunc palma.*"—In a short Account of the Kirk of Scotland, which I published some years ago, I applied these words to the two contending parties, and explained them thus: "The popular party has most eloquence; Dr. Robertson's party most influence."— I was very desirous to hear Dr. Johnson's explication.—Johnson. "I see no difficulty. Gilmour was admired for his parts; Nisbet carried his cause by his skill in law. *Palma* is victory."—I observed, that the character of Nicholson, in this book, resembled that of Burke: for it is said, in one place, "*in omnes lusos & jocos se sæpe resolvebat*;[1] and, in another, "*sea*

[1] He often indulged himself in every species of pleasantry and wit.

accipitris more e conspectu aliquando astantium sublimi se **Burke's**
protrahens volatu, in prædam miro impetu descendebat." [1]   **eloquence**
—JOHNSON. "No, sir ; I never heard Burke make a
good joke in my life."—BOSWELL. " But, sir, you will
allow he is a hawk."—Dr. Johnson, thinking that I
meant this of his joking, said, "No, sir, he is not
the hawk there. He is the beetle in the mire."—I
still adhered to my metaphor,—" But he *soars* as
the hawk."—JOHNSON. "Yes, sir ; but he catches
nothing."—M'Leod asked, what is the particular excellence of Burke's eloquence ?—JOHNSON. "Copiousness and fertility of allusion ; a power of diversifying
his matter, by placing it in various relations. Burke
has great information, and great command of language ;
though, in my opinion, it has not in every respect the
highest elegance."—BOSWELL. "Do you think, sir,
that Burke has read Cicero much ?"—JOHNSON. "I
don't believe it, sir. Burke has great knowledge, great
fluency of words, and great promptness of ideas, so that
he can speak with great illustration on any subject that
comes before him. He is neither like Cicero, nor like
Demosthenes, nor like any one else, but speaks as well
as he can."

In the 65th page of the first volume of Sir George
Mackenzie, Dr. Johnson pointed out a paragraph beginning with *Aristotle*, and told me there was an error
in the text, which he bade me try to discover. I was
lucky enough to hit it at once. As the passage is
printed, it is said that the devil answers *even* in *engines.*
I corrected it to—*ever* in *ænigmas.* "Sir, (said he,)
you are a good critick. This would have been a great
thing to do in the text of an ancient authour."

---

[1] But like the hawk, having soared with a lofty flight to
a height which the eye could not reach, he was wont to
swoop upon his quarry with wonderful rapidity.

**Natural
goodness**   *Thursday, 16th September.*

Last night much care was taken of Dr. Johnson,
who was still distressed by his cold. He had
hitherto most strangely slept without a night-cap.
Miss M'Leod made him a large flannel one, and he
was prevailed with to drink a little brandy when he
was going to bed. He has great virtue, in not drinking wine or any fermented liquor, because, as he
acknowledged to us, he could not do it in moderation.
—Lady M'Leod would hardly believe him, and said,
"I am sure, sir, you would not carry it too far."—
JOHNSON. "Nay, madam, it carried me. I took the
opportunity of a long illness to leave it off. It was
then prescribed to me not to drink wine; and having
broken off the habit, I have never returned to it."

In the argument on Tuesday night, about natural
goodness, Dr. Johnson denied that any child was better
than another, but by difference of instruction; though,
in consequence of greater attention being paid to instruction by one child than another, and of a variety of
imperceptible causes, such as instruction being counter-
acted by servants, a notion was conceived, that of two
children, equally well educated, one was naturally much
worse than another. He owned, this morning, that
one might have a greater aptitude to learn than another,
and that we inherit dispositions from our parents. "I
inherited, (said he,) a vile melancholy from my father,
which has made me mad all my life, at least not sober."
—Lady M'Leod wondered he should tell this.—
"Madam, (said I,) he knows that with that madness
he is superior to other men."

I have often been astonished with what exactness
and perspicuity he will explain the process of any art.
He this morning explained to us all the operation of

coining, and, at night, all the operation of brewing, so very clearly, that Mr. M'Queen said, when he heard the first, he thought he had been bred in the Mint; when he heard the second, that he had been bred a brewer.

I was elated by the thought of having been able to entice such a man to this remote part of the world. A ludicrous, yet just image presented itself to my mind, which I expressed to the company. I compared myself to a dog who has got hold of a large piece of meat, and runs away with it to a corner, where he may devour it in peace, without any fear of others taking it from him. " In London, Reynolds, Beauclerk, and all of them, are contending who shall enjoy Dr. Johnson's conversation. We are feasting upon it, undisturbed, at Dunvegan."

It was still a storm of wind and rain. Dr. Johnson however walked out with M'Leod, and saw Rorie More's cascade in full perfection. Colonel M'Leod, instead of being all life and gaiety, as I have seen him, was at present grave, and somewhat depressed by his anxious concern about M'Leod's affairs, and by finding some gentlemen of the clan by no means disposed to act a generous or affectionate part to their Chief in his distress, but bargaining with him as with a stranger. However, he was agreeable and polite, and Dr. Johnson said, he was a very pleasing man.—My fellow-traveller and I talked of going to Sweden; and, while we were settling our plan, I expressed a pleasure in the prospect of seeing the king.—Johnson. " I doubt, sir, if he would speak to us."—Colonel M'Leod said, " I am sure Mr. Boswell would speak to *him*." But, seeing me a little disconcerted by his remark, he politely added, " and with great propriety."—Here let me offer a short defence of that propensity in my disposi-

*H 387

tion, to which this gentleman alluded. It has procured me much happiness. I hope it does not deserve so hard a name as either forwardness or impudence. If I know myself, it is nothing more than an eagerness to share the society of men distinguished either by their rank or their talents, and a diligence to attain what I desire. If a man is praised for seeking knowledge, though mountains and seas are in his way, may he not be pardoned, whose ardour, in the pursuit of the same object, leads him to encounter difficulties as great, though of a different kind ?

After the ladies were gone from table, we talked of the Highlanders not having sheets ; and this led us to consider the advantage of wearing linen.—JOHNSON. "All animal substances are less cleanly than vegetables. Wool, of which flannel is made, is an animal substance ; flannel therefore is not so cleanly as linen. I remember I used to think tar dirty ; but when I knew it to be only a preparation of the juice of the pine, I thought so no longer. It is not disagreeable to have the gum that oozes from a plumb-tree upon your fingers, because it is vegetable ; but if you have any candle-grease, any tallow upon your fingers, you are uneasy till you rub it off.—I have often thought, that, if I kept a seraglio, the ladies should all wear linen gowns,—or cotton ;—I mean stuffs made of vegetable substances. I would have no silk ; you cannot tell when it is clean : It will be very nasty before it is perceived to be so. Linen detects its own dirtiness."

To hear the grave Dr. Samuel Johnson, "that majestick teacher of moral and religious wisdom," while sitting solemn in an arm-chair in the Isle of Sky, talk, *ex cathedra*, of his keeping a seraglio, and acknowledge that the supposition had *often* been in his

thoughts, struck me so forcibly with ludicrous con- Cunning
trast, that I could not but laugh immoderately.   He
was too proud to submit, even for a moment, to be the
object of ridicule, and instantly retaliated with such
keen sarcastick wit, and such a variety of degrading
images, of every one of which I was the object, that,
though I can bear such attacks as well as most men, I
yet found myself so much the sport of all the company,
that I would gladly expunge from my mind every
trace of this severe retort.

Talking of our friend Langton's house in Lincoln-
shire, he said, " the old house of the family was burnt.
A temporary building was erected in its room ; and to
this day they have been always adding as the family
increased.   It is like a shirt made for a man when he
was a child, and enlarged always as he grows older."

We talked to-night of Luther's allowing the Land-
grave of Hesse two wives, and that it was with the
consent of the wife to whom he was first married.—
JOHNSON.   " There was no harm in this, so far as she
was only concerned, because *volenti non fit injuria*.   But
it was an offence against the general order of society,
and against the law of the Gospel, by which one man
and one woman are to be united.   No man can have
two wives, but by preventing somebody else from
having one."

Friday, 17th September.

After dinner yesterday, we had a conversation upon
cunning.   M'Leod said that he was not afraid of
cunning people ; but would let them play their tricks
about him like monkeys.   " But, (said I,) they'll
scratch ; " and Mr. M'Queen added, " they'll in-
vent new tricks, as soon as you find out what they do."
—JOHNSON.   " Cunning has effect from the credulity

A curious
piece of
antiquity

of others, rather than from the abilities of those who are cunning. It requires no extraordinary talents to lie and deceive."—This led us to consider whether it did not require great abilities to be very wicked. —JOHNSON. "It requires great abilities to have the *power* of being very wicked; but not to *be* very wicked. A man who has the power, which great abilities procure him, may use it well or ill; and it requires more abilities to use it well, than to use it ill. Wickedness is always easier than virtue; for it takes the short cut to every thing. It is much easier to steal a hundred pounds, than to get it by labour, or any other way. Consider only what act of wickedness requires great abilities to commit it, when once the person who is to do it has the power; for *there* is the distinction. It requires great abilities to conquer an army, but none to massacre it after it is conquered."

The weather this day was rather better than any that we had since we came to Dunvegan. Mr. M'Queen had often mentioned a curious piece of antiquity near this, which he called a temple of the Goddess Anaitis. Having often talked of going to see it, he and I set out after breakfast, attended by his servant, a fellow quite like a savage. I must observe here, that in Sky there seems to be much idleness; for men and boys follow you, as colts follow passengers upon a road. The usual figure of a Sky-boy, is a *lown* with bare legs and feet, a dirty *kilt*, ragged coat and waistcoat, a bare head, and a stick in his hand, which, I suppose, is partly to help the lazy rogue to walk, partly to serve as a kind of a defensive weapon. We walked what is called two miles, but is probably four, from the castle, till we came to the sacred place. The country around is a black dreary moor on all sides, except to the sea-coast, towards which there is a view through a valley; and the farm of Bay shews some good land. The place itself is green ground, being well drained, by means of a deep glen on each side, in both of which there runs a rivulet with a good quantity of water, forming several cascades, which make a considerable appearance and sound. The first thing we came to was an earthen mound, or dyke, extending from the one precipice to the other. A little farther on, was a strong stone-wall, not high, but very thick, extending in the same manner. On the outside of it were the ruins of two houses, one on each side of the entry or gate to it. The wall is built all along of uncemented stones, but of so large a size as to make a very firm and durable rampart. It has been built all about the consecrated ground, except where the precipice is steep enough to form an enclosure of itself. The sacred spot contains more than two acres. There are within it the ruins of many houses, none of them large,—a *cairn*,—and many graves marked by clusters of stones. Mr. M'Queen insisted that the ruin of a small building, standing east and west, was actually the temple of the Goddess Anaitis, where her statue was kept, and from whence processions were made to wash it in one of the brooks. There is, it must be owned, a hollow road visible for a good way from the entrance; but Mr. M'Queen, with the keen eye of an antiquary, traced it much farther than I could perceive it. There is not above a foot and a half in height of the walls now remaining; and the whole extent of the building was never, I imagine, greater than an ordinary Highland house. Mr. M'Queen has collected a great deal of learning on the subject of the temple of Anaitis; and I had endeavoured, in my journal, to state such particulars as might give some idea of it, and of the surrounding scenery; but from the great difficulty of describing visible objects, I found my account so

Mr. Mac-Queen's conjecture

j

Family unsatisfactory, that my readers would probably have
portraits exclaimed

> "And write about it, *Goddess*, and about it;"

and therefore I have omitted it.

When we got home, and were again at table with
Dr. Johnson, we first talked of portraits. He agreed
in thinking them valuable in families. I wished to
know which he preferred, fine portraits, or those of
which the merit was resemblance.——JOHNSON. "Sir,
their chief excellence is being like."——BOSWELL. "Are
you of that opinion as to the portraits of ancestors,
whom one has never seen?"——JOHNSON. "It then becomes of more consequence that they should be like;
and I would have them in the dress of the times,
which makes a piece of history. One should like to
see how Rorie More looked. Truth, sir, is of the
greatest value in these things."——Mr. M'Queen observed, that if you think it of no consequence whether
portraits are like, if they are but well painted, you
may be indifferent whether a piece of history is true
or not, if well told.

Dr. Johnson said at breakfast to-day, "that it was
but of late that historians bestowed pains and attention
in consulting records, to attain to accuracy. Bacon,
in writing his History of Henry VII. does not seem
to have consulted any, but to have just taken what he
found in other histories, and blended it with what he
learnt by tradition." He agreed with me that there
should be a chronicle kept in every considerable family,
to preserve the characters and transactions of successive
generations.

After dinner I started the subject of the temple of
Anaitis. Mr. M'Queen had laid stress on the name
given to the place by the country people,——*Ainnit*;

and added, " I knew not what to make of this piece
of antiquity, till I met with the *Anaitidis delubrum* in
Lydia, mentioned by Pausanias and the elder Pliny."—
Dr. Johnson, with his usual acuteness, examined Mr.
M'Queen as to the meaning of the word *Ainnit*, in
Erse; and it proved to be a *water-place*, or a place
near water, "which," said Mr. M'Queen, "agrees with
all the descriptions of the temples of that goddess,
which were situated near rivers, that there might be
water to wash the statue."—JOHNSON. " Nay, sir, the
argument from the name is gone.   The name is exhausted by what we see.   We have no occasion to go
to a distance for what we can pick up under our feet.
Had it been an accidental name, the similarity between
it and Anaitis might have had something in it; but
it turns out to be a mere physiological name."—
Macleod said, Mr. M'Queen's knowledge of etymo-
logy had destroyed his conjecture.—JOHNSON. " Yes,
sir; Mr. M'Queen is like the eagle mentioned by
Waller, who was shot with an arrow feather'd from
his own wing."—Mr. M'Queen would not, however,
give up his conjecture.—JOHNSON. " You have one
possibility for you, and all possibilities against you.
It is possible it may be the temple of Anaitis.   But
it is also possible that it may be a fortification ;—or
it may be a place of Christian worship, as the first
Christians often chose remote and wild places, to make
an impression on the mind :—or, if it was a heathen
temple, it may have been built near a river, for the
purpose of lustration ; and there is such a multitude
of divinities, to whom it may have been dedicated,
that the chance of its being a temple of Anaitis is
hardly any thing.   It is like throwing a grain of sand
upon the sea-shore to-day, and thinking you may find
it to-morrow.   No, sir, this temple, like many an ill-

Mr. Mac-
Queen's
Temple
of Anaitis

The built edifice, tumbles down before it is roofed in."—
traveller In his triumph over the reverend antiquarian, he in-
Pennant dulged himself in a conceit; for, some vestige of the
altar of the goddess being much insisted on in support
of the hypothesis, he said, " Mr. M'Queen is fighting *pro* aris *et focis*."

It was wonderful how well time passed in a remote
castle, and in dreary weather. After supper, we talked
of Pennant. It was objected that he was superficial.
Dr. Johnson defended him warmly. He said, " Pennant has greater variety of enquiry than almost any man,
and has told us more than perhaps one in ten thousand
could have done, in the time that he took. He has not
said what he was to tell; so you cannot find fault with
him, for what he has not told. If a man comes to look
for fishes, you cannot blame him if he does not attend to
fowls."—" But," said Colonel M'Leod, " he mentions
the unreasonable rise of rents in the Highlands, and
says, ' the gentlemen are for emptying the bag, without
filling it;' for that is the phrase he uses. Why does
he not tell how to fill it?"—JOHNSON. " Sir, there is
no end of negative criticism. He tells what he ob-
serves, and as much as he chooses. If he tells what
is not true, you may find fault with him; but, though
he tells that the land is not well cultivated, he is not
obliged to tell how it may be well cultivated. If I
tell that many of the Highlanders go bare-footed, I am
not obliged to tell how they may get shoes. Pennant
tells a fact. He need go no farther, except he pleases.
He exhausts nothing; and no subject whatever has yet
been exhausted. But Pennant has surely told a great
deal. Here is a man six feet high, and you are angry
because he is not seven."—Notwithstanding this eloquent *Oratio pro Pennantio*, which they who have read
this gentleman's *Tours*, and recollect the Savage and

the Shopkeeper at Monboddo, will probably impute to Boswell's the spirit of contradiction, I still think that he had defence better have given more attention to fewer things, than of Dun- have thrown together such a number of imperfect vegan accounts.

Saturday, 18th September.

Before breakfast, Dr. Johnson came up to my room, to forbid me to mention that this was his birth-day; but I told him I had done it already; at which he was displeased; I suppose from wishing to have nothing particular done on his account. Lady M'Leod and I got into a warm dispute. She wanted to build a house upon a farm which she has taken, about five miles from the castle, and to make gardens and other ornaments there; all of which I approved of; but insisted that the seat of the family should always be upon the rock of Dunvegan.—JOHNSON. " Ay, in time we'll build all round this rock. You may make a very good house at the farm; but it must not be such as to tempt the Laird of M'Leod to go thither to reside. Most of the great families of England have a secondary residence, which is called a jointure-house : let the new house be of that kind."—The lady insisted that the rock was very inconvenient; that there was no place near it where a good garden could be made; that it must always be a rude place; that it was a Herculean labour to make a dinner here.—I was vexed to find the alloy of modern refinement in a lady who had so much old family spirit.—" Madam, (said I,) if once you quit this rock, there is no knowing where you may settle. You move five miles first;—then to St. Andrews, as the late Laird did;—then to Edinburgh;—and so on till you end at Hampstead, or in France. No, no; keep to the rock : it is the very jewel of the estate. It looks

as if it had been let down from heaven by the four
corners, to be the residence of a Chief.   Have all the
comforts and conveniencies of life upon it, but never
leave Rorie More's cascade."—" But, (said she,) is
it not enough if we keep it?   Must we never have
more convenience than Rorie More had? he had his
beef brought to dinner in one basket, and his bread in
another.   Why not as well be Rorie More all over,
as live upon his rock?   And should not we tire, in
looking perpetually on this rock?   It is very well for
you, who have a fine place, and every thing easy, to
talk thus, and think of chaining honest folks to a rock.
You would not live upon it yourself."—" Yes, madam,
(said I,) I would live upon it, were I Laird of
M'Leod, and should be unhappy if I were not upon
it."—JOHNSON. (with a strong voice, and most determined manner,) "Madam, rather than quit the old
rock, Boswell would live in the pit; he would make
his bed in the dungeon."—I felt a degree of elation,
at finding my resolute feudal enthusiasm thus confirmed
by such a sanction.   The lady was puzzled a little.
She still returned to her pretty farm,—rich ground,—
fine garden.—" Madam, (said Dr. Johnson,) were
they in Asia, I would not leave the rock."—My
opinion on this subject is still the same.   An ancient
family residence ought to be a primary object; and
though the situation of Dunvegan be such that little
can be done here in gardening, or pleasure-ground,
yet, in addition to the veneration acquired by the lapse
of time, it has many circumstances of natural grandeur,
suited to the seat of a Highland Chief: it has the sea,
—islands,—rocks,—hills,—a noble cascade; and when
the family is again in opulence, something may be done
by art.

Mr. Donald M'Queen went away to-day, in order

to preach at Bracadale next day. We were so comfortably situated at Dunvegan, that Dr. Johnson could
hardly be moved from it. I proposed to him that we
should leave it on Monday. "No, sir, (said he,) I
will not go before Wednesday. I will have some
more of this good."—However, as the weather was at
this season so bad, and so very uncertain, and we had
a great deal to do yet, Mr. M'Queen and I prevail'd
with him to agree to set out on Monday, if the day
should be good. Mr. M'Queen though it was inconvenient for him to be absent from his harvest, engaged
to wait on Monday at Ulinish for us. When he was
going away, Dr. Johnson said, "I shall ever retain a
great regard for you;" then asked him if he had the
Rambler.—Mr. M'Queen said, "No; but my brother
has it."—Johnson. "Have you the *Idler?*"—
M'Queen. "No, sir."—Johnson. "Then I will
order one for you at Edinburgh, which you will keep
in remembrance of me."—Mr. M'Queen was much
pleased with this. He expressed to me, in the strongest
terms, his admiration of Dr. Johnson's wonderful knowledge, and every other quality for which he is distinguished. I asked Mr. M'Queen, if he was satisfied
with being a minister in Sky. He said he was; but
he owned that his forefathers having been so long
there, and his having been born there, made a chief
ingredient in forming his contentment. I should have
mentioned, that on our left hand, between Portree and
Dr. Macleod's house, Mr. M'Queen told me there
had been a college of the Knights Templars; that
tradition said so; and that there was a ruin remaining
of their church, which had been burnt: but I confess
Dr. Johnson has weakened my belief in remote tradition. In the dispute about Anaitis, Mr. M'Queen
said, Asia Minor was peopled by Scythians, and, as

Lan-
guages
the pedi-
gree of
nations they were the ancestors of the Celts, the same religion might be in Asia Minor and Sky.—JOHNSON. " Alas! sir, what can a nation that has not letters tell of its original. I have always difficulty to be patient when I hear authors gravely quoted, as giving accounts of savage nations, which accounts they had from the savages themselves. What can the M'Craas tell about themselves a thousand years ago? There is no tracing the connection of ancient nations, but by language; and therefore I am always sorry when any language is lost, because languages are the pedigree of nations. If you find the same language in distant countries, you may be sure that the inhabitants of each have been the same people; that is to say, if you find the languages a good deal the same; for a word here and there being the same, will not do. Thus Butler, in his *Hudibras*, remembering that Penguin, in the Straits of Magellan, signifies a bird with a white head, and that the same word has, in Wales, the signification of a white-headed wench, (*pen* head, and *guin* white,) by way of ridicule, concludes that the people of those Straits are Welch."

A young gentleman of the name of M'Lean, nephew to the Laird of the isle of Muck, came this morning; and, just as we sat down to dinner, came the Laird of the isle of Muck himself, his lady, sister to Talisker, two other ladies their relations, and a daughter of the late M'Leod of Hamer, who wrote a treatise on the second sight, under the designation of *Theophilus Insulanus*. It was somewhat droll to hear this Laird called by his title. *Muck* would have sounded ill; so he was called *Isle of Muck*, which went off with great readiness. The name, as now written, is unseemly, but is not so bad in the original Erse, which is *Mouach*, signifying the Sows' Island. Buchanan calls it *Insula Porcorum*. It is so called from its

form.   Some call it Isle of *Monk*.   The Laird On choos-
insists that this is the proper name.   It was formerly ing a wife
church-land belonging to Icolmkill, and a hermit lived
in it.   It is two miles long, and about three quarters
of a mile broad.   The Laird said, he had seven score
of souls upon it.   Last year he had eighty persons
inoculated, mostly children, but some of them eighteen
years of age.   He agreed with the surgeon to come
and do it, at half a crown a head.——It is very fertile
in corn, of which they export some; and its coasts
abound in fish.   A taylor comes there six times in
a year.   They get a good blacksmith from the isle
of Egg.

Sunday, 19th September.

It was rather worse weather than any that we had
yet.   At breakfast Dr. Johnson said, "Some cunning
men choose fools for their wives, thinking to manage
them, but they always fail.   There is a spaniel fool and
a mule fool.   The spaniel fool may be made to do by
beating.   The mule fool will neither do by words or
blows; and the spaniel fool often turns mule at last:
and suppose a fool to be made do pretty well, you must
have the continual trouble of making her do.   Depend
upon it, no woman is the worse for sense and knowledge."——Whether afterwards he meant merely to say
a polite thing, or to give his opinion, I could not be
sure; but he added, "Men know that women are an
over-match for them, and therefore they choose the
weakest or most ignorant.   If they did not think so,
they never could be afraid of women knowing as much
as themselves."——In justice to the sex, I think it but
candid to acknowledge, that, in a subsequent conversation, he told me that he was serious in what he had
said.

Johnson
praises
Boswell's
Journal

He came to my room this morning before breakfast, to read my Journal, which he has done all along. He often before said, "I take great delight in reading it." To-day he said, "You improve: it grows better and better."—I observed, there was a danger of my getting a habit of writing in a slovenly manner.—"Sir," said he, "it is not written in a slovenly manner. It might be printed, were the subject fit for printing."[1]—While Mr. Beaton preached to us in the dining-room, Dr. Johnson sat in his own room, where I saw lying before him a volume of Lord Bacon's works, the *Decay of Christian Piety*, Monboddo's *Origin of Language*, and Sterne's Sermons.—He asked me to-day, how it happened that we were so little together: I told him, my Journal took up much time. Yet, on reflection, it appeared strange to me, that although I will run from one end of London to another, to pass an hour with him, I should omit to seize any spare time to be in his company, when I am settled in the same house with him. But my Journal is really a task of much time and labour, and he forbids me to contract it.

I omitted to mention, in its place, that Dr. Johnson told Mr. M'Queen that he had found the belief of the second sight universal in Sky, except among the clergy, who seemed determined against it. I took the liberty to observe to Mr. M'Queen, that the clergy were actuated by a kind of vanity. "The world, (say they,) takes us to be credulous men in a remote corner. We'll shew them that we are more enlightened than they think." The worthy man said, that his disbelief of it was from his not finding sufficient evidence; but I could perceive that he was prejudiced against it.

---

[1] As I have faithfully recorded so many minute particulars, I hope I shall be pardoned for inserting so flattering an encomium on what is now offered to the publick.

After dinner to-day, we talked of the extraordinary fact of Lady Grange's being sent to St. Kilda, and confined there for several years, without any means of relief.[1]   Dr. Johnson said, if M'Leod would let it be known that he had such a place for naughty ladies, he

The story of Lady Grange

[1] The true story of this lady, which happened in this century, is as frightfully romantick as if it had been the fiction of a gloomy fancy.   She was the wife of one of the Lords of Session in Scotland, a man of the very first blood of his country.   For some mysterious reasons, which have never been discovered, she was seized and carried off in the dark, she knew not by whom, and by nightly journies was conveyed to the Highland shores, from whence she was transported by sea to the remote rock of St. Kilda, where she remained, amongst its few wild inhabitants, a forlorn prisoner, but had a constant supply of provisions, and a woman to wait on her.   No inquiry was made after her, till she at last found means to convey a letter to a confidental friend, by the daughter of a Catechist, who concealed it in a clue of yarn. Information being thus obtained at Edinburgh, a ship was sent to bring her off; but intelligence of this being received, she was conveyed to M'Leod's island of Herries, where she died.

In *Carstares's State Papers*, we find an authentick narrative of Connor, a catholick priest, who turned protestant, being seized by some of Lord Seaforth's people, and detained prisoner in the island of Herries several years; he was fed with bread and water, and lodged in a house where he was exposed to the rains and cold.   Sir James Ogilvy writes, (June 18, 1667,) that the Lord Chancellor, the Lord Advocate, and himself, were to meet next day, to take effectual methods to have this redressed.   Connor was then still detained, p. 310.— This shews what private oppression might in the last century be practised in the Hebrides.

In the same collection, the Earl of Argyle gives a picturesque account of an embassy from *the great M'Neil of Barra*, as that insular Chief used to be denominated.—"I received a letter yesterday from M'Neil of Barra, who lives very far off, sent by a gentleman in all formality, offering his service, which had made you laugh to see his entry.   His style of his letter runs as if he were of another kingdom." —P. 643.

Prize-fighting might make it a very profitable island.—We had, in the course of our tour, heard of St. Kilda poetry. Dr. Johnson observed, "it must be very poor, because they have very few images."—BOSWELL. "There may be a poetical genius shewn in combining these, and in making poetry of them."—JOHNSON. "Sir, a man cannot make fire but in proportion as he has fuel. He cannot coin guineas but in proportion as he has gold."—At tea he talked of his intending to go to Italy in 1775. M'Leod said, he would like Paris better.—JOHNSON. "No, sir; there are none of the French literati now alive, to visit whom I would cross a sea. I can find in Buffon's book all that he can say." [1]

After supper he said, "I am sorry that prize-fighting is gone out; every art should be preserved, and the art of defence is surely important. It is absurd that our soldiers should have swords, and not be taught the use of them. Prize-fighting made people accustomed not to be alarmed at seeing their own blood, or feeling a little pain from a wound. I think the heavy glaymore was an ill-contrived weapon. A man could only strike once with it. It employed both his hands, and he must of course be soon fatigued with wielding it; so that if his antagonist could only keep playing a while, he was sure of him. I would fight with a dirk against Rorie More's sword. I could ward off a blow with a dirk, and then run in upon my enemy. When within that heavy sword, I have him; he is quite helpless, and I could stab him at my leisure, like a calf.—It is thought by sensible military men, that the English do

[1] I doubt the justice of my fellow-traveller's remark concerning the French literati, many of whom, I am told, have considerable merit in conversation, as well as in their writings. That of Monsieur de Buffon, in particular, I am well assured is highly instructive and entertaining.

not enough avail themselves of their superior strength of **Duelling**
body against the French; for that must always have a
great advantage in pushing with bayonets.   I have heard
an officer say, that if women could be made to stand,
they would do as well as men in a mere interchange of
bullets from a distance : but, if a body of men should
come close up to them, then to be sure they must be overcome ; now, (said he,) in the same manner the weaker-
bodied French must be overcome by our strong soldiers.''

The subject of duelling was introduced.—JOHNSON.
"There is no case in England where one or other of
the combatants *must* die : if you have overcome your
adversary by disarming him, that is sufficient, though
you should not kill him ; your honour, or the honour
of your family, is restored, as much as it can be by
a duel.   It is cowardly to force your antagonist to
renew the combat, when you know that you have the
advantage of him by superior skill.   You might just
as well go and cut his throat while he is asleep in his
bed.   When a duel begins, it is supposed there may
be an equality ; because it is not always skill that prevails.   It depends much on presence of mind ; nay on
accidents.   The wind may be in a man's face.   He
may fall.   Many such things may decide the superiority.—A man is sufficiently punished, by being called
out, and subjected to the risk that is in a duel.''—But
on my suggesting that the injured person is equally
subjected to risk, he fairly owned he could not explain the rationality of duelling.

Monday, 20th September.

When I awaked, the storm was higher still.   It
abated about nine, and the sun shone ; but it rained
again very soon, and it was not a day for travelling.

At breakfast, Dr. Johnson told us, "there was once
a pretty good tavern in Catharine-street in the Strand,
where very good company met in an evening, and
each man called for his own half-pint of wine, or gill,
if he pleased; they were frugal men, and nobody paid
but for what he himself drank. The house furnished
no supper; but a woman attended with mutton-pies,
which any body might purchase. I was introduced
to this company by Cumming the Quaker, and used
to go there sometimes when I drank wine. In the
last age, when my mother lived in London, there
were two sets of people, those who gave the wall, and
those who took it; the peaceable and the quarrelsome.
When I returned to Lichfield, after having been in
London, my mother asked me, whether I was one of
those who gave the wall, or those who took it. Now,
it is fixed that every man keeps to the right; or, if
one is taking the wall, another yields it, and it is never
a dispute."—He was very severe on a lady, whose
name was mentioned. He said, he would have sent
her to St. Kilda. That she was as bad as negative
badness could be, and stood in the way of what was
good: that insipid beauty would not go a great way;
and that such a woman might be cut out of a cabbage,
if there was a skilful artificer.

M'Leod was too late in coming to breakfast. Dr.
Johnson said, laziness was worse than the toothache.
—Boswell. "I cannot agree with you, sir; a bason
of cold water, or a horse whip, will cure laziness."—
Johnson. "No, sir; it will only put off the fit; it
will not cure the disease. I have been trying to cure
my laziness all my life, and could not do it."—
Boswell. "But if a man does in a shorter time
what might be the labour of a life, there is nothing to
be said against him."—Johnson (perceiving at once

that I alluded to him and his Dictionary). "Suppose that flattery to be true, the consequence would
be, that the world would have no right to censure a
man; but that will not justify him to himself."

After breakfast, he said to me, "A Highland
Chief should now endeavour to do every thing to
raise his rents, by means of the industry of his people.
Formerly, it was right for him to have his house full
of idle fellows; they were his defenders, his servants,
his dependants, his friends. Now they may be better
employed. The system of things is now so much
altered, that the family cannot have influence but by
riches, because it has no longer the power of ancient
feudal times. An individual of a family may have it;
but it cannot now belong to a family, unless you could
have a perpetuity of men with the same views. M'Leod
has four times the land that the Duke of Bedford has.
I think, with his spirit, he may in time make himself
the greatest man in the king's dominions; for land may
always be improved to a certain degree. I would
never have any man sell land, to throw money into
the funds, as is often done, or to try any other
species of trade. Depend upon it, this rage of trade
will destroy itself. You and I shall not see it; but
the time will come when there will be an end of it.
Trade is like gaming. If a whole company are game-
sters, play must cease; for there is nothing to be won.
When all nations are traders, there is nothing to be
gained by trade, and it will stop first where it is brought
to the greatest perfection. Then the proprietors of
land only will be the great men."—I observed, it was
hard that M'Leod should find ingratitude in so many
of his people.—JOHNSON. "Sir, gratitude is a fruit of
great cultivation; you do not find it among gross
people."—I doubt of this. Nature seems to have

Dun-
vegan
Castle

implanted gratitude in all living creatures. The lion, mentioned by Aulus Gellius, had it.[1] It appears to me that culture, which brings luxury and selfishness with it, has a tendency rather to weaken than promote this affection.

Dr. Johnson said this morning, when talking of our setting out, that he was in the state in which Lord Bacon represents kings. He desired the end, but did not like the means. He wished much to get home, but was unwilling to travel in Sky.—"You are like kings too in this, sir, (said I,) that you must act under the direction of others."

Tuesday, 21st September.

The uncertainty of our present situation having prevented me from receiving any letters from home for some time, I could not help being uneasy. Dr. Johnson had an advantage over me, in this respect, he having no wife or child to occasion anxious apprehensions in his mind.—It was a good morning; so we resolved to set out. But, before quitting this castle, where we have been so well entertained, let me give a short description of it.

Along the edge of the rock, there are the remains of a wall, which is now covered with ivy. A square court is formed by buildings of different ages, particularly some towers, said to be of great antiquity; and at one place there is a row of false cannon of stone. There is a very large unfinished pile, four stories high, which we were told was here when Leod, the first of this family, came from the Isle of Man, married the heiress of the M'Crails, the ancient possessors of Dunvegan, and afterwards acquired by conquest as much land

[1] Aul. Gellius, Lib. v. c. xiv.

as he had got by marriage. He surpassed the house
of Austria ; for he was *felix* both *bella gerere* et *nubere*.
John Breck M'Leod, the grandfather of the late laird,
began to repair the castle, or rather to complete it :
but he did not live to finish his undertaking. Not
doubting, however, that he should do it, he, like those
who have had their epitaphs written before they died,
ordered the following inscription, composed by the
minister of the parish, to be cut upon a broad stone
above one of the lower windows, where it still remains
to celebrate what was not done, and to serve as a
memento of the uncertainty of life, and the presumption
of man :

"Joannes Macleod Beganoduni Dominus gentis suæ
Philarchus, Durinesiæ Haraiæ Vaternesiæ, &c. : Baro
D. Floræ Macdonald matrimoniali vinculo conjugatus
turrem hanc Beganodunensem proavorum habitaculum
longe vetustissimum diu penitus labefectatam Anno æræ
vulgaris MDCLXXXVI instauravit.

"Quem stabilire juvat proavorum tecta vetusta,
    Omne scelus fugiat, justitiamque colat.
Vertit in aerias turres magalia virtus,
    Inque casas humiles tecta superba nefas."

M'Leod and Talisker accompanied us. We passed
by the parish church of Durinish. The church-yard
is not enclosed, but a pretty murmuring brook runs
along one side of it. In it is a pyramid erected to
the memory of Thomas Lord Lovat, by his son Lord
Simon, who suffered on Tower-hill. It is of free-
stone, and, I suppose, about thirty feet high. There is
an inscription on a piece of white marble inserted in it,
which I suspect to have been the composition of Lord
Lovat himself, being much in his pompous style :

Lord
Lovat's
pyramid

"This pyramid was erected by Simon Lord Fraser of Lovat, in honour of Lord Thomas his Father, a Peer of Scotland, and Chief of the great and ancient Clan of the Frasers. Being attacked for his birthright by the family of Atholl, then in power and favour with King William, yet, by the valour and fidelity of his clan, and the assistance of the Campbells, the old friends and allies of his family, he defended his birthright with such greatness and fermety of soul, and such valour and activity, that he was an honour to his name, and a good pattern to all brave Chiefs of clans. He died in the month of May, 1699, in the 63rd year of his age, in Dunvegan, the house of the Laird of Mac Leod, whose sister he had married: by whom he had the above Simon Lord Fraser, and several other children. And, for the great love he bore to the family of Mac Leod, he desired to be buried near his wife's relations, in the place where two of her uncles lay. And his son Lord Simon, to shew to posterity his great affection for his mother's kindred, the brave Mac Leods, chooses rather to leave his father's bones with them, than carry them to his own burial-place, near Lovat."

I have preserved this inscription, though of no great value, thinking it characteristical of a man who has made some noise in the world. Dr. Johnson said, it was poor stuff, such as Lord Lovat's butler might have written.

I observed, in this church-yard, a parcel of people assembled at a funeral, before the grave was dug. The coffin, with the corpse in it, was placed on the ground, while the people alternately assisted in making a grave. One man, at a little distance, was busy cutting a long turf for it, with the crooked spade which is used in Sky; a very aukward instrument. The iron part of it is like a plough-coulter. It has a rude tree for a Ulinish handle, in which a wooden pin is placed for the foot to press upon. A traveller might, without further enquiry, have set this down as the mode of burying in Sky. I was told, however, that the usual way is to have a grave previously dug.

I observed to-day, that the common way of carrying home their grain here is in loads on horseback. They have also a few sleds, or *cars*, as we call them in Ayrshire, clumsily made, and rarely used.

We got to Ulinish about six o'clock, and found a very good farm-house, of two stories. Mr. M'Leod of Ulinish, the sheriff-substitute of the island, was a plain honest gentleman, a good deal like an English justice of peace; not much given to talk, but sufficiently sagacious, and somewhat droll. His daughter, though she was never out of Sky, was a very well-bred woman.—Our reverend friend, Mr. Donald M'Queen, kept his appointment, and met us here.

Talking of Phipps's voyage to the North Pole, Dr. Johnson observed, that it "was conjectured that our former navigators have kept too near land, and so have found the sea frozen far north, because the land hinders the free motion of the tide; but, in the wide ocean, where the waves tumble at their full convenience, it is imagined that the frost does not take effect."

Wednesday, 22nd September.

In the morning I walked out, and saw a ship, the *Margaret* of Clyde, pass by with a number of emigrants on board. It was a melancholy sight.—After breakfast, we went to see what was called a subterraneous house, about a mile off. It was upon the side of a rising-ground. It was discovered by a fox's

A subter-
raneous
house

having taken up his abode in it, and in chacing him, they dug into it. It was very narrow and low, and seemed about forty feet in length. Near it, we found the foundations of several small huts, built of stone.—Mr. M'Queen, who is always for making every thing as ancient as possible, boasted that it was the dwelling of some of the first inhabitants of the island, and observed, what a curiosity it was to find here a specimen of the houses of the Aborigines, which he believed could be found no where else; and it was plain that they lived without fire.—Dr. Johnson remarked, that they who made this were not in the rudest state; for that it was more difficult to make *it* than to build a house; therefore certainly those who made it were in possession of houses, and had this only as a hiding-place.—It appeared to me, that the vestiges of houses, just by it, confirmed Dr. Johnson's opinion.

From an old tower, near this place, is an extensive view of Loch-Braccadil, and, at a distance, of the isles of Barra and South Uist; and on the land-side, the Cuillin, a prodigious range of mountains, capped with rocky pinnacles in a strange variety of shapes. They resemble the mountains near Corté in Corsica, of which there is a very good print. They make part of a great range for deer, which, though entirely devoid of trees, is in these countries called a *forest*.

In the afternoon, Ulinish carried us in his boat to an island possessed by him, where we saw an immense cave, much more deserving the title of *antrum immane* than that of the Sybil described by Virgil, which I likewise have visited. It is one hundred and eighty feet long, about thirty feet broad, and at least thirty feet high. This cave, we were told, had a remarkable echo; but we found none. They said it was owing to the great rains having made it damp. Such are the excuses by which the exaggeration of Highland narratives is palliated.—There is a plentiful garden at Ulinish, (a great rarity in Sky,) and several trees; and near the house is a hill, which has an Erse name, signifying "the hill of strife," where, Mr. M'Queen informed us, justice was of old administered. It is like the *mons placiti* of Scone, or those hills which are called *laws*, such as Kelly Law, North-Berwick Law, and several others. It is singular that this spot should happen now to be the sheriff's residence.

We had a very cheerful evening, and Dr. Johnson talked a good deal on the subject of literature.—Speaking of the noble family of Boyle, he said, that all the Lord Orrerys, till the present, had been writers. The first wrote several plays; the second was Bentley's antagonist; the third wrote the Life of Swift, and several other things; his son Hamilton wrote some papers in the *Adventurer* and *World*. He told us, he was well acquainted with Swift's Lord Orrery. He said, he was a feeble-minded man; that, on the publication of Dr. Delany's *Remarks* on his book, he was so much alarmed that he was afraid to read them. Dr. Johnson comforted him, by telling him they were both in the right; that Delany had seen most of the good side of Swift,—Lord Orrery most of the bad.—M'Leod asked, if it was not wrong in Orrery to expose the defects of a man with whom he lived in intimacy.—JOHNSON. "Why no, sir, after the man is dead; for then it is done historically." He added, "If Lord Orrery had been rich, he would have been a very liberal patron. His conversation was like his writings, neat and elegant, but without strength. He grasped at more than his abilities could reach; tried to pass for a better talker, a better writer, and a better thinker than he was. There was a quarrel between him and his father, in which his

Studied
con-
clusions
of letters
father was to blame; because it arose from the son's not allowing his wife to keep company with his father's mistress. The old lord shewed his resentment in his will, —leaving his library from his son, and assigning, as his reason, that he could not make use of it."

I mentioned the affectation of Orrery, in ending all his letters on the Life of Swift in studied varieties of phrase, and never in the common mode of "*I am*," &c. an observation which I remember to have been made several years ago by old Mr. Sheridan. This species of affectation in writing, as a foreign lady of distinguished talents once remarked to me, is almost peculiar to the English. I took up a volume of Dryden, containing the *Conquest of Granada*, and several other plays, of which all the dedications had such studied conclusions. Dr. Johnson said, such conclusions were more elegant, and, in addressing persons of high rank, (as when Dryden dedicated to the Duke of York,) they were likewise more respectful. I agreed that *there* it was much better: it was making his escape from the Royal presence with a genteel sudden timidity, in place of having the resolution to stand still, and make a formal bow.

Lord Orrery's unkind treatment of his son in his will, led us to talk of the dispositions a man should have when dying. I said, I did not see why a man should act differently with respect to those of whom he thought ill when in health, merely because he was dying.—JOHNSON. "I should not scruple to speak against a party, when dying; but should not do it against an individual.—It is told of Sixtus Quintus, that on his death-bed, in the intervals of his last pangs, he signed death-warrants."—Mr. M'Queen said, he should not do so; he would have more tenderness of heart.—JOHNSON. "I believe I should not

either; but Mr. M'Queen and I are cowards. It Bio-
would not be from tenderness of heart; for the heart graphy
is as tender when a man is in health as when he is
sick, though his resolution may be stronger. Sixtus
Quintus was a sovereign as well as a priest; and, if
the criminals deserved death, he was doing his duty to
the last. You would not think a judge died ill, who
should be carried off by an apoplectick fit while pro-
nouncing sentence of death. Consider a class of men
whose business it is to distribute death:—soldiers, who
die scattering bullets.—Nobody thinks they die ill on
that account."

Talking of Biography, he said, he did not think that
the life of any literary man in England had been well
written. Beside the common incidents of life, it should
tell us his studies, his mode of living, the means by
which he attained to excellence, and his opinion of his
own works. He told us, he had sent Derrick to
Dryden's relations, to gather materials for his Life;
and he believed Derrick had got all that he himself
should have got; but it was nothing. He added, he
had a kindness for Derrick, and was sorry he was dead.

His notion as to the poems published by Mr.
M'Pherson, as the works of Ossian, was not shaken
here. Mr. M'Queen always evaded the point of
authenticity, saying only that Mr. M'Pherson's pieces
fell far short of those he knew in Erse, which were
said to be Ossian's.—JOHNSON. "I hope they do. I
am not disputing that you may have poetry of great
merit; but that M'Pherson's is not a translation from
ancient poetry. You do not believe it. I say before
you, you do not believe it, though you are very willing
that the world should believe it."—Mr. M'Queen
made no answer to this.—Dr. Johnson proceeded,
"I look upon M'Pherson's *Fingal* to be as gross an

"Queen imposition as ever the world was troubled with.   Had
Eliza- it been really an ancient work, a true specimen how
beth's men thought at that time, it would have been a curiosity
Cham- of the first rate.   As a modern production, it is nothing."
pion" —He said, he could never get the meaning of an Erse
song explained to him.   They told him, the chorus
was generally unmeaning.   "I take it, (said he,) Erse
songs are like a song which I remember : it was composed in Queen Elizabeth's time, on the Earl of Essex;
and the burthen was

> "'Radaratoo, radarate, radara tàdara tandore.'"

"But surely," said Mr. M'Queen, "there were words
to it, which had meaning."—Johnson. "Why, yes,
sir ; I recollect a stanza, and you shall have it :

> "'O! then bespoke the prentices all,
>   Living in London, both proper and tall,
>   For Essex's sake they would fight all.
>   Radaratoo, radarate, radara, tadara, tandore.'"[1]

When Mr. M'Queen began again to expatiate on
the beauty of Ossian's poetry, Dr. Johnson entered into
no further controversy, but, with a pleasant smile, only
cried, "Ay, ay ; Radaratoo radarate."

---

[1] This droll quotation, I have since found, was from a song
in honour of the Earl of Essex, called "Queen Elizabeth's
Champion," which is preserved in a collection of Old Ballads,
in three volumes, published in London in different years,
between 1720 and 1730.   The full verse is as follows:

> "Oh! then bespoke the prentices all,
>   Living in London, both proper and tall,
>   In a kind letter sent straight to the Queen,
>   For Essex's sake they would fight all.
>   Raderer too, tandaro te,
>   Raderer, tandorer, tan do re."

Thursday, 23rd September.

I took *Fingal* down to the parlour in the morning, and tried a test proposed by Mr. Roderick M‘Leod, son to Ulinish. Mr. M‘Queen had said he had some of the poem in the original. I desired him to mention any passage in the printed book, of which he could repeat the original. He pointed out one in page 50 of the quarto edition, and read the Erse, while Mr. Roderick M‘Leod and I looked on the English ;— and Mr. M‘Leod said, that it was pretty like what Mr. M‘Queen had recited. But when Mr. M‘Queen read a description of Cuchullin's sword in Erse, together with a translation of it in English verse, by Sir James Foulis, Mr. M‘Leod said, that was much more like than Mr. M‘Pherson's translation of the former passage. Mr. M‘Queen then repeated in Erse a description of one of the horses in Cuchillin's car. Mr. M‘Leod said, Mr. M‘Pherson's English was nothing like it.

When Dr. Johnson came down, I told him that I had now obtained some evidence concerning Fingal; for that Mr. M‘Queen had repeated a passage in the original Erse, which Mr. M‘Pherson's translation was pretty like ; and reminded him that he himself had once said, he did not require Mr. M‘Pherson's Ossian to be more like the original than Pope's Homer.— Johnson. "Well, sir, this is just what I always maintained. He has found names, and stories, and phrases, nay passages in old songs, and with them has blended his own compositions, and so made what he gives to the world as the translation of an ancient poem."— If this was the case, I observed, it was wrong to publish it as a poem in six books.—Johnson. "Yes, sir ; and to ascribe it to a time too when the Highlanders knew nothing of *books*, and nothing of *six* ;—or perhaps

were got the length of counting six. We have been
told, by Condamine, of a nation that could count
no more than four. This should be told to Monboddo; it would help him. There is as much charity
in helping a man down-hill, as in helping him up-hill."
—BOSWELL. "I don't think there is as much charity."
—JOHNSON. "Yes, sir, if his *tendency* be downwards.
Till he is at the bottom, he flounders; get him once
there, and he is quiet. Swift tells, that Stella had a
trick, which she learned from Addison, of encourag-
ing a man in absurdity, instead of endeavouring to
extricate him."

Mr. M'Queen's answers to the inquiries concerning
Ossian were so unsatisfactory, that I could not help
observing, that, were he examined in a court of justice,
he would find himself under a necessity of being more
explicit.—JOHNSON. "Sir, he has told Blair a little
too much, which is published; and he sticks to it.
He is so much at the head of things here, that he has
never been accustomed to be closely examined; and
so he goes on quite smoothly."—BOSWELL. "He has
never had any body to work him."—JOHNSON. "No,
sir; and a man is seldom disposed to work himself;
though he ought to work himself, to be sure."—Mr.
M'Queen made no reply.[1]

Having talked of the strictness with which witnesses
are examined in courts of justice, Dr. Johnson told
us, that Garrick, though accustomed to face multi-
tudes, when produced as a witness in Westminster-
hall, was so disconcerted by a new mode of publick
appearance, that he could not understand what was

---

[1] I think it but justice to say, that I believe Dr. Johnson
meant to ascribe Mr. M'Queen's conduct to inaccuracy and
enthusiasm, and did not mean any severe imputation against
him.

asked. It was a cause where an actor claimed a *free benefit*; that is to say, a benefit without paying the expence of the house; but the meaning of the term was disputed. Garrick was asked, " Sir, have you a free benefit?"—"Yes."—"Upon what terms have you it?"—"Upon—the terms—of—a free benefit." —He was dismissed as one from whom no information could be obtained.—Dr. Johnson is often too hard on our friend Mr. Garrick. When I asked him, why he did not mention him in the Preface to his Shakspeare, he said, " Garrick has been liberally paid for any thing he has done for Shakspeare. If I should praise him, I should much more praise the nation who paid him. He has not made Shakspeare better known;[1] he cannot illustrate Shakspeare : So I have reasons enough against mentioning him, were reasons necessary. There should be reasons *for* it." —I spoke of Mrs. Montague's very high praises of

[1] It has been triumphantly asked, " Had not the plays of Shakspeare lain dormant for many years before the appear- ance of Mr Garrick? Did he not exhibit the most excellent of them frequently for thirty years together, and render them extremely popular by his own inimitable performance?" He undoubtedly did. But Dr. Johnson's assertion has been misunderstood. Knowing as well as the objectors what has been just stated, he must necessarily have meant, that " Mr. Garrick did not as a *critick* make Shakspeare better known ; he did not *illustrate* any one *passage* in any of his plays by acuteness of disquisition, or sagacity of conjecture: " and what had been done with any degree of excellence in *that* way was the proper and immediate subject of his preface. I may add in support of this explanation the following anecdote, related to me by one of the ablest commentators on Shakspeare, who knew much of Dr. Johnson: " Now I have quitted the theatre," cries Garrick, " I will sit down and read Shakspeare."—" 'Tis time you should," exclaimed Johnson, " for I much doubt if you ever examined one of his plays from the first scene to the last."

Garrick.—Johnson. "Sir, it is fit she should say so
much, and I should say nothing. Reynolds is fond
of her book, and I wonder at it; for neither I, nor
Beauclerk, nor Mrs. Thrale, could get through it." [1]

[1] No man has less inclination to controversy than I have,
particularly with a lady. But as I have claimed, and am
conscious of being entitled to, credit, for the strictest fidelity,
my respect for the publick obliges me to take notice of an
insinuation which tends to impeach it.

Mrs. Piozzi (late Mrs. Thrale), to her "Anecdotes of Dr.
Johnson," added the following postscript:

"*Naples, Feb.* 10, 1786.

"Since the foregoing went to the press, having seen a
passage from Mr. Boswell's 'Tour to the Hebrides,' in
which it is said, that *I could not get through Mrs. Montague's
'Essay on Shakspeare,'* I do not delay a moment to declare,
that, on the contrary, I have always commended it myself,
and heard it commended by every one else; and few things
would give me more concern than to be thought incapable
of tasting, or unwilling to testify my opinion of its excellence."

It is remarkable that this postscript is so expressed, as not
to point out the person who said that Mrs. Thrale could
not get through Mrs. Montague's book; and therefore I
think it necessary to remind Mrs. Piozzi, that the assertion
concerning her was Dr. Johnson's, and not mine. The
second observation that I shall make on this postscript is,
that it does not deny the fact asserted, though I must acknowledge from the praise it bestows on Mrs. Montague's
book, it may have been designed to convey that meaning.

What Mrs. Thrale's opinion is or was, or what she may
or may not have said to Dr. Johnson concerning Mrs. Montague's book, it is not necessary for me to enquire. It is
only incumbent on me to ascertain what Dr. Johnson said
to me. I shall therefore confine myself to a very short state
of the fact.

The unfavourable opinion of Mrs. Montague's book,
which Dr. Johnson is here reported to have given, is known
to have been that which he uniformly expressed, as many
of his friends well remember. So much for the authenticity
of the paragraph, as far as it relates to his own sentiments.
The words containing the assertion, to which Mrs. Piozzi

Last night Dr. Johnson gave us an account of the whole process of tanning,—and of the nature of milk, and the various operations upon it, as making whey, &c.   His variety of information is surprizing; and it gives one much satisfaction to find such a man bestowing his attention on the useful arts of life.   Ulinish was much struck with his knowledge; and said, " He is a great orator, sir; it is musick to hear this man speak."—A strange thought struck me, to try if he knew any thing of an art, or whatever it should be

Johnson's variety of information

objects, are printed from my manuscript Journal, and were taken down at the time.   The Journal was read by Dr. Johnson, who pointed out some inaccuracies, which I corrected, but did not mention any inaccuracy in the paragraph in question: and what is still more material, and very flattering to me, a considerable part of my Journal, containing this paragraph, *was read several years ago by Mrs. Thrale herself,* who had it for some time in her possession, and returned it to me, without intimating that Dr. Johnson had mistaken her sentiments.

When the first edition of my Journal was passing through the press, it occurred to me, that a peculiar delicacy was necessary to be observed in reporting the opinion of one literary lady concerning the performance of another; and I had such scruples on that head, that in the proof sheet I struck out the name of Mrs. Thrale from the above paragraph, and two or three hundred copies of my book were actually printed and published without it; of these Sir Joshua Reynolds's copy happened to be one.   But while the sheet was working off, a friend, for whose opinion I have great respect, suggested that I had no right to deprive Mrs. Thrale of the high honour which Dr. Johnson had done her, by stating her opinion along with that of Mr. Beauclerk, as coinciding with, and, as it were, sanctioning his own.   The observation appeared to me so weighty and conclusive, that I hastened to the printing-house, and, as a piece of justice, restored Mrs. Thrale to that place from which a too scrupulous delicacy had excluded her.

On this simple state of facts I shall make no observation whatever.

*I 387

called, which is no doubt very useful in life, but which
lies far out of the way of a philosopher and poet; I
mean the trade of a butcher. I enticed him into the
subject, by connecting it with the various researches
into the manners and customs of uncivilized nations,
that have been made by our late navigators into the
South Seas.—I began with observing, that Mr. (now
Sir Joseph) Banks tells us, that the art of slaughtering
animals was not known in Otaheite, for, instead of
bleeding to death their dogs, (a common food with
them,) they strangle them. This he told me himself;
and I supposed that their hogs were killed in the same
way. Dr. Johnson said, "This must be owing to
their not having knives,—though they have sharp
stones with which they can cut a carcase in pieces
tolerably." By degrees, he shewed that he knew
something even of butchery. "Different animals (said
he) are killed differently. An ox is knocked down,
and a calf stunned; but a sheep has its throat cut,
without any thing being done to stupify it. The
butchers have no view to the ease of the animals, but
only to make them quiet, for their own safety and
convenience. A sheep can give them little trouble.—
Hales is of opinion, that every animal should be
blooded, without having any blow given to it, because
it bleeds better."—BOSWELL. "That would be cruel."
—JOHNSON. "No, sir; there is not much pain, if the
jugular vein be properly cut."—Pursuing the subject,
he said, the kennels of Southwark ran with blood two
or three days in the week; that he was afraid there
were slaughter-houses in more streets in London than
one supposes; (speaking with a kind of horrour of
butchering;) and yet, he added, "any of us would
kill a cow, rather than not have beef."—I said we
could not.—"Yes, (said he,) any one may. The

business of a butcher is a trade indeed, that is to say, there is an apprenticeship served to it; but it may be learnt in a month."

I mentioned a club in London, at the Boar's Head in Eastcheap, the very tavern where Falstaff and his joyous companions met; the members of which all assume Shakspeare's characters. One is Falstaff, another Prince Henry, another Bardolph, and so on.— JOHNSON. "Don't be of it, sir. Now that you have a name, you must be careful to avoid many things, not bad in themselves, but which will lessen your character.[1] This every man who has a name must observe. A man who is not publickly known may live in London as he pleases, without any notice being taken of him; but it is wonderful how a person of any consequence is watched. There was a member of parliament, who wanted to prepare himself to speak on a question that was to come on in the House; and he and I were to talk it over together. He did not wish it should be known that he talked with me; so he would not let me come to his house, but came to mine. Some time after he had made his speech in the house, Mrs. Chol-mondeley, a very airy lady, told me, 'Well, you could make nothing of him!' naming the gentleman; which was a proof that he was watched.—I had once some business to do for government, and I went to Lord North's. Precaution was taken that it should not be known. It was dark before I went; yet a few days after I was told, 'Well, you have been with Lord North.' That the door of the prime minister should

---

[1] I do not see why I might not have been of this club without lessening my character. But Dr. Johnson's caution against supposing one's self concealed in London, may be very useful to prevent some people from doing many things, not only foolish, but criminal.

A fit of railing at the Scots

be watched, is not strange; but that a member of parliament should be watched, or that my door should be watched, is wonderful."

We set out this morning on our way to Talisker, in Ulinish's boat, having taken leave of him and his family. Mr. Donald M'Queen still favoured us with his company, for which we were much obliged to him. As we sailed along Dr. Johnson got into one of his fits of railing at the Scots. He owned that they had been a very learned nation for a hundred years, from about 1550 to about 1650; but that they afforded the only instance of a people among whom the arts of civil life did not advance in proportion with learning; that they had hardly any trade, any money, or any elegance, before the Union; that it was strange that, with all the advantages possessed by other nations, they had not any of those conveniencies and embellishments which are the fruit of industry, till they came in contact with a civilized people. "We have taught you, (said he,) and we'll do the same in time to all barbarous nations,—to the Cherokees,—and at last to the Ouran-Outangs;" laughing with as much glee as if Monboddo had been present.—BOSWELL. "We had wine before the Union."—JOHNSON. "No, sir; you had some weak stuff, the refuse of France, which would not make you drunk."—BOSWELL. "I assure you, sir, there was a great deal of drunkenness."—JOHNSON. "No, sir; there were people who died of dropsies, which they contracted in trying to get drunk."

I must here glean some of his conversation at Ulinish, which I have omitted. He repeated his remark, that a man in a ship was worse than a man in a jail. "The man in a jail, (said he,) has more room, better food, and commonly better company, and is in safety."—"Ay; but, (said Mr. M'Queen,) the man in the ship has the pleasing hope of getting Johnson's to shore."—JOHNSON. "Sir, I am not talking of a island man's getting to shore; but of a man while he is in a ship: and then, I say, he is worse than a man while he is in a jail. A man in a jail *may* have the 'pleasing hope' of getting out. A man confined for only a limited time, actually *has* it."—M'Leod mentioned his schemes for carrying on fisheries with spirit, and that he would wish to understand the construction of boats. I suggested that he might go to a dock-yard and work, as Peter the Great did.—JOHNSON. "Nay, sir, he need not work. Peter the Great had not the sense to see that the mere mechanical work may be done by any body, and that there is the same art in constructing a vessel, whether the boards are well or ill wrought. Sir Christopher Wren might as well have served his time to a bricklayer, and first, indeed, to a brickmaker."

There is a beautiful little island in the Loch of Dunvegan, called Isa. M'Leod said, he would give it to Dr. Johnson, on condition of his residing on it three months in the year; nay one month. Dr. Johnson was highly amused with the fancy. I have seen him please himself with little things, even with mere ideas like the present. He talked a great deal of this island;—how he would build a house there,—how he would fortify it,—how he would have cannon,—how he would plant,—how he would sally out, and *take* the isle of Muck;—and then he laughed with uncommon glee, and could hardly leave off. I have seen him do so at a small matter that struck him, and was a sport to no one else. Mr. Langton told me, that one night he did so while the company were all grave about him:— only Garrick, in his significant smart manner darting his eyes around, exclaimed, "*Very* jocose, to be sure!"

M'Leod
and his
clan

—M'Leod encouraged the fancy of Dr. Johnson's becoming owner of an island; told him, that it was the practice in this country to name every man by his lands; and begged leave to drink to him in that mode: "Island Isa, your health!"—Ulinish, Talisker, Mr. M'Queen, and I, all joined in our different manners, while Dr. Johnson bowed to each, with much good humour.

We had good weather, and a fine sail this day. The shore was varied with hills, and rocks, and corn-fields, and bushes, which are here dignified with the name of natural *wood*. We landed near the house of Ferneley, a farm possessed by another gentleman of the name of M'Leod, who, expecting our arrival, was waiting on the shore, with a horse for Dr. Johnson. The rest of us walked.—At dinner, I expressed to M'Leod the joy which I had in seeing him on such cordial terms with his clan. "Government (said he) has deprived us of our ancient power; but it cannot deprive us of our domestick satisfactions. I would rather drink punch in one of their houses, (meaning the houses of his people,) than be enabled by their hardships, to have claret in my own."—This should be the sentiment of every Chieftain. All that he can get by raising his rents, is more luxury in his own house. Is it not better to share the profits of his estate, to a certain degree, with his kinsmen, and thus have both social intercourse and patriarchal influence?

We had a very good ride, for about three miles, to Talisker, where Colonel M'Leod introduced us to his lady. We found here Mr. Donald M'Lean, the young Laird of Col, (nephew to Talisker,) to whom I delivered the letter with which I had been favoured by his uncle, Professor M'Leod, at Aberdeen. He was a little lively young man. We found he had been a good deal in Eng-

land, studying farming, and was resolved to improve the   Talisker
value of his father's lands, without oppressing his tenants,
or losing the ancient Highland fashions.

Talisker is a better place than one commonly finds
in Sky.   It is situated in a rich bottom.   Before it is
a wide expanse of sea, on each hand of which are immense rocks ;   and, at some distance in the sea, there
are three columnal rocks rising to sharp points.   The
billows break with prodigious force and noise on the
coast of Talisker.   There are here a good many well-
grown trees.   Talisker is an extensive farm.   The
possessor of it has, for several generations, been the
next heir to M'Leod, as there has been but one son
always in that family.   The court before the house is
most injudiciously paved with the round blueish-grey
pebbles which are found upon the sea-shore ; so that
you walk as if upon cannon-balls driven into the ground.

After supper, I talked of the assiduity of the Scottish clergy, in visiting and privately instructing their
parishioners, and observed how much in this they excelled the English clergy.   Dr. Johnson would not let
this pass.   He tried to turn it off, by saying, " There
are different ways of instructing.   Our clergy pray and
preach."—M'Leod and I pressed the subject, upon
which he grew warm, and broke forth : " I do not
believe your people are better instructed.   If they are,
it is the blind leading the blind ; for your clergy are
not instructed themselves."   Thinking he had gone a
little too far, he checked himself, and added, " When
I talk of the ignorance of your clergy, I talk of them
as a body : I do not mean that there are not individuals
who are learned (looking at Mr. M'Queen).   I suppose there are such among the clergy in Muscovy.
The clergy of England have produced the most valuable books in support of religion, both in theory and

practice. What have your clergy done, since you sunk into presbyterianism? Can you name one book of any value, on a religious subject, written by them?"—We were silent.—"I'll help you. Forbes wrote very well; but I believe he wrote before episcopacy was quite extinguished."—And then pausing a little, he said, "Yes, you have Wishart AGAINST Repentance."[1]—BOSWELL. "But, sir, we are not contending for the superior learning of our clergy, but for their superior assiduity."— He bore us down again, with thundering against their ignorance, and said to me, "I see you have not been well taught; for you have not charity."—He had been in some measure forced into this warmth, by the exulting air which I assumed; for, when he began, he said, "Since you *will* drive the nail!"—He again thought of good Mr. M'Queen, and, taking him by the hand, said, "Sir, I did not mean any disrespect to you."

Here I must observe, that he conquered by deserting his ground, and not meeting the argument as I had put it. The assiduity of the Scottish clergy is certainly greater than that of the English. His taking up the topick of their not having so much learning, was, though ingenious, yet a fallacy in logick. It was as if there should be a dispute whether a man's hair is well dressed, and Dr. Johnson should say, "Sir, his hair cannot be well dressed; for he has a dirty shirt. No man who has not clean linen has his hair well dressed."—When some days afterwards he read this passage, he said,

[1] This was a dexterous mode of description, for the purpose of his argument; for what he alluded to was, a Sermon published by the learned Dr. William Wishart, formerly principal of the college at Edinburgh, to warn men *against* confiding in a death-bed *repentance*, of the inefficacy of which he entertained notions very different from those of Dr. Johnson.

"No, sir; I did not say that a man's hair could not be well dressed because he has not clean linen, but because he is bald."

Johnson a foxhunter

He used one argument against the Scottish clergy being learned, which I doubt was not good. "As we believe a man dead till we know that he is alive; so we believe men ignorant till we know that they are learned." Now our maxim in law is, to presume a man alive, till we know he is dead. However, indeed, it may be answered, that we must first know he has lived; and that we have never known the learning of the Scottish clergy. Mr. M'Queen, though he was of opinion that Dr. Johnson had deserted the point really in dispute, was much pleased with what he said, and owned to me, he thought it very just; and Mrs. M'Leod was so much captivated by his eloquence, that she told me "I was a good advocate for a bad cause."

Friday, 24th September.

This was a good day. Dr. Johnson told us, at breakfast, that he rode harder at a fox chace than any body. "The English (said he) are the only nation who ride hard a-hunting. A Frenchman goes out upon a managed horse, and capers in the field, and no more thinks of leaping a hedge than of mounting a breach. Lord Powerscourt laid a wager, in France, that he would ride a great many miles in a certain short time. The French academicians set to work, and calculated that, from the resistance of the air, it was impossible. His lordship however performed it."

Our money being nearly exhausted, we sent a bill for thirty pounds, drawn on Sir William Forbes and Co. to Lochbraccadale, but our messenger found it very difficult to procure cash for it; at length, how-

ever, he got us value from the master of a vessel which
was to carry away some emigrants. There is a great
scarcity of specie in Sky. Mr. M'Queen said he had
the utmost difficulty to pay his servants' wages, or to
pay for any little thing which he has to buy. The
rents are paid in bills, which the drovers give. The
people consume a vast deal of snuff and tobacco, for
which they must pay ready money; and pedlers, who
come about selling goods, as there is not a shop in the
island, carry away the cash. If there were encourage-
ment given to fisheries and manufactures, there might
be a circulation of money introduced. I got one-and-
twenty shillings in silver at Portree, which was thought
a wonderful store.

Talisker, Mr. M'Queen, and I, walked out, and
looked at no less than fifteen different waterfalls
near the house, in the space of about a quarter of a
mile. We also saw Cuchillin's well, said to have been
the favourite spring of that ancient hero. I drank of
it. The water is admirable. On the shore are many
stones full of crystallizations in the heart.

Though our obliging friend, Mr. M'Lean, was but
the young laird, he had the title of Col constantly given
him. After dinner he and I walked to the top of
Prieshwell, a very high rocky hill, from whence there
is a view of Barra,—the Long Island,—Bernera,—the
Loch of Dunvegan,—part of Rum—part of Rasay,
and a vast deal of the isle of Sky. Col, though he
had come into Sky with an intention to be at Dunvegan, and pass a considerable time in the island, most
politely resolved first to conduct us to Mull, and then
to return to Sky. This was a very fortunate circumstance; for he planned an expedition for us of more
variety than merely going to Mull. He proposed we
should see the islands of Egg, Muck, Col, and Tyr-yi.

In all these islands he could shew us every thing worth **Men of** seeing; and in Mull he said he should be as if at home, **anecdote** his father having lands there, and he a farm.

Dr. Johnson did not talk much to-day, but seemed intent in listening to the schemes of future excursion, planned by Col. Dr. Birch, however, being mentioned, he said, he had more anecdotes than any man. I said, Percy had a great many; that he flowed with them like one of the brooks here.—JOHNSON. "If Percy is like one of the brooks here, Birch was like the river Thames. Birch excelled Percy in that, as much as Percy excels Goldsmith."—I mentioned Lord Hailes as a man of anecdote. He was not pleased with him, for publishing only such memorials and letters as were unfavourable for the Stuart family. "If, (said he,) a man fairly warns you, ' I am to give all the ill; do you find the good;' he may: but if the object which he professes be to give a view of a reign, let him tell all the truth. I would tell truth of the two Georges, or of that scoundrel, king William.—Granger's Biographical History is full of curious anecdote, but might have been better done. The dog is a Whig. I do not like much to see a Whig in any dress; but I hate to see a Whig in a parson's gown."

Saturday, 25th September.

It was resolved that we should set out, in order to return to Slate, to be in readiness to take boat whenever there should be a fair wind. Dr. Johnson remained in his chamber writing a letter, and it was long before we could get him into motion. He did not come to breakfast, but had it sent to him. When he had finished his letter, it was twelve o'clock, and we should

have set out at ten.   When I went up to him, he
said to me, "Do you remember a song which begins,

> " ' Every island is a prison
>   Strongly guarded by the sea ;
>   Kings and princes, for that reason,
>   Prisoners are, as well as we.' "

I suppose he had been thinking of our confined situation.   He would fain have gone in a boat from hence,
instead of riding back to Slate.   A scheme for it was
proposed.   He said, "We'll not be driven tamely
from it : "—but it proved impracticable.

We took leave of M'Leod and Talisker, from whom
we parted with regret.   Talisker, having been bred to
physick, had a tincture of scholarship in his conversation, which pleased Dr. Johnson, and he had some
very good books ; and being a colonel in the Dutch
service, he and his lady, in consequence of having
lived abroad, had introduced the ease and politeness of
the continent into this rude region.

Young Col was now our leader.   Mr. M'Queen
was to accompany us half a day more.   We stopped
at a little hut, where we saw an old woman grinding
with the *quern*, the ancient Highland instrument,
which it is said was used by the Romans, but which,
being very slow in its operation, is almost entirely gone
into disuse.

The walls of the cottages in Sky, instead of being
one compacted mass of stones, are often formed by
two exterior surfaces of stone, filled up with earth
in the middle, which makes them very warm.   The
roof is generally bad.   They are thatched, sometimes
with straw, sometimes with heath, sometimes with fern.
The thatch is secured by ropes of straw, or of heath ;
and, to fix the ropes, there is a stone tied to the end of

each. These stones hang round the bottom of the roof, and make it look like a lady's hair in papers; but I should think that, when there is wind, they would come down, and knock people on the head.

We dined at the inn at Sconser, where I had the pleasure to find a letter from my wife. Here we parted from our learned companion, Mr. Donald M'Queen. Dr. Johnson took leave of him very affectionately, saying, "Dear sir, do not forget me! "—We settled, that he should write an account of the Isle of Sky, which Dr. Johnson promised to revise. He said, Mr. M'Queen should tell all that he could; distinguishing what he himself knew, what was traditional, and what conjectural.

We sent our horses round a point of land, that we might shun some very bad road; and resolved to go forward by sea. It was seven o'clock when we got into our boat. We had many showers, and it soon grew pretty dark. Dr. Johnson sat silent and patient. Once he said, as he looked on the black coast of Sky, —black, as being composed of rocks seen in the dusk, —"This is very solemn." Our boatmen were rude singers, and seemed so like wild Indians, that a very little imagination was necessary to give one an impression of being upon an American river. We landed at Strolimus, from whence we got a guide to walk before us, for two miles, to Corrichatachin. Not being able to procure a horse for our baggage, I took one portmanteau before me, and Joseph another. We had but a single star to light us on our way. It was about eleven when we arrived. We were most hospitably received by the master and mistress, who were just going to bed, but, with unaffected ready kindness, made a good fire, and at twelve o'clock at night had supper on the table.

James Macdonald, of Knockow, Kingsburgh's brother, whom we had seen at Kingsburgh, was there. He shewed me a bond granted by the late Sir James Macdonald, to old Kingsburgh, the preamble of which does so much honour to the feelings of that much-lamented gentleman, that I thought it worth transcribing. It was as follows :

" I, Sir James Macdonald, of Macdonald, Baronet, now, after arriving at my perfect age, from the friendship I bear to Alexander Macdonald of Kingsburgh, and in return for the long and faithful services done and performed by him to my deceased father, and to myself during my minority, when he was one of my Tutors and Curators; being resolved, now that the said Alexander Macdonald is advanced in years, to contribute my endeavours for making his old age placid and comfortable,"—therefore he grants him an annuity of fifty pounds sterling.

Dr. Johnson went to bed soon. When one bowl of punch was finished, I rose, and was near the door, in my way up stairs to bed; but Corrichatachin said, it was the first time Col had been in his house, and he should have his bowl;—and would not I join in drinking it? The heartiness of my honest landlord, and the desire of doing social honour to our very obliging conductor, induced me to sit down again. Col's bowl was finished; and by that time we were well warmed. A third bowl was soon made, and that too was finished. We were cordial, and merry to a high degree; but of what passed I have no recollection, with any accuracy. I remember calling Corrichatachin by the familiar appellation of Corri, which his friends do. A fourth bowl was made, by which time Col, and young M'Kinnon, Corrichatachin's son, slipped away to bed.

I continued a little with *Corri* and *Knockow*; but at last I left them. It was near five in the morning when I got to bed.

Sunday, 26th September.

I awaked at noon, with a severe head-ach. I was much vexed that I should have been guilty of such a riot, and afraid of a reproof from Dr. Johnson. I thought it very inconsistent with that conduct which I ought to maintain, while the companion of the Rambler. About one he came into my room, and accosted me, " What, drunk yet ? " — His tone of voice was not that of severe upbraiding; so I was relieved a little.—" Sir, (said I), they kept me up." —He answered, " No, you kept them up, you drunken dog : "—This he said with good-humoured *English* pleasantry. Soon afterwards, Corrichatachin, Col, and other friends assembled round my bed. *Corri* had a brandy-bottle and glass with him, and insisted I should take a dram.—" Ay, (said Dr. Johnson), fill him drunk again. Do it in the morning, that we may laugh at him all day. It is a poor thing for a fellow to get drunk at night, and sculk to bed, and let his friends have no sport."—Finding him thus jocular, I became quite easy ; and when I offered to get up, he very good-naturedly said, " You need be in no such hurry now." [1]—I took my host's advice, and drank

[1] My ingenuously relating this occasional instance of intemperance has I find been made the subject both of serious criticism and ludicrous banter. With the banterers I shall not trouble myself, but I wonder that those who pretend to the appellation of serious criticks should not have had sagacity enough to perceive that here, as in every other part of the present work, my principal object was to delineate Dr. Johnson's manners and character. In justice to

A Jaco-
bite song

some brandy, which I found an effectual cure for my head-ach. When I rose, I went into Dr. Johnson's room, and taking up Mrs. M'Kinnon's Prayer-book, I opened it at the twentieth Sunday after Trinity, in the epistle for which I read, " And be not drunk with wine, wherein there is excess." Some would have taken this as a divine interposition.

Mrs. M'Kinnon told us at dinner, that old Kingsburgh, her father, was examined at Mugstot, by General Campbell, as to the particulars of the dress of the person who had come to his house in woman's clothes, along with Miss Flora M'Donald; as the General had received intelligence of that disguise. The particulars were taken down in writing, that it might be seen how far they agreed with the dress of the *Irish girl* who went with Miss Flora from the Long Island. Kingsburgh, she said, had but one song, which he always sung when he was merry over a glass. She dictated the words to me, which are foolish enough:

> Green sleeves and pudding pies,
> Tell me where my mistress lies,
> And I'll be with her before she rise,
> Fiddle and aw' together.

---

him I would not omit an anecdote, which, though in some degree to my own disadvantage, exhibits in so strong a light the indulgence and good humour with which he could treat those excesses in his friends, of which he highly disapproved.

In some other instances, the criticks have been equally wrong as to the true motive of my recording particulars, the objections to which I saw as clearly as they. But it would be an endless task for an authour to point out upon every occasion the precise object he has in view. Contenting himself with the approbation of readers of discernment and taste, he ought not to complain that some are found who cannot or will not understand him.

May our affairs abroad succeed,
And may our king come home with speed,
And all pretenders shake for dread,
And let *his* health go round.

Lady
Margaret
M'Donald

To all our injured friends in need,
This side and beyond the Tweed!——
Let all pretenders shake for dread,
And let *his* health go round.
     Green sleeves, &c.

While the examination was going on, the present
Talisker, who was there as one of M'Leod's militia,
could not resist the pleasantry of asking Kingsburgh,
in allusion to his only song, "Had she green sleeves?"
Kingsburgh gave him no answer. Lady Margaret
M'Donald was very angry at Talisker for joking on
such a serious occasion, as Kingsburgh was really in
danger of his life.——Mrs. M'Kinnon added that Lady
Margaret was quite adored in Sky. That when she
travelled through the island, the people ran in crowds
before her, and took the stones off the road, lest her
horse should stumble and she be hurt. Her husband,
Sir Alexander, is also remembered with great regard.
We were told that every week a hogshead of claret
was drunk at his table.

This was another day of wind and rain; but good
cheer and good society helped to beguile the time.
I felt myself comfortable enough in the afternoon.
I then thought that my last night's riot was no more
than such a social excess as may happen without much
moral blame; and recollected that some physicians maintained, that a fever produced by it was, upon the whole,
good for health : so different are our reflections on the
same subject, at different periods ; and such the excuses
with which we palliate what we know to be wrong.

Johnson's
convivi-
ality

Monday, 27th September.

Mr. Donald M'Leod, our original guide, who had
parted from us at Dunvegan, joined us again to-day.
The weather was still so bad that we could not travel.
I found a closet here, with a good many books, beside
those that were lying about. Dr. Johnson told me, he
found a library in his room at Talisker; and observed,
that it was one of the remarkable things of Sky, that
there were so many books in it.

Though we had here great abundance of provisions,
it is remarkable that Corrichatachin has literally no
garden: not even a turnip, a carrot or a cabbage.—
After dinner, we talked of the crooked spade used in
Sky, already described, and they maintained that it was
better than the usual garden-spade, and that there was
an art in tossing it, by which those who were accustomed
to it could work very easily with it.—"Nay, (said Dr.
Johnson,) it may be useful in land where there are many
stones to raise; but it certainly is not a good instrument
for digging good land. A man may toss it, to be sure;
but he will toss a light spade much better: its weight
makes it an incumbrance. A man *may* dig any land
with it; but he has no occasion for such a weight in
digging good land. You may take a field piece to shoot
sparrows; but all the sparrows you can bring home will
not be worth the charge."—He was quite social and
easy amongst them; and, though he drank no fermented
liquor, toasted Highland beauties with great readiness.
His conviviality engaged them so much, that they
seemed eager to shew their attention to him, and vied
with each other in crying out, with a strong Celtick
pronunciation, "Toctor Shonson, Toctor Shonson,
your health!"

This evening one of our married ladies, a lively *at Corri-* pretty little woman, good-humouredly sat down upon *chatachin* Dr. Johnson's knee, and, being encouraged by some of the company, put her hands round his neck, and kissed him.—" Do it again, (said he,) and let us see who will tire first."—He kept her on his knee some time, while he and she drank tea. He was now like a *buck* indeed. All the company were much entertained to find him so easy and pleasant. To me it was highly comick, to see the grave philosopher,—the Rambler,— toying with a Highland beauty!—But what could he do ? He must have been surly, and weak too, had he not behaved as he did. He would have been laughed at, and not more respected, though less loved.

He read to-night, to himself, as he sat in company, a great deal of my Journal, and said to me, " The more I read of this, I think the more highly of you."—The gentlemen sat a long time at their punch, after he and I had retired to our chambers. The manner in which they were attended struck me as singular :—The bell being broken, a smart lad lay on a table in the corner of the room, ready to spring up and bring the kettle, whenever it was wanted. They continued drinking, and singing Erse songs, till near five in the morning, when they all came into my room, where some of them had beds. Unluckily for me, they found a bottle of punch in a corner, which they drank ; and Corricha- tachin went for another, which they also drank. They made many apologies for disturbing me. I told them, that, having been kept awake by their mirth, I had once thoughts of getting up, and joining them again. Honest Corrichatachin said, " To have had you done so, I would have given a cow."

Tuesday, 28th September.

The weather was worse than yesterday. I felt as if imprisoned. Dr. Johnson said, it was irksome to be detained thus : yet he seemed to have less uneasiness, or more patience, than I had. What made our situation worse here was, that we had no rooms that we could command ; for the good people had no notion that a man could have any occasion but for a mere sleeping-place ; so, during the day, the bed chambers were common to all the house. Servants eat in Dr. Johnson's ; and mine was a kind of general rendezvous of all under the roof, children and dogs not excepted. As the gentlemen occupied the parlour, the ladies had no place to sit in, during the day, but Dr. Johnson's room. I had always some quiet time for writing in it, before he was up ; and, by degrees, I accustomed the ladies to let me sit in it after breakfast, at my Journal, without minding me.

Dr. Johnson was this morning for going to see as many islands as we could ; not recollecting the uncertainty of the season, which might detain us in one place for many weeks. He said to me, "I have more the spirit of adventure than you."—For my part, I was anxious to get to Mull, from whence we might almost any day reach the main land.

Dr. Johnson mentioned, that the few ancient Irish gentlemen yet remaining have the highest pride of family ; that Mr. Sandford, a friend of his, whose mother was Irish, told him, that O'Hara (who was true Irish, both by father and mother) and he, and Mr. Ponsonby, son to the Earl of Besborough, the greatest man of the three, but of an English family, went to see one of those ancient Irish, and that he distinguished

them thus : " O'Hara, you are welcome ! Mr. Sand- *Thresh-*
ford, your mother's son is welcome ! Mr. Ponsonby, *ing and*
you may sit down." *thatching*

He talked both of threshing and thatching. He
said, it was very difficult to determine how to agree
with a thresher. " If you pay him by the day's
wages, he will thresh no more than he pleases ; though,
to be sure, the negligence of a thresher is more easily
detected than that of most labourers, because he must
always make a sound while he works. If you pay
him by the piece, by the quantity of grain which he
produces, he will thresh only while the grain comes
freely, and, though he leaves a good deal in the ear, it
is not worth while to thresh the straw over again ; nor
can you fix him to do it sufficiently, because it is so
difficult to prove how much less a man threshes than
he ought to do. Here then is a dilemma : but, for
my part, I would engage him by the day ; I would
rather trust his idleness than his fraud." He said,
a roof thatched with Lincolnshire reeds would last
seventy years, as he was informed when in that county ;
and that he told this in London to a great thatcher,
who said, he believed it might be true.——Such are the
pains that Dr. Johnson takes to get the best information
on every subject.

He proceeded : " It is difficult for a farmer in England to find day-labourers, because the lowest manu-
facturers can always get more than a day-labourer. It
is of no consequence how high the wages of manu-
facturers are ; but it would be of very bad consequence
to raise the wages of those who procure the immediate
necessaries of life, for that would raise the price of
provisions. Here then is a problem for politicians. It
is not reasonable that the most useful body of men
should be the worst paid ; yet it does not appear how

Depar-
ture from
Corri-
chatachin
it can be ordered otherwise. It were to be wished, that
a mode for its being otherwise were found out. In the
mean time, it is better to give temporary assistance by
charitable contributions to poor labourers, at times when
provisions are high, than to raise their wages ; because, if
wages are once raised, they will never get down again."

Happily the weather cleared up between one and
two o'clock, and we got ready to depart ; but our kind
host and hostess would not let us go without taking a
snatch, as they called it ; which was in truth a very
good dinner. While the punch went round, Dr. Johnson kept a close whispering conference with Mrs.
M'Kinnon, which, however, was loud enough to let
us hear that the subject of it was the particulars of
Prince Charles's escape. The company were entertained and pleased to observe it. Upon that subject,
there was something congenial between the soul of Dr.
Samuel Johnson, and that of an isle of Sky farmer's wife.
It is curious to see people, how far soever removed
from each other in the general system of their lives,
come close together on a particular point which is
common to each. We were merry with Corrichatachin, on Dr. Johnson's whispering with his wife. She,
perceiving this, humourously cried, " I am in love with
him. What is it to live and not to love ? " Upon
her saying something, which I did not hear, or cannot
recollect, he seized her hand eagerly, and kissed it.

As we were going, the Scottish phrase of " *honest
man !* " which is an expression of kindness and regard,
was again and again applied by the company to Dr.
Johnson. I was also treated with much civility ; and
I must take some merit from my assiduous attention to
him, and from my contriving that he shall be easy
wherever he goes, that he shall not be asked twice to
eat or drink any thing, (which always disgusts him)

that he shall be provided with water at his meals, and many such little things, which, if not attended to would fret him. I also may be allowed to claim some merit in leading the conversation : I do not mean leading, as in an orchestra, by playing the first fiddle ; but leading as one does in examining a witness,—starting topics, and making him pursue them. He appears to me like a great mill, into which a subject is thrown to be ground. It requires, indeed, fertile minds to furnish materials for this mill. I regret whenever I see it unemployed ; but sometimes I feel myself quite barren, and having nothing to throw in.—I know not if this mill be a good figure ; though Pope makes his mind a mill for turning verses.

We set out about four. Young Corrichatachin went with us. We had a fine evening, and arrived in good time at Ostig, the residence of Mr. Martin M'Pherson, minister of Slate. It is a pretty good house, built by his father, upon a farm near the church. We were received here with much kindness by Mr. and Mrs. M'Pherson, and his sister, Miss M'Pherson, who pleased Dr. Johnson much, by singing Erse songs, and playing on the guittar. He afterwards sent her a present of his *Rasselas*. In his bed-chamber was a press stored with books, Greek, Latin, French, and English, most of which had belonged to the father of our host, the learned Dr. M'Pherson ; who, though his *Dissertations* have been mentioned in a former page as unsatisfactory, was a man of distinguished talents. Dr. Johnson looked at a Latin paraphrase of the song of Moses, written by him, and published in the *Scots Magazine* for 1747, and said, " It does him honour ; he has a great deal of Latin, and good Latin."— Dr. M'Pherson published also in the same magazine, June 1739, an original Latin ode, which he wrote from the isle of Barra, where he was minister for some years. It is very poetical, and exhibits a striking proof how much all things depend upon comparison: for Barra, it seems, appeared to him so much worse than Sky, his *natale solum*, that he languished for its "blessed mountains," and thought himself buried alive amongst barbarians where he was.—My readers will probably not be displeased to have a specimen of this ode:

"Hei mihi! quantos patior dolores,
Dum procul specto juga ter beata;
Dum feræ Barræ steriles arenas
Solus oberro.

Ingemo, indignor, crucior, quod inter
Barbaros Thulen lateam colentes;
Torpeo languens, morior sepultus,
Carcere cœco."

After wishing for wings to fly over to his dear country, which was in his view, from what he calls *Thule*, as being the most western isle of Scotland, except St. Kilda; after describing the pleasures of society, and the miseries of solitude, he at last, with becoming propriety, has recourse to the only sure relief of thinking men,—*Sursum corda*,—the hope of a better world, and disposes his mind to resignation:

"Interim fiat, tua, rex, voluntas:
Erigor sursum quoties subit spes
Certa migrandi Solymam supernam,
Numinis aulam."

He concludes in a noble strain of orthodox piety:

"Vita tum demum vocitanda vita est.
Tum licet gratos socios habere,
Seraphim et sanctos TRIADEM verendam
Concelebrantes."

Wednesday, 29th September.

After a very good sleep, I rose more refreshed than I had been for some nights. We were now at but a little distance from the shore, and saw the sea from our windows, which made our voyage seem nearer. Mr. M'Pherson's manners and address pleased us much. He appeared to be a man of such intelligence and taste as to be sensible of the extraordinary powers of his illustrious guest. He said to me, "Dr. Johnson is an honour to mankind; and, if the expression may be used, is an honour to religion."

Col, who had gone yesterday to pay a visit at Camus-cross, joined us this morning at breakfast. Some other gentlemen also came to enjoy the entertainment of Dr. Johnson's conversation.—The day was windy and rainy, so that we had just seized a happy interval for our journey last night. We had good entertainment here, better accommodation than at Corrichatachin, and time enough to ourselves. The hours slipped along imperceptibly. We talked of Shenstone. Dr. Johnson said, he was a good layer-out of land, but would not allow him to approach excellence as a poet. He said, he believed he had tried to read all his Love Pastorals, but did not get through them. I repeated the stanza,

> She gazed as I slowly withdrew;
>   My path I could hardly discern;
> So sweetly she bade me adieu,
>   I thought that she bade me return.

He said, "That seems to be pretty." I observed that Shenstone, from his short maxims in prose, appeared to have some power of thinking; but Dr. Johnson would not allow him that merit. He agreed, however, with

K 387

Night-
caps
Shenstone, that it was wrong in the brother of one of his correspondents to burn his letters; "for, (said he,) Shenstone was a man whose correspondence was an honour."—He was this afternoon full of critical severity, and dealt about his censures on all sides. He said, Hammond's Love Elegies were poor things. He spoke contemptuously of our lively and elegant, though too licentious, Lyrick bard, Hanbury Williams, and said, "he had no fame, but from boys who drank with him."

While he was in this mood, I was unfortunate enough, simply perhaps, but I could not help thinking, undeservedly, to come within "the whiff and wind of his fell sword." I asked him, if he had ever been accustomed to wear a night-cap. He said "No." I asked, if it was best not to wear one.—JOHNSON. "Sir, I had this custom by chance, and perhaps no man shall ever know whether it is best to sleep with or without a night-cap."—Soon afterwards he was laughing at some deficiency in the Highlands, and said, "One might as well go without shoes and stockings."—Thinking to have a little hit at his own deficiency, I ventured to add,—"or without a night-cap, sir." But I had better have been silent; for he retorted directly. "I do not see the connection there (laughing). Nobody before was ever foolish enough to ask whether it was best to wear a night-cap or not. This comes of being a little wrong-headed."—He carried the company along with him: and yet the truth is, that if he had always worn a night-cap, as is the common practice, and found the Highlanders did not wear one, he would have wondered at their barbarity; so that my hit was fair enough.

Thursday, 30th September.

There was as great a storm of wind and rain as I have almost ever seen, which necessarily confined us to the house; but we were fully compensated by Dr. Johnson's conversation. He said, he did not grudge Burke's being the first man in the House of Commons, for he was the first man every where; but he grudged that a fellow who makes no figure in company, and has a mind as narrow as the neck of a vinegar cruet, should make a figure in the House of Commons, merely by having the knowledge of a few forms, and being furnished with a little occasional information.[1]   He told us, the first time he saw Dr. Young was at the house of Mr. Richardson, the author of *Clarissa.*   He was sent for, that the doctor might read to him his *Conjectures on original Composition,* which he did, and Dr. Johnson made his remarks; and he was surprized to find Young receive as novelties, what he thought very common maxims. He said, he believed Young was not a great scholar, nor had studied regularly the art of writing; that there were very fine things in his *Night Thoughts,* though you could not find twenty lines together without some extravagance. He repeated two passages from his *Love of Fame,*—the characters of Brunetta and Stella, which he praised highly. He said Young pressed him much to come to Wellwyn. He always intended it, but never went. He was sorry when Young died. The cause of quarrel between Young and his son, he told us, was, that his son insisted Young should turn away a clergyman's widow, who

---

[1] He did not mention the name of any particular person; but those who are conversant with the political world will probably recollect more persons than one to whom this observation may be applied.

lived with him, and who, having acquired great influence over the father, was saucy to the son. Dr. Johnson said, she could not conceal her resentment at him, for saying to Young, that "an old man should not resign himself to the management of any body."—I asked him, if there was any improper connection between them.—"No, sir, no more than between two statues. —He was past fourscore, and she a very coarse woman. She read to him, and, I suppose, made his coffee, and frothed his chocolate, and did such things as an old man wishes to have done for him."

Dr. Doddridge being mentioned, he observed that "he was the author of one of the finest epigrams in the English language. It is in Orton's Life of him. The subject is his family-motto,—*Dum vivimus, vivamus*; which, in its primary signification, is, to be sure, not very suitable to a Christian divine; but he paraphrased it thus:

‘ Live, while you live, the *epicure* would say,
And seize the pleasures of the present day.
Live, while you live, the sacred *preacher* cries,
And give to God each moment as it flies.
Lord, in my views let both united be;
I live in *pleasure*, when I live to *thee.*’ ”

I asked if it was not strange that government should permit so many infidel writings to pass without censure. —Johnson. "Sir, it is mighty foolish. It is for want of knowing their own power. The present family on the throne came to the crown against the will of nine tenths of the people. Whether those nine tenths were right or wrong, it is not our business now to inquire. But such being the situation of the royal family, they were glad to encourage all who would be their friends. Now you know every bad man is a Whig; every man who has loose notions. The church was all against this family. They were, as I say, glad to encourage any friends; and therefore, since their accession, there is no instance of any man being kept back on account of his bad principles; and hence this inundation of impiety." I observed that Mr. Hume, some of whose writings were very unfavourable to religion, was, however, a Tory.—JOHNSON. "Sir, Hume is a Tory by chance, as being a Scotchman; but not upon a principle of duty; for he has no principle. If he is any thing, he is a Hobbist."

There was something not quite serene in his humour to-night, after supper; for he spoke of hastening away to London, without stopping much at Edinburgh. I reminded him, that he had General Oughton and many others to see.—JOHNSON. "Nay, I shall neither go in jest, nor stay in jest. I shall do what is fit."— BOSWELL. "Ay, sir, but all I desire is, that you will let me tell you when it is fit."—JOHNSON. "Sir, I shall not consult you."—BOSWELL. "If you are to run away from us, as soon as you get loose, we will keep you confined in an island."—He was, however, on the whole, very good company. Mr. Donald M'Leod expressed very well the gradual impression made by Dr. Johnson on those who are so fortunate as to obtain his acquaintance. "When you see him first, you are struck with awful reverence;—then you admire him;— and then you love him cordially."

I read this evening some part of Voltaire's History of the War in 1741, and of Lord Kames against Hereditary Indefeasible Right. This is a very slight circumstance, with which I should not trouble my reader, but for the sake of observing, that every man should keep minutes of whatever he reads. Every circumstance of his studies should be recorded; what

The advantage to authors books he has consulted; how much of them he has read; at what times; how often the same authors; and what opinions he formed of them, at different periods of his life.—Such an account would much illustrate the history of his mind.

Friday, 1st October.

I shewed to Dr. Johnson verses in a magazine, on his Dictionary, composed of uncommon words taken from it :

"Little of *Anthropopathy* has he," &c.

He read a few of them, and said, "I am not answerable for all the words in my Dictionary."—I told him, that Garrick kept a book of all who had either praised, or abused him.—On the subject of his own reputation, he said, "Now that I see it has been so current a topick, I wish I had done so too; but it could not well be done now, as so many things are scattered in news-papers."—He said he was angry at a boy of Oxford, who wrote in his defence against Kenrick; because it was doing him hurt to answer Kenrick. He was told afterwards, the boy was to come to him to ask a favour. He first thought to treat him rudely, on account of his meddling in that business; but then he considered, he had meant to do him all the service in his power, and he took another resolution; he told him he would do what he could for him, and did so; and the boy was satisfied. He said, he did not know how his pamphlet was done, as he had read very little of it. The boy made a good figure at Oxford, but died. He remarked, that attacks on authors did them much service. "A man who tells me my play is very bad, is less my enemy than he who lets it die in silence. A man, whose business it **of being** is to be talked of, is much helped by being attacked." **attacked** —Garrick, I observed, had been often so helped.— Johnson. " Yes, sir; though Garrick had more opportunities than almost any man, to keep the publick in mind of him, by exhibiting himself to such numbers, he would not have had so much reputation, had he not been so much attacked. Every attack produces a defence; and so attention is engaged. There is no sport in mere praise, when people are all of a mind." —Boswell. " Then Hume is not the worse for Beattie's attack?"—Johnson. " He is, because Beattie has confuted him. I do not say, but that there may be some attacks which will hurt an author. Though Hume suffered from Beattie, he was the better for other attacks." (He certainly could not include in that number those of Dr. Adams, and Mr. Tytler.) —Boswell. " Goldsmith is the better for attacks." —Johnson. " Yes, sir; but he does not think so yet. When Goldsmith and I published, each of us something, at the same time, we were given to understand that we might review each other. Goldsmith was for accepting the offer. I said, No; set Reviewers at defiance.—It was said to old Bentley, upon the attacks against him, 'Why, they'll write you down.' 'No, sir,' he replied; 'depend upon it, no man was ever written down but by himself.'" He observed to me afterwards, that the advantages authours derived from attacks, were chiefly in subjects of taste, where you cannot confute, as so much may be said on either side.—He told me he did not know who was the authour of the *Adventures of a Guinea*, but that the bookseller had sent the first volume to him in manuscript, to have his opinion if it should be printed; and he thought it should.

The learn-ing of manners The weather being now somewhat better, Mr. James M‘Donald, factor to Sir Alexander M‘Donald in Slate, insisted that all the company at Ostig should go to the house at Armidale, which Sir Alexander had left, having gone with his lady to Edinburgh, and be his guests, till we had an opportunity of sailing to Mull. We accordingly got there to dinner; and passed our day very cheerfully, being no less than fourteen in number.

Saturday, 2nd October.

Dr. Johnson said, that "a Chief and his Lady should make their house like a court. They should have a certain number of the gentlemen's daughters to receive their education in the family, to learn pastry and such things from the housekeeper, and manners from my lady. That was the way in the great families in Wales; at Lady Salisbury's, Mrs. Thrale's grand-mother's, and at Lady Philips's. I distinguish the families by the ladies, as I speak of what was properly their province. There were always six young ladies at Sir John Philips's: when one was married, her place was filled up. There was a large school-room, where they learnt needle-work and other things."—I observed, that, at some courts in Germany, there were academies for the pages, who are the sons of gentlemen, and receive their education without any expense to their parents. Dr. Johnson said, that manners were best learnt at those courts. "You are admitted with great facility to the prince's person, and yet must treat him with much respect. At a great court, you are at such a distance that you get no good."—I said, "Very true : a man sees the court of Versailles, as if he saw it on a theatre."—He said, "The best book that ever was written upon good breeding, *Il Corteggiano*, by

Castiglione, grew up at the little court of Urbino, and **Opinions** you should read it."—I am glad always to have his **on books** opinion of books. At Mr. M'Pherson's, he commended *Whitby's Commentary*, and said, he had heard him called rather lax ; but he did not perceive it. He had looked at a novel, called *The Man of the World*, at Rasay, but thought there was nothing in it. He said to-day, while reading my Journal, " This will be a great treasure to us some years hence."

Talking of a very penurious gentleman of our acquaintance, he observed, that he exceeded *L'Avare* in the play. I concurred with him, and remarked that he would do well, if introduced in one of Foote's farces ; that the best way to get it done, would be to bring Foote to be entertained at his house for a week, and then it would be *facit indignatio.*—JOHNSON. " Sir, I wish he had him. I, who have eaten his bread, will not give him to him ; but I should be glad he came honestly by him."

He said, he was angry at Thrale, for sitting at General Oglethorpe's without speaking. He censured a man for degrading himself to a non-entity. I observed, that Goldsmith was on the other extreme ; for he spoke at all ventures.—JOHNSON. " Yes, sir ; Goldsmith, rather than not speak, will talk of what he knows himself to be ignorant, which can only end in exposing him."—" I wonder, (said I,) if he feels that he exposes himself. If he was with two taylors "— " Or with two founders, (said Dr. Johnson, interrupting me,) he would fall a talking on the method of making cannon, though both of them would soon see that he did not know what metal a cannon is made of."—We were very social and merry in his room this forenoon. In the evening the company danced as usual. We performed, with much activity, a dance which, I

Emigra-
tion from
Sky

suppose, the emigration from Sky has occasioned. They call it *America*. Each of the couples, after the common *involutions* and *evolutions*, successively whirls round in a circle, till all are in motion; and the dance seems intended to shew how emigration catches, till a whole neighbourhood is set afloat.— Mrs. M'Kinnon told me, that last year when a ship sailed from Portree for America, the people on shore were almost distracted when they saw their relations go off; they lay down on the ground, tumbled, and tore the grass with their teeth.—This year there was not a tear shed. The people on shore seemed to think that they would soon follow. This indifference is a mortal sign for the country.

We danced to-night to the musick of the bagpipe, which made us beat the ground with prodigious force. I thought it better to endeavour to conciliate the kindness of the people of Sky, by joining heartily in their amusements, than to play the abstract scholar. I looked on this Tour to the Hebrides as a copartnership between Dr. Johnson and me. Each was to do all he could to promote its success; and I have some reason to flatter myself, that my gayer exertions were of service to us. Dr. Johnson's immense fund of knowledge and wit was a wonderful source of admiration and delight to them; but they had it only at times; and they required to have the intervals agreeably filled up, and even little elucidations of his learned text. I was also fortunate enough frequently to draw him forth to talk, when he would otherwise have been silent. The fountain was at times locked up, till I opened the spring.—It was curious to hear the Hebridians, when any dispute happened while he was out of the room, saying, "Stay till Dr. Johnson comes: say that to *him!*"

Yesterday Dr. Johnson said, " I cannot but laugh, to think of myself roving among the Hebrides at sixty. I wonder where I shall rove at fourscore ! "—This evening he disputed the truth of what is said, as to the people of St. Kilda catching cold whenever strangers come. " How can there (said he) be a physical effect without a physical cause ? "—He added, laughing, " the arrival of a ship full of strangers would kill them ; for, if one stranger gives them one cold, two strangers must give them two colds ; and so in proportion."—I wondered to hear him ridicule this, as he had praised M'Aulay for putting it in his book : saying, that it was manly in him to tell a fact, however strange, if he himself believed it. He said, the evidence was not adequate to the improbability of the thing ; that if a physician, rather disposed to be incredulous, should go to St. Kilda, and report the fact, then he would begin to look about him. They said, it was annually proved by M'Leod's steward, on whose arrival all the inhabitants caught cold. He jocularly remarked, " the steward always comes to demand something from them ; and so they fall a coughing. I suppose the people in Sky all take a cold, when ——— (naming a certain person) comes."—They said, he came only in summer.—JOHNSON. " That is out of tenderness to you. Bad weather and he, at the same time, would be too much."

Sunday, 3rd October.

Joseph reported that the wind was still against us. Dr. Johnson said, " A wind, or not a wind ? that is the question ; " for he can amuse himself at times with a little play of words, or rather sentences. I remember when he turned his cup at Aberbrothick, where we drank

The travellers leave Sky   tea, he muttered, *Claudite jam rivos, pueri.* I must again and again apologize to fastidious readers, for recording such minute particulars. They prove the scrupulous fidelity of my Journal. Dr. Johnson said it was a very exact picture of a portion of his life.

While we were chatting in the indolent stile of men who were to stay here all this day at least, we were suddenly roused at being told that the wind was fair, that a little fleet of herring-busses was passing by for Mull, and that Mr. Simpson's vessel was about to sail. Hugh M'Donald, the skipper, came to us, and was impatient that we should get ready, which we soon did. Dr. Johnson, with composure and solemnity, repeated the observation of Epictetus, that, "as man has the voyage of death before him,—whatever may be his employment, he should be ready at the master's call; and an old man should never be far from the shore, lest he should not be able to get himself ready." He rode, and I and the other gentlemen walked, about an English mile to the shore, where the vessel lay. Dr. Johnson said, he should never forget Sky, and returned thanks for all civilities. We were carried to the vessel in a small boat which she had, and we set sail very briskly about one o'clock. I was much pleased with the motion for many hours. Dr. Johnson grew sick, and retired under cover, as it rained a good deal. I kept above, that I might have fresh air, and finding myself not affected by the motion of the vessel, I exulted in being a stout seaman, while Dr. Johnson was quite in a state of annihilation. But I was soon humbled; for after imagining that I could go with ease to America or the East-Indies, I became very sick, but kept above board, though it rained hard.

As we had been detained so long in Sky by bad weather, we gave up the scheme that Col had planned

for us of visiting several islands, and contented our- A storm
selves with the prospect of seeing Mull, and Icolmkill off Ardna-
and Inchkenneth, which lie near to it. murchan

Mr. Simpson was sanguine in his hopes for awhile,
the wind being fair for us. He said, he would land
us at Icolmkill that night. But when the wind failed,
it was resolved we should make for the sound of Mull,
and land in the harbour of Tobermorie. We kept
near the five herring vessels for some time; but afterwards four of them got before us, and one little wherry
fell behind us. When we got in full view of the point
of Ardnamurchan, the wind changed, and was directly
against our getting into the sound. We were then
obliged to tack, and get forward in that tedious manner.
As we advanced, the storm grew greater, and the sea
very rough. Col then began to talk of making for
Egg, or Canna, or his own island. Our skipper said,
he would get us into the Sound. Having struggled
for this a good while in vain, he said, he would push
forward till we were near the land of Mull, where
we might cast anchor, and lie till the morning; for
although, before this, there had been a good moon, and
I had pretty distinctly seen not only the land of Mull,
but up the Sound, and the country of Morven as at one
end of it, the night was now grown very dark. Our
crew consisted of one M'Donald, our skipper, and two
sailors, one of whom had but one eye; Mr. Simpson
himself, Col, and Hugh M'Donald his servant, all
helped. Simpson said, he would willingly go for Col,
if young Col or his servant would undertake to pilot us
to a harbour; but, as the island is low land, it was
dangerous to run upon it in the dark. Col and his
servant appeared a little dubious. The scheme of
running for Canna seemed then to be embraced; but
Canna was ten leagues off, all out of our way; and

A dangerous voyage to Col

they were afraid to attempt the harbour of Egg. All these different plans were successively in agitation. The old skipper still tried to make for the land of Mull; but then it was considered that there was no place there where we could anchor in safety. Much time was lost in striving against the storm. At last it became so rough, and threatened to be so much worse, that Col and his servant took more courage, and said they would undertake to hit one of the harbours in Col. —" Then let us run for it in God's name," said the skipper; and instantly we turned towards it. The little wherry which had fallen behind us, had hard work. The master begged that, if we made for Col, we should put out a light to him. Accordingly one of the sailors waved a glowing peat for some time. The various difficulties that were started, gave me a good deal of apprehension, from which I was relieved, when I found we were to run for a harbour before the wind. But my relief was but of short duration; for I soon heard that our sails were very bad, and were in danger of being torn in pieces, in which case we should be driven upon the rocky shore of Col. It was very dark, and there was a heavy and incessant rain. The sparks of the burning peat flew so much about, that I dreaded the vessel might take fire. Then, as Col was a sportsman, and had powder on board, I figured that we might be blown up. Simpson and he appeared a little frightened, which made me more so; and the perpetual talking, or rather shouting, which was carried on in Erse, alarmed me still more. A man is always suspicious of what is saying in an unknown tongue; and, if fear be his passion at the time, he grows more afraid. Our vessel often lay so much on one side, that I trembled lest she should be overset, and indeed they told me afterwards, that they had run her sometimes

to within an inch of the water, so anxious were they
to make what haste they could before the night should
be worse.   I now saw what I never saw before, a
prodigious sea, with immense billows coming upon a
vessel, so as that it seemed hardly possible to escape.
There was something grandly horrible in the sight.   I
am glad I have seen it once.   Amidst all these terrifying circumstances, I endeavoured to compose my
mind.   It was not easy to do it; for all the stories
that I had heard of the dangerous sailing among the
Hebrides, which is proverbial, came full upon my recollection.   When I thought of those who were dearest
to me, and would suffer severely, should I be lost, I
upbraided myself, as not having a sufficient cause for
putting myself in such danger.   Piety afforded me
comfort; yet I was disturbed by the objections that
have been made against a particular providence, and by
the arguments of those who maintain that it is in vain
to hope that the petitions of an individual, or even of
congregations, can have any influence with the Deity;
objections which have been often made, and which Dr.
Hawkesworth has lately revived, in his Preface to the
Voyages to the South Seas; but Dr. Ogden's excellent
doctrine on the efficacy of intercession prevailed.

It was half an hour after eleven before we set ourselves in the course for Col.   As I saw them all busy
doing something, I asked Col, with much earnestness,
what I could do.   He, with a happy readiness, put
into my hand a rope, which was fixed to the top of one
of the masts, and told me to hold it till he bade me
pull.   If I had considered the matter, I might have
seen that this could not be of the least service; but his
object was to keep me out of the way of those who
were busy working the vessel, and at the same time to
divert my fear, by employing me, and making me think

that I was of use. Thus did I stand firm to my post,
while the wind and rain beat upon me, always expecting
a call to pull my rope.

The man with one eye steered; old M'Donald, and
Col and his servant, lay upon the fore-castle, looking
sharp out for the harbour. It was necessary to carry
much *cloth*, as they termed it, that is to say, much sail,
in order to keep the vessel off the shore of Col. This
made violent plunging in a rough sea. At last they
spied the harbour of Lochiern, and Col cried, "Thank
God, we are safe!" We ran up till we were opposite
to it, and soon afterwards we got into it, and cast
anchor.

Dr. Johnson had all this time been quiet and unconcerned. He had lain down on one of the beds, and
having got free from sickness, was satisfied. The
truth is, he knew nothing of the danger we were in;
but, fearless and unconcerned, might have said, in
the words which he has chosen for the motto to his
Rambler,

Quo me cunque rapit tempestas, deferor hospes. [1]

Once, during the doubtful consultations, he asked
whither we were going; and upon being told that it
was not certain whether to Mull or Col, he cried,
"Col for my money!"—I now went down, with Col
and Mr. Simpson, to visit him. He was lying in
philosophick tranquillity with a greyhound of Col's at
his back, keeping him warm. Col is quite the *Juvenis
qui gaudet canibus*. He had, when we left Talisker,
two greyhounds, two terriers, a pointer, and a large
Newfoundland water-dog. He lost one of his terriers
by the road, but had still five dogs with him. I was
very ill, and very desirous to get to shore. When I

[1] "For as the tempest drives, I shape my way."—FRANCIS.

was told that we could not land that night, as the storm
had now increased, I looked so miserably, as Col afterwards informed me, that what Shakspeare has made
the Frenchman say of the English soldiers, when scan-
tily dieted, " Piteous they will look, like drowned
mice! " might, I believe, have been well applied to
me.   There was in the harbour, before us, a Campbell-
town vessel, the *Betty*, Kenneth Morison master, taking
in kelp, and bound for Ireland.   We sent our boat to
beg beds for two gentlemen, and that the master would
send his boat, which was larger than ours.   He accordingly did so, and Col and I were accommodated
in his vessel till the morning.

The travellers land in Col

Monday, 4th October.

About eight o'clock we went in the boat to Mr.
Simpson's vessel, and took in Dr. Johnson.   He was
quite well, though he had tasted nothing but a dish of
tea since Saturday night.   On our expressing some
surprise at this, he said, that, " when he lodged in the
Temple, and had no regular system of life, he had
fasted for two days at a time, during which he had
gone about visiting, though not at the hours of dinner
or supper ; that he had drunk tea, but eaten no bread ;
that this was no intentional fasting, but happened just
in the course of a literary life."

There was a little miserable publick-house close
upon the shore, to which we should have gone, had
we landed last night : but this morning Col resolved
to take us directly to the house of Captain Lauchlan
M'Lean, a descendant of his family, who had acquired
a fortune in the East-Indies, and taken a farm in
Col.   We had about an English mile to go to it.   Col
and Joseph, and some others, ran to some little horses,

called here *Shelties*, that were running wild on a heath, and catched one of them. We had a saddle with us, which was clapped upon it, and a straw-halter was put on its head. Dr. Johnson was then mounted, and Joseph very slowly and gravely led the horse. I said to Dr. Johnson, "I wish, sir, *the club* saw you in this attitude." [1]

It was a very heavy rain, and I was wet to the skin. Captain M'Lean had but a poor temporary house, or rather hut; however, it was a very good haven to us. There was a blazing peat-fire, and Mrs. M'Lean, daughter of the minister of the parish, got us tea. I felt still the motion of the sea. Dr. Johnson said, it was not in imagination, but a continuation of motion on the fluids, like that of the sea itself after the storm is over.

There were some books on the board which served as a chimney-piece. Dr. Johnson took up Burnet's *History of his own Times.* He said, "The first part of it is one of the most entertaining books in the English language; it is quite dramatick: while he went about every where, saw every where, and heard every where. By the first part, I mean so far as it appears that Burnet himself was actually engaged in what he has told; and this may be easily distinguished." Captain M'Lean censured Burnet, for his high praise of Lauderdale in a dedication, when he shews him in his history to have been so bad a man.

---

[1] This curious exhibition may perhaps remind some of my readers of the ludicrous lines, made, during Sir Robert Walpole's administration, on Mr. George (afterwards Lord) Littelton, though the figures of the two personages must be allowed to be very different:

> "But who is this astride the pony;
>   So long, so lean, so lank, so bony?
>   Dat be de great orátor, Littletony."

—Johnson. "I do not myself think that a man
should say in a dedication what he could not say in a
history. However, allowance should be made; for
there is a great difference. The known style of a
dedication is flattery: it professes to flatter. There
is the same difference between what a man says in a
dedication, and what he says in a history, as between
a lawyer's pleading a cause, and reporting it."

The day passed away pleasantly enough. The
wind became fair for Mull in the evening, and Mr.
Simpson resolved to sail next morning: but having
been thrown into the island of Col, we were unwilling
to leave it unexamined, especially as we considered
that the Campbell-town vessel would sail for Mull in
a day or two, and therefore we determined to stay.

Tuesday, 5th October.

I rose, and wrote my Journal till about nine; and
then went to Dr. Johnson, who sat up in bed and
talked and laughed. I said, it was curious to look
back ten years, to the time when we first thought of
visiting the Hebrides. How distant and improbable
the scheme then appeared! Yet here we were
actually among them.—"Sir, (said he,) people may
come to do any thing almost, by talking of it. I
really believe, I could talk myself into building a
house upon island Isa, though I should probably never
come back again to see it. I could easily persuade
Reynolds to do it; and there would be no great sin in
persuading him to do it. Sir, he would reason thus:
'What will it cost me to be there once in two or three
summers?—Why, perhaps, five hundred pounds; and
what is that, in comparison of having a fine retreat,
to which a man can go, or to which he can send a

The minister of Col friend?' He would never find out that he may have this within twenty miles of London.—Then I would tell him, that he may marry one of the Miss M'Leods, a lady of great family.—Sir, it is surprising how people will go to a distance for what they may have at home. I knew a lady who came up from Lincoln-shire to Knightsbridge with one of her daughters and gave five guineas a week for a lodging and a warm bath; that is, mere warm water. That, you know, could not be had in Lincolnshire! She said, it was made either too hot or too cold there."

After breakfast, Dr. Johnson and I, and Joseph, mounted horses, and Col and the captain walked with us about a short mile across the island. We paid a visit to the Reverend Mr. Hector M'Lean. His parish consists of the islands of Col and Tyr-yi. He was about seventy-seven years of age, a decent eccle-siastick, dressed in a full suit of black clothes, and a black wig. He appeared like a Dutch pastor, or one of the assembly of divines at Westminster. Dr. Johnson observed to me afterwards, "that he was a fine old man, and was as well-dressed, and had as much dignity in his appearance as the dean of a cathedral." We were told, that he had a valuable library, though but poor accomodation for it, being obliged to keep his books in large chests. It was curious to see him and Dr. Johnson together. Neither of them heard very distinctly; so each of them talked in his own way, and at the same time. Mr. M'Lean said, he had a confutation of Bayle, by Leibnitz.—JOHNSON. "A confutation of Bayle, sir! What part of Bayle do you mean? The greatest part of his writings is not confutable: it is historical and critical."—Mr. M'Lean said, "the irreligious part;" and proceeded to talk of Leibnitz's controversy

with Clarke, calling Leibnitz a great man.—JOHNSON. **Leibnitz and Clarke**
"Why, sir, Leibnitz persisted in affirming that
Newton called space *sensorium numinis*, notwithstanding
he was corrected, and desired to observe that Newton's
words were QUASI *sensorium numinis*. No, sir ; Leibnitz was as paltry a fellow as I know. Out of respect
to Queen Caroline, who patronised him, Clarke treated
him too well."

During the time that Dr. Johnson was thus going
on, the old minister was standing with his back to the
fire, cresting up erect, pulling down the front of his
periwig, and talking what a great man Leibnitz
was. To give an idea of the scene, would require a
page with two columns ; but it ought rather to be represented by two good players. The old gentleman
said, Clarke was very wicked, for going so much into
the Arian system. "I will not say he was wicked,"
said Dr. Johnson ; "he might be mistaken."—
M'LEAN. "He was wicked, to shut his eyes against
the Scriptures ; and worthy men in England have
since confuted him to all intents and purposes."—
JOHNSON. "I know not *who* has confuted him to
all intents and *purposes*."—Here again there was a
double talking, each continuing to maintain his own
argument, without hearing exactly what the other said.

I regretted that Dr. Johnson did not practice the
art of accommodating himself to different sorts of
people. Had he been softer with this venerable old
man, we might have had more conversation ; but his
forcible spirit, and impetuosity of manner, may be said
to spare neither sex nor age. I have seen even Mrs.
Thrale stunned ; but I have often maintained, that it
is better he should retain his own manner. Pliability
of address I conceive to be inconsistent with that
majestick power of mind which he possesses, and which

Grissipol produces such noble effects. A lofty oak will not bend like a supple willow.

He told me afterwards, he liked firmness in an old man, and was pleased to see Mr. M'Lean so orthodox. " At his age, it is too late for a man to be asking himself questions as to his belief."

We rode to the northern part of the island, where we saw the ruins of a church or chapel. We then proceeded to a place called Grissipol, or the rough Pool.

At Grissipol we found a good farm house, belonging to the Laird of Col, and possessed by Mr. M'Sweyn. On the beach here there is a singular variety of curious stones. I picked up one very like a small cucumber. By the by, Dr. Johnson told me, that Gay's line in the *Beggar's Opera*, " As men should serve a cucumber," &c. has no waggish meaning, with reference to men flinging away cucumbers as too *cooling*, which some have thought; for it has been a common saying of physicians in England, that a cucumber should be well sliced, and dressed with pepper and vinegar, and then thrown out, as good for nothing.—Mr. M'Sweyn's predecessors had been in Sky from a very remote period, upon the estate belonging to M'Leod; probably before M'Leod had it. The name is certainly Norwegian, from *Sueno*, King of Norway. The present Mr. M'Sweyn left Sky upon the late M'Leod's raising his rents. He then got this farm from Col.

He appeared to be near fourscore; but looked as fresh, and was as strong as a man of fifty. His son Hugh looked older; and, as Dr. Johnson observed, had more the manners of an old man than he. I had often heard of such instances, but never saw one before. Mrs. M'Sweyn was a decent old gentlewoman. She was dressed in tartan, and could speak nothing but

Erse.   She said, she taught Sir James M'Donald Erse, *An*
and would teach me soon.   I could now sing a verse *ancient*
of the song *Hatyin foam'eri*, made in honour of Allan, *Highland*
the famous Captain of Clanranald, who fell at Sherrif- *custom*
muir ; whose servant, who lay on the field watching
his master's dead body, being asked next day who
that was, answered, " He was a man yesterday."

We were entertained here with a primitive heartiness.
Whisky was served round in a shell, according to the
ancient Highland custom.   Dr. Johnson would not
partake of it ; but, being desirous to do honour to the
modes " of other times," drank some water out of the
shell.

In the forenoon Dr. Johnson said, " it would require
great resignation to live in one of these islands."—
BOSWELL. " I don't know, sir ; I have felt myself at
times in a state of almost mere physical existence,
satisfied to eat, drink, and sleep, and walk about, and
enjoy my own thoughts ; and I can figure a continuation of this."—JOHNSON. " Ay, sir ; but if you were
shut up here, your own thoughts would torment you :
you would think of Edinburgh or London, and that
you could not be there."

We set out after dinner for Breacacha, the family
seat of the Laird of Col, accompanied by the young
laird, who had now got a horse, and by the younger
Mr. M'Sweyn, whose wife had gone thither before us,
to prepare every thing for our reception, the laird and
his family being absent at Aberdeen.   It is called
Breacacha, or the Spotted Field, because in summer
it is enamelled with clover and daisies, as young Col
told me.   We passed by a place where there is a very
large stone, I may call it a *rock* ;—" a vast weight for
Ajax."   The tradition is, that a giant threw such
another stone at his mistress, up to the top of a hill,

A sandy desert at a small distance; and that she in return, threw this mass down to him. It was all in sport.

Malo me petit lasciva puella.

As we advanced, we came to a large extent of plain ground. I had not seen such a place for a long time. Col and I took a gallop upon it by way of race. It was very refreshing to me, after having been so long taking short steps in hilly countries. It was like stretching a man's legs after being cramped in a short bed. We also passed close by a large extent of sand-hills, near two miles square. Dr. Johnson said, "he never had the image before. It was horrible, if barren-ness and danger could be so." I heard him, after we were in the house of Breacacha, repeating to himself, as he walked about the room,

"And smother'd in the dusty whirlwind, dies."

Probably he had been thinking of the whole of the simile in *Cato*, of which that is the concluding line; the sandy desert had struck him so strongly. The sand has of late been blown over a good deal of meadow; and the people of the island say, that their fathers remembered much of the space which is now covered with sand, to have been under tillage. Col's house is situated on a bay called Breacacha Bay. We found here a neat new-built gentleman's house, better than any we had been in since we were at Lord Errol's. Dr. Johnson relished it much at first, but soon re-marked to me, that "there was nothing becoming a Chief about it: it was a mere tradesman's box." He seemed quite at home, and no longer found any diffi-culty in using the Highland address; for, as soon as we arrived, he said, with a spirited familiarity, "Now, Col, if you could get us a dish of tea."——Dr. Johnson

and I had each an excellent bed-chamber. We had
a dispute which of us had the best curtains. His were
rather the best, being of linen; but I insisted that my
bed had the best posts, which was undeniable. "Well,
(said he,) if you *have* the best *posts*, we will have you
tied to them and whipped."—I mention this slight
circumstance, only to shew how ready he is, even in
mere trifles, to get the better of his antagonist, by
placing him in a ludicrous view. I have known him
sometimes use the same art, when hard pressed in serious
disputation. Goldsmith, I remember, to retaliate for
many a severe defeat which he has suffered from him,
applied to him a lively saying in one of Cibber's
comedies, which puts this part of his character in a
strong light.—"There is no arguing with Johnson;
for, *if his pistol misses fire, he knocks you down with the
but-end of it.*"

The old
castle of
Col

Wednesday, 6th October.

After a sufficiency of sleep, we assembled at breakfast. We were just as if in barracks. Every body
was master. We went and viewed the old castle of
Col, which is not far from the present house, near the
shore, and founded on a rock. It has never been a
larger feudal residence, and has nothing about it that
requires a particular description. Like other old inconvenient buildings of the same age, it exemplified
Gray's picturesque lines,

> "Huge windows that exclude the light,
> And passages that lead to nothing."

It may however be worth mentioning, that on the
second story we saw a vault, which was, and still is,
the family prison. There was a woman put into it by
the laird, for theft, within these ten years; and any

offender would be confined there yet; for, from the necessity of the thing, as the island is remote from any power established by law, the laird must exercise his jurisdiction to a certain degree.

We were shewn, in a corner of this vault, a hole, into which Col said greater criminals used to be put. It was now filled up with rubbish of different kinds. He said, it was of a great depth. " Ay, (said Dr. Johnson, smiling,) all such places, that *are filled up*, were of a great depth." He is very quick in shewing that he does not give credit to careless or exaggerated accounts of things. After seeing the castle, we looked at a small hut near it. It is called Teigh Franchich, *i.e.* the Frenchman's House. Col could not tell us the history of it. A poor man with a wife and children now lived in it. We went into it, and Dr. Johnson gave them some charity. There was but one bed for all the family, and the hut was very smoky. When he came out, he said to me, " *Et hoc secundum sententiam philosophorum est esse beatus.*"—BOSWELL. " The philosophers, when they placed happiness in a cottage, supposed cleanliness and no smoke."—JOHNSON. " Sir, they did not think about either."

We walked a little in the laird's garden, in which endeavours have been used to rear some trees; but, as soon as they got above the surrounding wall, they died. Dr. Johnson recommended sowing the seeds of hardy trees, instead of planting.

Col and I rode out this morning, and viewed a part of the island. In the course of our ride, we saw a turnip-field, which he had hoed with his own hands. He first introduced this kind of husbandry into the Western Islands. We also looked at an appearance of lead, which seemed very promising. It has been long known; for I found letters to the late laird, from Sir

John Areskine and Sir Alexander Murray, respecting it.

After dinner came Mr. M'Lean, of Corneck, brother
to Isle of Muck, who is a cadet of the family of Col.
He possesses the two ends of Col, which belong to the
Duke of Argyll.   Corneck had lately taken a lease of
them at a very advanced rent, rather than let the Campbells get a footing in the island, one of whom had
offered nearly as much as he.   Dr. Johnson well observed, that, "landlords err much when they calculate
merely what their land *may* yield.   The rent must be
in a proportionate ratio of what the land may yield,
and of the power of the tenant to make it yield.   A
tenant cannot make by his land, but according to the
corn and cattle which he has.   Suppose you should
give him twice as much land as he has, it does him no
good, unless he gets also more stock.   It is clear then,
that the Highland landlords, who let their substantial
tenants leave them, are infatuated ; for the poor small
tenants cannot give them good rents, from the very
nature of things.   They have not the means of raising
more from their farms."   Corneck, Dr. Johnson said,
was the most distinct man that he had met with in
these isles ; he did not shut his eyes, or put his fingers
in his ears, which he seemed to think was a good deal
the mode with most of the people whom we have seen
of late.

Highland
landlords
and their
rents

Thursday, 7th October.

Captain M'Lean joined us this morning at breakfast.
There came on a dreadful storm of wind and rain,
which continued all day, and rather increased at night.
The wind was directly against our getting to Mull.
We were in a strange state of abstraction from the
world : we could neither hear from our friends, nor

An im-   write to them. Col had brought Daille *on the Fathers*,
postor   Lucas *on Happiness*, and More's *Dialogues*, from the
Reverend Mr. M'Lean's, and Burnet's *History of his
own Times*, from Captain M'Lean's ; and he had of his
own some books of farming, and Gregory's *Geometry*.
Dr. Johnson read a good deal of Burnet, and of Gregory, and I observed he made some geometrical notes in
the end of his pocket-book. I read a little of Young's
Six Weeks Tour through the Southern Counties ; and
Ovid's Epistles, which I had bought at Inverness, and
which helped to solace many a weary hour.

We were to have gone with Dr. Johnson this morning to see the mine ; but were prevented by the storm.
While it was raging, he said, "We may be glad we
are not *damnati ad metalla*."

Friday, 8th October.

Dr. Johnson appeared to-day very weary of our
present confined situation. He said, "I want to be
on the main land, and go on with existence. This is
a waste of life."

I shall here insert, without regard to chronology,
some of his conversation at different times.

"There was a man some time ago, who was well
received for two years, among the gentlemen of Nor-
thamptonshire, by calling himself my brother. At
last he grew so impudent as by his influence to get
tenants turned out of their farms. Allen the Printer,
who is of that county, came to me, asking, with much
appearance of doubtfulness, if I had a brother ; and
upon being assured I had none alive, he told me of the
imposition, and immediately wrote to the country, and
the fellow was dismissed. It pleased me to hear that
so much was got by using my name. It is not every

name that can carry double; do both for a man's self
and his brother (laughing). I should be glad to see
the fellow. However, I could have done nothing
against him. A man can have no redress for his name
being used, or ridiculous stories being told of him in
the news-papers, except he can shew that he has suffered
damage.—Some years ago a foolish piece was published, said to be written 'by S. Johnson.' Some of
my friends wanted me to be very angry about this. I
said, it would be in vain; for the answer would be, ' S.
Johnson may be Simon Johnson, or Simeon Johnson,
or Solomon Johnson;' and even if the full name,
Samuel Johnson, had been used, it might be said; 'it
is not you; it is a much cleverer fellow.'

" Beauclerk and I, and Langton, and Lady Sydney
Beauclerk, mother to our friend, were one day driving
in a coach by Cuper's Gardens, which were then un-
occupied. I, in sport, proposed that Beauclerk and
Langton, and myself should take them; and we
amused ourselves with scheming how we should all
do our parts. Lady Sydney grew angry, and said, 'an
old man should not put such things in young people's
heads.' She had no notion of a joke, sir; had come
late into life, and had a mighty unpliable understanding.

" Carte's *Life of the Duke of Ormond* is considered
as a book of authority; but it is ill-written. The
matter is diffused in too many words; there is no
animation, no compression, no vigour. Two good
volumes in duodecimo might be made out of the two
in folio."

Talking of our confinement here, I observed, that
our discontent and impatience could not be considered
as very unreasonable; for that we were just in the state
of which Seneca complains so grievously, while in

exile in Corsica. "Yes, (said Dr. Johnson,) and he was not farther from home than we are." The truth is, he was much nearer.

There was a good deal of rain to-day, and the wind was still contrary. Corneck attended me, while I amused myself in examining a collection of papers belonging to the family of Col. The first laird was a younger son of the Chieftain M'Lean, and got the middle part of Col for his patrimony. Dr. Johnson having given a very particular account of the connection between this family and a branch of the family of Camerons, called M'Lonich, I shall only insert the following document, (which I found in Col's cabinet,) as a proof of its continuance, even to a late period :

"To the Laird of Col.

"DEAR SIR,

"THE long-standing tract of firm affectionate friendship 'twixt your worthy predecessors and ours affords us such assurance, as that we may have full relyance on your favour and undoubted friendship, in recommending the bearer, Ewen Cameron, our cousin, son to the deceast Dugall M'Connill of Innermaillie, sometime in Glenpean, to your favour and conduct, who is a man of undoubted honesty and discretion, only that he has the misfortune of being alledged to have been accessory to the killing of one of M'Martin's family about fourteen years ago, upon which alledgeance the M'Martins are now so sanguine on revenging, that they are fully resolved for the deprivation of his life ; to the preventing of which you are relyed on by us, as the only fit instrument, and a most capable person. Therefore your favour and protection is expected and intreated, during his good behaviour ; and failing of which behaviour, you'll please to use him as a most insignificant person deserves.

"Sir, he had, upon the alledgeance foresaid, been transported, at Lochiel's desire, to France, to gratify the M'Martins, and upon his return home, about five years ago, married : But now he is so much threatened by the M'Martins, that he is not secure enough to stay where he is, being Ardmurchan, which occasions this trouble to you.   Wishing prosperity and happiness to attend still yourself, worthy Lady, and good family, we are, in the most affectionate manner,

  "Dear Sir,
   "Your most obliged, affectionate,
     and most humble servants,
    "Dugall Cameron, of Strone.
    "Dugall Cameron, of Barr.
    "Dugall Cameron, of Inveriskvouilline.
    "Dugall Cameron, of Invinvalie."

"Strone, 11th March, 1737."

Ewen Cameron was protected, and his son has now a farm from the Laird of Col, in Mull.

The family of Col was very loyal in the time of the great Montrose, from whom I found two letters in his own hand-writing.   The first is as follows :

"For my very Loving Friend the Laird of Coall.
 "Sir,
  "I must heartily thank you for all your willing-ness and good affection to his Majesty's service, and particularly the sending alongs of your son, to who I will heave ane particular respect, hopeing also that you will still continue ane goode instrument for the advance-ing ther of the King's service, for which, and all your

Letters
from the
great
Montrose

former loyal carriages, be confident you shall find the effects of his Ma˜s favour, as they can be witnessed you by

"Your very faithful friende,

"MONTROSE."

"Strethearne, 20 *Jañ*. 1646."

The other is,

"FOR THE LAIRD OF COL.

"SIR,

"HAVING occasion to write to your fields, I cannot be forgetful of your willingness and good affection to his Majesty's service. I acknowledge to you, and thank you heartily for it, assuring, that in what lies in my power, you shall find the good. Mean while, I shall expect that you will continue your loyal endeavours, in wishing those slack people that are about you, to appear more obedient than they do, and loyal in their prince's service; whereby I assure you, you shall find me ever

"Your faithful friend,

"MONTROSE." [1]

"Petty, 17 *April*, 1646."

I found some uncouth lines on the death of the present laird's father, intituled "Nature's Elegy upon the Death of Donald Maclean of Col." They are not worth insertion. I shall only give what is called his Epitaph, which Dr. Johnson said, "was not so very bad."

"Nature's minion, Virtue's wonder,
    Art's corrective here lyes under."

---

[1] It is observeable that men of the first rank spelt very ill in the last century. In the first of these letters I have preserved the original spelling.

I asked, what "Art's corrective" meant. "Why, sir, (said he,) that the laird was so exquisite, that he set Art right, when she was wrong."

I found several letters to the late Col, from my father's old companion at Paris, Sir Hector M'Lean, one of which was written at the time of settling the colony in Georgia. It dissuades Col from letting people go there, and assures him there will soon be an opportunity of employing them better at home. Hence it appears that emigration from the Highlands, though not in such numbers at a time as of late, has always been practised. Dr. Johnson observed, that, "the Lairds, instead of improving their country, diminished their people."

There are several districts of sandy desart in Col. There are forty-eight lochs of fresh water; but many of them are very small,—mere pools. About one half of them, however, have trout and eel. There is a great number of horses in the island, mostly of a small size. Being over-stocked, they sell some in Tir-yi, and on the main land. Their black cattle, which are chiefly rough-haired, are reckoned remarkably good. The climate being very mild in winter, they never put their beasts in any house. The lakes are never frozen so as to bear a man; and snow never lies above a few hours. They have a good many sheep, which they eat mostly themselves, and sell but a few. They have goats in several places. There are no foxes; no serpents, toads, or frogs, nor any venomous creature. They have otters and mice here; but had no rats till lately that an American vessel brought them. There is a rabbit-warren on the north-east of the island, belonging to the Duke of Argyle. Young Col intends to get some hares, of which there are none at present. There are no black-cock, muir-fowl, nor partridges;

L 387

but there are snipe, wild-duck, wild-geese, and swans, in winter; wild-pidgeons, plover, and great number of starlings; of which I shot some, and found them pretty good eating. Woodcocks come hither, though there is not a tree upon the island. There are no rivers in Col; but only some brooks, in which there is a great variety of fish. In the whole isle there are but three hills, and none of them considerable, for a Highland country. The people are very industrious. Every man can tan. They get oak, and birch-bark, and lime, from the main land. Some have pits; but they commonly use tubs. I saw brogues very well tanned; and every man can make them. They all make candles of the tallow of their beasts, both moulded and dipped; and they all make oil of the livers of fish. The little fish called Cuddies produce a great deal. They sell some oil out of the island, and they use it much for light in their houses, in little iron lamps, most of which they have from England; but of late their own blacksmith makes them. He is a good workman; but he has no employment in shoeing horses, for they all go unshod here, except some of a better kind belonging to young Col, which were now in Mull. There are two carpenters in Col; but most of the inhabitants can do something as boat-carpenters. They can all dye. Heath is used for yellow; and for red, a moss which grows on stones. They make broad-cloth, and tartan, and linen, of their own wool and flax, sufficient for their own use; as also stockings. Their bonnets come from the main land. Hard-ware and several small articles are brought annually from Greenock, and sold in the only shop in the island, which is kept near the house, or rather hut, used for publick worship, there being no church in the island. —The inhabitants of Col have increased considerably within these thirty years, as appears from the parish registers.   There are but three considerable tacksmen on Col's part of the island : the rest is let to small tenants, some of whom pay so low a rent as four, three, or even two guineas.   The highest is seven pounds, paid by a farmer, whose son goes yearly on foot to Aberdeen for education, and in summer returns, and acts as a school-master in Col.   Dr. Johnson said, " There is something noble in a young man's walking two hundred miles and back again, every year, for the sake of learning."

This day a number of people came to Col, with complaints of each others' trespasses.   Corneck, to prevent their being troublesome, told them, that the lawyer from Edinburgh was here, and if they did not agree, he would take them to task.   They were alarmed at this ; said, they had never been used to go to law, and hoped Col would settle matters himself.—In the evening Corneck left us.

Saturday, 9th October.

As, in our present confinement, any thing that had even the name of curious was an object of attention, I proposed that Col should show me the great stone, mentioned in a former page, as having been thrown by a giant to the top of a mountain.   Dr. Johnson, who did not like to be left alone, said he would accompany us as far as riding was practicable.   We ascended a part of the hill on horseback, and Col and I scrambled up the rest.   A servant held our horses, and Dr. Johnson placed himself on the ground, with his back against a large fragment of rock.   The wind being high, he let down the cocks of his hat, and tied it with his handkerchief under his chin.   While we were employed in examining the stone, which did not repay our trouble in getting

Johnson's
avidity
for books

to it, he amused himself with reading *Gataker on Lots and on the Christian Watch*, a very learned book, of the last age, which had been found in the garret of Col's house, and which he said was a treasure here. When we descried him from above, he had a most eremitical appearance; and on our return told us, he had been so much engaged by Gataker, that he had never missed us. His avidity for variety of books, while we were in Col, was frequently expressed; and he often complained that so few were within his reach. Upon which I observed to him, that it was strange he should complain of want of books, when he could at any time make such good ones.

We next proceeded to the lead mine. In our way we came to a strand of some extent, where we were glad to take a gallop, in which my learned friend joined with great alacrity. Dr. Johnson, mounted on a large bay mare without shoes, and followed by a foal, which had some difficulty in keeping up with him, was a singular spectacle.

After examining the mine, we returned through a very uncouth district, full of sand hills; down which, though apparent precipices, our horses carried us with safety, the sand always gently sliding away from their feet. Vestiges of houses were pointed out to us, which Col, and two others who had joined us, asserted had been overwhelmed with sand blown over them. But, on going close to one of them, Dr. Johnson shewed the absurdity of the notion, by remarking, that "it was evidently only a house abandoned, the stones of which had been taken away for other purposes; for the large stones, which form the lower part of the walls, were still standing higher than the sand. If *they* were not blown over, it was clear nothing higher than they could be blown over." This was quite convincing to me; but it made not the least impression on Col and the others, who were not to be argued out of a Highland tradition.

We did not sit down to dinner till between six and seven. We lived plentifully here, and had a true welcome. In such a season, good firing was of no small importance. The peats were excellent, and burned cheerfully. Those at Dunvegan, which were damp, Dr. Johnson called "a sullen fuel."—Here a Scottish phrase was singularly applied to him. One of the company having remarked that he had gone out on a stormy evening, and brought in a supply of peats from the stack, old Mr. M'Sweyn said, "that was *main honest* !"

Blenheim being occasionally mentioned, he told me he had never seen it : he had not gone formerly ; and he would not go now, just as a common spectator, for his money : he would not put it in the power of some man about the Duke of Marlborough to say, "Johnson was here ; I knew him, but I took no notice of him." He said, he should be very glad to see it, if properly invited, which in all probability would never be the case, as it was not worth his while to seek for it.—I observed, that he might be easily introduced there by a common friend of ours, nearly related to the duke. He answered, with an uncommon attention to delicacy of feeling, " I doubt whether our friend be on such a footing with the duke as to carry any body there ; and I would not give him the uneasiness of seeing that I knew he was not, or even of being himself reminded of it."

Sunday, 10th October.

There was this day the most terrible storm of wind and rain that I ever remember. It made such an awful impression on us all, as to produce, for some time, a kind of dismal quietness in the house. The

The duty
of land-
lords

day was passed without much conversation : only, upon my observing that there must be something bad in a man's mind, who does not like to give leases to his tenants, but wishes to keep them in a perpetual wretched dependence on his will, Dr. Johnson said, " You are right : it is a man's duty to extend comfort and security among as many people as he can. He should not wish to have his tenants mere *Ephemeræ*,—mere beings of an hour."—BOSWELL. " But, sir, if they have leases, is there not some danger that they may grow insolent ? I remember you yourself once told me, an English tenant was so independent, that, if provoked, he would *throw* his rent at his landlord."—JOHNSON. " Depend upon it, sir, it is the landlord's own fault, if it is thrown at him. A man may always keep his tenants in dependence enough, though they have leases. He must be a good tenant indeed, who will not fall behind in his rent, if his landlord will let him ; and if he does fall behind, his landlord has him at his mercy. Indeed, the poor man is always much at the mercy of the rich ; no matter whether landlord or tenant. If the tenant lets his landlord have a little rent before-hand, or has lent him money, then the landlord is in his power. There cannot be a greater man than a tenant who has lent money to his landlord ; for he has under subjection the very man to whom he should be subjected."

Monday, 11th October.

We had some days ago engaged the Campbell-town vessel to carry us to Mull, from the harbour where she lay. The morning was fine, and the wind fair and moderate ; so we hoped at length to get away.

Mrs. M'Sweyn, who officiated as our landlady here, had never been on the main land. On hearing this,

Dr. Johnson said to me, before her, "That is rather being behind-hand with life. I would at least go and see Glenelg."—Boswell. "You yourself, sir, have never seen, till now, any thing but your native island." —Johnson. "But, sir, by seeing London, I have seen as much of life as the world can shew."—Boswell. "You have not seen Pekin."—Johnson. "What is Pekin? Ten thousand Londoners would drive all the people of Pekin: they would drive them like deer."

We set out about eleven for the harbour; but, before we reached it, so violent a storm came on, that we were obliged again to take shelter in the house of Captain M'Lean, where we dined, and passed the night.

Tuesday, 12th October.

After breakfast, we made a second attempt to get to the harbour; but another storm soon convinced us that it would be in vain. Captain M'Lean's house being in some confusion, on account of Mrs. M'Lean being expected to lie-in, we resolved to go to Mr. M'Sweyn's, where we arrived very wet, fatigued, and hungry. In this situation, we were somewhat disconcerted by being told that we should have no dinner till late in the evening; but should have tea in the mean time. Dr. Johnson opposed this arrangement; but they persisted, and he took the tea very readily. He said to me afterwards, "You must consider, sir, a dinner here is a matter of great consequence. It is a thing to be first planned, and then executed. I suppose the mutton was brought some miles off, from some place where they knew there was a sheep killed."

Talking of the good people with whom we were, he said, "Life has not got at all forward by a generation in M'Sweyn's family; for the son is exactly formed upon the father. What the father says, the son says; and what the father looks, the son looks."

There being little conversation to-night, I must endeavour to recollect what I may have omitted on former occasions.—When I boasted, at Rasay, of my independency of spirit, and that I could not be bribed, he said, "Yes, you may be bribed by flattery."—At the Reverend Mr. M'Lean's, Dr. Johnson asked him, if the people of Col had any superstitions. He said, "No." The cutting peats at the increase of the moon was mentioned as one; but he would not allow it, saying, it was not a superstition, but a whim. Dr. Johnson would not admit the distinction. There were many superstitions, he maintained, not connected with religion; and this was one of them.—On Monday we had a dispute at the Captain's, whether sand-hills could be fixed down by art. Dr. Johnson said, "How *the devil* can you do it?" but instantly corrected himself, "How can you do it?"—I never before heard him use a phrase of that nature.

He has particularities which it is impossible to explain. He never wears a night-cap, as I have already mentioned; but he puts a handkerchief on his head in the night.—The day that we left Talisker, he bade us ride on. He then turned the head of his horse back towards Talisker, stopped for some time; then wheeled round to the same direction with ours, and then came briskly after us. He sets open a window in the coldest day or night, and stands before it. It may do with his constitution; but most people, amongst whom I am one, would say, with the frogs in the fable, "This may be sport to you; but it is death to us."—It is in vain to try to find a meaning in every one of his particularities, which, I suppose, are mere habits, contracted by chance; of which every man has some that are more or less remarkable.   His speaking to himself, or **His dis-** rather repeating, is a common habit with studious men **like of** accustomed to deep thinking ; and, in consequence of **low life** their being thus rapt, they will even laugh by themselves, if the subject which they are musing on is a merry one.   Dr. Johnson is often uttering pious ejaculations, when he appears to be talking to himself ; for sometimes his voice grows stronger, and parts of the Lord's Prayer are heard.   I have sat beside him with more than ordinary reverence on such occasions.[1]

In our Tour, I observed that he was disgusted whenever he met with coarse manners.   He said to me, " I know not how it is, but I cannot bear low life : and I find others, who have as good a right as I to be fastidious, bear it better, by having mixed more with different sorts of men.   You would think that I have mixed pretty well too."

He read this day a good deal of my Journal, written in a small book with which he had supplied me, and was pleased, for he said, " I wish thy books were twice as big."   He helped me to fill up blanks which I had left in first writing it, when I was not quite sure of what he had said, and he corrected any mistakes that I had made.   " They call me a scholar, (said he,) and yet how very little literature is there in my conversation."—BOSWELL. " That, sir, must be according to your company.   You would not give literature to those who cannot taste it.   Stay till we meet Lord Elibank."

We had at last a good dinner, or rather supper, and were very well satisfied with our entertainment.

---

[1] It is remarkable, that Dr. Johnson should have read this account of some of his own peculiar habits, without saying any thing on the subject, which I hoped he would have done.

*L 387

Boswell's
bustling

Wednesday, 13th *October*.

Col called me up, with intelligence that it was a good day for a passage to Mull ; and just as we rose, a sailor from the vessel arrived for us.   We got all ready with dispatch.   Dr. Johnson was displeased at my bustling, and walking quickly up and down.   He said, " It does not hasten us a bit.   It is getting on horseback in a ship.   All boys do it ; and you are longer a boy than others."   He himself has no alertness, or whatever it may be called ; so he may dislike it, as *Oderunt hilarem tristes*.

Before we reached the harbour, the wind grew high again.   However, the small boat was waiting, and took us on board.   We remained for some time in uncertainty what to do : at last it was determined, that, as a good part of the day was over, and it was dangerous to be at sea at night, in such a vessel, and such weather, we should not sail till the morning tide, when the wind would probably be more gentle.   We resolved not to go ashore again, but lie here in readiness.   Dr. Johnson and I had each a bed in the cabbin.   Col sat at the fire in the forecastle, with the captain, and Joseph, and the rest.   I eat some dry oatmeal, of which I found a barrel in the cabbin.   I had not done this since I was a boy.   Dr. Johnson owned that he too was fond of it when a boy ; a circumstance which I was highly pleased to hear from him, as it gave me an opportunity of observing that, notwithstanding his joke on the article of OATS, he was himself a proof that this kind of *food* was not peculiar to the people of Scotland.

Thursday, 14th October.   Tober-
                                    morie

When Dr. Johnson awaked this morning, he called,
"Lanky!" having, I suppose, been thinking of Langton; but corrected himself instantly, and cried, "Bozzy!"
He has a way of contracting the names of his friends.
Goldsmith feels himself so important now, as to be displeased at it.   I remember one day, when Tom Davies
was telling that Dr. Johnson said, "We are all in labour
for a name to *Goldy's* play," Goldsmith cried, "I have
often desired him not to call me *Goldy*."

Between six and seven we hauled our anchor, and set
sail with a fair breeze; and, after a pleasant voyage, we
got safely and agreeably into the harbour of Tobermorie,
before the wind rose, which it always has done, for some
days, about noon.

Tobermorie is an excellent harbour.   An island lies
before it, and it is surrounded by a hilly theatre.   The
island is too low, otherwise this would be quite a secure
port; but, the island not being a sufficient protection,
some storms blow very hard here.   Not long ago, fifteen
vessels were blown from their moorings.   There are sometimes sixty or seventy sail here: to-day there were twelve
or fourteen vessels.   To see such a fleet was the next
thing to seeing a town.   The vessels were from different
places; Clyde, Campbelltown, Newcastle, &c.   One was
returning to Lancaster from Hamburgh.   After having
been shut up so long in Col, the sight of such an as-
semblage of moving habitations, containing such a variety
of people, engaged in different pursuits, gave me much
gaiety of spirit.   When we had landed, Dr. Johnson
said, "Boswell is now all alive.   He is like Antæus;
he gets new vigour whenever he touches the ground."
—I went to the top of a hill fronting the harbour, from
whence I had a good view of it.   We had here a toler-

able inn. Dr. Johnson had owned to me this morning, that he was out of humour. Indeed, he shewed it a good deal in the ship; for when I was expressing my joy on the prospect of our landing in Mull, he said, he had no joy, when he recollected that it would be five days before he should get to the main land. I was afraid he would now take a sudden resolution to give up seeing Icolmkill. A dish of tea, and some good bread and butter, did him service, and his bad humour went off. I told him, that I was diverted to hear all the people whom we had visited in our Tour, say, " Honest man! he's pleased with every thing; he's always content ! " —" Little do they know," said I. He laughed, and said, " You rogue ! "

We sent to hire horses to carry us across the island of Mull to the shore opposite to Inchkenneth, the residence of Sir Allan M'Lean, uncle to young Col, and Chief of the M'Leans, to whose house we intended to go the next day. Our friend Col went to visit his aunt, the wife of Dr. Alexander M'Lean, a physician, who lives about a mile from Tobermorie.

Dr. Johnson and I sat by ourselves at the inn, and talked a good deal.—I told him, that I had found, in Leandro Alberti's Description of Italy, much of what Addison has given us in his *Remarks*. He said, " The collection of passages from the Classicks has been made by another Italian: it is, however, impossible to detect a man as a plagiary in such a case, because all who set about making such a collection must find the same passages; but, if you find the same applications in another book, then Addison's learning in his *Remarks* tumbles down. It is a tedious book; and, if it were not attached to Addison's previous reputation, one would not think much of it. Had he written nothing else, his name would not have lived. Addison does not seem to

have gone deep in Italian literature : he shews nothing
of it in his subsequent writings. He shews a great deal
of French learning.—There is, perhaps, more knowledge circulated in the French language than in any
other. There is more original knowledge in English."—"But the French (said I) have the art of
accommodating literature." — JOHNSON. "Yes, sir ;
we have no such book as Moreri's Dictionary."—
BOSWELL. "Their *Ana* are good."—JOHNSON. "A
few of them are good ; but we have one book of that
kind better than any of them; Selden's *Table-talk*. As
to original literature, the French have a couple of tragick
poets who go round the world, Racine and Corneille,
and one comick poet, Moliere."—BOSWELL. "They
have Fenelon."—JOHNSON. "Why, sir, Telemachus
is pretty well."—BOSWELL. "And Voltaire, sir."
—JOHNSON. "He has not stood his trial yet. And
what makes Voltaire chiefly circulate is collection;
such as his *Universal History*."—BOSWELL. "What
do you say to the Bishop of Meaux ?"—JOHNSON.
"Sir, nobody reads him." [1]—He would not allow
Massillon and Bourdaloue to go round the world.
In general, however, he gave the French much praise
for their industry.

He asked me whether he had mentioned, in any of
the papers of the *Rambler*, the description in Virgil of
the entrance into Hell, with an application to the press ;
"for (said he) I do not much remember them." I
told him, "No." Upon which he repeated it :

Vestibulum ante ipsum, primisque in faucibus orci,
Luctus et ultrices posuere cubilia Curæ ;

---

[1] I take leave to enter my strongest protest against this
judgement. Bossuet I hold to be one of the first luminaries
of religion and literature. If there are who do not read him,
it is full time they should begin.

Pallentesque habitant Morbi, tristisque Senectus,
Et metus, et malesuada Fames, et turpis Egestas,
Terribiles visu formæ; Lethumque, Laborque.[1]

"Now, (said he), almost all these apply exactly to an
authour; all these are the concomitants of a printing-
house." I proposed to him to dictate an essay on it,
and offered to write it. He said, he would not do
it then, but perhaps would write one at some future
period.

The sunday evening that we sat by ourselves at
Aberdeen, I asked him several particulars of his life,
from his early years, which he readily told me; and I
wrote them down before him. This day I proceeded
in my inquiries, also writing them in his presence. I
have them on detached sheets. I shall collect authentick
materials for THE LIFE OF SAMUEL JOHNSON, LL.D.;
and, if I survive him, I shall be one who will most
faithfully do honour to his memory. I have now a
vast treasure of his conversation, at different times,
since the year 1762, when I first obtained his acquaintance; and, by assiduous inquiry, I can make up for not
knowing him sooner.[2]

A Newcastle ship-master, who happened to be in
the house, intruded himself upon us. He was much
in liquor, and talked nonsense about his being a man

---

[1] Just in the gate, and in the jaws of hell,
   Revengeful cares, and sullen sorrows dwell;
   And pale diseases, and repining age;
   Want, fear, and famine's unresisted rage;
   Here toils and death, and death's half-brother, sleep,
   Forms terrible to view, their sentry keep.—DRYDEN.

[2] It is no small satisfaction to me to reflect, that Dr.
Johnson read this, and, after being apprized of my intention, communicated to me, at subsequent periods, many
particulars of his life, which probably could not otherwise
have been preserved.

for *Wilkes and Liberty*, and against the ministry. Dr. Johnson's
Johnson was angry, that "a fellow should come into letter-
our company, who was fit for *no* company." He left writing
us soon.

Col returned from his aunt, and told us, she insisted
that we should come to her house that night. He
introduced to us Mr. Campbell, the Duke of Argyle's
factor in Tyr-yi. He was a genteel, agreeable man.
He was going to Inveraray, and promised to put letters
into the post-office for us. I now found that Dr.
Johnson's desire to get on the main land, arose from his
anxiety to have an opportunity of conveying letters to
his friends.

After dinner, we proceeded to Dr. M'Lean's, which
was about a mile from our inn. He was not at home,
but we were received by his lady and daughter, who
entertained us so well, that Dr. Johnson seemed quite
happy. When we had supped, he asked me to give
him some paper to write letters. I begged he would
write short ones, and not expatiate, as we ought to set
off early. He was irritated by this, and said, "What
must be done, must be done: the thing is past a
joke."—"Nay, sir, (said I,) write as much as you
please; but do not blame me, if we are kept six days
before we get to the main land. You were very impatient in the morning: but no sooner do you find
yourself in good quarters, than you forget that you are
to move." I got him paper enough, and we parted in
good humour.

Let me now recollect whatever particulars I have
omitted.—In the morning I said to him, before we
landed at Tobermorie, "We shall see Dr. M'Lean,
who has written the History of the M'Leans."—
Johnson. "I have no great patience to stay to hear
the history of the M'Leans. I would rather hear

the History of the Thrales."—When on Mull, I said,
" Well, sir, this is the fourth of the Hebrides that we
have been upon."—JOHNSON. " Nay, we cannot boast
of the number we have seen. We thought we should
see many more. We thought of sailing about easily
from island to island; and so we should, had we come
at a better season; but we, being wise men, thought it
would be summer all the year where *we* were. However, sir, we have seen enough to give us a pretty good
notion of the system of insular life."

Let me not forget, that he sometimes amused himself
with very slight reading; from which, however, his
conversation showed that he contrived to extract some
benefit. At Captain M'Lean's he read a good deal in
The Charmer, a collection of songs.

Friday, 15th October.

We this morning found that we could not proceed,
there being a violent storm of wind and rain, and the
rivers being impassable. When I expressed my discontent at our confinement, Dr. Johnson said, " Now
that I have had an opportunity of writing to the main
land, I am in no such haste." I was amused with his
being so easily satisfied; for the truth was, that the
gentleman who was to convey our letters, as I was now
informed, was not to set out for Inveraray for some
time; so that it was probable we should be there as
soon as he: however, I did not undeceive my friend,
but suffered him to enjoy his fancy.

Dr. Johnson asked, in the evening, to see Dr.
M'Lean's books. He took down Willis *de Anima
Brutorum*, and pored over it a good deal.

Miss M'Lean produced some Erse poems by John
M'Lean, who was a famous bard in Mull, and had

died only a few years ago. He could neither read nor
write. She read and translated two of them; one, a
kind of elegy on Sir John M'Lean's being obliged to
fly his country in 1715; another, a dialogue between
two Roman Catholick young ladies, sisters, whether it
was better to be a nun or to marry   I could not perceive much poetical imagery in the translation. Yet
all of our company who understood Erse, seemed
charmed with the original. There may, perhaps, be
some choice of expression, and some excellence of
arrangement, that cannot be shewn in translation.

After we had exhausted the Erse poems, of which
Dr. Johnson said nothing, Miss M'Lean gave us
several tunes on a spinnet, which, though made so long
ago as in 1667, was still very well toned. She sung
along with it. Dr. Johnson seemed pleased with the
musick, though he owns he neither likes it, nor has
hardly any perception of it. At Mr. M'Pherson's,
in Slate, he told us, that "he knew a drum from a
trumpet, and a bagpipe from a guittar, which was
about the extent of his knowledge of musick." To-
night he said, that, "if he had learnt musick, he
should have been afraid he would have done nothing
else but play. It was a method of employing the
mind, without the labour of thinking at all, and with
some applause from a man's self."

We had the musick of the bagpipe every day, at
Armidale, Dunvegan, and Col. Dr. Johnson appeared fond of it, and used often to stand for some
time with his ear close to the great drone.

The penurious gentleman of our acquaintance, formerly alluded to, afforded us a topick of conversation
to-night. Dr. Johnson said, I ought to write down a
collection of the instances of his narrowness, as they
almost exceeded belief. Col told us, that O'Kane,

Johnson's indifference to musick

the famous Irish harper, was once at that gentleman's
house. He could not find in his heart to give him any
money, but gave him a key for a harp, which was
finely ornamented with gold and silver, and with a
precious stone, and was worth eighty or a hundred
guineas. He did not know the value of it; and when
he came to know it, he would fain have had it back;
but O'Kane took care that he should not.—JOHNSON.
"They exaggerate the value; every body is so desirous
that he should be fleeced. I am very willing it
should be worth eighty or a hundred guineas; but I
do not believe it."—BOSWELL. "I do not think
O'Kane was obliged to give it back."—JOHNSON. "No,
sir. If a man with his eyes open, and without any
means used to deceive him, gives me a thing, I am not
to let him have it again when he grows wiser. I like
to see how avarice defeats itself: how, when avoiding
to part with money, the miser gives something more
valuable."—Col said, the gentleman's relations were
angry at his giving away the harp-key, for it had been
long in the family.—JOHNSON. "Sir, he values a new
guinea more than an old friend."

Col also told us, that the same person having come
up with a serjeant and twenty men, working on the
high road, he entered into discourse with the serjeant,
and then gave him sixpence for the men to drink. The
serjeant asked, "Who is this fellow?" Upon being
informed, he said, "If I had known who he was, I
should have thrown it in his face."—JOHNSON. "There
is much want of sense in all this. He had no business
to speak with the serjeant. He might have been in
haste, and trotted on. He has not learnt to be a
miser: I believe we must take him apprentice."—
BOSWELL. "He would grudge giving half a guinea to
be taught."—JOHNSON. "Nay, sir, you must teach him

gratis. You must give him an opportunity to practice your precepts."

Let me now go back, and glean *Johnsoniana.*—The Saturday before we sailed from Slate, I sat awhile in the afternoon with Dr. Johnson in his room, in a quiet serious frame. I observed, that hardly any man was accurately prepared for dying; but almost every one left something undone, something in confusion; that my father, indeed, told me he knew one man, (Carlisle of Limekilns,) after whose death all his papers were found in exact order; and nothing was omitted in his will.—JOHNSON. " Sir, I had an uncle who died so ; but such attention requires great leisure, and great firmness of mind. If one was to think constantly of death, the business of life would stand still. I am no friend to making religion appear too hard. Many good people have done harm, by giving severe notions of it. In the same way, as to learning : I never frighten young people with difficulties ; on the contrary, I tell them that they may very easily get as much as will do very well. I do not indeed tell them that they will be Bentleys."

The night we rode to Col's house, I said, " Lord Elibank is probably wondering what is become of us." —JOHNSON. " No, no ; he is not thinking of us."— BOSWELL. " But recollect the warmth with which he wrote. Are we not to believe a man, when he says he has a great desire to see another ? Don't you believe that I was very impatient for your coming to Scotland ? "—JOHNSON. " Yes, sir ; I believe you were; and I was impatient to come to you. A young man feels so, but seldom an old man." I however convinced him that Lord Elibank, who has much of the spirit of a young man, might feel so.—He asked me if our jaunt had answered expectation. I said it had much

Few men are prepared for dying

exceeded it. I expected much difficulty with him, and had not found it. " And (he added) wherever we have come, we have been received like princes in their progress."

He said, he would not wish not to be disgusted in the Highlands; for that would be to lose the power of distinguishing, and a man might then lie down in the middle of them. He wished only to conceal his disgust.

At Captain M'Lean's, I mentioned Pope's friend, Spence.—JOHNSON. " He was a weak conceited man." [1] —BOSWELL. " A good scholar, sir?" — JOHNSON. " Why, no, sir."—BOSWELL. " He was a pretty scholar."—JOHNSON. " You have about reached him."

Last night at the inn, when the factor in Tyr-yi spoke of his having heard that a roof was put on some part of the buildings at Icolmkill, I unluckily said, " It will be fortunate if we find a cathedral with a roof on it." I said this from a foolish anxiety to engage Dr. Johnson's curiosity more. He took me short at once. " What, sir? how can you talk so? If we shall *find* a cathedral roofed! as if we were going to a *terra incognita* : when everything that is at Icolmkill is so well known. You are like some New-England-men who came to the mouth of the Thames. 'Come, (said they,) let us go up and see what sort of inhabitants there are here.' They talked, sir, as if they had been to go up the Susquehannah, or any other American river."

[1] Mr. Langton thinks this must have been the hasty expression of a splenetick moment, as he has heard Dr. Johnson speak of Mr. Spence's judgement in criticism with so high a degree of respect, as to shew that this was not his settled opinion of him. Let me add that, in the preface to the *Preceptor*, he recommends Spence's *Essay on Pope's Odyssey*, and that his admirable Lives of the English Poets are much enriched by Spence's Anecdotes of Pope.

Saturday, 16th October.

This day there was a new moon, and the weather changed for the better. Dr. Johnson said of Miss M'Lean, " She is the most accomplished lady that I have found in the Highlands. She knows French, musick, and drawing, sews neatly, makes shell-work, and can milk cows; in short, she can do every thing. She talks sensibly, and is the first person whom I have found, that can translate Erse poetry literally."—We set out, mounted on little Mull horses. Mull corresponded exactly with the idea which I had always had of it; a hilly country, diversified with heath and grass, and many rivulets. Dr. Johnson was not in very good humour. He said, it was a dreary country, much worse than Sky. I differed from him. " O, sir, (said he,) a most dolorous country ! "

We had a very hard journey to-day. I had no bridle for my sheltie, but only a halter; and Joseph rode without a saddle. At one place, a loch having swelled over the road, we were obliged to plunge through pretty deep water. Dr. Johnson observed, how helpless a man would be, were he travelling here alone, and should meet with any accident; and said, " he longed to get to *a country of saddles and bridles.*" He was more out of humour to-day, than he has been in the course of our Tour, being fretted to find that his little horse could scarcely support his weight;—and having suffered a loss, which, though small in itself, was of some consequence to him, while travelling the rugged steeps of Mull, where he was at times obliged to walk. The loss that I allude to was that of the large oak-stick, which, as I formerly mentioned, he had brought with him from London. It was of great use to him in our wild peregrination; for, ever since

Johnson's his last illness in 1766, he has had a weakness in his
oak stick knees, and has not been able to walk easily.   It had
too the properties of a measure; for one nail was
driven into it at the length of a foot; another at that
of a yard.   In return for the services it had done him,
he said, this morning, he would make a present of it to
some Museum ; but he little thought he was so soon
to lose it.   As he preferred riding with a switch, it
was intrusted to a fellow to be delivered to our bag-
gage-man, who followed us at some distance , but we
never saw it more.   I could not persuade him out of a
suspicion that it had been stolen.   " No, no, my friend,
(said he,) it is not to be expected that any man in
Mull, who has got it, will part with it.   Consider,
sir, the value of such a *piece of timber* here ! "

As we travelled this forenoon, we met Dr. M'Lean,
who expressed much regret at his having been so unfortunate as to be absent while we were at his house.

We were in hopes to get to Sir Allan Maclean's at
Inchkenneth, to-night; but the eight miles, of which
our road was said to consist, were so very long, that
we did not reach the opposite coast of Mull till seven
at night, though we had set out about eleven in the
forenoon; and when we did arrive there, we found
the wind strong against us.   Col determined that we
should pass the night at M'Quarrie's, in the island of
Ulva, which lies between Mull and Inchkenneth; and
a servant was sent forward to the ferry, to secure the
boat for us : but the boat was gone to the Ulva side,
and the wind was so high that the people could not
hear him call; and the night so dark that they could
not see a signal.   We should have been in a very bad
situation, had there not fortunately been lying in the
little sound of Ulva an Irish vessel, the Bonnetta, of
Londonderry, Captain M'Lure, master.   He himself

was at M'Quarrie's; but his men obligingly came with their long-boat, and ferried us over.

M'Quarrie's house was mean; but we were agreeably surprised with the appearance of the master, whom we found to be intelligent, polite, and much a man of the world. Though his clan is not numerous, he is a very ancient Chief, and has a burial place at Icolmkill. He told us, his family had possessed Ulva for nine hundred years; but I was distressed to hear that it was soon to be sold for payment of his debts.

Captain M'Lure, whom we found here, was of Scotch extraction, and properly a M'Leod, being descended of some of the M'Leod's who went with Sir Normand of Bernera to the battle of Worcester; and after the defeat of the royalists, fled to Ireland, and, to conceal themselves, took a different name. He told me, there was a great number of them about Londonderry; some of good property. I said, they should now resume their real name. The Laird of M'Leod should go over, and assemble them, and make them all drink the large horn full, and from that time they should be M'Leods.—The captain informed us, he had named his ship the Bonnetta, out of gratitude to Providence; for once, when he was sailing to America with a good number of passengers, the ship in which he then sailed was becalmed for five weeks, and during all that time, numbers of the fish Bonnetta swam close to her, and were caught for food; he resolved therefore, that the ship he should next get, should be called the Bonnetta.

M'Quarrie told us a strong instance of the second sight. He had gone to Edinburgh, and taken a man-servant along with him. An old woman, who was in the house, said one day, "M'Quarrie will be at home to-morrow and will bring two gentlemen with him;"

Setting
aside
sales
and she said, she saw his servant return in red and
green. He did come home next day. He had two
gentlemen with him ; and his servant had a new red
and green livery, which M'Quarrie had bought for him
at Edinburgh, upon a sudden thought, not having the
least intention when he left home to put his servant in
livery ; so that the old woman could not have heard
any previous mention of it.   This, he assured us, was
a true story.

M'Quarrie insisted that the *Mercheta Mulierum*
mentioned in our old charters, did really mean the
privilege which a lord of a manor, or a baron, had, to
have the first night of all his vassal's wives. Dr.
Johnson said, the belief of such a custom having ex-
isted was also held in England, where there is a tenure
called *Borough English*, by which the eldest child
does not inherit, from a doubt of his being the son of
the tenant.[1] M'Quarrie told us, that still, on the
marriage of each of his tenants, a sheep is due to him ;
for which the composition is fixed at five shillings.
I suppose, Ulva is the only place where this custom
remains.

Talking of the sale of an estate of an ancient family,
which was said to have been purchased much under its
value by the confidential lawyer of that family, and it
being mentioned that the sale would probably be set
aside by a suit in equity, Dr. Johnson said, " I am
very willing that this sale should be set aside, but I
doubt much whether the suit will be successful ; for the
argument for avoiding the sale is founded on vague and
indeterminate principles,—as that the price was too low,

[1] Sir William Blackstone says in his COMMENTARIES, that
"he cannot find that ever this custom prevailed in England ; " and therefore he is of opinion that it could not have
given rise to *Borough-English*.

and that there was a great degree of confidence placed Inch-
by the seller in the person who became the purchaser. kenneth
Now, how low should a price be? or what degree of
confidence should there be to make a bargain be set
aside? a bargain, which is a wager of skill between
man and man.——If, indeed, any fraud can be proved,
that will do."

When Dr. Johnson and I were by ourselves at night,
I observed of our host, "*aspectum generosum habet;*"
—"*et generosum animum,*" he added.——For fear of
being overheard in the small Highland houses, I often
talked to him in such Latin as I could speak, and with
as much of the English accent as I could assume, so as
not to be understood, in case our conversation should
be too loud for the space.

We had each an elegant bed in the same room; and
here it was that a circumstance occurred, as to which he
has been strangely misunderstood. From his description
of his chamber, it has erroneously been supposed, that
his bed being too short for him, his feet, during the
night, were in the mire; whereas he has only said, that
when he undressed, he felt his feet in the mire: that
is, the clay-floor of the room, on which he stood upon
before he went into bed, was wet, in consequence of
the windows being broken, which let in the rain.

Sunday, 17th October.

Being informed that there was nothing worthy of
observation in Ulva, we took boat, and proceeded to
Inchkenneth, where we were introduced by our friend
Col to Sir Allan M'Lean, the Chief of his clan, and
to two young ladies, his daughters. Inchkenneth is a
pretty little island, a mile long, and about half a mile
broad, all good land.

Johnson's
Sunday
reading
As we walked up from the shore, Dr. Johnson's heart was cheered by the sight of a road marked with cart-wheels, as on the mainland; a thing which we had not seen for a long time. It gave us a pleasure similar to that which a traveller feels, when, whilst wandering on what he fears is a desert island, he perceives the print of human feet.

Military men acquire excellent habits of having all conveniencies about them. Sir Allan M'Lean, who had been long in the army, and had now a lease of the island, had formed a commodious habitation, though it consisted but of a few small buildings, only one story high. He had, in his little apartments, more things than I could enumerate in a page or two.

Among other agreeable circumstances, it was not the least, to find here a parcel of the *Caledonian Mercury*, published since we left Edinburgh; which I read with that pleasure which every man feels who has been for some time secluded from the animated scenes of the busy world.

Dr. Johnson found books here. He bade me buy Bishop Gastrell's *Christian Institutes*, which was lying in the room. He said, " I do not like to read any thing on a Sunday, but what is theological; not that I would scrupulously refuse to look at any thing which a friend should shew me in a newspaper; but in general, I would read only what is theological.—I read just now some of Drummond's Travels, before I perceived what books were here. I then took up Derham's Physico-Theology."

Every particular concerning this island having been so well described by Dr. Johnson, it would be superfluous in me to present the publick with the observations that I made upon it, in my journal.

I was quite easy with Sir Allan almost instantaneously.

He knew the great intimacy that had been between my Dr.
father and his predecessor, Sir Hector, and was himself John
of a very frank disposition.—After dinner, Sir Allan Campbell
said he had got Dr. Campbell about an hundred subscribers to his *Britannia Elucidata*, (a work since published under the title of *A Political Survey of Great
Britain*,) of whom he believed twenty were dead, the
publication having been so long delayed.—JOHNSON.
"Sir, I imagine the delay of publication is owing to
this;—that, after publication, there will be no more
subscribers, and few will send the additional guinea to
get their books: in which they will be wrong; for
there will be a great deal of instruction in the work.
I think highly of Campbell. In the first place, he
has very good parts. In the second place, he has
very extensive reading; not, perhaps, what is properly
called learning, but history, politicks, and, in short,
that popular knowledge which makes a man very useful.
In the third place, he has learned much by what is called
the *vox viva*. He talks with a great many people."

Speaking of this gentleman, at Rasay, he told us,
that he one day called on him, and they talked of
Tull's Husbandry. Dr. Campbell said something.
Dr. Johnson began to dispute it. "Come, (said Dr.
Campbell,) we do not want to get the better of one
another: we want to encrease each other's ideas."—
Dr. Johnson took it in good part, and the conversation
then went on coolly and instructively.—His candour
in relating this anecdote does him much credit, and
his conduct on that occasion proves how easily he
could be persuaded to talk from a better motive than
"for victory."

Dr. Johnson here shewed so much of the spirit of a
Highlander, that he won Sir Allan's heart: indeed, he
has shewn it during the whole of our Tour.—One

night, in Col, he strutted about the room with a broad
sword and target, and made a formidable appearance;
and, another night, I took the liberty to put a large
blue bonnet on his head. His age, his size, and his
bushy grey wig, with this covering on it, presented the
image of a venerable *Senachi*: and, however unfavourable to the Lowland Scots, he seemed much pleased
to assume the appearance of an ancient Caledonian.
We only regretted that he could not be prevailed with
to partake of the social glass. One of his arguments
against drinking, appears to me not convincing. He
urged, that, "in proportion as drinking makes a man
different from what he is before he has drunk, it is bad;
because it has so far affected his reason." But may it
not be answered, that a man may be altered by it *for
the better*; that his spirits may be exhilarated, without
his reason being affected? On the general subject of
drinking, however, I do not mean positively to take the
other side. I am *dubius, non improbus*.

In the evening, Sir Allan informed us that it was
the custom of his house to have prayers every Sunday;
and Miss M'Lean read the evening service, in which
we all joined. I then read Ogden's second and ninth
Sermons on Prayer, which, with their other distinguished excellence, have the merit of being short.
Dr. Johnson said, that it was the most agreeable
Sunday he had ever passed; and it made such an
impression on his mind, that he afterwards wrote the
following Latin verses upon Inchkenneth:

INSULA SANCTI KENNETHI

Parva quidem regio, sed relligione priorum
   Nota, Caledonias panditur inter aquas;
Voce ubi Cennethus populos domuisse feroces
   Dicitur, et vanos dedocuisse deos.

Huc ego delatus placido per cœrula cursu
   Scire locum volui quid daret ille novi.
Illic Leniades humili regnabat in aula,
   Leniades magnis nobilitatus avis :
Una duas habuit casa cum genitore puellas,
   Quas Amor undarum fingeret esse deas :
Non tamen inculti gelidis latuere sub antris,
   Accola Danubii qualia sævus habet ;
Mollia non deerant vacuæ solatia vitæ,
   Sive libros poscant otia, sive lyram.
Luxerat illa dies, legis gens docta supernæ
   Spes hominum ac curas cum procul esse jubet,
Ponti inter strepitus sacri non munera cultus
   Cessarunt ; pietas hic quoque cura fuit :
Quid quod sacrifici versavit femina libros,
   Legitimas faciunt pectora pura preces.
Quo vagor ulterius ? quod ubique requiritur hic est ;
   Hic secura quies, hic et honestus amor.

Young Col's merits

Monday, 18th October.

We agreed to pass this day with Sir Allan, and he engaged to have every thing in order for our voyage to-morrow.

Being now soon to be separated from our amiable friend young Col, his merits were all remembered. At Ulva he had appeared in a new character, having given us a good prescription for a cold. On my mentioning him with warmth, Dr. Johnson said, " Col does every thing for us: we will erect a statue to Col."—" Yes, (said I,) and we will have him with his various attributes and characters, like Mercury, or any other of the heathen gods. We will have him as a pilot; we will have him as a fisherman, as a hunter, as a husbandman, as a physician."

I this morning took a spade, and dug a little grave in the floor of a ruined chapel, near Sir Allan M'Lean's house, in which I buried some human bones I found there. Dr. Johnson praised me for what I had done, though he owned, he could not have done it. He shewed in the chapel at Rasay his horrour at dead men's bones. He shewed it again at Col's house. In the Charter-room there was a remarkable large shin-bone, which was said to have been a bone of John Garve, one of the lairds. Dr. Johnson would not look at it ; but started away.

At breakfast, I asked, "What is the reason that we are angry at a trader's having opulence?"—JOHNSON. "Why, sir, the reason is, (though I don't undertake to prove that there is a reason,) we see no qualities in trade that should entitle a man to superiority. We are not angry at a soldier's getting riches, because we see that he possesses qualities which we have not. If a man returns from a battle, having lost one hand, and with the other full of gold, we feel that he deserves the gold ; but we cannot think that a fellow, by sitting all day at a desk, is entitled to get above us."— BOSWELL. "But, sir, may we not suppose a merchant to be a man of an enlarged mind, such as Addison in the *Spectator* describes Sir Andrew Freeport to have been?"—JOHNSON. "Why, sir, we may suppose any fictitious character. We may suppose a philosophical day-labourer, who is happy in reflecting that, by his labour, he contributes to the fertility of the earth, and to the support of his fellow-creatures ; but we find no such philosophical day-labourer. A merchant may, perhaps, be a man of an enlarged mind ; but there is nothing in trade connected with an enlarged mind."

I mentioned that I had heard Dr. Solander say he was a Swedish Laplander.—JOHNSON. "Sir, I don't believe he is a Laplander. The Laplanders are not Johnson's much above four feet high. He is as tall as you; intre- and he has not the copper colour of a Laplander."— pidity Boswell. "But what motive could he have to make himself a Laplander?"—Johnson. "Why, sir, he must either mean the word Laplander in a very extensive sense, or may mean a voluntary degradation of himself. 'For all my being the great man that you see me now, I was originally a Barbarian;' as if Burke should say, 'I came over a wild Irishman,'— which he might say in his present state of exaltation."

Having expressed a desire to have an island like Inchkenneth, Dr. Johnson set himself to think what would be necessary for a man in such a situation. "Sir, I should build me a fortification, if I came to live here; for, if you have it not, what should hinder a parcel of ruffians to land in the night, and carry off every thing you have in the house, which, in a remote country, would be more valuable than cows and sheep? add to all this the danger of having your throat cut."—Boswell. "I would have a large dog."—Johnson. "So you may, sir; but a large dog is of no use but to alarm."—He, however, I apprehend, thinks too lightly of the power of that animal. I have heard him say, that he is afraid of no dog. "He would take him up by the hinder legs, which would render him quite helpless,—and then knock his head against a stone, and beat out his brains."—Topham Beauclerk told me, that at his house in the country, two large ferocious dogs were fighting. Dr. Johnson looked steadily at them for a little while; and then, as one would separate two little boys, who are foolishly hurting each other, he ran up to them, and cuffed their heads till he drove them asunder. But few men have his intrepidity, Herculean strength, or presence of mind.

Young
Col a
complete
islander

Most thieves or robbers would be afraid to encounter a mastiff.

I observed, that, when young Col talked of the lands belonging to his family, he always said, "*my* lands." For this he had a plausible pretence; for he told me, there has been a custom in this family, that the laird resigns the estate to the eldest son when he comes of age, reserving to himself only a certain life-rent. He said, it was a voluntary custom; but I think I found an instance in the charter-room, that there was such an obligation in a contract of marriage. If the custom was voluntary, it was only curious; but if founded on obligation, it might be dangerous; for I have been told, that in Otaheité, whenever a child is born, (a son, I think,) the father loses his right to the estate and honours, and that this unnatural, or rather absurd custom, occasions the murder of many children.

Young Col told us he could run down a greyhound; "for, (said he,) the dog runs himself out of breath, by going too quick, and then I get up with him." I accounted for his advantage over the dog, by remarking that Col had the faculty of reason, and knew how to moderate his pace, which the dog had not sense enough to do. Dr. Johnson said, "He is a noble animal. He is as complete an islander as the mind can figure. He is a farmer, a sailor, a hunter, a fisher: he will run you down a dog: if any man has a *tail*, it is Col. He is hospitable; and he has an intrepidity of talk, whether he understands the subject or not. I regret that he is not more intellectual."

Dr. Johnson observed, that there was nothing of which he would not undertake to persuade a Frenchman in a foreign country. "I'll carry a Frenchman to St. Paul's Church-yard, and I'll tell him, 'by our law you may walk half round the church; but, if you

walk round the whole, you will be punished capitally : ' His early
and he will believe me at once.   Now, no Englishman death
would readily swallow such a thing : he would go and
inquire of somebody else."—The Frenchman's credulity, I observed, must be owing to his being accustomed to implicit submission ; whereas every Englishman
reasons upon the laws of his country, and instructs his
representatives, who compose the legislature.

This day was passed in looking at a small island
adjoining Inchkenneth, which afforded nothing worthy
of observation ; and in such social and gay entertainments as our little society could furnish.

Tuesday, 19th October.

After breakfast we took leave of the young ladies,
and of our excellent companion Col, to whom we had
been so much obliged.   He had now put us under the
care of his Chief ; and was to hasten back to Sky.
We parted from him with very strong feelings of kindness and gratitude ; and we hoped to have had some
future opportunity of proving to him the sincerity of
what we felt ; but in the following year he was unfortunately lost in the Sound between Ulva and Mull ;
and this imperfect memorial, joined to the high honour
of being tenderly and respectfully mentioned by Dr.
Johnson, is the only return which the uncertainty of
human events has permitted us to make to this deserving
young man.

Sir Allan, who obligingly undertook to accompany
us to Icolmkill, had a strong good boat, with four stout
rowers.   We coasted along Mull till we reached Gribon,
where is what is called Mackinnon's cave, compared
with which that at Ulinish is inconsiderable.   It is in
a rock of a great height, close to the sea.   Upon the

M 387

Mac-
kinnon's
cave
left of its entrance there is a cascade, almost perpen-
dicular from the top to the bottom of the rock. There
is a tradition that it was conducted thither artificially,
to supply the inhabitants of the cave with water. Dr.
Johnson gave no credit to this tradition. As, on the
one hand, his faith in the Christian religion is firmly
founded upon good grounds; so, on the other, he is
incredulous when there is no sufficient reason for belief;
being in this respect just the reverse of modern infidels,
who, however nice and scrupulous in weighing the
evidences of religion, are yet often so ready to believe
the most absurd and improbable tales of another nature,
that Lord Hailes well observed, a good essay might be
written *Sur la credulité des Incredules.*

The height of this cave I cannot tell with any tolerable
exactness: but it seemed to be very lofty, and to be a
pretty regular arch. We penetrated, by candlelight,
a great way; by our measurement, no less than four
hundred and eighty-five feet. Tradition says, that a
piper and twelve men once advanced into this cave,
nobody can tell how far; and never returned At the
distance to which we proceeded the air was quite pure;
for the candle burned freely, without the least appearance of the flame growing globular; but as we had
only one, we thought it dangerous to venture farther,
lest, should it have been extinguished, we should have
had no means of ascertaining whether we could remain
without danger. Dr. Johnson said, this was the greatest
natural curiosity he had ever seen.

We saw the island of Staffa, at no very great distance, but could not land upon it, the surge was so high
on its rocky coast.

Sir Allan, anxious for the honour of Mull, was still
talking of its *woods,* and pointing them out to Dr.
Johnson, as appearing at a distance on the skirts of

that island, as we sailed along.—Johnson. "Sir, I saw at Tobermorie what they called a wood, which I unluckily took for *heath*. If you shew me what I shall take for *furze*, it will be something."

In the afternoon we went ashore on the coast of Mull, and partook of a cold repast, which we carried with us. We hoped to have procured some rum or brandy for our boatmen and servants, from a publick-house near where we landed; but unfortunately a funeral a few days before had exhausted all their store. Mr. Campbell however, one of the Duke of Argyle's tacks-men, who lived in the neighbourhood, on receiving a message from Sir Allan, sent us a liberal supply.

We continued to coast along Mull, and passed by Nuns' Island, which, it is said, belonged to the nuns of Icolmkill, and from which, we were told, the stone for the buildings there was taken. As we sailed along by moon-light, in a sea somewhat rough, and often between black and gloomy rocks, Dr. Johnson said, "If this be not *roving among the Hebrides*, nothing is."—The repetition of words which he had so often previously used, made a strong impression on my imagination; and, by a natural course of thinking, led me to consider how our present adventures would appear to me at a future period.

I have often experienced, that scenes through which a man has passed, improve by lying in the memory: they grow mellow. *Acti labores sunt jucundi.* This may be owing to comparing them with present listless ease. Even harsh scenes acquire a softness by length of time; [1] and some are like very loud sounds, which

---

[1] I have lately observed that this thought has been elegantly expressed by Cowley:

"Things which offend when present, and affright,
In memory, well painted, move delight."

The travellers land on Iona

do not please, or at least do not please so much, till you are removed to a certain distance. They may be compared to strong coarse pictures, which will not bear to be viewed near. Even pleasing scenes improve by time, and seem more exquisite in recollection, than when they were present; if they have not faded to dimness in the memory. Perhaps, there is so much evil in every human enjoyment, when present,—so much dross mixed with it, that it requires to be refined by time; and yet I do not see why time should not melt away the good and the evil in equal proportions;—why the shade should decay, and the light remain in preservation.

After a tedious sail, which, by our following various turnings of the coast of Mull, was extended to about forty miles, it gave us no small pleasure to perceive a light in the village at Icolmkill, in which almost all the inhabitants of the island live, close to where the ancient building stood. As we approached the shore, the tower of the cathedral, just discernible in the air, was a picturesque object.

When we had landed upon the sacred place, which, as long as I can remember, I had thought on with veneration, Dr. Johnson and I cordially embraced. We had long talked of visiting Icolmkill; and, from the lateness of the season, were at times very doubtful whether we should be able to effect our purpose. To have seen it, even alone, would have given me great satisfaction; but the venerable scene was rendered much more pleasing by the company of my great and pious friend, who was no less affected by it than I was; and who has described the impressions it should make on the mind, with such strength of thought, and energy of language, that I shall quote his words, as conveying my own sensations much more forcibly than I am capable of doing:

"We were now treading that illustrious Island, which was once the luminary of the Caledonian regions, whence savage clans and roving barbarians derived the benefits of knowledge, and the blessings of religion. To abstract the mind from all local emotion would be impossible, if it were endeavoured, and would be foolish if it were possible. Whatever withdraws us from the power of our senses, whatever makes the past, the distant, or the future, predominate over the present, advances us in the dignity of thinking beings. Far from me, and from my friends, be such frigid philosophy as may conduct us indifferent and unmoved over any ground which has been dignified by wisdom, bravery or virtue. That man is little to be envied, whose patriotism would not gain force upon the plain of *Marathon*, or whose piety would not grow warmer among the ruins of *Iona!*" [1]

A passage from Johnson's "Journey"

Upon hearing that Sir Allan M'Lean was arrived, the inhabitants, who still consider themselves as the people of M'Lean, to whom the island formerly belonged, though the Duke of Argyle has at present possession of it, ran eagerly to him.

We were accommodated this night in a large barn, the island affording no lodging that we should have liked so well. Some good hay was strewed at one end of it, to form a bed for us, upon which we lay with our clothes on; and we were furnished with blankets from the village. Each of us had a portmanteau for a pillow. When I awaked in the morn-

---

[1] Had our Tour produced nothing else but this sublime passage, the world must have acknowledged that it was not made in vain. The present respectable President of the Royal Society was so much struck on reading it, that he clasped his hands together, and remained for some time in an attitude of silent admiration.

The ruins of Iona ing, and looked round me, I could not help smiling at the idea of the chief of the M'Leans, the great English Moralist, and myself, lying thus extended in such a situation.

Wednesday, 20th October.

Early in the morning we surveyed the remains of antiquity at this place, accompanied by an illiterate fellow, as *Cicerone*, who called himself a descendant of a cousin of Saint Columba, the founder of the religious establishment here. As I knew that many persons had already examined them, and as I saw Dr. Johnson inspecting and measuring several of the ruins of which he has since given so full an account, my mind was quiescent; and I resolved to stroll among them at my ease, to take no trouble to investigate minutely, and only receive the general impression of solemn antiquity, and the particular ideas of such objects as should of themselves strike my attention.

We walked from the monastery of Nuns to the great church or cathedral, as they call it, along an old broken causeway. They told us, that this had been a street; and that there were good houses built on each side. Dr. Johnson doubted if it was any thing more than a paved road for the nuns. The convent of Monks, the great church, Oran's chapel, and four other chapels, are still to be discerned. But I must own that Icolmkill did not answer my expectations; for they were high, from what I had read of it, and still more from what I had heard and thought of it, from my earliest years. Dr. Johnson said, it came up to his expectations, because he had taken his impression from an account of it subjoined to Sacheverel's History of the Isle of Man, where it is said, there is

not much to be seen here. We were both disappointed, when we were shewn what are called the
monuments of the kings of Scotland, Ireland, and
Denmark, and of a King of France. There are only
some grave-stones flat on the earth, and we could see
no inscriptions. How far short was this of marble
monuments, like those in Westminster-Abbey, which
I had imagined here! The grave-stones of Sir Allan
M'Lean's family, and of that ot M'Quarrie, had as
good an appearance as the royal grave-stones; if they
were royal, we doubted.

My easiness to give credit to what I heard in the
course of our Tour was too great. Dr. Johnson's
peculiar accuracy of investigation detected much traditional fiction, and many gross mistakes. It is not to
be wondered at, that he was provoked by people care-
lessly telling him, with the utmost readiness and confidence, what he found, on questioning them a little
more, was erroneous. Of this there were innumerable
instances.

I left him and Sir Allan at breakfast in our barn,
and stole back again to the cathedral, to indulge in
solitude and devout meditation. While contemplating
the venerable ruins, I reflected with much satisfaction,
that the solemn scenes of piety never lose their sanctity
and influence, though the cares and follies of life may
prevent us from visiting them, or may even make us
fancy that their effects are only " as yesterday, when it
is past," and never again to be perceived. I hoped,
that, ever after having been in this holy place, I should
maintain an exemplary conduct. One has a strange
propensity to fix upon some point of time from whence
a better course of life may begin.

Being desirous to visit the opposite shore of the
island, where Saint Columba is said to have landed, I

Boswell's
solitary
medita-
tion

The Chieftain's feudal authority

procured a horse from one M'Ginnis, who ran along as my guide. The M'Ginnises are said to be a branch of the clan of M'Lean. Sir Allan had been told that this man had refused to send him some rum, at which the knight was in great indignation. "You rascal! (said he,) don't you know that I can hang you, if I please?"—Not adverting to the Chieftain's power over his clan, I imagined that Sir Allan had known of some capital crime that the fellow had committed, which he could discover, and so get him condemned; and said, "How so?"—"Why, (said Sir Allan,) are they not all my people?"—Sensible of my inadvertency, and most willing to contribute what I could towards the continuation of feudal authority, "Very true," said I.—Sir Allan went on: "Refuse to send rum to me, you rascal! Don't you know that, if I order you to go and cut a man's throat, you are to do it?"—"Yes, an't please your honour! and my own too, and hang myself too."—The poor fellow denied that he had refused to send the rum. His making these professions was not merely a pretence in presence of his Chief; for after he and I were out of Sir Allan's hearing, he told me, "Had he sent his dog for the rum, I would have given it: I would cut my bones for him."—It was very remarkable to find such an attachment to a Chief, though he had then no connection with the island, and had not been there for fourteen years.—Sir Allan, by way of upbraiding the fellow, said, "I believe you are a *Campbell*."

The place which I went to see is about two miles from the village. They call it *Portawherry*, from the wherry in which Columba came; though, when they shew the length of his vessel, as marked on the beach by two heaps of stones, they say, "Here is the length of the *Currach*," using the Erse word.

Icolmkill is a fertile island. The inhabitants export A talk
some cattle and grain; and I was told, they import upon
nothing but iron and salt. They are industrious, and politicks
make their own woollen and linen cloth; and they
brew a good deal of beer, which we did not find in
any of the other islands.

We set sail again about mid-day, and in the evening
landed on Mull, near the house of the Reverend Mr.
Neal M'Leod, who having been informed of our coming,
by a message from Sir Allan, came out to meet us.
We were this night very agreeably entertained at his
house. Dr. Johnson observed to me, that he was the
cleanest-headed man that he had met with in the
Western islands. He seemed to be well acquainted
with Dr. Johnson's writings, and courteously said, "I
have been often obliged to you, though I never had the
pleasure of seeing you before."

He told us, he had lived for some time in St. Kilda,
under the tuition of the minister or catechist there, and
had there first read Horace and Virgil. The scenes
which they describe must have been a strong contrast
to the dreary waste around him.

Thursday, 21st October.

This morning the subject of politicks was introduced.
—JOHNSON. "Pulteney was as paltry a fellow as could
be. He was a Whig, who pretended to be honest;
and you know it is ridiculous for a Whig to pretend to
be honest. He cannot hold it out." He called Mr.
Pitt a meteor; Sir Robert Walpole a fixed star.—
He said, "It is wonderful to think that all the force
of government was required to prevent Wilkes from
being chosen the chief magistrate of London, though

*M 387

Mr.
Wilkes the liverymen knew he would rob their shops,—knew he would debauch their daughters." [1]

BOSWELL. "The History of England is so strange, that, if it were not so well vouched as it is, it would hardly be credible."—JOHNSON. "Sir, if it were told as shortly, and with as little preparation for introducing the different events, as the History of the Jewish Kings, it would be equally liable to objections of improbability."—Mr. M'Leod was much pleased with the justice and novelty of the thought.—Dr. Johnson illustrated what he had said, as follows : " Take, as an instance, Charles the First's concessions to his parliament, which were greater and greater, in proportion as the parliament grew more insolent, and less deserving of trust. Had these concessions been related nakedly, without any

[1] I think it incumbent on me to make some observation on this strong satirical sally on my classical companion, Mr. Wilkes. Reporting it lately from memory, in his presence, I expressed it thus :—" They knew he would rob their shops, *if he durst*; they knew he would debauch their daughters, *if he could*;" which, according to the French phrase, may be said *renchérir* on Dr. Johnson ; but on looking into my Journal, I found it as above, and would by no means make any addition. Mr. Wilkes received both readings with a good humour that I cannot enough admire. Indeed both he and I (as, with respect to myself, the reader has more than once had occasion to observe in the course of this Journal,) are too fond of a *bon mot*, not to relish it, though we should be ourselves the object of it.

Let me add, in justice to the gentleman here mentioned, that at a subsequent period, he *was* elected chief magistrate of London, and discharged the duties of that high office with great honour to himself, and advantage to the city.—Some years before Dr. Johnson died, I was fortunate enough to bring him and Mr. Wilkes together; the consequence of which was, that they were ever afterwards on easy and not unfriendly terms. The particulars I shall have great pleasure in relating at large in my LIFE OF DR. JOHNSON.

detail of the circumstances which generally led to them, they would not have been believed."

Sir Allan M'Lean bragged, that Scotland had the advantage of England, by its having more water. JOHNSON. "Sir we would not have your water, to take the vile bogs which produce it. You have too much! A man who is drowned has more water than either of us;"—and then he laughed.—(But this was surely robust sophistry: for the people of taste in England, who have seen Scotland, own that its variety of rivers and lakes makes it naturally more beautiful than England, in that respect.)—Pursuing his victory over Sir Allan, he proceeded: "Your country consists of two things, stone and water. There is, indeed, a little earth above the stone in some places, but a very little; and the stone is always appearing. It is like a man in rags; the naked skin is still peeping out."

He took leave of Mr. M'Leod, saying, "Sir, I thank you for your entertainment, and your conversation."

Mr. Campbell, who had been so polite yesterday, came this morning on purpose to breakfast with us, and very obligingly furnished us with horses to proceed on our journey to Mr. M'Lean's of Lochbuy, where we were to pass the night. We dined at the house of Dr. Alexander M'Lean, another physician in Mull, who was so much struck with the uncommon conversation of Dr. Johnson, that he observed to me, "This man is just a *hogshead* of sense."

Dr. Johnson said of the *Turkish Spy*, which lay in the room, that it told nothing but what every body might have known at that time; and that what was good in it, did not pay you for the trouble of reading to find it.

After a very tedious ride, through what appeared to

Johnson a "hogshead of sense"

The me the most gloomy and desolate country I had ever
Laird of beheld, we arrived, between seven and eight o'clock,
Lochbuy at Moy, the seat of the Laird of Lochbuy.—*Buy*, in
Erse, signifies yellow, and I at first imagined that the
loch or branch of the sea here, was thus denominated,
in the same manner as the Red Sea; but I afterwards learned that it derived its name from a hill
above it, which being of a yellowish hue, has the
epithet of Buy.

We had heard much of Lochbuy's being a great
roaring braggadocio, a kind of Sir John Falstaff, both
in size and manners; but we found that they had
swelled him up to a fictitious size, and clothed him
with imaginary qualities.—Col's idea of him was
equally extravagant, though very different: he told
us, he was quite a Don Quixote; and said, he would
give a great deal to see him and Dr. Johnson together. The truth is, that Lochbuy proved to be
only a bluff, comely, noisy old gentleman, proud of
his hereditary consequence, and a very hearty and
hospitable landlord. Lady Lochbuy was sister to
Sir Allan M'Lean, but much older. He said to me,
"They are quite *Antediluvians*." Being told that
Dr. Johnson did not hear well, Lochbuy bawled out
to him, " Are you of the Johnstons of Glencro, or of
Ardnamurchan?"—Dr. Johnson gave him a significant look, but made no answer; and I told Lochbuy
that he was not John*ston*, but John*son*, and that he was
an Englishman.

Lochbuy some years ago tried to prove himself a
weak man, liable to imposition, or, as we term it in
Scotland, a *facile* man, in order to set aside a lease
which he had granted; but failed in the attempt. On
my mentioning this circumstance to Dr. Johnson, he
seemed much surprized that such a suit was admitted

by the Scottish law, and observed, that "in England **Cold**
no man is allowed to *stultify* himself." [1] **sheep's-**

Sir Allan, Lochbuy, and I, had the conversation **head**
chiefly to ourselves to-night : Dr. Johnson, being extremely weary, went to bed soon after supper.

Friday, 22nd October.

Before Dr. Johnson came to breakfast, Lady Lochbuy said. "he was a *dungeon* of wit ; " a very common
phrase in Scotland to express a profoundness of intellect,
though he afterwards told me, that he never had heard
it. She proposed that he should have some cold
sheep's-head for breakfast. Sir Allan seemed displeased at his sister's vulgarity, and wondered how
such a thought should come into her head. From a
mischievous love of sport, I took the lady's part ; and
very gravely said, "I think it is but fair to give him
an offer of it. If he does not choose it, he may let
it alone."—"I think so," said the lady, looking at
her brother with an air of victory. Sir Allan, finding
the matter desperate, strutted about the room, and
took snuff. When Dr. Johnson came in, she called
to him, "Do you choose any cold sheep's-head, sir ? "
—"No, madam," said he, with a tone of surprise and
anger.—"It is here, sir," said she, supposing he had
refused it to save the trouble of bringing it in. They
thus went on at cross purposes, till he confirmed his
refusal in a manner not to be misunderstood ; while I
sat quietly by, and enjoyed my success.

After breakfast, we surveyed the old castle, in the
pit or dungeon of which Lochbuy had some years

[1] This maxim, however, has been controverted. See Blackstone's COMMENTARIES, Vol. II. p. 292 ; and the authorities
there quoted.

The main
land at
last

before taken upon him to imprison several persons; and though he had been fined in a considerable sum by the Court of Justiciary, he was so little affected by it, that while we were examining the dungeon, he said to me, with a smile, "Your father knows something of this;" (alluding to my father's having sat as one of the judges on his trial.) Sir Allan whispered me, that the laird could not be persuaded, that he had lost his heritable jurisdiction.

We then set out for the ferry, by which we were to cross to the main land of Argyleshire. Lochbuy and Sir Allan accompanied us. We were told much of a war-saddle, on which this reputed Don Quixote used to be mounted; but we did not see it, for the young laird had applied it to a less noble purpose, having taken it to Falkirk fair *with a drove of black cattle.*

We bade adieu to Lochbuy, and to our very kind conductor, Sir Allan M'Lean, on the shore of Mull, and then got into the ferry-boat, the bottom of which was strewed with branches of trees or bushes, upon which we sat. We had a good day and a fine passage, and in the evening landed at Oban, where we found a tolerable inn. After having been so long confined at different times in islands, from which it was always uncertain when we could get away, it was comfortable to be now on the main land, and to know that, if in health, we might get to any place in Scotland or England in a certain number of days.

Here we discovered from the conjectures which were formed, that the people on the main land were intirely ignorant of our motions; for in a Glasgow news-paper we found a paragraph, which, as it contains a just and well-turned compliment to my illustrious friend, I shall here insert:

"We are well assured that Dr. Johnson is confined

by tempestuous weather to the isle of Sky; it being Gold-
unsafe to venture, in a small boat upon such a stormy smith's
surge as is very common there at this time of the year. "Tra-
Such a philosopher, detained on an almost barren veller"
island, resembles a whale left upon the strand. The
latter will be welcome to every body, on account of
his oil, his bone, &c. and the other will charm his
companions, and the rude inhabitants, with his superior
knowledge and wisdom, calm resignation, and un-
bounded benevolence."

Saturday, 23rd October.

After a good night's rest, we breakfasted at our
leisure. We talked of Goldsmith's *Traveller*, of which
Dr. Johnson spoke highly; and, while I was helping
him on with his great coat, he repeated from it the
character of the British nation, which he did with such
energy, that the tear started into his eye :

" Stern o'er each bosom reason holds her state.
With daring aims irregularly great,
Pride in their port, defiance in their eye,
I see the lords of humankind pass by,
Intent on high designs, a thoughtful band,
By forms unfashion'd, fresh from nature's hand ;
Fierce in their native hardiness of soul,
True to imagin'd right, above control,
While ev'n the peasant boasts these rights to scan,
And learns to venerate himself as man."

We could get but one bridle here, which, according
to the maxim *detur digniori*, was appropriated to Dr.
Johnson's sheltie. I and Joseph rode with halters.
We crossed in a ferry-boat a pretty wide lake, and on

Pope and
Cowley

the farther side of it, close by the shore, found a hut for our inn. We were much wet. I changed my clothes in part, and was at pains to get myself well dried. Dr. Johnson resolutely kept on all his clothes, wet as they were, letting them steam before the smoky turf fire. I thought him in the wrong; but his firmness was, perhaps, a species of heroism.

I remember but little of our conversation. I mentioned Shenstone's saying of Pope, that he had the art of condensing sense more than any body. Dr. Johnson said, "It is not true, sir. There is more sense in a line of Cowley than in a page (or a sentence, or ten lines,—I am not quite certain of the very phrase) of Pope." He maintained that Archibald, Duke of Argyle, was a narrow man. I wondered at this; and observed, that his building so great a house at Inveraray was not like a narrow man. "Sir, (said he,) when a narrow man has resolved to build a house, he builds it like another man. But Archibald, Duke of Argyle, was narrow in his ordinary expences, in his quotidian expences."

The distinction is very just. It is in the ordinary expences of life that a man's liberality or narrowness is to be discovered.—I never heard the word *quotidian* in this sense, and I imagined it to be a word of Dr. Johnson's own fabrication; but I have since found it in *Young's Night Thoughts*, (Night fifth,)

"Death's a destroyer of quotidian prey,"

and in my friend's Dictionary, supported by the authorities of Charles I. and Dr. Donne.

It rained very hard as we journied on after dinner. The roar of torrents from the mountains, as we passed along in the dusk, and the other circumstances attend-

ing our ride this evening, have been mentioned with
so much animation by Dr. Johnson, that I shall not
attempt to say any thing on the subject.

Johnson
tastes
whisky

We got at night to Inveraray, where we found
an excellent inn. Even here, Dr. Johnson would not
change his wet clothes.

The prospect of good accommodation cheered us
much. We supped well; and after supper, Dr. Johnson, whom I had not seen taste any fermented liquor
during all our travels, called for a gill of whisky.
"Come, (said he,) let me know what it is that makes
a Scotchman happy!" He drank it all but a drop,
which I begged leave to pour into my glass, that I
might say we had drunk whisky together. I proposed
Mrs. Thrale should be our toast. He would not have
her drunk in whisky, but rather "some insular lady;"
so we drank one of the ladies whom we had lately
left.—He owned to-night, that he got as good a room
and bed as at an English inn.

I had here the pleasure of finding a letter from
home, which relieved me from the anxiety I had suffered, in consequence of not having received any
account of my family for many weeks. I also found
a letter from Mr. Garrick, which was a regale as
agreeable as a pine-apple would be in a desert. He
had favoured me with his correspondence for many
years; and when Dr. Johnson and I were at Inverness, I had written to him as follows:

"Inverness, Sunday, 29 August, 1773.

"MY DEAR SIR,

"HERE I am, and Mr. Samuel Johnson actually
with me. We were a night at Fores, in coming to
which, in the dusk of the evening, we passed over the
bleak and blasted heath where Macbeth met the witches.

Your old preceptor repeated, with much solemnity, the speech—

> "'How far is't called to Fores? What are these,
> So wither'd and so wild in their attire,' &c.

This day we visited the ruins of Macbeth's castle at Inverness. I have had great romantick satisfaction in seeing Johnson upon the classical scenes of Shakspeare in Scotland; which I really looked upon as almost as improbable as that 'Birnam wood should come to Dunsinane.' Indeed, as I have always been accustomed to view him as a permanent London object, it would not be much more wonderful to me to see St. Paul's church moving along where we now are. As yet we have travelled in post-chaises; but to-morrow we are to mount on horseback, and ascend into the mountains by Fort Augustus, and so on to the ferry, where we are to cross to Sky. We shall see that Island fully, and then visit some more of the Hebrides; after which we are to land in Argyleshire, proceed by Glasgow to Auchinleck, repose there a competent time, and then return to Edinburgh, from whence the Rambler will depart for old England again, as soon as he finds it convenient. Hitherto we have had a very prosperous expedition. I flatter myself, *servetur ad imum, qualis ab incepto processerit*. He is in excellent spirits, and I have a rich journal of his conversation. Look back, *Davy*,[1] to Litchfield;— run up through the time that has elapsed since you first knew Mr. Johnson,—and enjoy with me his present extraordinary Tour. I could not resist the impulse of

---

[1] I took the liberty of giving this familiar appellation to my celebrated friend, to bring in a more lively manner to his remembrance the period when he was Dr. Johnson's pupil.

writing to you from this place. The situation of the Garrick's
old castle corresponds exactly to Shakspeare's de- reply
scription. While we were there to-day, it happened
oddly, that a raven perched upon one of the chimney-
tops, and croaked. Then I in my turn repeated—

> " 'The raven himself is hoarse,
> That croaks the fatal entrance of Duncan,
> Under my battlements.'

"I wish you had been with us. Think what enthusiastick happiness I shall have to see Mr. Samuel
Johnson walking among the romantick rocks and woods
of my ancestors at Auchinleck! Write to me at Edinburgh. You owe me his verses on great George and
tuneful Cibber, and the bad verses which led him to
make his fine ones on Philips the musician. Keep
your promise, and let me have them. I offer my very
best compliments to Mrs. Garrick, and ever am

"Your warm admirer and friend,

"JAMES BOSWELL."

"To David Garrick, Esq. London."

His answer was as follows;

"Hampton, September 14, 1773.

"DEAR SIR,

"You stole away from London, and left us all
in the lurch; for we expected you one night at the
club, and knew nothing of your departure. Had I
payed you what I owed you, for the book you bought
for me, I should only have grieved for the loss of your
company, and slept with a quiet conscience; but,
wounded as it is, it must remain so till I see you
again, though I am sure our good friend Mr. Johnson
will discharge the debt for me, if you will let him.—

Your account of your journey to Fores, the raven, old
castle, &c. &c. made me half mad. Are you not
rather too late in the year for fine weather, which is
the life and soul of seeing places?—I hope your pleasure
will continue *qualis ab incepto*, &c.

"Your friend [1]——— threatens me much. I only
wish that he would put his threats in execution, and, if
he prints his play, I will forgive him. I remember he
complained to you, that his bookseller called for the
money for some copies of his ———, which I subscribed for, and that I desired him to call again.—The
truth is, that my wife was not at home, and that for
weeks together I have not ten shillings in my pocket.
—However, had it been otherwise, it was not so
great a crime to draw his poetical vengeance upon me.
—I despise all that he can do, and am glad that I can
so easily get rid of him and his ingratitude.—I am
hardened both to abuse and ingratitude.

"You, I am sure, will no more recommend your
poetasters to my civility and good offices.

"Shall I recommend to you a play of Eschylus,
(the Prometheus,) published and translated by poor
old Morell, who is a good scholar, and an acquaintance of mine? It will be but half a guinea, and your

[1] I have suppressed my friend's name from an apprehension
of wounding his sensibility; but I would not withhold from
my readers a passage which shews Mr. Garrick's mode of
writing as the Manager of a Theatre, and contains a pleasing trait of his domestick life. His judgment of dramatick
pieces, so far as concerns their exhibition on the stage,
must be allowed to have considerable weight. But from the
effect which a perusal of the tragedy here condemned had
upon myself, and from the opinions of some eminent criticks,
I venture to pronounce that it has much poetical merit; and
its authour has distinguished himself by several performances
which shew that the epithet *poetaster* was, in the present
instance, much misapplied.

name shall be put in the list I am making for him.

"Now for the Epitaphs!

[These, together with the verses on George the
     Second, and Colley Cibber, as his Poet Laureat,
     of which imperfect copies are gone about, will
     appear in my Life of Dr. Johnson.]

"I have no more paper, or I should have said more
to you.   My love and respects to Mr. Johnson.
                                   "Yours ever,
                                        "D. GARRICK."

"I can't write.   I have the gout in my hand."

"To James Boswell, Esq. Edinburgh."

Sunday, 24th October.

We passed the forenoon calmly and placidly.   I
prevailed on Dr. Johnson to read aloud Ogden's sixth
Sermon on Prayer, which he did with a distinct expression, and pleasing solemnity.   He praised my
favourite preacher, his elegant language, and remarkable acuteness; and said, he fought infidels with their
own weapons.

As a specimen of Ogden's manner, I insert the
following passage from the sermon which Dr. Johnson
now read.   The preacher, after arguing against that
vain philosophy which maintains, in conformity with
the hard principle of eternal necessity, or unchangeable
predetermination, that the only effect of prayer for
others, although we are exhorted to pray for them,

Hervey's "Meditations" is to produce good dispositions in ourselves towards them; thus expresses himself:

"A plain man may be apt to ask, But if this then, though enjoined in the holy scriptures, is to be my real aim and intention, when I am taught to pray for other persons, why is it that I do not plainly so express it? Why is not the form of the petition brought nearer to the meaning? Give them, say I to our heavenly father, what is good. But this, I am to understand, will be as it will be, and is not for me to alter. What is it then that I am doing? I am desiring to become charitable myself; and why may I not plainly say so? Is there shame in it, or impiety? The wish is laudable: why should I form designs to hide it?

"Or is it, perhaps, better to be brought about by indirect means, and in this artful manner? Alas! who is it that I would impose on? From whom can it be, in this commerce, that I desire to hide any thing? When, as my Saviour commands me, I have *entered into my closet, and shut my door*, there are but two parties privy to my devotions, GOD and my own heart; which of the two am I deceiving?"

He wished to have more books, and, upon inquiring if there were any in the house, was told that a waiter had some, which were brought to him; but I recollect none of them, except Hervey's *Meditations*. He thought slightingly of this admired book. He treated it with ridicule, and would not allow even the scene of the dying Husband and Father to be pathetick. I am not an impartial judge; for Hervey's *Meditations* engaged my affections in my early years.—He read a passage concerning the moon, ludicrously, and shewed how easily he could, in the same style, make reflections on that planet, the very reverse of Hervey's, representing her as treacherous to mankind. He did this with much humour; but I have not preserved the particulars. He then indulged a playful fancy, in making a *Meditation on a Pudding*, of which I hastily wrote down, in his presence, the following note; which, though imperfect, may serve to give my readers some idea of it.

A Meditation on a Pudding

MEDITATION ON A PUDDING

" Let us seriously reflect of what a pudding is composed. It is composed of flour that once waved in the golden grain, and drank the dews of the morning; of milk pressed from the swelling udder by the gentle hand of the beauteous milkmaid, whose beauty and innocence might have recommended a worse draught; who, while she stroked the udder, indulged no ambitious thoughts of wandering in palaces, formed no plans for the destruction of her fellow-creatures: milk, which is drawn from the cow, that useful animal, that eats the grass of the field, and supplies us with that which made the greatest part of the food of mankind in the age which the poets have agreed to call golden. It is made with an egg, that miracle of nature, which the theoretical Burnet has compared to creation. An egg contains water within its beautiful smooth surface; and an unformed mass, by the incubation of the parent, becomes a regular animal, furnished with bones and sinews, and covered with feathers.—Let us consider; can there be more wanting to complete the Meditation on a Pudding? If more is wanting, more may be found. It contains salt, which keeps the sea from putrefaction: salt, which is made the image of intellectual excellence, contributes to the formation of a pudding."

In a Magazine I found a saying of Dr. Johnson's, something to this purpose; that the happiest part of a man's life is what he passes lying awake in bed in the morning. I read it to him. He said, " I may, perhaps, have said this ; for nobody, at times, talks more laxly than I do." I ventured to suggest to him, that this was dangerous from one of his authority.

I spoke of living in the country, and upon what footing one should be with neighbours. I observed that some people were afraid of being on too easy a footing with them, from an apprehension that their time would not be their own. He made the obvious remark, that it depended much on what kind of neighbours one has, whether it was desirable to be on an easy footing with them, or not. I mentioned a certain baronet, who told me, he never was happy in the country, till he was not on speaking terms with his neighbours, which he contrived in different ways to bring about. " Lord ——— (said he) stuck long ; but at last the fellow pounded my pigs, and then I got rid of him."—Johnson. " Nay, sir, My Lord got rid of Sir John, and shewed how little he valued him, by putting his pigs in the pound."

I told Dr. Johnson I was in some difficulty how to act at Inveraray. I had reason to think that the Duchess of Argyle disliked me, on account of my zeal in the Douglas cause ; but the Duke of Argyle had always been pleased to treat me with great civility. They were now at the castle, which is a very short walk from our inn ; and the question was, whether I should go and pay my respects there. Dr. Johnson, to whom I had stated the case, was clear that I ought ; but, in his usual way, he was very shy of discovering a desire to be invited there himself. Though from a conviction of the benefit of subordination to society, he has always shewn great respect to persons of high rank, when he happened to be in their company, yet his pride of character has ever made him guard against any appearance of courting the **Boswell** great. Besides, he was impatient to go to Glasgow, **calls at** where he expected letters. At the same time he was, **the Castle** I believe, secretly not unwilling to have attention paid him by so great a Chieftain, and so exalted a nobleman. He insisted that I should not go to the castle this day before dinner, as it would look like seeking an invitation. " But, (said I,) if the duke invites us to dine with him to-morrow, shall we accept?"—"Yes, sir;" I think he said, "to be sure." But, he added, "He won't ask us!"—I mentioned, that I was afraid my company might be disagreeable to the duchess. He treated this objection with a manly disdain : "*That*, sir, he must settle with his wife."—We dined well. I went to the castle just about the time when I supposed the ladies would be retired from dinner. I sent in my name; and, being shewn in, found the amiable duke sitting at the head of his table with several gentlemen. I was most politely received, and gave his grace some particulars of the curious journey which I had been making with Dr. Johnson. When we rose from table, the duke said to me, "I hope you and Dr. Johnson will dine with us to-morrow." I thanked his grace; but told him, my friend was in a great hurry to get back to London. The duke, with a kind complacency, said, "He will stay one day; and I will take care he shall see this place to advantage." I said, I should be sure to let him know his grace's invitation.—As I was going away, the duke said, "Mr. Boswell, won't you have some tea?"—I thought it best to get over the meeting with the duchess this night; so respectfully agreed. I was conducted to the drawing-room by the duke, who announced my name; but the duchess, who was sitting with her daughter, Lady Betty Hamilton, and some other ladies, took not the least notice of me. I should

The in-fluence of peers at elections have been mortified at being thus coldly received by a lady of whom I, with the rest of the world, have always entertained a very high admiration, had I not been consoled by the obliging attention of the duke.

When I returned to the inn, I informed Dr. Johnson of the Duke of Argyle's invitation, with which he was much pleased, and readily accepted of it.—We talked of a violent contest which was then carrying on, with a view to the next general election for Ayrshire; where one of the candidates, in order to undermine the old and established interest, had artfully held himself out as a champion for the independency of the county against aristocratic influence, and had persuaded several gentlemen into a resolution to oppose every candidate who was supported by peers.—" Foolish fellows! (said Dr. Johnson,) don't they see that they are as much dependent upon the peers one way as the other. The peers have but to *oppose* a candidate, to ensure him success. It is said, the only way to make a pig go forward, is to pull him back by the tail. These people must be treated like pigs."

Monday, 25th October.

My acquaintance, the Reverend Mr. John M'Aulay, one of the Ministers of Inveraray, and brother to our good friend at Calder, came to us this morning, and accompanied us to the castle, where I presented Dr. Johnson to the Duke of Argyle. We were shewn through the house; and I never shall forget the impression made upon my fancy by some of the ladies' maids tripping about in neat morning dresses. After seeing for a long time little but rusticity, their lively manner, and gay inviting appearance, pleased me so much, that I thought, for the moment, I could have been a **The** knight-errant for them.[1] **travellers**

We then got into a low one-horse chair, ordered for **at Inver-** us by the duke, in which we drove about the place. Dr. **aray** Johnson was much struck by the grandeur and elegance **Castle** of this princely seat. He thought, however, the castle too low, and wished it had been a story higher.—He said, "What I admire here, is the total defiance of expence." I had a particular pride in shewing him a great number of fine old trees, to compensate for the nakedness which had made such an impression on him on the eastern coast of Scotland.

When we came in, before dinner, we found the duke and some gentlemen in the hall. Dr. Johnson took much notice of the large collection of arms, which are excellently disposed there. I told what he had said to Sir Alexander M'Donald, of his ancestors not suffering their arms to rust. "Well, (said the doctor,) but let us be glad we live in times when arms *may* rust. We can sit to-day at his grace's table, without any risk of being attacked, and perhaps sitting down again wounded or maimed." The duke placed Dr. Johnson next himself at table. I was in fine spirits; and though sensible that I had the misfortune of not being in favour with the duchess, I was not in the least disconcerted, and offered her grace some of the dish that was before me. It must be owned that I was in the right to be quite unconcerned, if I could. I was the Duke of Argyle's guest; and I had no reason to suppose that he adopted the prejudices and resentments of the Duchess of Hamilton.

I knew it was the rule of modern high life not to drink to any body; but, that I might have the satisfac-

---

[1] On reflection, at the distance of several years, I wonder that my venerable fellow-traveller should have read this passage without censuring my levity.

Boswell
drinks the
Duchess's
health

tion for once to look the duchess in the face, with a glass
in my hand, I with a respectful air addressed her,—
"My Lady Duchess, I have the honour to drink your
grace's good health."—I repeated the words audibly,
and with a steady countenance. This was, perhaps,
rather too much; but some allowance must be made
for human feelings.

The duchess was very attentive to Dr. Johnson.   I
know not how a *middle state* came to be mentioned.   Her
grace wished to hear him on that point. "Madam, (said
he,) your own relation, Mr. Archibald Campbell, can
tell you better about it than I can.   He was a bishop
of the nonjuring communion, and wrote a book upon
the subject." [1]—He engaged to get it for her grace.
He afterwards gave a full history of Mr. Archibald
Campbell, which I am sorry I do not recollect particularly.   He said, Mr. Campbell had been bred a
violent Whig, but afterwards "kept *better company*,
and became a Tory."   He said this with a smile, in
pleasant allusion, as I thought, to the opposition between

[1] As this book is now become very scarce, I shall subjoin
the title, which is curious :
"The Doctrines of a Middle State between Death and the
Resurrection : Of Prayers for the Dead : And the Necessity
of Purification ; plainly proved from the holy Scriptures, and
the Writings of the Fathers of the Primitive Church : And
acknowledged by several learned Fathers and great Divines
of the Church of England and others since the Reformation.
To which is added, an Appendix concerning the Descent of
the Soul of Christ into Hell, while his Body lay in the Grave
Together with the Judgment of the Reverend Dr. Hickes concerning this Book, so far as relates to a Middle State, particular Judgment, and Prayers for the Dead as it appeared in
the first Edition.   And a Manuscript of the Right Reverend
Bishop Overall upon the Subject of a Middle State, and never
before printed.   Also, a Preservative against several of the
Errors of the Roman Church, in six small Treatises.   By
the Honourable Archibald Campbell."   Folio, 1721.

his own political principles and those of the duke's clan. The
He added that Mr. Campbell, after the Revolution, was Hon.
thrown into gaol on account of his tenets; but, on appli- Archibald
cation by letter to the old Lord Townshend, was released: Campbell
that he always spoke of his Lordship with great gratitude,
saying, "though a *Whig*, he had humanity."

Dr. Johnson and I passed some time together, in
June 1784, at Pembroke College, Oxford, with the
Reverend Dr. Adams, the master; and I having expressed a regret that my note relative to Mr. Archibald
Campbell was imperfect, he was then so good as to write
with his own hand, on the blank page of my Journal,
opposite to that which contains what I have now mentioned, the following paragraph; which, however, is not
quite so full as the narrative he gave at Inveraray:

"The Honourable Archibald Campbell was, I believe,
the nephew of the Marquis of Argyle. He began life
by engaging in Monmouth's rebellion, and, to escape the
law, lived some time in Surinam. When he returned,
he became zealous for episcopacy and monarchy; and
at the Revolution adhered not only to the Nonjurors,
but to those who refused to communicate with the Church
of England, or to be present at any worship where the
usurper was mentioned as king. He was, I believe,
more than once apprehended in the reign of King
William, and once at the accession of George. He
was the familiar friend of Hicks and Nelson; a man
of letters, but injudicious; and very curious and inquisi-
tive, but credulous. He lived in 1743, or 44, about
75 years old."

The subject of luxury having been introduced, Dr.
Johnson defended it. "We have now (said he) a splendid
dinner before us; Which of all these dishes is unwhol-

Luxury some?" The duke asserted, that he had observed the grandees of Spain diminished in their size by luxury. Dr. Johnson politely refrained from opposing directly an observation which the duke himself had made; but said, "Man must be very different from other animals, if he is diminished by good living; for the size of all other animals is increased by it." I made some remark that seemed to imply a belief in second sight. The duchess said, "I fancy you will be a *Methodist.*"— This was the only sentence her grace deigned to utter to me; and I take it for granted, she thought it a good hit on my *credulity* in the Douglas cause.

A gentleman in company, after dinner, was desired by the duke to go to another room, for a specimen of curious marble, which his grace wished to shew us. He brought a wrong piece, upon which the duke sent him back again. He could not refuse; but, to avoid any appearance of servility, he whistled as he walked out of the room, to show his independency. On my mentioning this afterwards to Dr. Johnson, he said, it was a nice trait of character.

Dr. Johnson talked a great deal, and was so entertaining, that Lady Betty Hamilton, after dinner, went and placed her chair close to his, leaned upon the back of it, and listened eagerly. It would have made a fine picture to have drawn the Sage and her at this time in their several attitudes. He did not know, all the while, how much he was honoured. I told him afterwards. I never saw him so gentle and complaisant as this day.

We went to tea. The duke and I walked up and down the drawing-room, conversing. The duchess still continued to show the same marked coldness for me; for which, though I suffered from it, I made every allowance, considering the very warm part that I had taken for Douglas, in the cause in which she thought her son deeply interested. Had not her grace discovered some displeasure towards me, I should have suspected her of insensibility or dissimulation.

Her grace made Dr. Johnson come and sit by her, and asked him why he made his journey so late in the year. "Why, madam (said he,) you know Mr. Boswell must attend the Court of Session, and it does not rise till the twelfth of August."—She said, with some sharpness, "I *know nothing* of Mr. Boswell." Poor Lady Lucy Douglas, to whom I mentioned this, observed, "She knew *too much* of Mr. Boswell." I shall make no remark on her grace's speech. I indeed felt it as rather too severe; but when I recollected that my punishment was inflicted by so dignified a beauty, I had that kind of consolation which a man would feel who is strangled by a *silken cord*. Dr. Johnson was all attention to her grace. He used afterwards a droll expression, upon her enjoying the three titles of Hamilton, Brandon, and Argyle. Borrowing an image from the Turkish empire, he called her a *Duchess* with *three tails*.

He was much pleased with our visit at the castle of Inveraray. The Duke of Argyle was exceedingly polite to him, and, upon his complaining of the shelties which he had hitherto ridden being too small for him, his grace told him he should be provided with a good horse to carry him next day.

Mr. John M'Aulay passed the evening with us at our inn. When Dr. Johnson spoke of people whose principles were good, but whose practice was faulty, Mr. M'Aulay said, he had no notion of people being in earnest in their good professions, whose practice was not suitable to them. The Doctor grew warm, and said, "Sir, are you so grossly ignorant of human nature, as not to know that a man may be very sincere in good principles, without having good practice?"

Dr.   Dr. Johnson was unquestionably in the right; and
Beattie's   whoever examines himself candidly, will be satisfied
pension   of it, though the inconsistency between principles and
practice is greater in some men than in others.

I recollect very little of this night's conversation. I
am sorry that indolence came upon me towards the
conclusion of our journey, so that I did not write
down what passed with the same assiduity as during
the greatest part of it.

Tuesday, 26th October.

Mr. M'Aulay breakfasted with us, nothing hurt or
dismayed by his last night's correction. Being a man
of good sense, he had a just admiration of Dr. Johnson.

Either yesterday morning, or this, I communicated
to Dr. Johnson, from Mr. M'Aulay's information,
the news that Dr. Beattie had got a pension of two
hundred pounds a year. He sat up in his bed, clapped
his hands, and cried, " O brave we ! "—a peculiar
exclamation of his when he rejoices.[1]

As we sat over our tea, Mr. Home's Tragedy of
Douglas was mentioned. I put Dr. Johnson in mind,
that once, in a coffee-house at Oxford, he called to old
Mr. Sheridan, " How came you, Sir, to give Home a
gold medal for writing that foolish play ? " and defied
Mr. Sheridan to shew ten good lines in it. He did
not insist they should be together; but that there
were not ten good lines in the whole play. He
now persisted in this. I endeavoured to defend that
pathetick and beautiful tragedy, and repeated the following passage :

---

[1] Having mentioned, more than once, that my Journal
was perused by Dr. Johnson, I think it proper to inform my
readers that this is the last paragraph which he read.

> " Sincerity,
> Thou first of virtues ! let no mortal leave
> Thy onward path, although the earth should gape,
> And from the gulph of hell destruction cry,
> To take dissimulation's winding way."

JOHNSON. "That will not do, sir. Nothing is good but what is consistent with truth or probability, which this is not. Juvenal, indeed, gives us a noble picture of inflexible virtue :

> "'*Esto bonus miles, tutor bonus, arbiter idem*
> *Integer : ambiguæ si quando citabere testis,*
> *Incertæque rei, Phalaris licet imperet, ut sis*
> *Falsus, et admoto dictet perjuria tauro,*
> *Summum crede nefas animam præferre pudori,*
> *Et propter vitam vivendi perdere causas.*' " [1]

He repeated the lines with great force and dignity ; then added, " And, after this, comes Johnny Home, with his *earth gaping*, and his *destruction crying* :— Pooh ! " [2]

---

[1] An honest guardian, arbitrator just,
Be thou ; thy station deem a sacred trust.
With thy good sword maintain thy country's cause,
In every action venerate its laws :
The lie suborn'd if falsely urg'd to swear,
Though torture wait thee, torture firmly bear ;
To forfeit honour, think the highest shame,
And life too dearly bought by loss of fame ;
Nor, to preserve it, with thy virtue give
That for which only man should wish to live.
For this and the other translations to which no signature is affixed, I am indebted to the friend whose observations are mentioned in the notes, pp. 62 and 390.

[2] I am sorry that I was unlucky in my quotation. But notwithstanding the acuteness of Dr. Johnson's criticism, and the power of his ridicule, the Tragedy of Douglas still continues to be generally and deservedly admired.

The chapel of Holyrood

While we were lamenting the number of ruined religious buildings which we had lately seen, I spoke with peculiar feeling of the miserable neglect of the chapel belonging to the palace of Holyrood-house, in which are deposited the remains of many of the Kings of Scotland, and of many of our nobility. I said, it was a disgrace to the country that it was not repaired: and particularly complained that my friend Douglas, the representative of a great house, and proprietor of a vast estate, should suffer the sacred spot where his mother lies interred, to be unroofed, and exposed to all the inclemencies of the weather. Dr. Johnson, who, I know not how, had formed an opinion on the Hamilton side, in the Douglas cause, slily answered, "Sir, sir, don't be too severe upon the gentleman; don't accuse him of want of filial piety! Lady Jane Douglas was not *his* mother."—He roused my zeal so much that I took the liberty to tell him he knew nothing of the cause; which I do most seriously believe was the case.

We were now "in a country of bridles and saddles," and set out fully equipped. The Duke of Argyle was obliging enough to mount Dr. Johnson on a stately steed from his grace's stable. My friend was highly pleased, and Joseph said, "He now looks like a bishop."

We dined at the inn at Tarbat, and at night came to Rosedow, the beautiful seat of Sir James Colquhoun, on the banks of Lochlomond, where I, and any friends whom I have introduced, have ever been received with kind and elegant hospitality.

Wednesday, 27th October.

When I went into Dr. Johnson's room this morning, I observed to him how wonderfully courteous he had been at Inveraray, and said, "You were quite a

fine gentleman, when with the duchess." He answered, **Johnson's**
in good humour, " Sir, I look upon myself as a very **politeness**
polite man : " and he was right, in a proper manly
sense of the word. As an immediate proof of it, let
me observe, that he would not send back the Duke
of Argyle's horse without a letter of thanks, which I
copied.

"To his Grace the Duke of Argyle.

" my lord,

"That kindness which disposed your grace to
supply me with the horse, which I have now returned,
will make you pleased to hear that he has carried me
well.

" By my diligence in the little commission with
which I was honoured by the duchess, I will endeavour to shew how highly I value the favours
which I have received, and how much I desire to
be thought,

" My lord,

" Your grace's most obedient,

" and most humble servant,

" Sam. Johnson."

" Rosedow, Oct. 29, 1773."

The duke was so attentive to his respectable guest,
that on the same day, he wrote him an answer, which
was received at Auchinleck :

"To Dr. Johnson, Auchinleck, Ayrshire.

" sir,

" I am glad to hear your journey from this place
was not unpleasant, in regard to your horse. I wish I
could have supplied you with good weather, which I
am afraid you felt the want of.

" The Duchess of Argyle desires her compliments

**Loch-
lomond** to you, and is much obliged to you for remembering
her commission.

"I am, sir,
  "Your most obedient humble servant,
                                        "ARGYLE."
"Inveraray, Oct. 29, 1773."

I am happy to insert every memorial of the honour
done to my great friend.   Indeed, I was at all times
desirous to preserve the letters which he received from
eminent persons, of which, as of all other papers, he
was very negligent; and I once proposed to him, that
they should be committed to my care, as his *Custos
Rotulorum*.   I wish he had complied with my request,
as by that means many valuable writings might have
been preserved, that are now lost.[1]

After breakfast, Dr. Johnson and I were furnished
with a boat, and sailed about upon Lochlomond, and
landed on some of the islands which are interspersed.
He was much pleased with the scene, which is so well
known by the accounts of various travellers, that it is
unnecessary for me to attempt any description of it.

I recollect none of his conversation, except that,
when talking of dress, he said, "Sir, were I to have
any thing fine, it should be very fine.   Were I to wear
a ring, it should not be a bauble, but a stone of great
value.   Were I to wear a laced or embroidered waist-

[1] As a remarkable instance of his negligence, I remember
some years ago to have found lying loose in his study, and
without the cover, which contained the address, a letter to
him from Lord Thurlow, to whom he had made an application as Chancellor, in behalf of a poor literary friend.   It
was expressed in such terms of respect for Dr. Johnson, that,
in my zeal for his reputation, I remonstrated warmly with
him oh his strange inattention, and obtained his permission
to take a copy of it; by which probably it has been preserved, as the original I have reason to suppose is lost.

coat, it should be very rich.   I had once a very rich laced **Forms of**
waistcoat, which I wore the first night of my tragedy." **prayer**

Lady Helen Colquhoun being a very pious woman,
the conversation, after dinner, took a religious turn.
Her ladyship defended the presbyterian mode of publick worship; upon which Dr. Johnson delivered those
excellent arguments for a form of prayer which he has
introduced into his "Journey."   I am myself fully
convinced that a form of prayer for publick worship is
in general most decent and edifying.   *Solennia verba*
have a kind of prescriptive sanctity, and make a deeper
impression on the mind than extemporaneous effusions,
in which, as we know not what they are to be, we
cannot readily acquiesce.   Yet I would allow also of a
certain portion of extempore address, as occasion may
require.   This is the practice of the French Protestant
churches.   And although the office of forming sup-
plications to the throne of Heaven is, in my mind,
too great a trust to be indiscriminately committed to
the discretion of every minister, I do not mean to deny
that sincere devotion may be experienced when joining
in prayer with those who use no Liturgy.

We were favoured with Sir James Colquhoun's coach
to convey us in the evening to Cameron, the seat of
Commissary Smollet.   Our satisfaction of finding ourselves again in a comfortable carriage was very great.
We had a pleasing conviction of the commodiousness
of civilization, and heartily laughed at the ravings of
those absurd visionaries who have attempted to persuade
us of the superior advantages of a *state of nature.*

Mr. Smollet was a man of considerable learning,
with abundance of animal spirits; so that he was a
very good companion for Dr. Johnson, who said to
me, "We have had more solid talk here than at any
place where we have been."

The monument to Smollet   I remember Dr. Johnson gave us this evening an able and eloquent discourse on the *Origin of Evil*, and on the consistency of moral evil with the power and goodness of God.   He shewed us how it arose from our free agency, an extinction of which would be a still greater evil than any we experience.   I know not that he said anything absolutely new, but he said a great deal wonderfully well ; and perceiving us to be delighted and satisfied, he concluded his harangue with an air of benevolent triumph over an objection which has distressed many worthy minds : " This then is the answer to the question, Ποθεν το Κακον ? "—Mrs. Smollet whispered me, that it was the best sermon she had ever heard.   Much do I upbraid myself for having neglected to preserve it.

Thursday, 28th October.

Mr. Smollet pleased Dr. Johnson, by producing a collection of news-papers in the time of the Usurpation, from which it appeared that all sorts of crimes were very frequent during that horrible anarchy.   By the side of the high road to Glasgow, at some distance from his house, he had erected a pillar to the memory of his ingenious kinsman, Dr. Smollet ; and he consulted Dr. Johnson as to an inscription for it.   Lord Kames, who, though he had a great store of knowledge, with much ingenuity, and uncommon activity of mind, was no profound scholar, had it seems recommended an English inscription.   Dr. Johnson treated this with great contempt, saying, " An English inscription would be a disgrace to Dr. Smollet ; " and, in answer to what Lord Kames had urged, as to the advantage of its being in English, because it would be generally understood, I observed, that all to whom Dr. Smollet's merit could be an object of respect and imitation, would understand it as well in Latin; and that surely it was not meant for the Highland drovers, or other such people, who pass and repass that way. Johnson
revises
the in-
scription

We were then shewn a Latin inscription, proposed for this monument. Dr. Johnson sat down with an ardent and liberal earnestness to revise it, and greatly improved it by several additions and variations. I unfortunately did not take a copy of it, as it originally stood; but I have happily preserved every fragment of what Dr. Johnson wrote:

> *Quisquis ades, viator,*
> *Vel mente felix, vel studiis cultus,*
> *Immorare paululum memoriæ*
> **TOBIÆ SMOLLET M.D.**
> *Viri iis virtutibus*
> *Quas in homine et cive*
> *Et laudes, et imiteris,*
> * * * * *
>
> *Postquam mira* * * *
> *Se* * * * * * * * * *
> * * * *
>
> *Tali tantoque viro, suo patrueli,*
> * * * * * *
>
> *Hanc columnam,*
> *Amoris eheu! inane monumentum,*
> *In ipsis Leviniæ ripis,*
> *Quas primis infans vagitibus personuit,*
> *Versiculisque jam fere moriturus illustravit,*
> *Ponendam curavit* [1]
> * * * * * *

---

[1] The epitaph which has been inscribed on the pillar erected on the banks of the Leven, in honour of Dr. Smollet, is as follows. The part which was written by Dr. Johnson,

We had this morning a singular proof of Dr. Johnson's quick and retentive memory.   Hay's translation
of Martial was lying in a window.   I said, I thought
it was pretty well done, and shewed him a particular

it appears, has been altered; whether for the better, the
reader will judge.   The alterations are distinguished by
Italicks.

Siste viator!
Si lepores ingeniique venam benignam,
Si morum callidissimum pictorem,
Unquam es miratus,
Immorare paululum memoriæ
T O B I Æ   S M O L L E T, M.D.
Viri virtutibus *hisce*
Quas in homine et cive
Et laudes et imiteris,
Haud mediocriter ornati:
Qui in literis variis versatus,
Postquam felicitate *sibi propria*
Sese posteris commendaverat,
Morte acerba raptus
Anno ætatis 51
Eheu! quam procul a patria!
Prope Liburni portum in Italia,
Jacet sepultus.
Tali tantoque viro, patrueli suo,
Cui in decursu lampada
Se potius tradidisse decuit,
Hanc Columnam,
Amoris, eheu! inane monumentum
In ipsis Leviniæ ripis,
Quas *versiculis sub exitu vitæ illustratas*
Primis infans vagitibus personuit,
Ponendam curavit
J A C O B U S   S M O L L E T de Bonhill
Abi et reminiscere,
Hoc quidem honore,
Non modo defuncti memoriæ,
Verum etiam exemplo, prospectum esse
Aliis enim, si modo digni sint,
Idem erit virtutis præmium!

epigram, I think, of ten, but am certain of eight, lines. Johnson's
He read it, and tossed away the book, saying—" No, activity
it is *not* pretty well." As I persisted in my opinion,
he said, " Why, sir, the original is thus,"—(and he
repeated it;) "and this man's translation is thus,"—
and then he repeated that also, exactly, though he had
never seen it before, and read it over only once, and
that too, without any intention of getting it by heart.

Here a post-chaise, which I had ordered from Glasgow, came for us, and we drove on in high spirits. We
stopped at Dunbarton, and though the approach to the
castle there is very steep, Dr. Johnson ascended it with
alacrity, and surveyed all that was to be seen. During
the whole of our Tour he shewed uncommon spirit,
could not bear to be treated like an old or infirm man,
and was very unwilling to accept of any assistance, insomuch that, at our landing at Icolmkill, when Sir
Allan M'Lean and I submitted to be carried on men's
shoulders from the boat to the shore, as it could not be
brought quite close to land, he sprang into the sea, and
waded vigorously out.

On our arrival at the Saracen's Head Inn, at Glasgow, I was made happy by good accounts from home;
and Dr. Johnson, who had not received a single letter
since we left Aberdeen, found here a great many, the
perusal of which entertained him much. He enjoyed
in imagination the comforts which we could now command, and seemed to be in high glee. I remember, he
put a leg up on each side of the grate, and said, with a
mock solemnity, by way of soliloquy, but loud enough
for me to hear it, " Here am I, an ENGLISH man, sitting
by a *coal* fire."

*N 387

Friday, 29th October.

The professors of the university being informed of
our arrival, Dr. Stevenson, Dr. Reid, and Mr. Anderson, breakfasted with us.   Mr. Anderson accompanied
us while Dr. Johnson viewed this beautiful city.   He
had told me, that one day in London, when Dr. Adam
Smith was boasting of it, he turned to him and said,
" Pray, sir, have you ever seen Brentford ? "—This
was surely a strong instance of his impatience, and spirit
of contradiction.   I put him in mind of it to-day, while
he expressed his admiration of the elegant buildings, and
whispered him, " Don't you feel some remorse ? "

We were received in the college by a number of the
professors, who shewed all due respect to Dr. Johnson ;
and then we paid a visit to the principal, Dr. Leechman, at his own house, where Dr. Johnson had the
satisfaction of being told that his name had been gratefully celebrated in one of the parochial congregations in
the Highlands, as the person to whose influence it was
chiefly owing, that the New Testament was allowed to
be translated into the Erse language.   It seems some
political members of the Society in Scotland for pro-
pagating Christian Knowledge, had opposed this pious
undertaking, as tending to preserve the distinction between the Highlanders and Lowlanders.   Dr. Johnson
wrote a long letter upon the subject to a friend, which
being shewn to them, made them ashamed, and afraid
of being publickly exposed ; so they were forced to a
compliance.   It is now in my possession, and is, perhaps, one of the best productions of his masterly pen.

Professors Reid and Anderson, and the two Messieurs
Foulis, the Elzevirs of Glasgow, dined and drank tea
with us at our inn, after which the professors went

away; and I, having a letter to write, left my fellow-traveller with Messieurs Foulis. Though good and ingenious men, they had that unsettled speculative mode of conversation which is offensive to a man regularly taught at an English school and university. I found that, instead of listening to the dictates of the Sage, they had teazed him with questions and doubtful disputations. He came in a flutter to me, and desired I might come back again, for he could not bear these men. "O ho! sir, (said I,) you are flying to me for refuge!" He never, in any situation, was at a loss for a ready repartee. He answered, with quick vivacity, "It is of two evils choosing the least." I was delighted with this flash bursting from the cloud which hung upon his mind, closed my letter directly, and joined the company. *The Glasgow professors*

We supped at Professor Anderson's. The general impression upon my memory is, that we had not much conversation at Glasgow, where the professors, like their brethren at Aberdeen, did not venture to expose themselves much to the battery of cannon which they knew might play upon them. Dr. Johnson, who was fully conscious of his own superior powers, afterwards praised Principal Robertson for his caution in this respect. He said to me, "Robertson, sir, was in the right. Robertson is a man of eminence, and the head of a college at Edinburgh. He had a character to maintain, and did well not to risk its being lessened."

Saturday, 30th October.

We set out towards Ayrshire. I sent Joseph on to Loudoun, with a message, that, if the earl was at home, Dr. Johnson and I would have the honour to dine with him. Joseph met us on the road, and reported that the

The Earl of Loudoun

earl "*jumped for joy*," and said, "I shall be very happy to see them."—We were received with a most pleasing courtesy by his lordship, and by the countess his mother, who, in her ninety-fifth year, had all her faculties quite unimpaired. This was a very cheering sight to Dr. Johnson, who had an extraordinary desire for long life. Her ladyship was sensible and well-informed, and had seen a great deal of the world. Her lord had held several high offices, and she was sister to the great Earl of Stair.

I cannot here refrain from paying a just tribute to the character of John Earl of Loudoun, who did more service to the county of Ayr in general, as well as to individuals in it, than any man we have ever had. It is painful to think that he met with much ingratitude from persons both in high and low rank : but such was his temper, such his knowledge of "base mankind," [1] that, as if he had expected no other return, his mind was never soured, and he retained his good-humour and benevolence to the last. The tenderness of his heart was proved in 1745-6, when he had an important command in the Highlands, and behaved with a generous humanity to the unfortunate. I cannot figure a more honest politician ; for, though his interest in our county was great, and generally successful, he not only did not deceive by fallacious promises, but was anxious that people should not deceive themselves by too sanguine expectations. His kind and dutiful attention to his mother was unremitted. At his house was true hospitality ; a plain but a plentiful table ; and every guest, being left at perfect freedom, felt himself quite easy and happy. While I live, I shall honour the memory of this amiable man.

At night, we advanced a few miles farther, to the

[1] "The unwilling gratitude of base mankind."—Pope.

house of Mr. Campbell of Treesbank, who was married   Thought-
to one of my wife's sisters, and were entertained very   less
agreeably by a worthy couple.   charity

Sunday, 31st October.

We reposed here in tranquillity.   Dr. Johnson was
pleased to find a numerous and excellent collection of
books, which had mostly belonged to the Reverend Mr.
John Campbell, brother of our host.   I was desirous
to have procured for my fellow-traveller, to-day, the
company of Sir John Cuninghame, of Caprington,
whose castle was but two miles from us.   He was
a very distinguished scholar, was long abroad, and
during part of the time lived much with the learned
Cuninghame, the opponent of Bentley as a critick upon
Horace.   He wrote Latin with great elegance, and,
what is very remarkable, read Homer and Ariosto
through every year.   I wrote to him to request he
would come to us; but unfortunately he was prevented
by indisposition.

Monday, 1st November.

Though Dr. Johnson was lazy, and averse to move,
I insisted that he should go with me, and pay a visit to
the Countess of Eglintoune, mother of the late and
present earl.   I assured him, he would find himself
amply recompensed for the trouble; and he yielded to
my solicitations, though with some unwillingness.   We
were well mounted, and had not many miles to ride.
He talked of the attention that is necessary in order to
distribute our charity judiciously.   " If thoughtlessly
done, we may neglect the most deserving objects; and,
as every man has but a certain proportion to give, if it

Dundon-
ald Castle is lavished upon those who first present themselves, there may be nothing left for such as have a better claim.   A man should first relieve those who are nearly connected with him, by whatever tie ; and then, if he has any thing to spare, may extend his bounty to a wider circle."

As we passed very near the castle of Dundonald, which was one of the many residencies of the kings of Scotland, and in which Robert the Second lived and died, Dr. Johnson wished to survey it particularly.   It stands on a beautiful rising ground, which is seen at a great distance on several quarters, and from whence there is an extensive prospect of the rich district of Cuninghame, the western sea, the isle of Arran, and a part of the northern coast of Ireland.   It has long been unroofed ; and, though of considerable size, we could not, by any power of imagination, figure it as having been a suitable habitation for majesty.   Dr. Johnson, to irritate my *old Scottish* enthusiasm, was very jocular on the homely accommodation of " King *Bob*," and roared and laughed till the ruins echoed.

Lady Eglintoune, though she was now in her eighty-fifth year, and had lived in the retirement of the country for almost half a century, was still a very agreeable woman.   She was of the noble house of Kennedy, and had all the elevation which the consciousness of such birth inspires.   Her figure was majestick, her manners high-bred, her reading extensive, and her conversation elegant.   She had been the admiration of the gay circles of life, and the patroness of poets.   Dr. Johnson was delighted with his reception here.   Her principles in church and state were congenial with his. She knew all his merit, and had heard much of him from her son, Earl Alexander, who loved to cultivate the acquaintance of men of talents, in every department

All who knew his lordship, will allow that his under-standing and accomplishments were of no ordinary rate. From the gay habits which he had early acquired, he spent too much of his time with men, and in pursuits far beneath such a mind as his. He afterwards became sensible of it, and turned his thoughts to objects of importance; but was cut off in the prime of his life. I cannot speak, but with emotions of the most affectionate regret, of one, in whose company many of my early days were passed, and to whose kindness I was much indebted.

Johnson and Lady Eglintoune

Often must I have occasion to upbraid myself, that soon after our return to the main land, I allowed in-dolence to prevail over me so much, as to shrink from the labour of continuing my journal with the same minuteness as before; sheltering myself in the thought, that we had done with the *Hebrides*; and not con-sidering, that Dr. Johnson's *Memorabilia* were likely to be more valuable when we were restored to a more polished society. Much has thus been irrecoverably lost.

In the course of our conversation this day, it came out, that Lady Eglintoune was married the year before Dr. Johnson was born; upon which she graciously said to him, that she might have been his mother; and that she now adopted him; and when we were going away, she embraced him, saying, "My dear son, fare-well!"—My friend was much pleased with this day's entertainment, and owned that I had done well to force him out.

Tuesday, 2nd November.

We were now in a country not only "of saddles and bridles," but of post-chaises; and having ordered one from Kilmarnock, we got to Auchinleck before dinner.

My father was not quite a year and a half older

Boswell's
account
of his
father

than Dr. Johnson; but his conscientious discharge of his laborious duty as a judge in Scotland, where the law proceedings are almost all in writing,—a severe complaint which ended in his death,—and the loss of my mother, a woman of almost unexampled piety and goodness,— had before this time in some degree affected his spirits, and rendered him less disposed to exert his faculties: for he had originally a very strong mind, and cheerful temper. He assured me, he never had felt one moment of what is called low spirits, or uneasiness, without a real cause. He had a great many good stories, which he told uncommonly well, and he was remarkable for " humour, *incolumi gravitate*," as Lord Monboddo used to characterise it. His age, his office, and his character, had long given him an acknowledged claim to great attention, in whatever company he was; and he could ill brook any diminution of it. He was as sanguine a Whig and Presbyterian, as Dr. Johnson was a Tory and church of England man: and as he had not much leisure to be informed of Dr. Johnson's great merits by reading his works, he had a partial and unfavourable notion of him, founded on his supposed political tenets; which were so discordant to his own, that, instead of speaking of him with that respect to which he was entitled, he used to call him "a Jacobite fellow." Knowing all this, I should not have ventured to bring them together, had not my father, out of kindness to me, desired me to invite Dr. Johnson to his house.

I was very anxious that all should be well; and begged of my friend to avoid three topicks, as to which they differed very widely; Whiggism, Presbyterianism, and—Sir John Pringle. He said courteously, " I shall certainly not talk on subjects which I am told are disagreeable to a gentleman under whose roof I am; especially, I shall not do so to *your father.*"

Our first day went off very smoothly. It rained, and we could not get out; but my father shewed Dr. Johnson his library, which, in curious editions of the Greek and Roman classicks, is, I suppose, not excelled by any private collection in Great Britain. My father had studied at Leyden, and been very intimate with the Gronovii, and other learned men there. He was a sound scholar, and, in particular, had collated manuscripts and different editions of Anacreon, and others of the Greek Lyrick poets, with great care; so that my friend and he had much matter for conversation, without touching on the fatal topicks of difference.

Rainy days at Auchinleck

Dr. Johnson found here Baxter's *Anacreon*, which he told me he had long enquired for in vain, and began to suspect there was no such book. Baxter was the keen antagonist of Barnes. His life is in the *Biographia Britannica*. My father has written many notes on this book, and Dr. Johnson and I talked of having it reprinted

Wednesday, 3rd November.

It rained all day, and gave Dr. Johnson an impression of that incommodiousness of climate in the west, of which he has taken notice in his "Journey;" but, being well accommodated, and furnished with variety of books, he was not dissatisfied.

Some gentlemen of the neighbourhood came to visit my father; but there was little conversation. One of them asked Dr. Johnson how he liked the Highlands. The question seemed to irritate him, for he answered, "How, sir, can you ask me what obliges me to speak unfavourably of a country where I have been hospitably entertained? Who *can* like the Highlands?— I like the inhabitants very well."—The gentleman asked no more questions.

"Her-
mes"
Harris
Let me now make up for the present neglect, by
again gleaning from the past.   At Lord Monboddo's,
after the conversation upon the decrease of learning
in England, his Lordship mentioned *Hermes* by Mr.
Harris of Salisbury, as the work of a living authour,
for whom he had a great respect.   Dr. Johnson said
nothing at the time; but when we were in our post-
chaise, told me, he thought Harris "a coxcomb."
This he said of him, not as a man, but as an authour;
and I give his opinions of men and books, faithfully,
whether they agree with my own, or not.   I do admit,
that there always appeared to me something of affectation in Mr. Harris's manner of writing; something of
a habit of clothing plain thoughts in analytick and
categorical formality.   But all his writings are imbued
with learning; and all breathe that philanthropy and
amiable disposition, which distinguished him as a man.[1]

At another time, during our Tour, he drew the
character of a rapacious Highland Chief with the
strength of Theophrastus or La Bruyere; concluding
with these words: "Sir, he has no more the soul of a

---

[1] This gentleman, though devoted to the study of
grammar and dialecticks, was not so absorbed in it as to be
without a sense of pleasantry, or to be offended at his
favourite topicks being treated lightly.   I one day met him
in the street, as I was hastening to the House of Lords, and
told him, I was sorry I could not stop, being rather too late
to attend an appeal of the Duke of Hamilton against
Douglas.   "I thought (said he) their contest had been over
long ago."   I answered, "The contest concerning Douglas's
filiation was over long ago; but the contest now is, who
shall have the estate."   Then, assuming the air of "an
antient sage philosopher," I proceeded thus: "Were I to
predicate concerning him, I should say, the contest formerly
was, What *is* he?   The contest now is, What *has* he?"—
"Right, (replied Mr. Harris, smiling,) you have done with
quality, and have got into *quantity*."

Chief, than an attorney who has twenty houses in a street, and considers how much he can make by them."

The old castle of Auchinleck

He this day, when we were by ourselves, observed, how common it was for people to talk from books; to retail the sentiments of others, and not their own; in short, to converse without any originality of thinking. He was pleased to say, "You and I do not talk from books."

Thursday, 4th November.

I was glad to have at length a very fine day, on which I could shew Dr. Johnson the Place of my family, which he has honoured with so much attention in his "Journey." He is, however, mistaken in thinking that the Celtick name, *Auchinleck*, has no relation to the natural appearance of it. I believe every Celtick name of a place will be found very descriptive. *Auchinleck* does not signify a stony field, as he has said, but a *field of flag stones*; and this place has a number of rocks, which abound in strata of that kind. The "sullen dignity of the old castle," as he has forcibly expressed it, delighted him exceedingly. On one side of the rock on which its ruins stand, runs the river Lugar, which is here of considerable breadth, and is bordered by other high rocks, shaded with wood. On the other side runs a brook, skirted in the same manner, but on a smaller scale. I cannot figure a more romantick scene.

I felt myself elated here, and expatiated to my illustrious Mentor on the antiquity and honourable alliances of my family, and on the merits of its founder, Thomas Boswell, who was highly favoured by his sovereign, James IV. of Scotland, and fell with him at the battle of Flodden-field; and in the glow of what, I am sensible, will, in a commercial age, be considered as genealogical enthusiasm, did not omit to mention what I was sure my friend would not think lightly of, my relation to the Royal Personage, whose liberality, on his accession to the throne, had given him comfort and independence. I have, in a former page, acknowledged my pride of ancient blood, in which I was encouraged by Dr. Johnson : my readers therefore will not be surprised at my having indulged it on this occasion.

Not far from the old castle is a spot of consecrated earth, on which may be traced the foundations of an ancient chapel, dedicated to St. Vincent, and where in old times " was the place of graves " for the family. It grieves me to think that the remains of sanctity here, which were considerable, were dragged away, and employed in building a part of the house of Auchinleck, of the middle age ; which was the family residence, till my father erected that "elegant modern mansion," of which Dr. Johnson speaks so hand- somely. Perhaps this chapel may one day be restored.

Dr. Johnson was pleased, when I shewed him some venerable old trees, under the shade of which my ancestors had walked. He exhorted me to plant assiduously, as my father had done to a great extent.

As I wandered with my reverend friend in the groves of Auchinleck, I told him, that, if I survived him, it was my intention to erect a monument to him here, among scenes which, in my mind, were all classical ; for in my youth I had appropriated to them many of the descriptions of the Roman poets. He could not bear to have death presented to him in any shape ; for his constitutional melancholy made the king of terrours more frightful. He turned off the subject, saying, " Sir, I hope to see your grand-children ! "

This forenoon he observed some cattle without **Cattle** horns, of which he has taken notice in his "Journey," **without** and seems undecided whether they be of a particular **horns** race. His doubts appear to have had no foundation; for my respectable neighbour, Mr. Fairlie, who, with all his attention to agriculture, finds time both for the classicks and his friends, assures me they are a distinct species, and that, when any of their calves have horns, a mixture of breed can be traced. In confirmation of his opinion, he pointed out to me the following passage in Tacitus,—"*Ne armentis quidem suus honor, aut gloria frontis;*" (De mor. Germ. § 5.) which he wondered had escaped Dr. Johnson.

On the front of the house of Auchinleck is this inscription:

Quod petis, hic est ;
Est Ulubris ; animus si te non deficit æquus.

It is characteristick of the founder; but the *animus æquus* is, alas! not inheritable, nor the subject of devise. He always talked to me as if it were in a man's own power to attain it; but Dr. Johnson told me that he owned to him, when they were alone, his persuasion that it was in a great measure constitutional, or the effect of causes which do not depend on ourselves, and that Horace boasts too much, when he says, *æquum mi animum ipse parabo*.

Friday, 5th November.

The Reverend Mr. Dun, our parish minister, who had dined with us yesterday, with some other company, insisted that Dr. Johnson and I should dine with him to-day. This gave me an opportunity to shew my friend the road to the church, made by my father at a great expence, for above three miles, on his own estate,

An alter-
cation
between
Johnson

through a range of well enclosed farms, with a row of trees on each side of it. He called it the *Via sacra*, and was very fond of it. Dr. Johnson, though he held notions far distant from those of the Presbyterian clergy, yet could associate on good terms with them. He indeed occasionally attacked them. One of them discovered a narrowness of information concerning the dignitaries of the church of England, among whom may be found men of the greatest learning, virtue, and piety, and of a truly apostolic character. He talked before Dr. Johnson, of fat bishops and drowsy deans; and, in short, seemed to believe the illiberal and profane scoffings of professed satyrists, or vulgar railers. Dr. Johnson was so highly offended, that he said to him, " Sir, you know no more of our church than a Hottentot."—I was sorry that he brought this upon himself.

Saturday, 6th November.

I cannot be certain, whether it was on this day, or a former, that Dr. Johnson and my father came in collision. If I recollect right, the contest began while my father was shewing him his collection of medals; and Oliver Cromwell's coin unfortunately introduced Charles the First, and Toryism. They became exceedingly warm, and violent, and I was very much distressed by being present at such an altercation between two men, both of whom I reverenced; yet I durst not interfere. It would certainly be very unbecoming in me to exhibit my honoured father, and my respected friend, as intellectual gladiators, for the entertainment of the publick; and therefore I suppress what would, I dare say, make an interesting scene in this dramatick sketch,— this account of the transit of Johnson over the Caledonian Hemisphere.

Yet I think I may, without impropriety, mention one circumstance, as an instance of my father's address. Dr. Johnson challenged him, as he did us all at Talisker, to point out any theological works of merit written by Presbyterian ministers in Scotland. My father, whose studies did not lie much in that way, owned to me afterwards, that he was somewhat at a loss how to answer, but that luckily he recollected having read in catalogues the title of *Durham on the Galatians* ; upon which he boldly said, "Pray, sir, have you read Mr. Durham's excellent commentary on the Galatians?" —"No, sir," said Dr. Johnson. By this lucky thought my father kept him at bay, and for some time enjoyed his triumph; but his antagonist soon made a retort, which I forbear to mention.

In the course of their altercation, Whiggism and Presbyterianism, Toryism and Episcopacy, were terribly buffeted. My worthy hereditary friend, Sir John Pringle, never having been mentioned, happily escaped without a bruise.

My father's opinion of Dr. Johnson may be conjectured from the name he afterwards gave him, which was URSA MAJOR. But it is not true, as has been reported, that it was in consequence of my saying that he was a *constellation* of genius and literature. It was a sly abrupt expression to one of his brethren on the bench of the Court of Session, in which Dr. Johnson was then standing; but it was not said in his hearing.

Sunday, 7th November.

My father and I went to publick worship in our parish-church, in which I regretted that Dr. Johnson would not join us; for, though we have there no form of prayer, nor magnificent solemnity, yet, as GOD is

and Lord Auchinleck

Johnson and Lord Auchinleck worshipped in spirit and in truth, and the same doctrines preached as in the church of England, my friend would certainly have shewn more liberality, had he attended. I doubt not, however, but he employed his time in private to very good purpose. His uniform and fervent piety was manifested on many occasions during our Tour, which I have not mentioned.—His reason for not joining in Presbyterian worship has been recorded in a former page.[1]

Monday, 8th November.

Notwithstanding the altercation that had passed, my father, who had the dignified courtesy of an old Baron, was very civil to Dr. Johnson, and politely attended him to the post-chaise, which was to convey us to Edinburgh.

Thus they parted.—They are now in another, and a higher, state of existence : and as they were both worthy christian men, I trust they have met in happiness. But I must observe, in justice to my friend's political principles, and my own, that they have met in a place where there is no room for *Whiggism*.

We came at night to a good inn at Hamilton.—I recollect no more.

Tuesday, 9th November.

I wished to have shewn Dr. Johnson the Duke of Hamilton's house, commonly called the Palace of Hamilton, which is close by the town. It is an object which, having been pointed out to me as a splendid edifice, from my earliest years, in travelling between Auchinleck and

[1] P. 103.

Edinburgh, has still great grandeur in my imagination. Lord Elibank
My friend consented to stop, and view the outside of it,
but could not be persuaded to go into it.

We arrived this night at Edinburgh, after an absence
of eighty-three days. For five weeks together, of the
tempestuous season, there had been no account received
of us. I cannot express how happy I was on finding
myself again at home.

Wednesday, 10th November.

Old Mr. Drummond, the bookseller, came to breakfast. Dr. Johnson and he had not met for ten years.
There was respect on his side, and kindness on Dr.
Johnson's. Soon afterwards Lord Elibank came in,
and was much pleased at seeing Dr. Johnson in Scotland. His lordship said, "hardly any thing seemed to
him more improbable." Dr. Johnson had a very high
opinion of him. Speaking of him to me, he characterized
him thus : " Lord Elibank has read a great deal. It is
true, I can find in books all that he has read ; but he
has a great deal of what is in books, proved by the test
of real life."—Indeed, there have been few men whose
conversation discovered more knowledge enlivened by
fancy. He published several small pieces of distinguished
merit ; and has left some in manuscript, in particular an
account of the expedition against Carthagena, in which
he served as an officer in the army. His writings deserve
to be collected. He was the early patron of Dr. Robertson, the historian, and Mr. Home, the tragick poet ;
who, when they were ministers of country parishes, lived
near his seat. He told me, " I saw these lads had talents,
and they were much with me."—I hope they will pay
a grateful tribute to his memory.

The morning was chiefly taken up by Dr. Johnson's

A Scotch-
man's
noblest
prospect

giving him an account of our Tour.—The subject of
difference in political principles was introduced.—JOHN-
SON. "It is much increased by opposition.   There was
a violent Whig, with whom I used to contend with great
eagerness.   After his death I felt my Toryism much
abated."—I suppose he meant Mr. Walmsley of Lichfield, whose character he has drawn so well in his life
of Edmund Smith.

Mr. Nairne came in, and he and I accompanied Dr.
Johnson to Edinburgh castle, which he owned was "a
great place."   But I must mention, as a striking instance
of that spirit of contradiction to which he had a strong
propensity, when Lord Elibank was some days after talking of it with the natural elation of a Scotchman, or of
any man who is proud of a stately fortress in his own
country, Dr. Johnson affected to despise it, observing
that, "it would make a good *prison* in ENGLAND."

Lest it should be supposed that I have suppressed
one of his sallies against my country, it may not be
improper here to correct a mistaken account that has
been circulated, as to his conversation this day.   It has
been said, that being desired to attend to the noble prospect from the Castle-hill, he replied, "Sir, the noblest
prospect that a Scotchman ever sees, is the high road
that leads him to London."—This lively sarcasm was
thrown out at a tavern in London, in my presence, many
years before.

We had with us to day at dinner, at my house, the
Lady Dowager Colvill, and Lady Anne Erskine, sisters
of the Earl of Kelly; the Honourable Archibald Erskine, who has now succeeded to that title; Lord Elibank;
the Reverend Dr. Blair; Mr. Tytler, the acute vindi-
cator of Mary Queen of Scots, and some other friends.

Fingal being talked of, Dr. Johnson, who used to
boast that he had, from the first, resisted both Ossian

and the Giants of Patagonia, averred his positive disbelief of its authenticity. Lord Elibank said, " I am
sure it is not M'Pherson's. Mr. Johnson, I keep company a great deal with you; it is known I do. I may
borrow from you better things than I can say myself,
and give them as my own; but, if I should, every
body will know whose they are."—The Doctor was
not softened by this compliment. He denied merit
to *Fingal*, supposing it to be the production of a man
who has had the advantages that the present age affords;
and said, " nothing is more easy than to write enough in
that style if once you begin." [1]—One gentleman in company expressing his opinion "that *Fingal* was certainly
genuine, for that he had heard a great part of it repeated
in the original," Dr. Johnson indignantly asked him,
whether he understood the original; to which an answer
being given in the negative, "Why then, (said Dr. Johnson,) we see to what *this* testimony comes:—thus it is."

I mentioned this as a remarkable proof how liable the
mind of man is to credulity, when not guarded by such
strict examination as that which Dr. Johnson habitually
practised. The talents and integrity of the gentleman
who made the remark, are unquestionable; yet, had not
Dr. Johnson made him advert to the consideration, that
he who does not understand a language, cannot know
that something which is recited to him is in that language,
he might have believed, and reported to this hour, that
he had "heard a great part of *Fingal* repeated in the
original."

For the satisfaction of those on the north of the
Tweed, who may think Dr. Johnson's account of

[1] I desire not to be understood as agreeing *entirely* with the
opinions of Dr. Johnson, which I relate without any remark.
The many imitations, however, of *Fingal*, that have been published, confirm this observation in a considerable degree.

The
authen-
ticity of
"Fingal"

Caledonian credulity and inaccuracy too strong, it is
but fair to add, that he admitted the same kind of
ready belief might be found in his own country.
"He would undertake, (he said) to write an epick
poem on the story of Robin Hood, and half England, to whom the names and places he should mention
in it are familiar, would believe and declare they had
heard it from their earliest years."

One of his objections to the authenticity of *Fingal*,
during the conversation at Ulinish, is omitted in my
Journal, but I perfectly recollect it.—"Why is not the
original deposited in some publick library, instead of
exhibiting attestations of its existence? Suppose there
were a question in a court of justice, whether a man be
dead or alive: You aver he is alive, and you bring fifty
witnesses to swear it: I answer, 'Why do you not
produce the man?'"—This is an argument founded
on one of the first principles of the law of evidence
which Gilbert would have held to be irrefragable.

I do not think it incumbent on me to give any precise
decided opinion upon this question, as to which I believe
more than some, and less than others. The subject
appears to have now become very uninteresting to the
publick. That *Fingal* is not from beginning to end
a translation from the Gallick, but that *some* passages
have been supplied by the editor to connect the whole,
I have heard admitted by very warm advocates for its
authenticity. If this be the case, why are not these
distinctly ascertained? Antiquaries, and admirers of
the work, may complain, that they are in a situation similar to that of the unhappy gentleman whose
wife informed him, on her death-bed, that one of
their reputed children was not his; and, when he
eagerly begged her to declare which of them it
was, she answered, "*That* you shall never know;"

and expired, leaving him in irremediable doubt as to Second
them all.   sight

I beg leave now to say something upon second sight,
of which I have related two instances, as they impressed
my mind at the time.   I own, I returned from the
Hebrides with a considerable degree of faith in the
many stories of that kind which I heard with a too
easy acquiescence, without any close examination of
the evidence : but, since that time, my belief in those
stories has been much weakened, by reflecting on the
careless inaccuracy of narrative in common matters, from
which we may certainly conclude that there may be
the same in what is more extraordinary.—It is but
just, however, to add, that the belief in second sight
is not peculiar to the Highlands and Isles.

Some years after our Tour, a cause was tried in the
Court of Session, where the principal fact to be ascertained was, whether a ship-master, who used to frequent
the Western Highlands and Isles, was drowned in one
particular year, or in the year after.   A great number
of witnesses from those parts were examined on each
side, and swore directly contrary to each other, upon
this simple question.   One of them, a very respectable
Chieftain, who told me a story of second sight, which
I have not mentioned, but which I too implicitly believed, had in this case, previous to this publick examination, not only said, but attested under his hand, that
he had seen the ship-master in the year subsequent to
that in which the court was finally satisfied he was
drowned.   When interrogated with the strictness of
judicial inquiry, and under the awe of an oath, he
recollected himself better, and retracted what he had
formerly asserted, apologising for his inaccuracy, by
telling the judges, " A man will *say* what he will not
s*wear*."—By many he was much censured, and it was

Garrick
and
Foote
maintained that every gentleman would be as attentive to truth without the sanction of an oath, as with it. Dr. Johnson, though he himself was distinguished at all times by a scrupulous adherence to truth, controverted this proposition; and, as a proof that this was not, though it ought to be, the case, urged the very different decisions of elections under Mr. Grenville's Act, from those formerly made. "Gentlemen will not pronounce upon oath, what they would have said, and voted in the house, without that sanction."

However difficult it may be for men who believe in preternatural communications, in modern times, to satisfy those who are of a different opinion, they may easily refute the doctrine of their opponents, who impute a belief in second sight to superstition. To entertain a visionary notion that one sees a distant or future event, may be called superstition; but the correspondence of the fact or event with such an impression on the fancy, though certainly very wonderful, *if proved*, has no more connection with superstition, than magnetism or electricity.

After dinner, various topicks were discussed; but I recollect only one particular. Dr. Johnson compared the different talents of Garrick and Foote, as companions, and gave Garrick greatly the preference for elegance, though he allowed Foote extraordinary powers of entertainment. He said, "Garrick is restrained by some principle; but Foote has the advantage of an unlimited range. Garrick has some delicacy of feeling; it is possible to put him out; you may get the better of him; but Foote is the most incompressible fellow that I ever knew: when you have driven him into a corner, and think you are sure of him, he runs through between your legs, or jumps over your head, and makes his escape."

Dr. Erskine and Mr. Robert Walker, two very re-   **The**
spectable ministers of Edinburgh, supped with us, as did   **Metho-**
the Reverend Dr. Webster.—The conversation turned   **dists**
on the Moravian missions, and on the Methodists. Dr.
Johnson observed in general, that missionaries were too
sanguine in their accounts of their success among savages,
and that much of what they tell is not to be believed.
He owned that the Methodists had done good; had
spread religious impressions among the vulgar part of
mankind: but, he said, they had great bitterness against
other Christians, and that he never could get a Methodist to explain in what he excelled others; that it
always ended in the indispensable necessity of hearing
one of their preachers.

Thursday, 11th November.

Principal Robertson came to us as we sat at breakfast; he advanced to Dr. Johnson, repeating a line of
Virgil, which I forget. I suppose, either

> *Post varios casus, per tot discrimina rerum,*[1]

or

> *—multum ille et terris jactatus, et alto.*[2]

Every body had accosted us with some studied compliment on our return. Dr. Johnson said, " I am really
ashamed of the congratulations which we receive. We
are addressed as if we had made a voyage to Nova
Zembla, and suffered five persecutions in Japan." And
he afterwards remarked, that, " to see a man come up
with a formal air, and a Latin line, when we had no
fatigue and no danger, was provoking."—I told him,

---

[1] Through various hazards and events we move.
[2] "Long labours both by sea and land he bore."—DRYDEN.

Collect-
ing
materials
for
history

he was not sensible of the danger, having lain under cover in the boat during the storm : he was like the chicken, that hides its head under its wing, and then thinks itself safe.

Lord Elibank came to us, as did Sir William Forbes. The rash attempt in 1745 being mentioned, I observed, that it would make a fine piece of History. Dr. Johnson said it would. Lord Elibank doubted whether any man of this age could give it impartially.—JOHNSON. "A man, by talking with those of different sides, who were actors in it, and putting down all that he hears, may in time collect the materials of a good narrative. You are to consider, all history was at first oral. I suppose Voltaire was fifty years in collecting his *Louis XIV.*, which he did in the way that I am proposing."— ROBERTSON. "He did so. He lived much with all the great people who were concerned in that reign, and heard them talk of every thing ; and then either took Mr. Boswell's way, of writing down what he heard, or, which is as good, preserved it in his memory ; for he has a wonderful memory."—With the leave, how- ever, of this elegant historian, no man's memory can preserve facts or sayings with such fidelity as may be done by writing them down when they are recent.— Dr. Robertson said, "it was now full time to make such a collection as Dr. Johnson suggested ; for many of the people who were then in arms, were dropping off ; and both Whigs and Jacobites were now come to talk with moderation."—Lord Elibank said to him, "Mr. Robertson, the first thing that gave me a high opinion of you, was your saying in the Select Society,[1] while parties ran high, soon after the year 1745, that you did not think worse of a man's moral character for

[1] A society for debate in Edinburgh, consisting of the most eminent men.

his having been in rebellion. This was venturing to utter a liberal sentiment, while both sides had a detestation of each other.''

Dr. Johnson observed, that being in rebellion from a notion of another's right, was not connected with depravity; and that we had this proof of it, that all mankind applauded the pardoning of rebels; which they would not do in the case of robbers and murderers. He said, with a smile, that, "he wondered that the phrase of *unnatural* rebellion should be so much used, for that all rebellion was natural to man.''

As I kept no Journal of any thing that passed after this morning, I shall, from memory, group together this and the other days, till that on which Dr. Johnson departed for London. They were in all nine days; on which he dined at Lady Colvill's, Lord Hailes's, Sir Adolphus Oughton's, Sir Alexander Dick's, Principal Robertson's, Mr. M'Laurin's, and thrice at Lord Elibank's seat in the country, where we also passed two nights. He supped at the Honourable Alexander Gordon's, now one of our judges, by the title of Lord Rockville; at Mr. Nairne's, now also one of our judges, by the title of Lord Dunsinan; at Dr. Blair's, and Mr. Tytler's; and at my house thrice, one evening with a numerous company, chiefly gentlemen of the law; another with Mr. Menzies of Culdares, and Lord Monboddo, who disengaged himself on purpose to meet him; and the evening on which we returned from Lord Elibank's, he supped with my wife and me by ourselves.

He breakfasted at Dr. Webster's, at old Mr. Drummond's, and at Dr. Blacklock's; and spent one forenoon at my uncle Dr. Boswell's, who shewed him his curious museum; and, as he was an elegant scholar,

Lord
Mansfield
and a physician bred in the school of Boerhaave, Dr.
Johnson was pleased with his company.

On the mornings when he breakfasted at my house,
he had, from ten o'clock till one or two, a constant
levee of various persons, of very different characters
and descriptions. I could not attend him, being
obliged to be in the Court of Session; but my wife
was so good as to devote the greater part of the morning
to the endless task of pouring out tea for my friend and
his visitors.

Such was the disposition of his time at Edinburgh.
He said one evening to me, in a fit of languor, " Sir,
we have been harassed by invitations." I acquiesced.
" Ay, sir," he replied; " but how much worse would
it have been, if we had been neglected ? "

From what has been recorded in this Journal, it may
well be supposed that a variety of admirable conversation has been lost, by my neglect to preserve it.—I
shall endeavour to recollect some of it, as well as I can.

At Lady Colvill's, to whom I am proud to introduce
any stranger of eminence, that he may see what dignity
and grace is to be found in Scotland, an officer observed,
that he had heard Lord Mansfield was not a great
English lawyer.—JOHNSON. " Why, sir, supposing Lord
Mansfield not to have the splendid talents which he
possesses, he must be a great English lawyer, from
having been so long at the bar, and having passed
through so many of the great offices of the law. Sir, you
may as well maintain that a carrier, who has driven a
packhorse between Edinburgh and Berwick for thirty
years, does not know the road, as that Lord Mansfield
does not know the law of England."

At Mr. Nairne's, he drew the character of Richard-
son, the author of *Clarissa*, with a strong yet delicate
pencil. I lament much that I have not preserved it :

I only remember that he expressed a high opinion of his talents and virtues ; but observed, that "his perpetual study was to ward off petty inconveniencies, and procure petty pleasures ; that his love of continual superiority was such, that he took care to be always surrounded by women, who listened to him implicitly, and did not venture to controvert his opinions ; and that his desire of distinction was so great, that he used to give large vails to the Speaker Onslow's servants, that they might treat him with respect." Samuel Richard-son

On the same evening, he would not allow that the private life of a judge, in England, was required to be so strictly decorous as I supposed. "Why then, sir, (said I,) according to your account, an English judge may just live like a gentleman."—JOHNSON. "Yes, sir, —if he *can*."

At Mr. Tytler's, I happened to tell that one evening, a great many years ago, when Dr. Hugh Blair and I were sitting together in the pit of Drury-lane playhouse, in a wild freak of youthful extravagance, I entertained the audience prodigiously, by imitating the lowing of a cow. A little while after I had told this story, I differed from Dr. Johnson, I suppose too confidently, upon some point, which I now forget. He did not spare me. "Nay, sir, (said he,) if you cannot talk better as a man, I'd have you bellow like a cow."[1]

---

[1] As I have been scrupulously exact in relating anecdotes concerning other persons, I shall not withhold any part of this story, however ludicrous.—I was so successful in this boyish frolick, that the universal cry of the galleries was, "*Encore* the cow ! *Encore* the cow ! " In the pride of my heart, I attempted imitations of some other animals, but with very inferior effect. My reverend friend, anxious for my *fame*, with an air of the utmost gravity and earnestness, addressed me thus : "My dear sir, I would *confine* myself to the *cow* ! "

At Dr. Webster's, he said, that he believed hardly any man died without affectation. This remark appears to me to be well founded, and will account for many of the celebrated death-bed sayings which are recorded.

On one of the evenings at my house, when he told that Lord Lovat boasted to an English nobleman, that though he had not his wealth, he had two thousand men whom he could at any time call into the field, the Honourable Alexander Gordon observed, that those two thousand men brought him to the block.——"True, sir, (said Dr. Johnson :) but you may just as well argue, concerning a man who has fallen over a precipice to which he has walked too near,—'His two legs brought him to that,' is he not the better for having two legs?"

At Dr. Blair's I left him, in order to attend a consultation, during which he and his amiable host were by themselves. I returned to supper, at which were Principal Robertson, Mr. Nairne, and some other gentlemen. Dr. Robertson and Dr. Blair, I remember, talked well upon subordination and government; and, as my friend and I were walking home, he said to me, " Sir, these two doctors are good men, and wise men."——I begged of Dr. Blair to recollect what he could of the long conversation that passed between Dr. Johnson and him alone, this evening, and he obligingly wrote to me as follows:

"*March* 3, 1785.

"DEAR SIR,

"As so many years have intervened, since I chanced to have that conversation with Dr. Johnson in my house, to which you refer, I have forgotten most of what then passed, but remember that I was both instructed and entertained by it. Among other subjects, the discourse happening to turn on modern Latin poets, the Doctor expressed a very favourable opinion of Buchanan, and instantly repeated, from beginning to end, an ode of his, intituled *Calendæ Maiæ*, (the eleventh in his *Miscellaneorum Liber*,) beginning with these words, '*Salvete sacris deliciis sacræ*,' with which I had formerly been unacquainted; but upon perusing it, the praise which he bestowed upon it, as one of the happiest of Buchanan's poetical compositions, appeared to me very just. He also repeated to me a Latin ode he had composed in one of the western islands, from which he had lately returned. We had much discourse concerning his excursion to those islands, with which he expressed himself as having been highly pleased; talked in a favourable manner of the hospitality of the inhabitants; and particularly spoke much of his happiness in having you for his companion; and said, that the longer he knew you, he loved and esteemed you the more. This conversation passed in the interval between tea and supper, when we were by ourselves. You, and the rest of the company who were with us at supper, have often taken notice that he was uncommonly bland and gay that evening, and gave much pleasure to all who were present.— This is all that I can recollect distinctly of that long conversation.

"Yours sincerely,
"HUGH BLAIR."

Dr. Blair's letter to Boswell

At Lord Hailes's, we spent a most agreeable day; but again I must lament that I was so indolent as to let almost all that passed evaporate into oblivion. Dr. Johnson observed there, that " it is wonderful how ignorant many officers of the army are, considering how much leisure they have for study, and the acquisition of knowledge." I hope he was mistaken; for he maintained that many of them were ignorant of things belonging

An academy for the deaf and dumb

immediately to their own profession; "for instance, many cannot tell how far a musket will carry a bullet;" in proof of which, I suppose, he mentioned some particular person, for Lord Hailes, from whom I solicited what he could recollect of that day, writes to me as follows:

"As to Dr. Johnson's observation about the ignorance of officers, in the length that a musket will carry, my brother, Colonel Dalrymple, was present, and he thought that the doctor was either mistaken, by putting the question wrong, or that he had conversed on the subject with some person out of service.

"Was it upon that occasion that he expressed no curiosity to see the room at Dumfermline, where Charles I. was born? 'I know that he was born, (said he;) no matter where.'—Did he envy us the birth-place of the king?"

Near the end of his "Journey," Dr. Johnson has given liberal praise to Mr. Braidwood's academy for the deaf and dumb. When he visited it, a circumstance occurred which was truly characteristical of our great Lexicographer. "Pray, (said he,) can they pronounce any *long* words?"—Mr. Braidwood informed him they could. Upon which Dr. Johnson wrote one of his *sesquipedalia verba*, which was pronounced by the scholars, and he was satisfied.—My readers may perhaps wish to know what the word was; but I cannot gratify their curiosity. Mr. Braidwood told me, it remained long in his school, but had been lost before I made my inquiry.[1]

[1] One of the best criticks of our age "does not wish to prevent the admirers of the incorrect and nerveless style which generally prevailed for a century before Dr. Johnson's

Dr. Johnson one day visited the Court of Session.
He thought the mode of pleading there too vehement,
and too much addressed to the passions of the judges.
"This (said he) is not the Areopagus."

At old Mr. Drummond's, Sir John Dalrymple
quaintly said, the two noblest animals in the world
were, a Scotch Highlander and an English Sailor.
"Why, sir, (said Dr. Johnson,) I shall say nothing
as to the Scotch Highlander; but as to the English
Sailor, I cannot agree with you."—Sir John said, he
was generous in giving away his money.—Johnson.
"Sir, he throws away his money, without thought,
and without merit. I do not call a tree generous, that
sheds its fruit at every breeze."—Sir John having
affected to complain of the attacks made upon his
Memoirs, Dr. Johnson said, "Nay, sir, do not complain. It is advantageous to an authour, that his book
should be attacked as well as praised. Fame is a
shuttlecock. If it be struck only at one end of the
room, it will soon fall to the ground. To keep it up, it
must be struck at both ends."—Often have I reflected
on this since; and, instead of being angry at many of
those who have written against me, have smiled to
think that they were unintentionally subservient to my
fame, by using a battledoor to make me *virum volitare
per ora*.

At Sir Alexander Dick's, from that absence of

energetick writings were known, from enjoying the laugh
that this story may produce, in which he is very ready to
join them." He, however, requests me to observe, that
"my friend very properly chose a *long* word on this occasion,
not, it is believed, from any predilection for polysyllables,
(though he certainly had a due respect for them,) but in order
to put Mr. Braidwood's skill to the strictest test, and to try
the efficacy of his instruction by the most difficult exertion of
the organs of his pupils."

A hand-
some
compli-
ment

mind to which every man is at times subject, I told,
in a blundering manner, Lady Eglintoune's complimentary adoption of Dr. Johnson as her son; for I
unfortunately stated that her ladyship adopted him as
her son, in consequence of her having been married the
year *after* he was born.   Dr. Johnson instantly corrected me.   "Sir, don't you perceive that you are
defaming the countess?   For, supposing me to be her
son, and that she was not married till the year after my
birth, I must have been her *natural* son."   A young lady
of quality, who was present, very handsomely said,
"Might not the son have justified the fault."—My
friend was much flattered by this compliment, which
he never forgot.   When in more than ordinary spirits,
and talking of his journey in Scotland, he has called
to me, "Boswell, what was it that the young lady of
quality said of me at Sir Alexander Dick's?"   Nobody will doubt that I was happy in repeating it.

My illustrious friend, being now desirous to be again
in the great theatre of life and animated exertion, took a
place in the coach, which was to set out for London on
Monday the 22nd of November.   Sir John Dalrymple
pressed him to come on the Saturday before, to his
house at Cranston, which being twelve miles from Edinburgh, upon the middle road to Newcastle, (Dr. Johnson had come to Edinburgh by Berwick, and along
the naked coast,) it would make his journey easier, as
the coach would take him up at a more seasonable hour
than that at which it sets out.   Sir John, I perceived,
was ambitious of having such a guest; but, as I was
well assured, that at this very time he had joined with
some of his prejudiced countrymen in railing at Dr.
Johnson, and had said, "he wondered how any gentleman of Scotland could keep company with him," I
thought he did not deserve the honour: yet, as it

might be a convenience to Dr. Johnson, I contrived *Roslin* that he should accept the invitation, and engaged to *and Haw-* conduct him.   I resolved that, on our way to Sir *thornden* John's, we should make a little circuit by Roslin Castle, and Hawthornden, and wished to set out soon after breakfast; but young Mr. Tytler came to shew Dr. Johnson some essays which he had written; and my great friend, who was exceedingly obliging when thus consulted, was detained so long that it was, I believe, one o'clock before we got into our post-chaise. I found that we should be too late for dinner at Sir John Dalrymple's, to which we were engaged : but I would by no means lose the pleasure of seeing my friend at Hawthornden,—of seeing *Sam Johnson* at the very spot where *Ben Jonson* visited the learned and poetical Drummond.

We surveyed Roslin Castle, the romantick scene around it, and the beautiful Gothick chapel, and dined and drank tea at the inn; after which we proceeded to Hawthornden, and viewed the caves; and I all the while had *Rare Ben* in my mind, and was pleased to think that this place was now visited by another celebrated wit of England.

By this time "the waning night was growing old," and we were yet several miles from Sir John Dalrymple's. Dr. Johnson did not seem much troubled at our having treated the baronet with so little attention to politeness; but when I talked of the grievous disappointment it must have been to him that we did not come to the *feast* that he had prepared for us, (for he told us he had killed a seven-year-old sheep on purpose,) my friend got into a merry mood, and jocularly said, " I dare say, sir, he has been very sadly distressed : Nay, we do not know but the consequence may have been fatal.   Let me try to describe his situation in his own

*O 387

Dal-
rymple's
"Me-
moirs"
parodied

historical style. I have as good a right to make him
think and talk, as he has to tell us how people thought
and talked a hundred years ago, of which he has no
evidence. All history, so far as it is not supported by
contemporary evidence, is romance.—Stay now.—Let
us consider!"—He then (heartily laughing all the
while) proceeded in his imitation, I am sure to the
following effect, though now, at the distance of almost
twelve years, I cannot pretend to recollect all the precise words :

"Dinner being ready, he wondered that his guests
were not yet come. His wonder was soon succeeded
by impatience. He walked about the room in anxious
agitation ; sometimes he looked at his watch, sometimes
he looked out at the window with an eager gaze of
expectation, and revolved in his mind the various accidents of human life. His family beheld him with mute
concern. 'Surely (said he, with a sigh,) they will
not fail me.'—The mind of man can bear a certain
pressure ; but there is a point when it can bear no
more. A rope was in his view, and he died a Roman
death." [1]

It was very late before we reached the seat of Sir
John Dalrymple, who, certainly with some reason, was
not in very good humour. Our conversation was not
brilliant. We supped, and went to bed in ancient

[1] "Essex was at that time confined to the same chamber
of the Tower from which his father Lord Capel had been led
to death, and in which his wife's grandfather had inflicted
a voluntary death upon himself. When he saw his friend
carried to what he reckoned certain fate, their common
enemies enjoying the spectacle, and reflected that it was he
who had forced Lord Howard upon the confidence of Russel,
he retired, and, by a *Roman death*, put an end to his misery."
—Dalrymple's Memoirs of Great Britain and Ireland, vol. i.
p. 36.

rooms, which would have better suited the climate of
Italy in summer, than that of Scotland in the month
of November.

I recollect no conversation of the next day, worth
preserving, except one saying of Dr. Johnson, which
will be a valuable text for many decent old dowagers,
and other good company, in various circles to descant
upon.—He said, " I am sorry I have not learned to
play at cards.   It is very useful in life : it generates
kindness, and consolidates society."—He certainly
could not mean deep play.

My friend and I thought we should be more comfortable at the inn at Blackshields, two miles farther
on.   We therefore went thither in the evening, and he
was very entertaining ; but I have preserved nothing
but the pleasing emembrance, and his verses on George
the Second and Cibber, and his epitaph on Parnell,
which he was then so good as to dictate to me.   We
breakfasted together next morning, and then the coach
came, and took him up.   He had, as one of his companions in it, as far as Newcastle, the worthy and
ingenious Dr. Hope, botanical professor at Edinburgh.
Both Dr. Johnson and he used to speak of their good
fortune in thus accidentally meeting ; for they had
much instructive conversation, which is always a most
valuable enjoyment, and, when found where it is not
expected, is peculiarly relished.

I have now completed my account of our Tour to
the Hebrides.   I have brought Dr. Johnson down to
Scotland, and seen him into the coach which in a few
hours carried him back into England.   He said to me
often, that the time he spent in this Tour was the
pleasantest part of his life, and asked me if I would
lose the recollection of it for five hundred pounds.   I
answered I would not ; and he applauded my setting

Johnson's
"Jour-
ney"
praised

such a value on an accession of new images in my mind.

Had it not been for me, I am persuaded Dr. Johnson never would have undertaken such a journey; and I must be allowed to assume some merit from having been the cause that our language has been enriched with such a book as that which he published on his return; a book which I never read but with the utmost admiration, as I had such opportunities of knowing from what very meagre materials it was composed.

But my praise may be supposed partial; and therefore I shall insert two testimonies, not liable to that objection, both written by gentlemen of Scotland, to whose opinions I am confident the highest respect will be paid, Lord Hailes, and Mr. Dempster.

"To James Boswell, Esq.

"Sir,

"I have received much pleasure and much instruction, from perusing 'The Journey' to the Hebrides.

"I admire the elegance and variety of description, and the lively picture of men and manners. I always approve of the moral, often of the political, reflections. I love the benevolence of the authour.

"They who search for faults, may possibly find them in this, as well as in every other work of literature.

"For example, the friends of the old family say that *the æra of planting* is placed too late, at the Union of the two kingdoms. I am known to be no friend of the old family; yet I would place the æra of planting at the Restoration; after the murder of Charles I. had been expiated in the anarchy which succeeded it.

"Before the Restoration, few trees were planted, unless by the monastick drones: their successors, (and worthy patriots they were,) the barons, first cut down the trees, and then sold the estates. The gentlemen at St. Andrews, who said that there were but two trees in Fife, ought to have added, that the Elms of Balmerino were sold within these twenty years, to make pumps for the fire-engines.

"In J. Major *de Gestis Scotorum*, L. i. C. 2. last edition, there is a singular passage:

"'Davidi Cranstoneo conterraneo, dum de prima theologiæ licentia foret, duo ei consocii et familiares, et mei cum eo in artibus auditores, scilicet Jacobus Almain Senonensis, et Petrus Bruxcellensis, Prædicatoris ordinis, in Sorbonæ curia die Sorbonico commilitonibus suis publice objecerunt, *quod pane avenaceo plebeii Scoti, sicut a quodam religioso intellexerant, vescebantur, ut virum, quem cholericum noverant, honestis salibus tentarent, qui hoc inficiari tanquam patriæ dedecus nisus est.*'

"Pray introduce our countryman, Mr. Licentiate David Cranston, to the acquaintance of Mr. Johnson.

"The syllogism seems to have been this:

"They who feed on oatmeal are barbarians;
But the Scots feed on oatmeal:
Ergo—

"The licentiate denied the *minor*.
          "I am, Sir,
                    "Your most obedient servant,
                              "DAV. DALRYMPLE."

"Newhailes, 6th Feb. 1775."

To James Boswell, Esq. Edinburgh.

"Dunnichen, 16th February, 1775.

" my dear boswell,

" I cannot omit a moment to return you my best
thanks for the entertainment you have furnished me,
my family, and guests, by the perusal of Dr. Johnson's
'Journey to the Western Islands;' — and now for
my sentiments of it.—I was well entertained. His
descriptions are accurate and vivid. He carried me
on the Tour along with him. I am pleased with the
justice he has done to your humour and vivacity.
'The noise of the wind being all its own,' is a *bon-
mot*, that it would have been a pity to have omitted,
and a robbery not to have ascribed to its author.

"There is nothing in the book, from beginning to
end, that a Scotchman need to take amiss. What he
says of the country is true, and his observations on the
people are what must naturally occur to a sensible,
observing, and reflecting inhabitant of a *convenient*
Metropolis, where a man on thirty pounds a year may
be better accommodated with all the little wants of
life, than Col or Sir Allan. He reasons candidly
about the second sight; but I wish he had enquired
more, before he ventured to say he even doubted of
the possibility of such an unusual and useless deviation
from all the known laws of nature. The notion of the
second sight I consider as a remnant of superstitious
ignorance and credulity, which a philosopher will set
down as such, till the contrary is clearly proved, and
then it will be classed among the other certain, though
unaccountable, parts of our nature, like dreams, and—I
do not know what.

" In regard to the language, it has the merit of being
all his own. Many words of foreign extraction are

used, where, I believe, common ones would do as well, letter to
especially on familiar occasions. Yet I believe he Boswell
could not express himself so forcibly in any other stile.
I am charmed with his researches concerning the Erse
language, and the antiquity of their manuscripts. I am
quite convinced; and I shall rank *Ossian*, and his
Fingals and *Oscars*, amongst the Nursery Tales, not
the true history of our country, in all time to come.

"Upon the whole, the book cannot displease, for
it has no pretensions. The author neither says he is
a Geographer, nor an Antiquarian, nor very learned
in the History of Scotland, nor a Naturalist, nor a
Fossilist. The manners of the people, and the face of
the country, are all he attempts to describe, or seems
to have thought of. Much were it to be wished,
that they who have travelled into more remote, and
of course more curious, regions, had all possessed his
good sense. Of the state of learning, his observations
on Glasgow university shew he has formed a very
sound judgement. He understands our climate too,
and he has accurately observed the changes, however
slow and imperceptible to us, which Scotland has
undergone, in consequence of the blessings of liberty
and internal peace. I could have drawn my pen
through the story of the old woman at St. Andrews,
being the only silly thing in the book. He has taken
the opportunity of ingrafting into the work several
good observations, which I dare say he had made upon
men and things, before he set foot on Scotch ground,
by which it is considerably enriched.[1] A long journey,

---

[1] Mr Orme, one of the ablest historians of this age, is of
the same opinion. He said to me, "There are in that book
thoughts, which, by long revolution in the great mind of
Johnson, have been formed and polished—like pebbles rolled
in the ocean!"

like a tall may-pole, though not very beautiful itself, yet is pretty enough, when ornamented with flowers and garlands: it furnishes a sort of cloak-pins for hanging the furniture of your mind upon; and whoever sets out upon a journey, without furnishing his mind previously with much study and useful knowledge, erects a may-pole in December, and puts up very useless cloak-pins.

"I hope the book will induce many of his countrymen to make the same jaunt, and help to intermix the more liberal part of them still more with us, and perhaps abate somewhat of that virulent antipathy which many of them entertain against the Scotch; who certainly would never have formed those *combinations* which he takes notice of, more than their ancestors, had they not been necessary for their mutual safety, at least for their success, in a country where they are treated as foreigners. They would find us not deficient, at least in point of hospitality, and they would be ashamed ever after to abuse us in the mass.

"So much for the Tour.—I have now, for the first time in my life, passed a winter in the country; and never did three months roll on with more swiftness and satisfaction. I used not only to wonder at, but pity, those whose lot condemned them to winter any where but in either of the capitals. But every place has its charms to a cheerful mind. I am busy planting and taking measures for opening the summer campaign in farming; and I find I have an excellent resource, when revolutions in politicks perhaps, and revolutions of the sun for certain, will make it decent for me to retreat behind the ranks of the more forward in life.

"I am glad to hear the last was a very busy week with you. I see you as counsel in some causes which must have opened a charming field for your humourous vein. As it is more uncommon, so I verily believe it is more useful than the more serious exercise of reason; and, to a man who is to appear in publick, more eclat is to be gained, sometimes more money too, by a *bon-mot*, than a learned speech. It is the fund of natural humour which Lord North possesses, that makes him so much the favourite of the house, and so able, because so amiable, a leader of a party.

"I have now finished *my* Tour of *Seven Pages*. In what remains, I beg leave to offer my compliments, and those of *ma tres chere femme*, to you and Mrs. Boswell. Pray unbend the busy brow, and frolick a little in a letter to,

> "My dear Boswell,
> > "Your affectionate friend,
> > > "GEORGE DEMPSTER."[1]

I shall also present the publick with a correspondence with the Laird of Rasay, concerning a passage in the *Journey to the Western Islands*, which shews Dr. Johnson in a very amiable light.

"TO JAMES BOSWELL, ESQ.

"Rasay, April 10th, 1775.

"DEAR SIR,

"I TAKE this occasion of returning you my most hearty thanks for the civilities shown to my daughter by you and Mrs. Boswell. Yet, though she has

[1] Every reader will, I am sure, join with me in warm admiration of the truly patriotick writer of this letter. I know not which most to applaud,—that good sense and liberality of mind, which could see and admit the defects of his native country, to which no man is a more zealous friend;—or that candour, which induced him to give just praise to the minister whom he honestly and strenuously opposed.

informed me that I am under this obligation, I should
very probably have deferred troubling you with making
my acknowledgments at present, if I had not seen Dr.
Johnson's 'Journey to the Western Isles,' in which
he has been pleased to make a very friendly mention
of my family, for which I am surely obliged to him,
as being more than an equivalent for the reception you
and he met with. Yet there is one paragraph I should
have been glad he had omitted, which I am sure was
owing to misinformation; that is, that I had acknowledged M'Leod to be my chief, though my ancestors
disputed the pre-eminence for a long tract of time.

"I never had occasion to enter seriously on this
argument with the present laird or his grandfather, nor
could I have any temptation to such a renunciation
from either of them. I acknowledge, the benefit of
being chief of a clan is in our days of very little signi-
ficancy, and to trace out the progress of this honour to
the founder of a family, of any standing, would perhaps
be a matter of some difficulty.

"The true state of the present case is this: the
M'Leod family consists of two different branches; the
M'Leods of Lewis, of which I am descended, and the
M'Leods of Harris. And though the former have
lost a very extensive estate by forfeiture in king James
the sixth's time, there are still several respectable
families of it existing, who would justly blame me for
such an unmeaning cession, when they all acknowledge
me head of that family; which though in fact it be
but an ideal point of honour, is not hitherto so far disregarded in our country, but it would determine some
of my friends to look on me as a much smaller man
than either they or myself judge me at present to be. I
will, therefore, ask it as a favour of you to acquaint the
Doctor with the difficulty he has brought me to. In

travelling among rival clans, such a silly tale as this
might easily be whispered into the ear of a passing
stranger; but as it has no foundation in fact, I hope
the Doctor will be so good as to take his own way in
undeceiving the publick, I principally mean my friends
and connections, who will be first angry at me, and
next sorry to find such an instance of my littleness
recorded in a book which has a very fair chance of being
much read.   I expect you will let me know what he
will write you in return, and we here beg to make
offer to you and Mrs. Boswell of our most respectful
compliments.   I am,

> " Dear sir,
> " Your most obedient humble servant,
> > "JOHN M'LEOD."

" To THE LAIRD OF RASAY.

> " London, May 8, 1775.

" DEAR SIR,
   " THE day before yesterday I had the honour to
receive your letter, and I immediately communicated
it to Dr. Johnson.   He said he loved your spirit,
and was exceedingly sorry that he had been the cause
of the smallest uneasiness to you.   There is not a
more candid man in the world than he is, when
properly addressed, as you will see from his letter to
you, which I now enclose.   He has allowed me to take
a copy of it, and he says you may read it to your clan,
or publish it if you please.   Be assured, sir, that I shall
take care of what he has entrusted to me, which is to
have an acknowledgment of his errour inserted in the
Edinburgh newspapers.   You will, I dare say, be fully
satisfied with Dr. Johnson's behaviour.   He is desirous
to know that you are; and therefore when you have

read his acknowledgement in the papers, I beg you may write to me; and if you choose it, I am persuaded a letter from you to the Doctor also will be taken kind. I shall be at Edinburgh the week after next.

"Any civilities which my wife and I had in our power to shew to your daughter, Miss M'Leod, were due to her own merit, and were well repaid by her agreeable company. But I am sure I should be a very unworthy man if I did not wish to shew a grateful sense of the hospitable and genteel manner in which you were pleased to treat me. Be assured, my dear sir, that I shall never forget your goodness, and the happy hours which I spent in Rasay.

"You and Dr. M'Leod were both so obliging as to promise me an account in writing, of all the particulars which each of you remember, concerning the transactions of 1745-6. Pray do not forget this, and be as minute and full as you can; put down every thing; I have a great curiosity to know as much as I can, authentically.

"I beg that you may present my best respects to Lady Rasay, my compliments to your young family, and to Dr. M'Leod; and my hearty good wishes to Malcolm, with whom I hope again to shake hands cordially. I have the honour to be,

> "Dear sir,
> "Your obliged and faithful humble servant,
> "JAMES BOSWELL."

ADVERTISEMENT, written by Dr. Johnson, and inserted by his desire in the Edinburgh newspapers:— Referred to in the foregoing letter.[1]

"THE authour of the *Journey to the Western Islands*, having related that the M'Leods of Rasay acknowledge

---

[1] The original MS. is now in my possession.

the chieftainship or superiority of the M'Leods of Sky, finds that he has been misinformed or mistaken. He means in a future edition to correct his errour, and wishes to be told of more, if more have been discovered." Johnson's letter to Rasay

Dr. Johnson's letter was as follows :

" To the Laird of Rasay.

" DEAR SIR,

" MR. BOSWELL has this day shewn me a letter, in which you complain of a passage in the 'Journey to the Hebrides.' My meaning is mistaken. I did not intend to say that you had personally made any cession of the rights of your house, or any acknowledgement of the superiority of M'Leod of Dunvegan. I only designed to express what I thought generally admitted, —that the house of Rasay allowed the superiority of the house of Dunvegan. Even this I now find to be erroneous, and will therefore omit or retract it in the next edition.

" Though what I had said had been true, if it had been disagreeable to you, I should have wished it unsaid ; for it is not my business to adjust precedence. As it is mistaken, I find myself disposed to correct, both by my respect for you, and my reverence for truth.

" As I know not when the book will be reprinted, I have desired Mr. Boswell to anticipate the correction in the Edinburgh papers. This is all that can be done.

" I hope I may now venture to desire that my compliments may be made, and my gratitude expressed, to Lady Rasay, Mr. Malcolm M'Leod, Mr. Donald M'Queen, and all the gentlemen and all the ladies

whom I saw in the island of Rasay ; a place which I remember with too much pleasure and too much kindness,
not to be sorry that my ignorance, or hasty persuasion,
should, for a single moment, have violated its tranquillity.

"I beg you all to forgive an undesigned and involuntary injury, and to consider me as,

"Sir, your most obliged,

"and most humble servant,

"SAM. JOHNSON." [1]

"London, May 6, 1775."

It would be improper for me to boast of my own
labours ; but I cannot refrain from publishing such
praise as I received from such a man as Sir William
Forbes, of Pitsligo, after the perusal of the original
manuscript of my Journal.

"TO JAMES BOSWELL, ESQ.

"Edinburgh, March 7, 1777.

"MY DEAR SIR,

"I OUGHT to have thanked you sooner, for your
very obliging letter, and for the singular confidence
you are pleased to place in me, when you trust me
with such a curious and valuable deposit as the papers
you have sent me.[2]   Be assured I have a due sense

[1] Rasay was highly gratified, and afterwards visited and
dined with Dr. Johnson, at his house in London.

[2] In justice both to Sir William Forbes and myself, it is
proper to mention, that the papers which were submitted
to his perusal contained only an account of our Tour from
the time that Dr. Johnson and I set out from Edinburgh
(p. 37), and consequently did not contain the eulogium on
Sir William Forbes (p. 12), which he never saw till this book
appeared in print ; nor did he even know, when he wrote
the above letter, that this Journal was to be published.

of this favour, and shall faithfully and carefully return
them to you.   You may rely that I shall neither copy
any part, nor permit the papers to be seen.

    "They contain a curious picture of society, and
form a journal on the most instructive plan that can
possibly be thought of; for I am not sure that an
ordinary observer would become so well acquainted
either with Dr. Johnson, or with the manners of the
Hebrides, by a personal intercourse, as by a perusal of
your Journal.

      "I am very truly, Dear Sir,
        "Your most obedient,
           "And affectionate humble servant,
                "WILLIAM FORBES."

The
faculty of
recording
conversa-
tions

    When I consider how many of the persons men-
tioned in this Tour are now gone to "that undiscovered
country, from whose bourne no traveller returns," I
feel an impression at once awful and tender.—*Re-
quiescant in pace!*

    It may be objected by some persons, as it has been
by one of my friends, that he who has the power of thus
exhibiting an exact transcript of conversations is not
a desirable member of society.   I repeat the answer
which I made to that friend :—"Few, very few,
need be afraid that their sayings will be recorded.
Can it be imagined that I would take the trouble to
gather what grows on every hedge, because I have
collected such fruits as the *Nonpareil* and the BON
CHRETIEN ?"

    On the other hand, how useful is such a faculty, if
well exercised!   To it we owe all those interesting
apothegms and *memorabilia* of the ancients, which
Plutarch, Xenophon, and Valerius Maximus, have
transmitted to us.   To it we owe all those instructive

and entertaining collections which the French have
made under the title of *Ana*, affixed to some celebrated
name.   To it we owe the *Table-Talk* of Selden, the
Conversation between Ben Jonson and Drummond of
Hawthornden, Spence's *Anecdotes* of Pope, and other
valuable remains in our own language. How delighted
should we have been, if thus introduced into the company of Shakspeare and of Dryden, of whom we know
scarcely any thing but their admirable writings ! What
pleasure would it have given us, to have known their
petty habits, their characteristick manners, their modes
of composition, and their genuine opinion of preceding
writers and of their contemporaries !   All these are
now irrecoverably lost.—Considering how many of
the strongest and most brilliant effusions of exalted
intellect must have perished, how much is it to be
regretted that all men of distinguished wisdom and wit
have not been attended by friends, of taste enough to
relish, and abilities enough to register their conversation;

> *Vixere fortes ante Agamemnona*
> *Multi, sed omnes illacrymabiles*
> *Urgentur, ignotique longa*
> *Nocte, carent quia vate sacro.*

They whose inferiour exertions are recorded, as
serving to explain or illustrate the sayings of such men,
may be proud of being thus associated, and of their
names being transmitted to posterity, by being appended
to an illustrious character.

Before I conclude, I think it proper to say, that
I have suppressed[1] every thing which I thought could

[1] Having found, on a revision of the first edition of this
work, that, notwithstanding my best care, a few observations
had escaped me, which arose from the instant impression,
the publication of which might perhaps be considered as

really hurt any one now living.   Vanity and self- **Passages**
conceit indeed may sometimes suffer.   With respect **sup-**
to what *is* related, I considered it my duty to "ex- **pressed**
tenuate nothing, nor set down aught in malice ; " and
with those lighter strokes of Dr. Johnson's satire,
proceeding from a warmth and quickness of imagination, not from any malevolence of heart, and which,
on account of their excellence, could not be omitted, I
trust that they who are the subject of them have good
sense and good temper enough not to be displeased.

I have only to add, that I shall ever reflect with
great pleasure on a Tour, which has been the means of
preserving so much of the enlightened and instructive
conversation of one whose virtues will, I hope, ever be
an object of imitation, and whose powers of mind were
so extraordinary, that ages may revolve before such a
man shall again appear.

passing the bounds of a strict decorum, I immediately ordered
that they should be omitted in the subsequent editions.   I
was pleased to find that they did not amount in the whole
to a page.   If any of the same kind are yet left, it is owing
to inadvertence alone, no man being more unwilling to give
pain to others than I am.

A contemptible scribbler, of whom I have learned no
more than that, after having disgraced and deserted the
clerical character, he picks up in London a scanty livelihood
by scurrilous lampoons under a feigned name, has impudently
and falsely asserted that the passages omitted were *defamatory*,
and that the omission was not voluntary, but compulsory.
The last insinuation I took the trouble publickly to dis-
prove ; yet, like one of Pope's dunces, he persevered in
" the lie o'erthrown."   As to the charge of defamation,
there is an obvious and certain mode of refuting it.   Any
person who thinks it worth while to compare one edition
with the other, will find that the passages omitted were not
in the least degree of that nature, but exactly such as I have
represented them in the former part of this note, the hasty
effusion of momentary feelings, which the delicacy of politeness should have suppressed.

APPENDIX

No. I.

Dr. Black-lock's In justice to the ingenious DR. BLACKLOCK, I publish the following letter from him, relative to a passage in p. 33 :—

"To JAMES BOSWELL, ESQ.

"DEAR SIR,

"HAVING lately had the pleasure of reading your account of the journey which you took with Dr. Samuel Johnson to the Western Isles, I take the liberty of transmitting my ideas of the conversation which happened between the doctor and myself concerning Lexicography and Poetry, which, as it is a little different from the delineation exhibited in the former edition of your Journal, cannot, I hope, be unacceptable ; particularly since I have been informed that a second edition of that work is now in contemplation, if not in execution : and I am still more strongly tempted to encourage that hope, from considering that, if every one concerned in the conversations related, were to send you what they can recollect of these colloquial entertainments, many curious and interesting particulars might be recovered, which the most assiduous attention could not observe, nor the most tenacious memory retain. A little reflection, sir, will convince you, that there is not an axiom in Euclid more intuitive nor more evident than the doctor's assertion that poetry was of much easier execution than lexicography. Any mind therefore endowed with common sense, must have been

extremely absent from itself, if it discovered the least letter to
astonishment from hearing that a poem might be Boswell
written with much more facility than the same quantity
of a dictionary.

" The real cause of my surprise was what appeared to
me much more paradoxical, that he could write a sheet
of dictionary *with as much pleasure* as a sheet of poetry.
He acknowledged, indeed, that the latter was much
easier than the former. For in the one case, books
and a desk were requisite; in the other, you might
compose when lying in bed, or walking in the fields,
&c. He did not, however, descend to explain, nor to
this moment can I comprehend, how the labours of a
mere Philologist, in the most refined sense of that term,
could give equal pleasure with the exercise of a mind
replete with elevated conceptions and pathetic ideas,
while taste, fancy, and intellect were deeply enamoured
of nature, and in full exertion. You may likewise,
perhaps, remember, that when I complained of the
ground which Scepticism in religion and morals was
continually gaining, it did not appear to be on my own
account, as my private opinions upon these important
subjects had long been inflexibly determined. What
I then deplored, and still deplore, was the unhappy
influence which that gloomy hesitation had, not only
upon particular characters, but even upon life in general;
as being equally the bane of action in our present state,
and of such consolations as we might derive from the
hopes of a future.

" I have the pleasure of remaining with sincere esteem
and respect,

" Dear Sir,
" Your most obedient humble servant,
" THOMAS BLACKLOCK."

" Edinburgh, Nov. 12, 1785."

I am very happy to find that Dr. Blacklock's apparent uneasiness on the subject of Scepticism was not on
his own account, (as I supposed,) but from a benevolent concern for the happiness of mankind.   With
respect, however, to the question concerning poetry,
and composing a dictionary, I am confident that my
state of Dr. Johnson's position is accurate.   One may
misconceive the motive by which a person is induced
to discuss a particular topick (as in the case of Dr.
Blacklock's speaking of Scepticism) ; but an assertion,
like that made by Dr. Johnson, cannot be easily mistaken.   And indeed it seems not very probable, that
he who so pathetically laments the *drudgery* to which
the unhappy lexicographer is doomed, and is known
to have written his splendid imitation of Juvenal with
astonishing rapidity, should have had " as much pleasure
in writing a sheet of a dictionary as a sheet of poetry."
Nor can I concur with the ingenious writer of the foregoing letter, in thinking it an axiom as evident as any
in Euclid, that " poetry is of easier execution than
lexicography."   I have no doubt that Bailey, and the
" mighty blunderbuss of law," Jacob, wrote ten pages
of their respective Dictionaries with more ease than
they could have written five pages of poetry.

If this book should again be reprinted, I shall, with
the utmost readiness, correct any errours I may have
committed, in stating conversations, provided it can be
clearly shewn to me that I have been inaccurate.   But
I am slow to believe, (as I have elsewhere observed,)
that any man's memory, at the distance of several years,
can preserve facts or sayings with such fidelity as may
be done by writing them down when they are recent :
and I beg it may be remembered, that it is not upon
memory, but upon what was *written at the time*, that the
authenticity of my Journal rests.

No. II.

VERSES WRITTEN BY SIR ALEXANDER (NOW LORD) MACDONALD;

ADDRESSED AND PRESENTED TO DR. JOHNSON, AT
ARMIDALE IN THE ISLE OF SKY.

Viator, o qui nostra per æquora
Visurus agros Skiaticos venis,
   En te salutantes tributim
      Undique conglomerantur oris.

Donaldiani,—quotquot in insulis
Compescit arctis limitibus mare ;
   Alitque jamdudum, ac alendos
      Piscibus indigenas fovebit.

Ciere fluctus siste, Procelliger,
Nec tu laborans perge, precor, ratis,
   Ne conjugem plangat marita,
      Ne doleat soboles parentem.

Nec te vicissim pæniteat virum
Luxisse ;—vestro scimus ut æstuant
   In corde luctantes dolores,
      Cum feriant inopina corpus.

Quidni ! peremptum clade tuentibus
Plus semper illo qui moritur pati
   Datur, doloris dum profundos
      Pervia mens àperit recessus.

Valete luctus ;—hinc lacrymabiles
Arcete visus :—ibimus, ibimus
   Superbienti qua theatro
      Fingaliæ memorantur aulæ.

Sir Alex-
ander
Mac-
donald's
verses

Illustris hospes ! mox spatiabere
Qua mens ruinæ ducta meatibus
Gaudebit explorare cætus,
Buccina qua cecinit triumphos ;

Audin ? resurgens spirat anhelita
Dux usitato, suscitat efficax
Poeta manes, ingruitque
Vi solitâ redivivus horror.

Ahæna quassans tela gravi manu
Sic ibat atrox Ossiani pater :
Quiescat urnâ, stet fidelis
" Phersonius vigil ad favillam."

MADE AT THE
TEMPLE PRESS   LETCHWORTH
IN GREAT BRITAIN